INSIGHT GUIDES
POLAND

Discovery CHANNEL

APA PUBLICATIONS

Part of the Langenscheidt Publishing Group

INSIGHT GUIDE
POLAND

Editorial
Project Editor
Clare Griffiths
Series Editor
Dorothy Stannard

Distribution

UK & Ireland
GeoCenter International Ltd
Meridian House, Churchill Way West
Basingstoke, Hampshire RG21 6YR
Fax: (44) 1256 817988

United States
Langenscheidt Publishers, Inc.
36–36 33rd Street 4th Floor
Long Island City, NY 11106
Fax: 1 (718) 784 0640

Australia
Universal Publishers
1 Waterloo Road
Macquarie Park, NSW 2113
Fax: (61) 2 9888 9074

New Zealand
Hema Maps New Zealand Ltd (HNZ)
Unit 2, 10 Cryers Road
East Tamaki, Auckland 2013
Fax: (64) 9 273 6479

Worldwide
Apa Publications GmbH & Co.
Verlag KG (Singapore branch)
38 Joo Koon Road, Singapore 628990
Tel: (65) 6865 1600. Fax: (65) 6861 6438

Printing

Insight Print Services (Pte) Ltd
38 Joo Koon Road, Singapore 628990
Tel: (65) 6865 1600. Fax: (65) 6861 6438

©2009 Apa Publications GmbH & Co.
Verlag KG (Singapore branch)
All Rights Reserved
First Edition 1991
Second Edition 2000
Updated 2008

CONTACTING THE EDITORS
We would appreciate it if readers
would alert us to errors or out-
dated information by writing to:
**Insight Guides, P.O. Box 7910,
London SE1 1WE, England.
Fax: (44) 20 7403 0290.
insight@apaguide.co.uk**

www.insightguides.com

ABOUT THIS BOOK

The first Insight Guide pioneered
the use of creative full-colour
photography in travel guides in
1970. Since then, we have
expanded our range to cater for our
readers' need not only for reliable
information about their chosen destination but also for a real understanding of the culture and workings
of that destination. Now, when the
internet can supply inexhaustible
(but not always reliable) facts, our
books marry text and pictures to
provide those much more elusive
qualities: knowledge and discern-
ment. To achieve this, they rely
heavily on the authority of
locally based writers
and photographers.

This fully updated
edition of *Insight
Guide: Poland* is
carefully structured
to convey an understanding of
Poland and its culture as well as to
guide readers through its sights
and activities:

◆ The **Features** section, indicated
by a yellow bar at the top of each
page, covers the history and culture
of the country in a series of informative essays.

◆ The main **Places** section, indicated by a blue bar, is a complete
guide to all the sights and areas
worth visiting. Places of special
interest are coordinated by number
with the maps.

◆ The **Travel Tips** listings section,
with an orange bar, provides
all the practical infor-
mation you will need for
a trip to Poland. It is
divided in six key secti-
ons; transport, accom-
modation, eating out,

activities, and an A–Z listing of practical tips, and a language and further reading guide. An easy-to-find contents list for Travel Tips is printed on the back flap.

The contributors
This new edition of *Insight Guide: Poland* was edited by **Clare Griffiths** and builds on the work of the original editor **Alfred Horn**, who also contributed the original one-page story on concentration camps.

The history section, written originally by **Waldemar Paclawski**, was revised by **Lieutenant Colonel P.A. Szudek**, retired. Szudek was born in Poland in 1921 and served in the Polish forces between 1939 and 1947. He is a member of the Military Commentators' Circle and Honourary secretary of the Polish Forces Historical Commission.

The combined chapters on the arts was significantly revised by **Michal Gieleta** who has translated several plays and musicals into Polish and contributed work to a variety of Polish magazines. His work is based on the original features on Polish literature, by **Ewa Malicka-Kingston**, and Polish art by **Dr Thomas Strauss**.

The majority of the remaining feature essays were brought up-to-date and revised by **Kristina Rees** of the Polish Tourist Board in London. Original contributors to the features section of the book include **Waldemar Paclawski; Tomasz Parteka; Jacek Ziarno** and **Mariusz Urbanek**.

The in-depth places section of the book was thoroughly revised by London-based freelance food, drink and travel writer, **Ian Wisniewski**, who is a frequent visitor to Poland and Eastern Europe. Wisniewski also extended and revised the essay on food and drink and wrote the text for the *Insight On...* picture stories.

Original contributors to the places section include **Professor Jachowitz; Jacek Ziarno; Maria and Przemyslaw Pilicki; Stanislaw Klos; Lidia Dlugolecka; Maciej Pinkwart; Lech Szaranieç; Wlobziemierz Lekki; Janusz Umiński; Jan Baldowski** and **Thomas Urban**.

This book was updated by **Craig Turp** who has spent most of his adult life studying languages and peoples of Central and Eastern Europe. He has written a number of books on the region.

Jerry Dennis; Michael Jenner, Corrie Wingate and **Gregory Wrona** contributed the bulk of the new photographic material for this edition. Indexing was done by **Helen Peters**, and **Paula Soper** edited the book.

Map Legend

– – – –	Province Boundary
	National Park/Reserve
– – – –	Ferry Route
⊖	Border Crossing
✈ ✈	Airport: International/Regional
▭	Bus Station
Ⓜ	Metro
❶	Tourist Information
✉	Post Office
✝ ✝	Church/Ruins
✝	Monastery
✡	Synagogue
☾	Mosque
∴	Archaeological Site
∩	Cave
⚊	Statue/Monument
★	Place of Interest

113

The main places of interest in the Places section are coordinated by number with a full-colour map (e.g. ❶), and a symbol at the top of every right-hand page tells you where to find the map.

INSIGHT GUIDE
POLAND

CONTENTS

Maps

The 17th-century
sundial featuring
Choronos the
God of Time, at
Wilanów Palace,
Warsaw

Insight on ...

Information panels

Travel Tips

◆ **Full Travel Tips index
is on page 371**

Places

THE BEST OF POLAND

Warsaw and its high-rise skyline, the miraculously preserved Old Town of Kraków,
Baltic beaches, chilling memorials and mountain trails...
here at a glance are our recommendations for your trip

BEST CATHEDRALS AND CHURCHES

● **Kraków Cathedral** *(see page 210–11)* Kraków Cathedral is a Gothic masterpiece, worthy of as much time as you can afford it. Do not miss the Sigismund Chapel or the labyrinthine crypt.

● **St. Mary's Church**, Kraków *(see page 205)* The lush interior decoration of this 14th-century building was added over the course of the centuries by great artists of the day. Look out for frescos by Veit Stoss and Jan Metejko.

● **Tyniec Abbey** *(see page 214)* Sitting imposingly on the banks of the Vistula, the partly-ruined Benedictine Abbey at

Tyniec plays host to a series of summer organ concerts which attract large crowds.

● **Gniezno Cathedral** *(see page 303)* The biggest Gothic church in Poland stands proudly in the centre of what was Poland's first capital. The highlight being a magnificent pair of Romanesque bronze doors.

● **Church of St Mary Magdalene**, Wrocław *(see page 272)* Famed for its Romanesque sandstone portal, which dates from the 12th century, St Mary's is a triple-naved red-brick church with flying buttresses.

WARSAW RISING

● **Wilanów Palace** *(see page 173)* Summer residence of Jan III Sobieski, Wilanów dates from 1679 and is the finest Baroque building in Poland.

● **The Palace of Culture and Science** *(see page 168)* Built at great human cost from the rubble of a Warsaw destroyed in World War II, the PKiN is now the symbol of the city and offers great views from its top floors.

● **Old Town** *(see page 158)* Warsaw's Unesco protected, Old

Town was painstakingly rebuilt and meticulously restored in 1945, taking about 30 years. Somehow that only makes it even more impressive.

● **Łazienki Park** *(see page 166)* Anyone who still thinks Warsaw is a grey, concrete jungle has never visited Poland's greatest public park, home to numerous palaces, and the city's botanical gardens. Half of Warsaw visits on summer Sundays, yet still there is more than enough room for everyone.

LEFT: the sumptuous carved altarpiece by master craftsman, Veit Stoss at St Mary's Church, Kraków.
ABOVE: the high-rise skyline of Warsaw.

THE GREAT OUTDOORS

- **Tatra Mountains** *(see page 245)* With their spectacular peaks, the Tatras are a mountaineer's paradise and a haven for wildlife. There are also excellent trails for hikers.
- **Słowiński National Park** *(see page 331)* The main attraction of this biosphere reserve is its shifting sand dunes. The park also includes two large lakes, Lake Łebsko and Lake Gardno.
- **The Mazurian Lakes** *(see page 361)* The Mazurian landscape is made up of thousands of lakes and hills.
- **Karkonosze Mountains** *(see page 282)* The Karkonosze straddle the Polish-Czech border, and offer great hiking. They host some of the most majestic waterfalls in Europe.

ONLY IN POLAND

- **The Górals** *(see page 242)* The mountain Górals are one of Poland's minorities. They have preserved their culture which is today thriving. Taste their cuisine in the resort of Zakopane, and the villages of the High Tatras.
- **Wieliczka Salt Mine** *(see page 214)* dates from the 12th century. A fascinating tour takes you down several levels to view the amazing churches, chapels and even chandeliers carved out of the salt by miners over the centuries.
- **Bison** European Bison roam wild in the forests of both Northern and Eastern Poland.
- ***Pierogi*** Tasty Polish treats eaten for breakfast, lunch or dinner. A little like ravioli, *pierogi* can be filled with cheese, spinach, cabbage or even fruits.

PICTURESQUE POLAND

- **Zamość** *(see page 231)* The small Renaissance town of Zamość is one of Poland's little gems. The arcaded houses are painted vivid yellow, brick-red and blue, with Oriental detailing of 17th-century Armenian merchants.
- **Poznań** *(see page 289)* is one of Poland's oldest cities with a wealth of Gothic, Renaissance and neo-Classical architecture. The Old Market Square is one of the largest and finest in Poland.
- **Kazimierz Dolny** *(see page 234)* One of the most beautiful places in Poland. The small, mercantile town is a confection of elaborate Renaissance and Mannerist houses.

ABOVE: Zakopane and the Tatra Mountains.
ABOVE LEFT: selling smoked cheese in Zakopane.
BELOW: the Old Town Square of Zamość. is lined with ornately painted burghers' houses.

JEWISH HISTORY AND CULTURE

- **Kazimierz** *(see page 211)* Poland was once a place of refuge for Europe's Jews, who prospered in Kazimerz, in Kraków, and in Łodz especially. Though almost wiped out in the Holocaust, Jews are slowly returning to Poland; Kazimierz's revival echoes this flourishing of Jewish culture.

- **Auschwitz** *(see page 258)* Now a place of pilgrimage and remembrance for Jews, Gypsies and any number of nationalities who suffered here, modern-day Auschwitz is a solemn yet compelling place that should be visited by all.

- **Radegast Station**, Łodz *(see page 191)* Like Auschwitz, this moving memorial has become a site of pilgrimage for many Jews. The original, empty cattle trucks which sit at the platform – once used to carry Jews from here to the death camps – are eerily poignant and loaded with meaning.

- **The Old Synagogue**, Kraków *(see page 212)* Dating from the early 15th century, the Old Synagogue is the oldest surviving Jewish house of worship in Poland. Today, this Gothic synagogue houses a superb exhibition of Polish-Jewish history and the culture that once flourished here.

- **Ariel**, Kraków *(see page 391)* Though not entirely kosher, the Ariel restaurant offers the best range of Jewish specialities in the country and stocks a fabulous selection of kosher wines in the cellar.

ABOVE: Kraków's Main Market Square.
BELOW: the infamous Nazi death camp, Auschwitz, is now a Unesco World Heritage Site and museum.

IMPERIAL KRAKÓW

- **Rynek Głowny** *(see page 203)* Kraków's Main Market Square never fails to amaze and inspire. Miraculously spared the ravages of both war and Communism, the mix of Baroque and Art Nouveau architecture is a joy to behold, especially early in the morning before the hordes arrive.

- **Wawel Castle** *(see page 209)* The Royal Castle was the seat of power for centuries of Polish kings. Wawel towers over Kraków to this day, a symbol not just of the city but of Polish greatness. Visit the sumptuous royal apartments and admire the wealth of jewels in the treasury.

- **Czartoryski Museum** *(see page 207)* The priceless *Lady with an Ermine* by Leonardo da Vinci is the prize exhibit that brings the visitors in, but there are thousands of other works of art to enjoy in this stunning museum.

- **Planty Park** *(see page 206)* The old city walls of Kraków were demolished in the 19th century and laid to lawns. The result is Planty, a glorious green oasis that circumnavigates the old city centre.

- **Dragon's Cave** *(see page 211)* The kids will love this one; the spooky home of Kraków's legendary fire-breathing dragon who was eventually killed by a lowly shoemaker. After descending into the cave you emerge on the banks of the Vistula River.

BALTIC BEAUTIES

●**Amber** *(see page 338)* Take a walk along Mariacka in Gdańsk, one of the city's most beautiful streets, given over almost entirely to the sale of amber, known in these parts as Baltic Gold.

●**Sopot** *(see page 342)* Poland's most swish and fashionable beach resort is a refuge for

the country's rich and famous. Expensive yachts line the shore, in full view of the balconies of the Grand Hotel, historically Poland's best and most expensive.

●**Gdańsk Maritime Museum** *(see page 339)* Admire the Gdańsk Crane (Żuraw Gdański), used since the 15th century to raise the masts of the tall ships that docked in the harbour. Opposite is the *Sołdek*, the first ship built in Gdańsk's reopened shipyards after World War II.

●**Wolin** *(see page 328)* Site of one of the earliest Slavic settlements on Polish territory, this small town lies on an island at the heart of a mini-lake district. Today it is a nature reserve for a number of species of birds.

●**Hel Peninsula** *(see page 345)* Take the ferry from Gdynia to the Hel Peninsula, site of Poland's sandiest beaches and home to the country's best seafood.

ABOVE: arts, leisure and shopping, all under one roof at Manufaktura in Łodz.
BELOW LEFT: people promenading on the pier in the Baltic resort of Sopot.

CONTEMPORARY POLAND

●**Manufaktura**, Łodz *(see page 191)* Carving the future out of the past, this massive recreational complex makes unique use of a former textile mill.

●**Nowy Świat**, Warsaw *(see page 164)* Poland's best address. Lined with smart cafés and restaurants, this elegant street is proof that Poland's darkest years are well and truly behind it.

●**Roads to Freedom** *(see page 340)* The fall of the Berlin Wall and the end of the Soviet Empire began right here, at the Gdańsk Shipyards. Visit the Roads to Freedom museum, opposite the shipyard gates, for a fascinating modern history lesson.

● **Nowa Huta** *(see page 213)* A visit to this surreal place in Kraków gives an insight into the kind of world the Stalinists who ruled Eastern Europe for much of the latter 20th century wanted to create.

MONEY-SAVING TIPS

Poland is not by most standards an expensive country to visit, but with prices rising all the time it's useful to know where and how you can save a few pennies.

Museums Almost all Polish museums offer free entrance one day a week.

Hotels Never turn up on spec at a Polish hotel and expect a bargain. Most hotels have high rack rates which are heavily discounted for visitors booking via the hotel's website. Try the Poland specialist; www.staypoland.com for the best deals.

Use public tranport With taxis relatively expensive, you are advised to stick to public transport. Most Polish cities have excellent public transport networks. Trams especially are clean, reliable and usually fast.

Eating Out Many restaurants in the biggest cities, especially Warsaw, charge very high prices. To eat cheaply, look out for places off the main tourist routes, or for *pierogi* bars, where tasty little Polish ravioli can be bought for next to nothing.

THE APPEAL OF POLAND

Often caught between the geopolitical forces of east and west,
Poland has mastered the subtle arts of survival

For more than a millennium, Poland has played a vital role in European history. The country's position in the heart of Europe has always made it a bridge between the two great cultures on its eastern and western flanks. The resulting diversity of influences has helped to shape the mentality of the people, who are tolerant of differing opinions and ways of life, yet open-minded about new ideas and hospitable towards strangers.

Neither oppression nor the centuries of brutal violence perpetrated by neighbouring countries have succeeded in stifling Poland's liberal spirit. Even during times of upheaval, when the country was obliterated from the map of Europe, the safeguarding of national culture, the recollection of a glorious past, Christian-humanistic traditions and solidarity remained at the forefront of the collective memory. These values still abound, and in such a climate there has never been room for any one "truth" or a monopoly of any one doctrine. The Poles have never allowed their liberty to be curtailed.

Poland has so much to offer – seaside resorts by the Baltic, hillwalking in the High Tatra Mountains, canoeing on the rivers and lakes of Mazuria, strolling through the Old Town in the historic city of Gdańsk, touring the monuments in Kraków or enjoying a beer in Old Market Square in Warsaw, the nation's capital. In recent years, Poland's appeal as a holiday destination has grown, as the range of accommodation has improved. Now the choice runs from luxury hotel with swimming pool and fitness suite to rooms in a private house, living with a Polish family, to camping by a lake.

If you are looking for some adventurous outdoor activities, then Poland is just the place. You can explore the countryside on foot, by bike, on horseback or by boat. Hunters and anglers have also discovered the special attractions that Poland can offer. If wildlife is one of your passions, then there is a good chance that you will catch a glimpse of some unusual species. Storks, for example, are very much in evidence in Mazuria, while bison, elk and tarpan, a kind of wild horse once thought to be extinct, are much rarer.

As well as these natural treasures, Poland possesses some imposing buildings: the Teutonic Knights' castle at Malbork or the magnificent complex on the Wawel in Kraków. The Old Town in Warsaw and the heart of ancient Gdańsk have been rebuilt to their former splendour. ❑

PRECEDING PAGES: freshly-painted townhouses in Zamość; sheep grazing in the Podhale region.
LEFT: flute-player in youth orchestra.

Decisive Dates

6th century AD The Slavonic tribe Polanie appeared on the Warta, an eastern tributary of the Oder. Related tribes occupy the Vistula basin.

966 The Polish court adopts Christianity. Count Mieszko unifies Polanie and neighbouring tribes.

1000 The first Polish church province is established in Gniezno.

1024 Bolesław I Chrobry is crowned King of Poland.

1138 Duke Bolesław Krzywousty divides the country into provinces, which are then ruled by his sons.

1226 Duke Konrad Mazowiecki asks the Teutonic

Order of Knights to Poland to join him against the Prussians. The knights then establish their own state and rule over large areas of the eastern Baltic.

1241 The Mongols raze Kraków and invade Silesia. Silesian duke Henryk Pobożny dies in battle at Legnica. The Mongols later withdraw from Poland.

1320 Duke Władysław I Łokietek is crowned king of Poland, having partly reunified the country.

1333–1370 Łokietek's son, King Kazimierz III Wielki, last in the Piast dynasty, consolidates his father's territory. Poland becomes an regional power broker and begins its expansion eastwards.

1386 11-year-old Hungarian princess Jadwiga is crowned queen of Poland and two years later marries the Lithuanian Grand Duke Jagiełło. Process of unification of Poland and Lithuania is initiated.

1410 Defeat of the Teutonic Order of Knights allows greater expansion of power in the unified realm.

1466 In the second Peace of Toruń, the Teutonic Knights recognise the sovereignty of the Polish kings and cede territory, including the city of Gdańsk, to Poland. The Jagiellons now rule from the Baltic Sea to the Black Sea.

1505 At the Diet or Sejm of Radom the king grants unprecedented rights to the nobility, establishing the "rule of nobility" as a Polish form of government.

1525 The "Knights' State", which has been secularised in the wake of the Reformation, becomes the Duchy of Prussia, a fiefdom of the Polish crown, under Duke Albrecht of Hohenzollern.

1543 Copernicus publishes his book *De revolutionibus orbium Coelestium* on planetary motion.

1552 An Imperial Council grants the right to religious freedom. Poland is a centre of tranquillity in the turmoil of the European religious wars.

1564 Bishop Hosius of Ermland invites the Jesuits into Poland. The Counter-Reformation starts.

1569 Under the Union of Lublin, Poland and Lithuania are united to form an "inseparable whole".

1572 The death of Zygmunt August brings an end to the Jagiellon dynasty.

1618 The state of Brandenburg-Prussia is born.

1648–54 Rebellion of the Dnieper Cossacks under Bogdan Chmielnicki (Khmelnytsky) brings an army of Cossacks and Tartars up to the banks of Vistula.

1655–60 A Swedish invasion drives the King Jan Kazimierz into exile. The Swedes are eventually expelled but the peace treaty of Oliwa ends Polish domination in northeast Europe.

1683 King John III of Poland (Jan Sobieski) is given the credit for expelling the Turks from Vienna.

1772 The First Partition of Poland.

1791 King Stanisław II, head of a Polish reform movement, proclaims a liberal constitution.

1795 In the Third Partition, Austria, Prussia and Russia occupy Poland despite fierce resistance.

1830–32 The November uprising against Russia, to restore the commonwealth of Poland-Lithuania, is crushed. 10,000 insurgents go to France and many more march to Siberia.

1863-64 The January rising against tsarist rule ends with the execution of its leaders at the Warsaw citadel and 80,000 Poles go to Siberia.

1918 With military defeat of the three occupying forces, an independent Polish state is declared on 7 October. In November, Józef Piłsudski, as a provisional Leader of the State, assumes military and political control over re-emerging Poland.

1920 Under President Piłsudski, Poland stops the advance of the Red Army at the Vistula and occupies part of the Ukraine and Lithuania. Under the Treaty of Versailles, Gdańsk becomes a "Free City".
1921 After a Polish uprising, Upper Silesia is divided between Poland and Germany.
1926 Piłsudski regains power in coup; his method of government becomes ever-more authoritarian.
1939 On 1 September World War II starts with the German assault on the Polish garrison on the Westerplatte off Gdańsk. On 17 September, the Soviet Union attacks eastern areas of Poland. Hitler and Stalin then divide the country.
1944 The Warsaw rebellion – the culmination of an embittered and protracted resistance to Nazi rule – is led by partisans and the Polish *Armia Krajowa*, backed by the government-in-exile in London.
1945 The "Lublin Committee" proclaims itself the provisional government. Supported by the Soviet army, the communists suppress all opposition. The Soviet economic system is introduced. At the Yalta and Potsdam conferences Poland's territory is extended westwards. In the east large territories fall to the Soviet Union and their republics.
1955 Founding of the "Warsaw Pact" and "Treaty of Friendship, Co-operation and Mutual Assistance" with the Soviet Union and other Eastern bloc states in reply to the founding of NATO. A year later, after strikes and unrest in Poznań, the National Communist Gomulka assumes leadership of the country.
1970 The Federal Republic of Germany and Poland sign a treaty restoring normal relations.
1980 Strikes in Gdańsk spread country-wide. Formation of an independent trades union known as "Solidarność" or Solidarity.
1981 General Jaruzelski declares martial law on 13 December to pre-empt an invasion by the Warsaw Pact. The opposition goes underground.
1989 The communist leadership agrees to share power with the opposition headed by Lech Wałęsa. Solidarity candidate Tadeusz Mazowiecki becomes leader of the new government.
1990 Following unification, Germany formally recognises Poland's western border. Lech Wałęsa wins the presidential elections by a narrow majority.
1993 The country's first woman prime minister, Hanna Suchocka, resigns. Soviet troops leave Poland. After four Solidarity governments, the left-wing government of Waldemar Pawlak takes over.

PRECEDING PAGES: Warsaw at the start of the 20th century. **LEFT:** Traditional religious wood carving. **RIGHT:** Prime Minister, Donald Tusk.

1995 Alexander Kwaśniewski, a junior minister in Poland's last communist government, defeats Lech Wałęsa in a presidential election.
1997 Solidarity Electoral Action (AWS), the political wing of the Solidarity trade union, wins the general election and forms a new government. Jerzy Buzek becomes prime minister and oversees the introduction of a new constitution later in the year.
1998 President Kwaśniewski vetoes a law which proposed allowing all Poles free access to their secret police files.
1999 Poland joins NATO.
2000 Kwaśniewski wins a second term in office in October's presidential election.

2001 The Democratic Left Alliance wins parliamentary elections, with the centre-right Civic Platform becoming the main opposition party. Solidarity fails to win a single seat.
2004 Poland joins the EU.
2005 The right-wing Lech Kaczyński is elected president after defeating Civic Platform candidate Donald Tusk in a run-off election. In parliamentary elections Kaczyński's Law and Justice party win the most seats. Kaczyński's twin brother Jarosław is named prime minister.
2007 Jarosław Kaczyński's deeply unpopular government is forced to resign, prompting a general election. The Civic Platform is returned as the largest party, and Tusk is named prime minister. ❏

A GLORIOUS PAST

During this period of history the newly formed Polish nation consolidated

its power and took on much of its present-day territorial form

The vast plain between the Odra and Vistula rivers, which flow from the Carpathian and the Sudeten mountains as far the Baltic Sea, has been at the interface between two great cultures ever since the Stone Age. After a period of Celtic influences, west Slavic tribes settled here. They had already mastered the skills of iron-making and had nurtured good relations with the countries of southern Europe.

The Ślężanie, the Mazowszanie, the Pomorzanie and the Wiślanie – the tribes who inhabited the area we now know as Silesia (in the southwest), Pomerania (in the north) and Mazovia (the region around Warsaw) – combined to form a defensive pact. To protect their settlements, which quickly developed into centres of craftsmanship and trade, they surrounded them with strong defensive walls.

The early state

The ruler Mieszko I, a member of the Piast dynasty, united the Polanie tribe of the Warta Valley with other groups that were linguistically and culturally related. The land occupied by these tribes was bordered to the south and west by Christian states that were closely tied to Rome. In order to project his state onto the European stage, Mieszko was subsequently baptised, together with his subjects. He married the Czech princess Dobrava, thereby securing the southern borders of his territory. Mieszko's son, Bolesław I Chrobry (the Brave), established an independent, ecclesiastical administration which – enlightened yet rigidly centralised – set about integrating the component parts of the state.

In AD 1000, the Holy Roman Emperor Otto III was received with great pomp at Gniezno, the then capital of Poland. When Chrobry took over the Bohemian throne in 1003, it brought him into conflict with Otto's successor – Heinrich II, who

---

LEFT: *The Black Madonna of Częstochowa,* a Byzantine icon of unknown age.

RIGHT: Madonna figure on the clock of St Mary's church, Gdańsk.

invaded Poland on several occasions. The protracted war ended with the peace treaty of Bautzen (Budziszyn) in 1018, which established Polish control in Lausitz (Łużyce), west of the River Oder. (History repeated itself just under 1,000 years later, when a German invasion of Poland culminated in a similar conclusion.)

The proud victor was not content with stopping there. He wanted to expand eastwards too – in the name of Christianity. Bolesław annexed Ruthenia (present-day Ukraine) with its capital of Kiev to Poland. In 1025 he was rewarded by the Pope, who presented him with the royal insignia. Poland had become a fully-fledged member of the Christian community of states.

The Piast dynasty

Throughout his lifetime Bolesław III Krzywousty (the wry-mouthed) tightened the bonds between Pomerania and the Polish state, but in his will he divided the country among his four sons. Soon the brothers and their successors were engaged in unseemly disputes over royal titles, leadership claims and commercial advantages. The centre of political life moved from Wielkopolska (Great Poland) to Małopolska (Little Poland) in the southeast. Its capital, Kraków, lay in a favourable position on the trade route from Regensburg and Vienna to Kiev and Byzantium.

> **NATIONAL TRIBE**
>
> The Polanie tribe, who lived in the Warta valley not far from Poznań, were the peoples who gave Poland its name.

Immigrants soon arrived in great numbers from northern Germany and the Netherlands. Thousands of Jews, persecuted elsewhere in Europe, sought refuge in a part of the continent

dangerous to Mazovia. In 1226, Duke Konrad of Mazovia who bore the brunt of their constant raids, invited the German Order of Teutonic Knights to assist him (*see page 263*). The Order had just been expelled from the Holy Land after the failure of the last crusade and was ready to take any employment. The Order carried out the task by wiping out the Prussians and establishing a state of their own in the conquered land, but this soon began to threaten Poland. In 1308 it took over Gdańsk and massacred its popula-

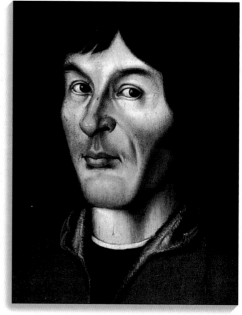

that had by then become renowned for religious tolerance. They did not arrive empty-handed, but brought new tools and new ways of doing business. Before long, Kraków was enjoying a period of unrivalled commercial prosperity and cultural richness. Nor was the development of the Polish state seriously impeded by the Mongol invasions of the 13th century. It was during this time that Wrocław, Kraków and Poznań decided to adopt the Magdeburg municipal law, which afforded good conditions for economic development.

In the north, Poland bordered with Prussian pagan tribes. They resisted all previous Polish missionary attempts and were particularly

tion. In the wars between 1327 and 1333 it laid waste large parts of Wielkopolska.

Nevertheless, the old Piast dynasty managed to uphold the idea of a united Polish state during two centuries of feudal dismemberment. By the end of the 12th century, the kingdom consolidated itself again. The difficult task was successfully concluded when in 1320 Władysław Łokietek was crowned in Kraków as an undisputed king of the united kingdom.

The restored *Corona Regni Poloniae* received a modern constitution and a stable currency during the reign of his son Kazimierz III Wielki (Casimir the Great). It was said that he had found Poland built in wood, and left it built in stone. During Kazimierz's reign (1333–70) the full "polonisation" of Małopolska was finally completed.

The most important development, however, was that of establishing the Polish identity as firmly belonging to the western European civilisation. As the last Piast king, Kazimierz may have achieved much on the domestic front, but was less successful from a military point of view. He had a dense network of fortified castles built throughout the country, but the expansion to the eastern territories left other areas of the kingdom vulnerable and resulted in the loss of the whole of Silesia.

Teutonic Knights. Despite the spectacular victory of the union's army at Grunwald in 1410, the military power of the Order was not broken until the 1454–66 war. From then on Gdańsk was to have the special status of a free city state ruled by the kings of Poland.

The new king, Kazimierz Jagiellończyk (1445–92) became known as the "Father of Europe". Of his 11 children, one son became a cardinal, four became kings, one was canonised and the three daughters were married off to become the mothers of the heirs of some of the greatest dynasties in western Europe. Nevertheless, Jagiellończyk and his successors did

The Jagiellons

After the death of the last Piast king, the Polish throne fell to the Hungarian line of the royal family of d'Anjou. Soon afterwards, however, the kingdom was united with the Grand Duchy of Lithuania. The new ruler, the Grand Duke of Lithuania, Władysław Jagiełło and his subjects converted to Christianity and Jagiełło married the Polish queen Jadwiga d'Anjou. The immediate reason for this union was the continuing threat posed by the German Order of

FAR LEFT: trade flourished during the Middle Ages.
LEFT: portrait of Nicholas Copernicus.
ABOVE: defeat of the Teutonic Order at Grunwald, 1410.

NICHOLAS COPERNICUS

Mikołaj Kopernik (Nicholas Copernicus) was born in Toruń in 1473. In 1491 he enrolled at the Jagiellonian University in Kraków, and studied in Italy before becoming a priest.

However, in true Renaissance fashion, his interests far exceeded the narrow confines of the church and he became particularly interested in astronomy. While canon of Frombork he constructed an observatory and from here discovered that it was the sun at the centre of the universe, not the Earth as previously thought. He published his findings as *De Revolutionibus Orbium Celestium* in 1543 but died later that year. The treatise was later banned by the Pope.

not manage to convert these exceedingly favourable family connections into real political power. This was primarily due to the very strong economic position of the nobility, which, as a reward for its participation in wars, was granted numerous and far-reaching privileges.

Around 1500, the population of the multinational, multi-faith Polish-Lithuanian Commonwealth stood at around 7.5 million in an area of about 1.1 million sq km (420,000 sq miles). Ethnic Poles made up only about 50 percent of

RENAISSANCE ERA

The Renaissance period was influential in Poland, largely because of its connections with Italy. Many Italianate buildings survive in Polish towns and cities.

dynasty of Germany, who were supporters of the Lutheran doctrines, and closely aligned with the house of Brandenburg.

Even though religious wars were raging in the west, the traditional and reformed religious denominations continued to live amicably in the territory ruled by the Polish crown. Religious tolerance was a central element of the "golden period of liberty", as the Polish state ideology was known at the time.

In 1569 the union of the Polish crown with

the total population. However, during the reign of the last Jagiellons – Zygmunt Stary (1506–48) and Zygmunt August (1548–72) – the country once more enjoyed a cultural and political boom, known in history as the "Golden Age of Poland". Polish language became the *lingua franca* of the eastern European nobility. The Polish, Lithuanian and Ruthenian gentry, which was quite used to the cohabitation of people of different denominations, readily accepted the revolutionary teachings of Luther and Calvin.

At the time of the Reformation, the Teutonic Order of Knights was also secularised. In effect, this meant it was subjugated to the secular administration of the Hohenzollern

Lithuania was renewed and a "Republic of Two Nations" was proclaimed.

An elective monarchy

In the mid-16th century, political and economic life had been characterised by the growing power of the Lithuanian and Ruthenian aristocratic families. Their huge estates in the east afforded them economic independence and enabled them to rise to the highest official posts. There they pursued solely their own interests, without any consideration of matters of state. At the same time powerful and aggressive forces developed within the adjoining states: in the west the Habsburgs, in the southeast Turkey, with its ambitions to conquer the continent, Moscow under the rule of Ivan the Terrible in the east, and Sweden in the north.

When the Jagiellon dynasty came to an end, the *Sejm,* the Polish parliament, introduced an elective monarchy. However, Henri de Valois, the first king to be elected (in 1573) decided to return to France to rule there as King Henry III. The next king, Stefan Batory, Duke of Transylvania (1576–86) was a superb military strategist, but constantly had to struggle to find sufficient funds to wage war: the powerful nobility evaded all state taxes and the war treasury was bankrupt. In spite of all this, he

elected for life. Although the electorate was limited to the gentry, they formed more than 20 percent of the population, comprising not only large landowners and numerous owners of one to three villages, but also (by far the largest group) those possessing a homestead with a few acres of arable land, which they tilled themselves. Their financial status may have been as low as that of an average peasant, but their social standing was as high as any magnate with thousands of peasants working his estate.

In effect, the size of the electorate in Poland in the 17th century was not equalled by the rest of Europe until the second half of the 19th

won the war with Russia and consolidated Poland's position in the east of Europe by annexing Livonia.

In 1587 a member of the Swedish Vasa dynasty was elected King of Poland. Zygmunt III Vasa and his successors Władysław IV and Jan Kazimierz ruled Poland until 1668, but the country's economy continued to decline.

In the 17th century, the Polish political system became fully established. Kings of Poland were

LEFT: Duke Albrecht of Prussia, Grand Master of the Teutonic Order, swears allegiance to King Zygmunt II.
ABOVE: King Stefan Batory receives the surrender of Pskov.

century. In the absence of modern communications, new members of parliament were elected by local county assemblies *(Sejmiki).* Their number varied from 65 to 75 and they elected new members of parliament at special sessions, which were, in fact, congresses of the county gentry. The assemblies' role was not limited to the election of members of parliament. Their main political task was to discuss, approve or veto any new government measures and legislation. The elected members were then issued with instructions on how to vote in parliament. In this way members of parliament truly represented the general electorate. The powers of local assemblies were considerable: they could impose their own local taxes or even raise their own county troops. The system was not only well established, but worked as efficiently as only parliamentary systems can. It was a supreme exponent of the "golden liberty of Poland", the pride of every Pole and, without doubt, the only system of its kind in Europe.

The system, based on the representation of local interests which strongly resembled a federation, more than any other demanded the universal acceptance of laws by all component parties. Consequently, it was argued that only total unanimity of all members could be just to all. This ideal was often reached after many

rest of Europe. The political systems of the west were steadily moving towards strengthening the power of central authorities, until what became known as "absolutist monarchies" were established. Whether they called themselves "enlightened" or not, any form of absolute power in the hands of central government was totally alien to the spirit of Poland. In this respect, the gap between Poland and the rest of Europe was growing.

Terror of the Turks

The Polish parliament was parsimonious in their expenditure on armed forces and each

long debates, but unfortunately it became a parliamentary tradition which, in turn, developed into a principle. Worse consequences followed. In 1652 a member of parliament protested against some matters under discussion and left the House. A baffled speaker suspended the session, and such was the enormous power of the parliamentary precedent that henceforward, one member vetoing the proceedings could cause suspension of the session, thus nullifying all laws proposed for that session by the government. The principle of *liberum veto* (veto of the free) was born, with disastrous consequences.

Whatever merits or demerits of the system, its direction was diametrically opposite to the

Commander-in-Chief, or Grand Hetman of the Republic had to fight hard to defend his army estimates and was lucky to get half of the money he needed. Consequently, the aim was to command a small but extremely efficient force. The peace establishment of the armed forces never exceeded 20,000, grouped exclusively in the Ukraine (Ukraina meaning "borderland") under the name of a Mobile Defence Force. Mobile they had to be to meet the annual raids of Tartars, Cossacks and later Ottoman Turks. The war establishment also comprised foreign mercenary troops or, in the last resort, a General Levy of all the gentry, raised under the banners of their own counties.

The army compensated its numerical weakness by its high combat effectiveness, which allowed Poland to emerge victorious from numerous wars of the 17th century. It scored resounding victories over the Russians, Turks, Cossacks, Tartars and even over the large and efficient armies of Sweden. It also produced outstanding commanders. One of them, Grand Hetman Jan Sobieski, was rewarded for his victories with the royal crown of Poland.

During the 17th century, the Ottoman Empire was steadily enlarging its Balkan possessions, aiming at the conquest of Europe. After suffering serious reverses in wars against Poland, the tember 1683, was fought one of the most decisive battles of the world – had the Turks been victorious, it is possible that Islam would have become the ruling religion of Europe. After preliminary artillery fire and infantry skirmishes, Sobieski unleashed the charge of his dreaded, winged hussars. The charge broke through the Turkish lines and in a matter of two hours, the Turkish army was annihilated. Its commander fled the field and the green standard of the Prophet fell into Polish hands. As a trophy, it was sent to Rome. The Turkish might was broken and it ceased to present a threat to European civilisation. ❑

Turks changed their strategic direction and aimed at the very heart of Europe. After defeating the field army of the German Empire, they laid siege to Vienna. With a force of some 140,000 men, they were masters of the situation and in the summer of 1683 Vienna was in dire straits. Envoys sent by the Austrian emperor to Sobieski begged him to rescue the city and the empire. Sobieski, already known throughout Europe as the "Terror of the Turks", sent 29,000 men to Vienna. There, on 12 Sep-

LEFT: an ambassador from Vienna begs for Polish help against the Turks.
ABOVE: Jan Sobieski at the siege of Vienna, 1683.

A CONGENIAL RACE

The *Description of Poland*, Oxford 1733, has this to say about the "Disposition of the Inhabitants": "The Polandres are generally of good complexion. Flaxen-hair'd, and tall of stature. The men… corpulent and personable. The women slender and beautiful, disdaining the help of art… They are naturally open-hearted and candid, more apt to be deceived then to deceive; not so easily provoked as appea'd; neither arrogant, nor obstinate; but very tractable if they be gently managed. They are chiefly led by example; are dutiful to their Princes and magistrates; inclined to civility and hospitality, especially to strangers; whose customs and manners they are forward to imitate…"

DEPENDENCY AND DIVISION

Poland's decline during the 18th century lead to its third partition in 1795.

An independent Polish state didn't exist again until 1918

Poland emerged victorious from the 17th century wars but was economically ruined. Large tracts of land were laid waste. The treasury was empty; the people were exhausted, both materially and spiritually. Polish links with Saxony had always been very close and it seemed propitious to elect a Saxon king on the death of the great Jan Sobieski. Augustus II the Strong, of the House of Wettins, was duly elected King of Poland in 1697.

Russia's dominance

Unfortunately, Augustus II was an adherent of absolutist ideas and his main endeavour was directed towards strengthening his personal power in Poland. He also sought to use the military power of the Republic primarily in promoting the interests of Saxony. To this end, he embroiled Poland in the disastrous second Northern War, which lasted for 20 years and turned the country into a battleground for the armies of Saxony, Russia, Prussia and Sweden. In 1704, under pressure from King Charles XII of Sweden, the exasperated gentry revolted and dethroned Augustus II, electing in his place a Pole, Stanisław Leszczyński. This gave rise to further disturbances and neighbouring powers had the opportunity to intervene in support of either king. This war, in which the Poles were most unwilling participants, brought about devastation on a vast scale and reduced the country to total penury. Army discipline, which only played a marginal role in the war, disintegrated.

As a result of war, Russia emerged as the dominant power. The parliamentary session which was held in Warsaw in 1717 bore the full imprint of its new might. Called the "silent" session because no member was allowed to speak, it marked the beginning of Russian rule over Poland, under the guise of protecting the old liberties of the Republic. Under Russian pressure, all gentry privileges were confirmed and even extended. It was Russia which officially became

the guarantor of the "golden liberty" of the Poles and any true or imaginary infringement would give it a pretext for military intervention. The total strength of the army was permanently fixed at 24,000, a ridiculous figure in comparison to standing armies of more than 200,000 each of Russia, Austria and Prussia.

Under these prevailing conditions, effective governing of the state was impossible for the king or any other body. With the rapid disintegration of its domestic market and lack of organised foreign trade relations, the state had been heading for bankruptcy since the beginning of the century. Like the sword of Damocles, the threatening coalition of neighbouring states was hanging over Poland.

In 1764, Stanisław August of the Poniatowski family was elected king. He has been brought up in the spirit of French enlightenment and he did his best to revitalise the state. His endeavours at reform and in inspiring a cultural movement that had a decidedly nat-

LEFT: Canaletto's view of Warsaw.
RIGHT: Mural on shop wall, Wolin.

ional character received much support from the intellectuals and the gentry. First successes were soon apparent: some form of discipline returned to parliament and the tax system was reformed. But the new custom offices, which were to provide the treasury with additional income, were prevented from functioning through intervention from Berlin. In 1768, in the town of Bar (in present-day Ukraine) a patriotic confederation was formed chiefly by conservative elements, directed against Russian

COMMENDING BRAVERY

The world's first Order for Bravery for all ranks in the field was the *Order Viruti Militari* (for Military Virtue), instituted by Stanisław August during the 1792 war with Russia.

sq km (31,623 sq miles) and Russia 93,000 sq km (35,908 sq miles). This annexation by the coalition of three powers became known as the First Partition of Poland. The Republic had no means of defending itself against the onslaught, but it was immediately realised that in order to survive, comprehensive reforms were imperative and the king became the leading spirit of far-reaching changes in political and social fields. A strong government was set up comprising, among other bodies, the Min-

dominance. It formed its own army, which attacked Russian garrisons in Poland. The confederation's struggle lasted for four years and effectively put a stop to economic revival and turned the country once more into a battlefield. Eventually, Russian military might prevailed and confederates were crushed.

The partition of Poland

The events served as a pretext for a Russian diplomatic initiative to partition Poland between the three powers: Russia, Austria and Prussia. In 1772 these powers annexed large parts of the state of Poland: Prussia gained 36,300 sq km (14,016 sq miles) Austria 81,900

istry of Education, the first ministry of its kind in the world, preceding other European states by almost a century.

The session of parliament which began in 1788 lasted for four years and reformed the political system of Poland. When the session ended, the country had acquired the most modern framework of political law in Europe, including that of revolutionary France.

This was embodied in the new constitution of 3 May 1791 which granted more power to all citizens, allowed greater autonomy to towns and gave full legal protection to the peasant class. "The Great *Sejm*", as the session was called, fixed the number of the standing army at 100,000 men. Again, it was Stanisław August who led the reform. The influence of his intellect was felt in all spheres of social and cultural life.

Kościuszko and the peasants

Russia took these manifestations of Poland's revival as a serious threat. Empress Catherine II decided to take immediate action. First she mobilised her own adherents who belonged to the most conservative elements in Poland. On her orders, they formed a Confederation in Targowica and declared the Constitution null and void. Following this they requested Russian

States' War of Independence. The other general was Prince Józef Poniatowski, nephew of the king: when in the king's view the war became hopeless, he ordered capitulation and submitted to humiliating conditions by the victors.

There followed the Second Partition of Poland. But even the small part of the country nominally left free was occupied by Russia, with strong garrisons in all towns. They were there primarily to supervise the total disbandment of the Polish army, but the army, though beaten in the field, retained its high morale. Its officers, supported by large numbers of citizens, requested General Kościuszko to lead

military intervention, which the Tsarina was only too eager to grant. The Russian army invaded Poland. The invasion was staunchly resisted by the army which was still far from the numerical strength as fixed by the Great *Sejm*. The war lasted several months, during which two generals became known throughout Europe. One was Tadeusz Kościuszko, who had already distinguished himself during the United

FAR LEFT: Stanisław Poniatowski, the last king of Poland. **LEFT:** detail from Jan Matejko's painting portraying the 1773 partition of Poland.
ABOVE: a cartoon depicting the occupation of Wrocław by hostile forces (1741).

them in a new, full-scale war. He promptly agreed, and in March 1794 he stood in the old marketplace in Kraków and proclaimed a national insurrection against the invaders. This scene, immortalised in contemporary prints and subsequent paintings, is known to every child in Poland – it is a part of national consciousness.

Being short of arms and ammunition, Kościuszko called upon volunteers from villages in the Kraków district; they eagerly answered his call. Their weapons were scythes, fixed vertically to shafts. With a few battalions of regular troops, squadrons of cavalry and a battalion of Kraków scythemen, Kościuszko marched to meet the Russian Army Corps. They met head on near the village of Racławice. The battle took the usual shape of the times, opening with the artillery bombardment and infantry on both sides trying to seize commanding positions. At midday, Kościuszko personally led the attack with his scythemen against a strong battery of Russian guns. The attack was delivered in the only way known to this improvised infantry: at the double and in loose column. The gunners had time for one salvo only, after which they met their deaths from terrible weapons in the hands of the scythemen. The Russian line broke and soon the whole corps was in full flight.

News of victory, the first since the relief of Vienna, was greeted throughout the country with enthusiasm. However soon afterwards, the uprising was crushed by the Russians which led to the Third Partition of the country, finally blotting out Poland from the map of Europe.

The Napoleonic era

When the last shots of the war were fired in Poland, the name of General Bonaparte was beginning to be well-known in Europe. This young general of the French revolutionary army, was fighting one of the enemies of Poland in Italy. Indeed, he had already had several astonishing successes against the Austrians.

1794 UPRISING AND MASSACRE

While Kościuszko and his men were fighting in the field, the citizens of Warsaw rose against the Russian garrison and expelled it after murderous street battles. The same happened in Wilno. Prussia sent its army to assist the hard-pressed Russians and both armies laid siege to Warsaw. After a few unsuccessful attempts at storming the city, they had to abandon the siege.

So far the uprising was victorious, but in October 1794, Kościuszko personally took command of a division with the intention of intercepting the Russians at the crossing of the Vistula at Maciejowice. Faulty intelligence caused him to meet an enemy double in numbers to his own army.

Wounded, Kościuszko fell into Russian hands and, now leaderless, the Polish army suffered reverses. A new Russian army, commanded by General Suvoroff, approached Warsaw. The right bank suburb of Praga was hastily fortified and defended by General Jasinski, the liberator of Wilno. The Russians overwhelmed the defenders by sheer numbers and butchered the civilian population. They murdered every man, woman and child in an orgy of killing which lasted throughout the day and following night.

The massacre of Warsaw's civilian population, unheard of in Europe since the Tartar invasions, shook the entire civilised world.

One of the first Poles to arrive in Italy was a general who had distinguished himself during the Insurrection. His name was Jan Dąbrowski. His plan, speedily agreed by Bonaparte and the French government, was to form a Polish Army as a force allied to the French Republic. Polish Legions in Italy – as they were called – relied on the Austrians to supply them with men. Sure enough, thousands of Poles who had been pressed into the Austrian army soon filled the ranks of the Legions, in addition to thousands of other volunteers escaping from occupied Poland. The Legions fought with distinction not only against the Austrians, but also against the Russians who invaded Italy to assist the hard-pressed Imperial Austrian Army. The Russians were led by the man known as the "butcher of Warsaw", Field-Marshall Suvoroff.

For the rest of the Napoleonic period, Poles fought alongside the French army in all its campaigns. Their hopes were dashed though when after the defeat of Prussia and Russia, Poland was not allowed to be rebuilt but only to form a small state called the Duchy of Warsaw.

Nevertheless it was a good foundation for the state which was to arise after the defeat of Russia in the "Second Polish War" which began in 1812. The Polish army, commanded by Prince Józef Poniatowski, marched to the campaign full of enthusiasm and hope. Unfortunately, the campaign ended in a disastrous retreat of the Grand Army and with this ended all hopes of the resurrection of the Polish Republic. But the army remained true to its allies. During the "Battle of Nations", at Leipzig in October 1813, Prince Józef, by then Marshall of France, fell commanding the rear guard of the army.

Unsettled century

The Congress of Vienna which ended the Napoleonic wars, reconstituted a small Polish state, more or less within the frontiers of the former Duchy of Warsaw. It was a constitutional monarchy, with the Tsar of Russia as its king.

LEFT: the Cossack massacre during the January Uprising of 1863.
RIGHT: statue of Prince Józef Poniatowski outside Radziwiłł Palace in Warsaw.

NATIONAL ANTHEM

The "Song of the Legions of Italy", in the rhythm of the mazurka, declared "Poland shall not die as long as we live". The song was sung in occupied Poland and was soon elevated to national anthem.

The Poles used a few liberties that were afforded them by the Congress of Vienna to help carry out the variety of tasks specified in the Constitution of 3 May 1791.

In 1816, a university was founded in Warsaw, which soon became a decisive factor in the promotion of scientific and cultural contacts with other academic centres in Europe. Russia did not yet have a single university. The idea of a national revival was also evident in the establishment of an independent, domestic industry and the

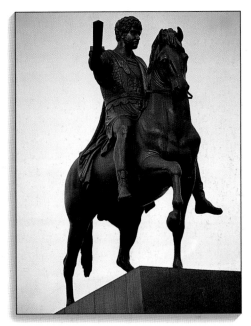

administration structures of a modern state.

However, there were frequent conflicts with Russia's stifling bureaucracy. The sharpest conflicts were those in the army whose Commander-in-Chief, Grand Duke Constantine, was brother of the tsar. The prince attempted to introduce Russian forms of discipline into the Polish army, built on principles of military honour and patriotic duty. He had failed to introduce corporal punishment, but he interfered personally with the minutiae of army routine, driving both officers and men to distraction. This resulted in several cases of suicide among the officers each year. Secret, patriotic associations sprang up everywhere, particularly in the army. The conflicts were growing and finally they erupted in a national uprising in November 1830. The Russians replied with a general offensive which was broken at the gates of Warsaw and for almost a year the Poles were victorious in every engagement. However, Russia's overwhelming superiority in numbers began to be felt and this, coupled with strategic errors by the Polish High Command, brought them back to Warsaw.

In October 1831, Warsaw fell after a short siege and Poland, once again, disappeared from the map of Europe. One of the positive effects of the resultant new wave of emigrants was admiration in western Europe for the freedom

fight in Poland. In the European revolution year of 1848, Poles sought to re-establish their national sovereignty, but were unsuccessful, as were all other revolutionary movements.

Thirty years later, new generations of Poles again took up the armed struggle for freedom. In 1863, circumstances were far less favourable than those in 1830. The armed uprising was prepared after years of secretly gathering arms and of secret training in their use. Secondly, the Russian terror and the vigilance of the secret police made the preparations risky and difficult. The date of the uprising, in January 1863, was necessitated by the Russian plan to draft most of the young men into the Russian army

for 20 years' service from which very few returned alive. In spite of adverse circumstances, the January 1863 uprising lasted longer than the preceding ones. The insurgents continued fighting, even when members of the national government in Warsaw, were captured and executed. Without central direction, the guerrilla type of operations lasted well into 1865, with Lithuanian groups being the most effective. A wave of terror followed the end of the uprising. The Russian governor of Wilno, Muravief, gained for himself special distinction by being known as "Muravief the Hangman".

World War I

It was in the Austrian-occupied part of Poland, with centres in Lwów and Kraków, that the first Polish military organisation since the 1863 uprising was born. It was allowed by the authorities under the guise of a voluntary rifle association. It was a paramilitary organisation, but its secret work aimed at the training of officers and men for the future army of the independent Poland. The man who organised and subsequently commanded all "Riflemen" was Józef Piłsudski, born in Lithuania and an ex-convict in Siberia, where he had served a sentence for anti-Russian activities (*see page 38*).

When war, which everyone in Poland expected, broke out in the summer 1914, he led his riflemen across the line of partition to fight the Russians. When, as a result of German victories in 1916, most of Poland was cleared of Russian armies, Piłsudski launched a new, secret Polish Military Organisation, to which he transferred his best officers. They were to command the forces designated to liberate Poland when Germany and Austria were next beaten by the western Allies. For his refusal to co-operate with the Austro-German authorities, Piłsudski was arrested and imprisoned in the fortress of Magdeburg for the rest of the war.

Meanwhile, in 1917, the US president Woodrow Wilson included independent Poland in one of the US war aims. With the disintegration of Austria first, members of the Polish Military Organisation took to arms. Sharp fighting started first in Lwów which the Ukrainians, armed by the Austrians, tried to seize. ❑

LEFT: picture postcard details of Kraków before 1918.
RIGHT: a patriotic portrayal of the historic ties between Gdańsk and Poland.

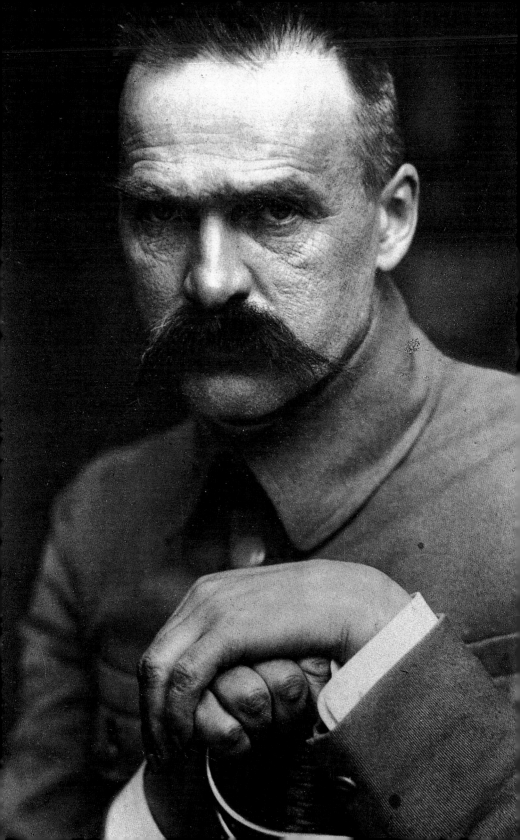

REBIRTH: THE SECOND REPUBLIC

The inter-war years were marked by the re-establishment and expansion of the Polish state under the authoritarian leadership of Józef Piłsudski

In 1918 the banners of rebellion fluttered over the debris of the dynastic empires throughout Europe. Liberty was writ large – larger than it had ever been after 1848 and before 1989.

Now regionally organised, in November 1918 the Poles disarmed the Germans and Austrians, whose leadership had been overthrown and who were too exhausted even to consider a continuation of hostilities. In Poznań weapons for a Polish rebellion were collected. A national government, free from all Bolshevik ambition, was established in Lublin and in Lwów fervently patriotic high school pupils fought street battles with the Ukrainians, who had also started an uprising.

On 7 October 1918, the Regency Council met in Warsaw and proclaimed the Independence of Poland. On 10 November, released from prison, Piłsudski arrived in Warsaw. The Regency Council relinquished its power into his hands, with the title of "Naczelnik", first given to Kościuszko. This made him a virtual dictator. On 11 November 1918 Independence was officially proclaimed and world governments were accordingly notified. The reborn Republic of Poland had no frontiers, no army and no treasury, but universal enthusiasm and the well-known organisational abilities of the Poles remedied many shortcomings. Time was short, with a new danger looming across the temporary demarcation lines in the east.

The Red threat

Hard on the heels of the retreating German army came a new enemy: the Red Army. It represented a new force in world politics – that of the Communist revolution – with its aim to spread its preaching throughout Europe and to create one universal "State of Workers and Peasants". Piłsudski, by then Head of State and Commander-in Chief with the rank of Marshal of Poland, realised the imminent danger. Pił-

LEFT: Józef Piłsudski led the Second Republic to independence.
RIGHT: J. Malczewski, *Bowing before Polonia*.

sudski was a patriot through and through, but neither in the Polish nor the Lithuanian tradition. His lodestar was the Jagiellonian idea of creating a strong political and military structure, capable of forming a strong barrier against any aggression from the east. In modern terms, he was a federalist on the old Polish principle of

the "Free Union of the Free People".

For centuries, the vast lands of the Ukraine, originally populated by nomads from the east, had been the grain store for Poland, and later for the ever more powerful Russian empire. Piłsudski supported the Ukrainian nationalists and, together with allied Ukrainian forces commanded by Ataman Petlura, the Polish army marched into the capital city of Kiev. Unfortunately, the bulk of the Ukrainian population did not support their new government with sufficient strength. While Polish lines were extended, the Red Army launched a major offensive in the north. Under the command of General Tukhachevsky, the Red Army broke through the thinly held Polish front and marched west. The aim of the offensive was to turn Leon Trotsky's command into reality. "Over the corpse of bourgeois Poland" they were to march into Berlin – in socialist hands at the time – to add impetus to the expected Red world revolution.

Under this concentrated offensive, the Polish army retreated. Slowly, one after another, the intended lines of defence were broken. In the south, the dreaded cavalry army, led by Budyonny, spread havoc and panic; in the north, the relentless pressure of the main Russian force, led by Tukhachevsky, turned an

organised retreat into headlong flight. This group of armies had outflanked Warsaw defences from the north, cutting off the lines of supply from Gdańsk and crossing the Vistula at Płock. Seemingly, there was nothing to stop the Red Army from its conquest of Europe, over the dead body of Poland.

But Marshal Piłsudski was not idle. To the southeast of Warsaw he concentrated a group of armies which he decided to command in person. On 16 August 1920 Piłsudski struck due northeast. His attack drove a wedge between the Russian forces and cut Tuhatchevski's lines of communications and their centre gave way.

PIŁSUDSKI – POLAND'S MILITARY HERO

Józef Piłsudski (1867–1935), born in Lithuania into a noble but impoverished Polish family, began his career as a revolutionary. But as far as his political inclination was concerned, he was a pragmatist. Throughout the last 10 years of his life he had a formative influence on the power structure of the state. In theory the structure of the democratic order remained untouched. In practice, however, all the key positions in the army and the administration were held by fervent Piłsudski supporters. A loyal élite was forged from the group of erstwhile soldiers who had fought for independence under his command. A large portion of the intelligentsia were employed in the state administration.

Also, the influence of the aristocracy, who for centuries had owned the landed estates, increased. The socialists in turn – initially supporters of Piłsudski – soon lost any illusions they may have had and joined the opposition. The undoubted charisma of the Marshal was cleverly marketed and his political premises were popularised. The equality of all religious denominations – specified in the constitution – was retained due to his political dexterity. His *savoir-vivre*, his adherence to the traditions of the Polish multinational state, his preference for horses, sabres and swords; all this fused in the eyes of his countrymen to make him the embodiment of a popular hero.

With Polish offensive pressing on, the whole right wing of the Russian army was annihilated. A general rout of the Red Army followed. Marshal Tukhachevsky wrote: "There is not the slightest doubt that, had we been victorious on the Vistula, the revolution would have set light to the entire continent of Europe." The British ambassador in Warsaw, Lord D'Abernon, set down his judgement, as follows: "The history of contemporary civilisation knows no event of greater importance than the Battle of Warsaw."

MUSICAL POWER

In 1919 the acclaimed concert pianist, Ignacy Jan Paderewski, became Poland's second prime minister. He later lived in the United States.

A new democracy

In 1921 a general political consensus resulted in the acceptance of a democratic constitution, based on the French model. After the election victory of the right-wing National Democrats in 1922, Gabriel Narutowicz became the first president of the new republic, elected with votes by the left, centre and national minority parties. Piłsudski was compelled to tender his resignation. Narutowicz did not last long: he was assassinated some days later. When Sikorski became

Major General J.F.C. Fuller, in his work *The Battle of Warsaw* (1920), concurred with this opinion: "It should be the task of political writers to explain to European opinion that Poland saved Europe in 1920, and that it is necessary to keep Poland powerful and in harmonious relations with western European civilisation, for Poland is the barrier to the everlasting peril of an Asiatic invasion... by shielding Central Europe from the full blast of Marxist contagion, the Battle of Warsaw set back the Bolshevik clock."

LEFT: Lviv was a centre for politics and the arts.
ABOVE: the port of Gdynia – gateway to world trade.

prime minister, a new president, Stanisław Wojciechowski, was elected and eventually a degree of stability was once more restored to the political scene.

Although the parliamentary constitution protected the fledgling democracy from the monopolistic claims of the central executive, it had insufficient control to afford total political freedom. The coalition governments of the 1920s worked in an atmosphere of mutual distrust and disunity. Their attempt to turn high-flying modernisation plans into reality did not really get off the ground – not surprising, considering the vast number of problems the country faced.

Currency reform ultimately proved advantageous, but it entailed an unpopular limitation of social rights. As was the case in other European states, this in turn encouraged radical political groupings to start to question the legitimacy and leadership mandate of parliament.

Only within the army did a strong, supraregional link to the new, united state emerge. In the spring of 1926, the economic conditions worsened with increased inflation and unemployment. In May, the new centre-right government of Wincenty Witos met strong opposition from the socialists and from Piłsudski, who was also deeply dissatisfied with the

to enable Poland in the long run to play a mediating role between the so-called "wild east" and the "civilised west". With the creation of a Non-Partisan Bloc for Cooperation with the Government, parliament was left with only a very few legislative functions.

Using an impending coup as a pretext, legal proceedings were instigated against the socialist deputies. The judiciary managed to save face by remaining independent and passing purely symbolic sentences, but nevertheless the young democracy lost much of its credibility.

Piłsudski not only sanctioned this development, he even consented to the new, restrictive

existing structure of the high military command. On May 12 Piłsudski decided to lead his loyal military units into Warsaw. After several days of street battles the coup succeeded and Piłsudski once again managed to gain total control. A new political strategy of restructuring, that went under the name of *"Sanacja"* ("Recovery"), was introduced.

Piłsudski's paternalistic leadership ideal was underscored by a cult of strict bureaucracy and the reliance on the obedient and loyal citizen. The encouragement of such characteristics in the national consciousness was not only designed to guarantee survival for a nation wedged between "traditional enemies", but also

constitution during his final hours on his deathbed. On his death in 1935, he left a vacuum that was filled by the somewhat weaker General Edward Rydz-Śmigly took over from him.

Racial tensions

The only significant opposition against the Piłsudski clan came from the National Democracy Party. Particularly in rural areas, this movement was inseparably linked with the Roman Catholic hierarchy. It propagated the concept that people had a natural right to their land, language and traditions. Roman Dmowski, the chief ideologist and strategist of this movement at that time, deemed the search for an ultimate solution to the nationality conflicts the most important task of any political agenda. The various peoples were to be settled on their own respective territories and a system of peaceful co-existence established. The movement also called for racial purity.

The Jewish community, who made up more than eight percent of the population, were the prime target of attack. But in addition, loyal, often non-denominational citizens whose families may have been "polonised" for centuries, became the victims of these persecutions. The main pretext for the attacks were the utopian-socialist ideas propagated by promi-

Economic struggles

In the period between the two world wars, Poland had become a relatively homogeneous economic unit. But radical change was needed to enable this to happen.

Provinces that for centuries had been characterised by totally diverse influences had to be economically integrated, plus a combination of radically different cultural elements within Polish society had to be assimilated: the efficient "Prussian-style" industrial machine, an easy-going "Austrian" Bohemian way of life and "Russian" dynamism, which all had to be brought under one roof. This process of assim-

nent members of the Jewish intellectual scene.

When in the late 1930s the feeling of external threat increased, it soon became clear that Poland lacked anyone of the calibre of Piłsudski; the kind of figure required to maintain the integrity of the state. Nationalism grew apace and the government became ever more aligned with the National Democratic Party. On the extreme right of these groups, fascist tendencies became evident. Violence against minority groups was no longer an isolated occurrence.

LEFT: the Polish parliament on the eve of war in 1939.
ABOVE: a 100 mark note, post World War I Polish currency replaced by the złoty in 1924.

THE IDEA OF A STATE

In 1921 the idea of a state was a very modern concept for Poles. The aim was to create a democratic political system, which withstood the efforts of the church to raise Catholicism to a state religion. Liberation from patriotic obligations was endemic in intellectual circles and there appeared to be a cultural renaissance. Through contact with the west, the belief that Poland was, once again, a member of the European family was strengthened. The cinema became the main attraction in large cities; small theatres in Warsaw flourished. The nightlife in large cities was on a par with any that may have been offered in Paris or London.

ilation – particularly with regard to legislation and infrastructure – took time to achieve. A port was built in Gdynia and linked to industrialised Silesia by miles of railway track.

Nevertheless, even during the years of economic growth there was a dearth of funds to enable independent Polish investment. Heavy industry, for example, remained controlled by France and Germany.

At this time, the annual capital transfer to foreign banks was five times higher than any investments made at home. Moreover, the primitive banking system levied the highest interest rates in Europe; the prime lending rate

was three times higher than in the United Kingdom or in Switzerland. Even in 1939 it was still not possible to regain pre-World War I levels of industrial production.

Almost 65 percent of the population lived tied to the land in rural areas. With the exception of Greater Poland and Pomerania, the agricultural structure remained backward without modern machinery or outside investment. Seven-tenths of the rural population was only marginally involved in the circulation of goods and currency. As well as this sluggish pace of industrialisation, a catastrophically high birth rate caused a drastic decline in the overall standard of living and triggered a fresh wave of

emigration. During the time leading up to the Great Depression (1926–30) approximately 200,000 people left Poland annually to start a new life somewhere else, with the Untied States being a popular destination. In subsequent years, over-population led to further subdivision of rural estates and thus to lower revenues for those who made their living from the soil. The rural population, which was largely illiterate and highly indebted to provincial usurers, remained in a suffering, seemingly divinely ordained state of lethargy.

Controlling eastern Europe

In the 1930s Poland's foreign policy situation deteriorated rapidly. Stuck in the doldrums of the world economic crisis of 1929, the country's plans for rapid modernisation and social improvements collapsed. After 1935, the government, which was having to rely even more strongly than before on the traditional forces of the army and the landed gentry, passed a new, far more authoritarian, constitution.

In Warsaw the popular slogan of a "superpower Poland" found favour among the masses. Despite all endeavours to achieve a national consensus, in this tense situation there was far too little freedom of movement for such a conflict to be resolved. As far as the propagandists were concerned, the Polish "superpower" should, with the assistance of its culture, influence the whole of central and eastern Europe and, at the same time, form a military protection wall to the east.

An alliance with Berlin or Moscow was out of the question, but when Hitler occupied Bohemia and Moravia after the Munich agreement, Marshal Edward Rydz-Śmigły, in turn, gave orders to reclaim part of the territory of Polish Silesia which Czechoslovakia had annexed in 1920.

In this optimistic atmosphere, a young generation of Poles waited for a solution to the mystery of independence. On 11 November 1939, it intended to celebrate its 21st birthday, together with the republic. But, as it happened, matters were to turn out very differently. Another power sought to find its *lebensraum* (living space) in the east. ❑

LEFT: The Pilot monument, originally designed by E. Wittig and reconstructed after World War II, can be seen at Warsaw airport

Lviv and Vilnius

The reunification of Germany brought about an unequivocal renunciation of the former East German territories. At the same time Poland has gained a secure western border and millions of new Polish citizens in Wrocław, Malbork and Szczecin are guaranteed a right to their homeland. Many of these people had had to leave their homes either as part of the resettlement policies within the Polish state or when they were expelled from the former Polish eastern territories, now part of Lithuania, Russia and the Ukraine. Luckily, nobody in Poland today has any intention of reclaiming these territories and triggering yet another tragic migration of the region's peoples. Instead, it is becoming apparent that only through intercultural exchange and overcoming isolationist tactics will there be common access to regions characterised by centuries of shared cultural history.

This point is clearly demonstrated by the former Polish cities Vilnius/Wilno and Lviv/Lwów, with their rich multi-cultural traditions. In free Poland during the inter-war years both cities developed into centres of intellectual life. Regaining them had been a considerable task for the young Poland. Vilnius, although largely inhabited by Poles, was regarded by the Lithuanian republic as their true capital and Lviv, also with a Polish majority, had to be defended against claims from the Ukraine.

Lviv was founded in the mid-13th century by the son of Prince Daniil of Galicia, who built a fort on the site of the present-day town. In the years of Polish partition, Lwów became an important city: it was located at the junction of major trade routes and its population was made up of a variety of cultures and nationalities.

In the 19th century, trade, transport and industry developed rapidly and in 1894 an electric tram system was in operation. Science and literature were allowed to flourish and the university, renamed in 1919 after King Jan Kazimierz, produced great humanists. The town also became a meeting place for Ukranians, Poles and Jews and prominent cultural and political leaders lived here towards the end of the 19th century, including Ivan Franko and Mykhailo Hrushevsky. The mathematics department of Lwów University, founded by Stefan Banach and Hugo Steinhaus, was once the leading institute of its kind in the world. It was in Lviv that

RIGHT: the Church of St Michael in Vilnius.

Rudolf Weigl developed the vaccine against typhoid. The theatre was deemed one of the best in the country and two legendary Polish actors, Leon Schiller and Wilam Horzyca, were members of its company.

Vilnius, now capital of Lithuania, is one of the country's oldest cities, founded in 1323 by Gediminas, a Lithuanian duke. After protracted disputes the former capital of the Grand Duchy of Lithuania was returned to Poland in 1922. Interaction between these two cultures determined the stature of this city. Piłsudski was a descendant of Lithuanian dukes; Adam Mickiewicz, the Polish national poet, began his epic poem *Pan Tadeusz*

with the exclamation: "Lithuania, my fatherland!" The literary tradition was further developed by Czesław Miłosz, who was awarded the Nobel Prize for Literature in 1980. Antoni Gołubiew and Paweł Jasienica were also active in Vilnius during the inter-war years. Stanisław Mackiewicz, prime minister of the government-in-exile after World War II period, began his political career in the city.

Both Lviv and Vilnius retain evidence of this multicultural diversity. In Vilnius the Górny Zamek Giedymina, the Church of St Casimir and St Anne's Church characterise the landscape. In Lwów there are Armenian, Greek Orthodox and Roman Catholic cathedrals and it was the only city in Poland to be the seat of three archbishops. ❑

WORLD WAR II AND ITS AFTERMATH

When Germany invaded Poland in 1939 it set off a catastrophic chain of events that were to change the world – and totally transform Poland

In autumn 1938, the German Reich under Adolf Hitler summarily confronted Poland with a number of political demands, including the return of the "free city" of Gdańsk, access via a motorway to East Prussia across the so-called Polish corridor and a realignment of Polish foreign policy towards the Third Reich, namely signing up to the Anti-Comintern Pact.

Neither Great Britain nor France made any attempt to halt the growing expansion of the Third Reich to the east. The only obstruction to Hitler's plans was uncertainty about how the Soviet Union would react to these claims.

In fact, after Hitler's troops invaded Czechoslovakia in March 1939, the Soviet Union agreed to collaborate with the "Greater German Reich". In response, Great Britain and France concluded a treaty with Poland, assuring each other of mutual military assistance in case of a German attack on any one of the countries. It entailed a huge risk of world war.

Defeat and partition

On 23 August 1939, Germany and the Soviet Union concluded a "non-aggression pact". In an additional, secret protocol both countries specified their territorial claims against Poland: Eastern Poland was assigned to the Soviet Union, while the remainder – the whole of the western and central territories – was to come under Hitler's control.

In the late evening of 31 August 1939, the Soviet parliament ratified the Hitler-Stalin pact; only a few hours later, without making any declaration of war, the German Wehrmacht marched into Poland, the first country to offer military resistance to Nazi aggression.

Polish troops were mobilised in a matter of hours, but the unprepared soldiers faced a German army that was both numerically and technically superior. Attempts to resist the

German advance in the north, west and south, over a front some 1,600 km (990 miles) in length, were in vain. A popular myth has grown up that the Polish cavalry charged German tanks. What really happened was that detachments of mounted infantry and cavalry met German panzer divisions. The cavalry, whose

duty it was to charge the infantry following behind the tanks, naturally had to gallop towards oncoming armour in order to attempt this objective.

By the terms of their mutual defence pacts with Poland, Britain and France were duty-bound to immediately declare war on Germany, but they were procrastinating. Only on the third day of the invasion, 3 September 1939, did they make their declarations official. According to additional military clauses of the pact, Britain was to start a bombing offensive on Germany without delay, while France was to attack Germany "with the bulk of her forces" by 15 September. Neither obligation was kept.

LEFT: the free city of Gdańsk – a calamitous bone of contention between Germany and Poland.
RIGHT: Hitler crosses the Czech border in 1939.

Cut off from the rest of the country by the Russian invasion, the Polish government crossed the frontier of allied Romania to carry on the war from abroad. However, instead of being given opportunity to travel to France, the Romanians interned the allied government of Poland. Nevertheless, the armed forces continued to fight. Warsaw capitulated only after the last rounds of ammunition were fired and the city itself was turned to rubble under air and artillery bombardment. The last group, surrounded by Germans and

FLYING SKILLS

The Polish soldiers who trained with the British Royal Air Force were later to win great fame at the Battle of Britain.

these began almost immediately. Their target was France, where in October 1939 a new government of Poland was formed, headed by General Władysław Sikorski. A new army was also being organised there. Part of the Polish Air Force personnel was directed to England, where they began training on the British aircraft. Another strong group of Polish Forces formed in Syria, then a French protectorate. By the spring of 1940, Polish Forces gathered in France had already reached the 100,000 mark.

Russians, gave up the unequal contest on 5 October. As the post-war testimonies of German generals make plain, the war could have ended in 1939 because almost the entire German army and practically the entire air force were thrown against Poland, leaving only an insignificant screen in the west. Had the Western allies intervened, as they were obliged to do by their treaties with Poland, Germany would certainly have been crushed.

Polish Army in exile

The remnants of the Polish army which crossed the Romanian and Hungarian frontiers, were put in internment camps, but mass escapes from

The first Polish group to go into action against Germany was the so-called "Podhale Brigade" which formed part of the allied expeditionary force in Norway. Some units of the Polish Navy had been in constant action already under the tactical command of the Royal Navy. It was the submarine *Orzeł*, which, after her epic escape from the Baltic, torpedoed a German troop transport, thus first signalling their invasion of Norway.

Two Polish infantry divisions and one armoured brigade also fought side by side with the allies to the bitter end during the French campaign of 1940. The remnants of the army were then evacuated to Great Britain.

The Home Army

While Warsaw was still under siege in 1939, the first steps were taken to create an underground army. It was to this end that General Tokarzewski-Karaszewicz was appointed its Commander-in-Chief and given appropriate staff, with such funds as were available. This Organisation formed the basis of the future Home Army (*Armia Krajowa* or AK), which incorporated a great many clandestine groups, formed spontaneously all over Poland. The Home Army formed an integral part of the Polish Forces, subordinate to the government, first in France, later in Great Britain.

and the most effective underground army in Europe. They were armed with what they had taken from Germans and also by a continuous stream of supplies delivered by air from Britain, mostly by the Polish air-crews. Towards the end of 1943, the blowing up of bridges and rail tracks disrupted German supply lines with the Russian front to such an extent that it had begun to play a substantial part in their defeat, Finally, the Home Army power revealed itself in full force in its attempt to liberate the capital city of Poland, Warsaw.

During the last week of September, a treaty was concluded between the Soviet Union and

As part of the Armed Forces of Poland, the Home Army carried out the war against Germany, as distinct from what is called "the resistance", in which almost every Polish man and woman took part. The primary targets of the Home Army were the German forces and German police, which were kept on constant alert by the activities of partisan detachments.

By 1944, the Home Army numbered 350,000 men in active formations – by far the largest

LEFT: Home Army detachment during the 1944 Warsaw Uprising.
ABOVE: schoolgirls delivering mail at a Home Army fieldpost.

UNDERGROUND RESISTANCE

Among civilians there was a great deal of activity under German Occupation. The Poles were not allowed to receive higher education but were to remain on a barely literate level to provide labour. The vast Organisation of the "Underground State" clandestinely arranged for young Poles to obtain diplomas and university education. An underground administration and press continued; there was even a police force and law courts. It was to the nameless authorities of this State that Poles owed their allegiance, at the risk of death or concentration camps. It may be said that at no other time was national cohesion stronger than under the German occupation.

the German Reich and German and Soviet soldiers fraternised on Polish soil. In the subsequent months, the German Wehrmacht occupied Denmark and Norway and conquered France. The Soviet Union occupied the Baltic states and eventually large areas of Finland and Romania too.

Once the Polish campaign had come to an end, West Prussia, Greater Poland and Upper Silesia were swallowed up by the German Reich. After various unsuccessful

> **CULTURAL DEATH**
>
> Craftsmen and labourers were deported to do forced labour in the Reich. Artists, scientists and priests were taken into "protective custody", often a synonym for concentration camps.

attempts to establish a puppet state, Germany declared the rest of occupied Poland a "General Government" with its administrative seat located in Kraków. Its powers were limitless, its subjects stateless.

Hitler's reign of terror

Hitler exploited for his own ends the anti-Semitism that had long been latent throughout Europe. With the help of chauvinistic propaganda, the party apparatus and its organisations – above all the Waffen SS and the Gestapo – he ruthlessly applied his theories concerning racial purity. The final victory would give the German "master race" *leben-*

sraum in territory that stretched as far as the Urals. This aim was to be achieved in accordance with a "legal punishment system", which could be interpreted so broadly that in the occupied areas the decisions of an SS commander could never be challenged.

In accordance with the guidelines of the propaganda ministry, Poles were regarded as *untermenschen* – a sub-human species. The final aim of national socialist policy was the destruction of the Polish people, their expulsion or "germanisation", the extermination of Jews and gypsies as well as the settlement of Germans in the newly "liberated" areas. Any racial group that was deported from the provinces within the German Reich in the course of the ethnic cleansing process was to be concentrated in the General Government. The racially pure were to be resettled in the new provinces, and the "inferior races" dispatched to Kraków, where they would face an uncertain fate.

Anyone who attempted to resist had to reckon with brutal retaliation. Mass executions were the order of the day. In 1940 the Germans established a number of camps on Polish territory (*see page 54*), which, in January 1942, were semi-officially refashioned and enlarged to function as extermination camps. People deported to these camps were officially described as "vermin". Before being killed, they were abused as slave workers and used for medical experiments. From 1942 onwards the prisoners of these camps were killed by poison gas and the corpses incinerated. Of more than five million people interned in Polish concentration camps, more than 3.5 million were killed – three million of those as a consequence of the *endlösung* (Final Solution) policy that had been planned for the Jews.

In conjunction with the executions in the camps, there was also the *Aktion Reinhard,* which simply meant that those who had been condemned to death were first relieved of any valuables they may have had. In the fiscal year 1943–44 this brought the Deutsche Reichsbank an incredible net profit totalling over 100 million Reichsmarks.

The military and political collapse of Poland was a severe shock for the Polish people and it forced them into a painful reappraisal of their situation. Terror, torture, death and starvation, and the suppression of any independence movements, further intensified the general feeling of hopelessness. Corruption and human rights abuses were rife.

Soviet control

In tandem with the German terrorising campaign, the Soviet Union set about the annexation of occupied East Poland and began with the "russification" of its newly won territory. This was personally undertaken by the head of the Communist Party in the Ukraine at the time, Nikita Khrushchev, who later, on

In February 1940 the deportation of Polish citizens to Kazakhstan, to the Russian Arctic and to Siberia commenced. Stalin was of the opinion that it was possible to expel anyone or anything: the nation from its identity and its land, the family from home and hearth. His aim was that ultimately people would lose their self-esteem and all sense of personal identity.

Stalin's method of control was based on rather different premises from Hitler's reign of terror. He believed that in the end his victims would surrender to a system in which they were forced to do slave labour and were pressured day and night by functionaries or police.

Stalin's death, became the first Secretary of the Soviet Communist Party. In Moscow, Stalin propagated the occupation of Poland as an "act of liberation from the capitalist system by a fraternal nation". A precise census was carried out, and subsequently the Soviet administration foisted Soviet passports on every east Polish citizen. The occupied regions were designated as "western Ukraine" and "western Belorussia". After a manipulated "referendum" on 1 and 2 November both were incorporated into the two Soviet republics.

LEFT: Home Army patrol.
ABOVE: the German menace in World War II.

MASS DEPORTATIONS

One Stalinist method that was especially successful was the expulsion of whole sections of the Polish population from their traditional homelands. State officials, judges, foresters and small farmers were the first to be deported. Eventually whole families, merchants, members of the self-employed classes, professors and teachers followed. In one year almost 1.65 million Polish citizens were deported in cattle wagons, many of them refugees who had recently arrived from central and eastern Poland. A large percentage were taken to concentration camps for "re-education". By 1942 more than half of the people who had been deported were dead.

Sikorski versus the Communists

The Polish government-in-exile under General Sikorski was not just involved in military matters, but was also active politically. As early as 20 December 1939 and despite the harsh realities of the situation, it was calling for the liberation of Poland from enemy occupation, pleading for boundaries that would guarantee Polish security. When Hitler attacked the Soviet Union in June 1941, Sikorski, met with Stalin and was granted the concession that a number of Poles who had been deported to Soviet camps should be released in order to set up a Polish army. Stalin was even prepared to annul the earlier pact with

Meanwhile in Russia, the Germans discovered the mass graves of Polish officers, murdered on Stalin's orders. They were the bodies in Katyń of officers unaccounted for during the formation of the army in the USSR. Understandably, German propaganda was making the best possible use of the discovery. To put an end to it, the Polish Government proposed that a neutral Red Cross commission should investigate the matter. This proposal was met with a furious Russian reaction. They accused the Polish Government of siding with the Germans and, using it as a pretext, Russia broke off diplomatic relations with Poland.

Hitler concerning the partition of Poland, but he peremptorily rejected the Polish demand to be allowed to re-establish its pre-World War I border (see page 42).

Eventually, about 100,000 soldiers, women and children were safely evacuated to the Middle East via Iran. Men, armed and equipped by the British, formed the Second Army Corps of the Polish Forces, which subsequently landed in Italy. The Corps, commanded by General Władysław Anders, played a prominent part in the Italian campaign. Its successes included breaking through "Hitler's Line", with its key position at Monte Cassino, one of the great battles of World War II.

At the time Stalin was totally convinced of his victory over Germany and he believed that the Soviet expansion to the west would obliterate any memory of Katyń. He even had the temerity to invite Polish Communists to Moscow. Just a few years previously many of them had barely escaped the execution that Stalin had ordered for all members of the Polish Communist Party. (In 1938 the Polish Communist Party, at the time illegal, had been disbanded because of a "betrayal of the world revolution"; the party had collaborated with the Socialist Party and the Peasant Party in Poland. Some 5,000 comrades invited to the Soviet Union were murdered on Stalin's orders).

Those members of the Polish Communist Party who had formed a pro-Soviet wing in the years before 1939 – Bierut, Minc, Ochab, Gomułka and others – now made it clear that they were ready to co-operate with Moscow. In March 1943, they combined to establish the Union of Polish Patriots and, as far as Stalin was concerned, were the "true representatives of the Polish people". In autumn 1943, the newly organised Polish divisions fought side by side with the Soviet army at the Eastern front. As a sign of

LAYING BOUNDARIES

At the Tehran Conference in November 1943 Stalin made it clear to Britain and the US that most of post-war Poland would become part of the Soviet Union.

in-exile was looking towards the restitution of the 1921 borders and the return of the areas annexed by the Soviet Union; while the pro-Soviet Poles, on the other hand, now preferred the so-called Stalin Compensation Plan. Within the guideline of this plan, in return for shifting the western border to the Oder-Neisse line, the Poles would give up claims to the eastern regions and Polish territory would, in addition, include Gdańsk and southern East Prussia.

The Allied forces found these ongoing

their identity, these soldiers wore the Piast eagle – without the crown – on their helmets.

Government-in-exile isolated

While fighting was continuing on various fronts around Poland, tough negotiations on the borders for the future of the Polish state were continuing at a diplomatic level. Various differing views existed at that time regarding mainly the eastern border. The government-

LEFT: Polish Prime Minister Stanisław Mikołajczyk (1901–66) in London, 1944.
ABOVE: a cabinet meeting of the Polish government-in-exile.

disputes increasingly embarrassing, as the demands of the Polish government-in-exile conflicted with those of their military alliance with the Soviet Union. By the autumn of 1943, the government-in-exile found itself dangerously out on a limb.

The Warsaw Uprising

In January 1944, the Soviet army had reached the pre-war frontiers of Poland. After the death of General Sikorski in an air crash in Gibraltar on 4 July 1943, Stanisław Mikołajczyk became the Prime Minister. He instructed the Home Army command to liberate parts of Poland from the Germans before the Red Army arrived and to co-operate with the Russians afterwards.

The plan worked well in the Vilno district, which was liberated by the Home Army division. However, when according to government instructions, the division made contact with the Russians to plan future co-operation, the officers were immediately imprisoned and their units disarmed. So ended another attempt to establish friendly relations with the Russians. But there still remained the slight chance to liberate the capital city of Poland, Warsaw, before the

> ### BITTER RETALIATION
>
> Enraged by the activities of the Warsaw Uprising, Hitler demanded that the city be razed to the ground, hoping to leave the rubble to the awaiting Red Army.

tory. So, in spite of the sacrifice of many a brave air-crew, mainly Polish and South African, the uprising slowly died.

When the Home Army capitulated on 2 October 1944, the casualties among the civilian population amounted to around 180,000 and 85 per cent of the city was totally destroyed.

However tragic the fate of the city, the uprising had succeeded in halting the Red Army's progress into Europe for at least two months, while it waited for the Germans to eliminate the Poles. Given these

arrival of the Red Army and thus make it the true seat of government of Poland.

With this in view, on 1 August 1944, the Home Army attacked the German garrison in Warsaw. Eventually, considerable forces of the German 9th Army had to be diverted into the battle for Warsaw. It lasted for 63 days, with the Russian Army impassively observing it from across the River Vistula.

The Home Army needed ammunition most of all, but the air supplies from Italy and England were difficult over such long distances, in the face of alerted German anti-aircraft defences. The Russians flatly refused to allow allied aircraft to refuel on their terri-

two months, it is reasonable to suppose that the Red Army would have met the Western Allies on the Rhine and Germany as a whole, not only its eastern part, would then have become a People's Republic.

Yalta and Potsdam conferences

In mid-December 1944, the Russians decided to fix the western Polish border along the line of the rivers Oder and Neisse. Soon afterwards they elevated the committee of the Polish Communists to the government of Poland, with its seat at Lublin.

By the time of the conference in Yalta, in February 1945, Russian troops had already reached this line, thus cleverly presenting Roosevelt and Churchill with a *fait accompli*. According to Russian plans, this shift of Polish frontiers to the west would have been a compensation for the lands of Eastern Poland, invaded in 1939 as a result of Ribbentropp–Molotov agreement. This plan received a tacit approval from Roosevelt and Churchill, although the final decisions were postponed until the end of the war. It is certainly notable, however, that the Government of Poland, still residing in exile in London, was not once consulted on matters concerning the frontiers of its country at this time.

As was expected, the Potsdam conference, which began on 17 July 1945, ended in complete political victory for Soviet Russia. It approved the Soviet solution for the post-war frontiers of Europe and consigned half of its countries into Soviet overlordship. The Western allies, surprisingly, also agreed to the Russian method of settling nationality problems, first used in Poland, where about two million people were forcibly removed from their homes and sent to labour camps in Russia. In the same way, Germans east of the Oder-Neisse line, were to be resettled in the new People's Republic of Germany. In Churchill's opinion, this was the only way to bring lasting peace to the region.

Polish Forces disbanded

In 1945, Polish forces numbered 250,000 men, spread between the army, navy and air force. They had fought on all major fronts of the war, in the air over Great Britain and Germany and on the seas and oceans. The Second Army Corps took part in the African and Italian campaigns, ending the last named in liberating the city of Bologna.

The First Corps, with its rear echelons in Great Britain, took part in the invasion of the Continent. Its famous armoured division covered itself in glory at Falaise, while the Parachute Brigade fought with distinction at Arnhem. Ever since the conferences in Tehran and Yalta, every soldier knew that he would have had no country to return to. In spite of that, the soldiers remained loyal to their allies and fought to the last day of the war with their

customary bravery. In 1947, all units of the Polish forces were concentrated in Great Britain, where they were disbanded on the orders of the British Government. A small percentage of men returned to Poland, but the great majority remained in Great Britain to seek civilian employment and start a new life.

No nation throughout the world was to suffer more than Poland in the machinations of World War II. Although Hitler was clearly defeated, he had decimated the population through his racist policies and ethnic cleansing by almost 25 percent, many of the victims being among Poland's brightest and most creative pre-war

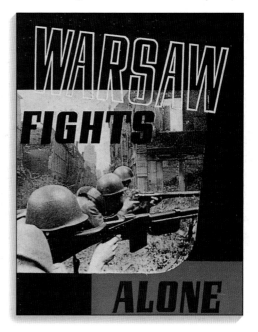

citizens. The cities and landscape were ravaged by war and the evil testaments to Hitler's "Final Solution" still haunt the country dotted with barren and eerie land that once supported his death camps. Stalin, however, far from being defeated, had gained his original aims, shifting the borders of eastern Europe and infiltrating greater areas with his politics.

Poland lost great cities, rural communities and a strong pre-war sense of national identity, despite participating bravely in a war that had begun in its defence by its Allies. It would take many decades of hardship and political struggle before the Polish nation would regain its former strength. ❑

LEFT: monument to the Warsaw Uprising in Warsaw.
RIGHT: World War II propaganda.

The Concentration Camps

The Russo-German alliance of August 1939, known as the Ribbentrop Molotov pact, had a double purpose. Its most immediate aim was a joint invasion of Poland, whereas its long term purpose was the annihilation of the Polish nation. It was put in operation after the end of the September 1939 campaign on Poland, when the secret police of both aggressors (Gestapo for Germany and NKVD for the Soviet Union) had

established friendly co-operation. In the autumn of 1939, the Gestapo carried out the first of its mass arrests comprising of people prominent in politics and the arts who were subsequently murdered or sent to concentration camps to await a slower form of death.

To provide for the fast growing number of prisoners, a new concentration camp was established in Poland, near the town of Oświęcim. It became known under its German name of Auschwitz, as the most dreaded "*Vernichtungslager*", or extermination camp in Europe. It was built to provide a killing ground for Poles, but it grew steadily between 1940 and 1945, to accommodate and destroy people of many nationalities. It is calculated that 1.5 million people perished there, mostly Jews from Poland and all over Europe.

It was the only German concentration camp, which tattooed identity numbers on prisoner's forearms. However, the number of prisoners thus marked did not exceed 200,000. The rest ended up in gas chambers straight from their trains, without being registered. The first test killing by the gas Cyclon B, was carried out in September 1941. After that date, additional gas chambers were constantly constructed. The camp was greatly enlarged by adding new areas near the village of Brzezinka (German Birkenau). The gas chambers of Birkenau became the central extermination camp, established for the Jews.

On 18th January 1945, the camp was evacuated and 60,000 prisoners were marched on foot, in scanty clothing without food and in the depths of the winter to concentration camps in Germany. Most perished before they reached their destination. Another major concentration camp was built in Poland, near Lublin. At least 1 million people (almost all Polish Jews) died in Majdanek and Treblinka – but it was the name Auschwitz that became a symbol of martyrdom, not only for Poles, but for the mass extermination of countless European Jews.

In the Russian occupied part of Poland, the NKVD began arrests of the "enemies of the people". As in German-occupied Poland, the term embraced people prominent in their professional capacity, with the addition of property owners. In fact, it meant anyone suspicious in the eyes of local NKVD agents, without any reference to their past, social or economic standing. Those arrested were sent to the Russian equivalents of German concentration camps, the so-called "labour camps" in Siberia, where their chances of survival were minimal. Polish prisoners of war were also sent to these camps or *gulags*, with the exception of officers. At the beginning of 1940, the mass deportations of entire families began. It is estimated that 1.5 million adults and children were deported to remote parts of Russia, in what is now known as "ethnic cleansing".

The army officers, taken prisoners of war during the defence of Poland, were imprisoned in three camps: Kozielsk and Ostaszkow near Smolensk and Starobielsk near Kharkov. Their total number in these camps amounted to 15,570. As might be expected, the majority were reserve officers, representing many professions, including 800 medical doctors. All but 448 were murdered during April 1940, on orders from the Soviet Government.

Two years later, the bodies of officers from Kozielsk camp, were accidentally discovered by German army personnel, in a wood near the village of Katyń. All had been killed with a single pistol shot to the base of the skull. Goebels enthusiastically embraced this golden opportunity for German propaganda.

At the time, it was assumed that all 15,000 were killed there, and Katyń Forest became known as a scene of the greatest single war crime committed in modern history. German forensic authorities established the date of the crime as spring 1940. The Soviet government, however, denied any complicity and, in turn, accused the Germans. It was Germans who were subsequently accused during the Nuremberg war crime trials in 1945 and since adequate proof was lacking, the case against Germany was dropped. This didn't prevent the allied governments from supporting the Soviet version of events, right down to the end of the Soviet State.

It was only after the collapse of the Soviet Union, that the Russian authorities admitted responsibility for the crime and published the relevant orders which originated from the "Politburo", the supreme organ of the Soviet Government, presided over by Stalin himself. Only then it was possible to seek the graves of thousands of missing officers who were not buried at Katyń Forest. Those from Ostaszków and Starobielsk were found at various sites and in all, 15,000 murdered prisoners of war were finally accounted for. Like Auschwitz in German-occupied Poland, so Katyń Forest became a symbol of the martyrdom suffered by the Poles at the hands of the Russians.

The concentration camp at Treblinka provides one of the most chilling reminders of the Nazi atrocities: the site was strategically

well chosen, about 100 km (60 miles) to the northeast of Warsaw, with its rail terminal linked with the international rail network to Russia. At the junction there was a large supply depot for the German advance to the east. It is almost certain that the two extermination camps, Treblinka I and II, were built along the demarcation line that the German Reich and Russia had drawn through Poland when they divided the country between them. In 1943 when the mass graves of Katyń were accidentally discovered, where Stalin had interred 4,000 Polish officers, the Germans made use of the massacre to their own end.

By then, the military situation had changed.

The Nazis closed the Treblinka camps in November 1943 and obliterated their bloody traces. Before the closure they had committed 2,400 murders per day. Documents were rapidly burned, all possible eye-witnesses were liquidated: the SS literally tried to let grass grow over the horrors they had committed. But their attempts at a cover-up failed – a few dozen eye-witnesses escaped and conveyed the cruel truths about the camps to the rest of the world. In 1964 a commemorative site was inaugurated that tried to do some justice to the human tragedy that this place represents. ❑

LEFT: concentration camp victims.
RIGHT: the site of the crematorium at Treblinka is covered with basalt rocks, melted and fused at 2,000°C (3632°F) to form a memorial to indescribable suffering.

THE COMMUNIST STATE

The rise of Stalin at the end of World War II saw the whole of Eastern Europe

ruled by the restrictive and often terrifying Communist regime

W hen in the summer of 1944 the Soviet army liberated parts of Poland from the German occupying forces, the generals immediately set about installing a Polish Communist administration. That same year the "Manifesto for Progress" appeared with proposals for a new social and economic order. Slogans urged Poles to welcome plans for agrarian reform, the state ownership of industry and a transformation in society, accompanied by justice and democracy. With the strong support of the Soviet army, Polish Communists began establishing a totalitarian dictatorship along Russian lines.

Communists seize power

This "revolution from outside" was not accepted passively by the Poles. Units of the Home Army were still active and considerable forces were needed to put them out of action, As Stalin had no faith in the Polish Communists, he wasted no time in putting Russian secret police in the front line. Their job was to insure the loyalty of the Polish population to Russia and to the Communist party. Those who dissented were either executed or imprisoned. In an atmosphere of terror, the Provisional Government of National Unity was set up. Bolesław Beirut became president and Osóbka-Morawski became prime minister.

Open political opposition to the Communists came mainly from the Polish Peasant Party (PSL) with Mikołajczyk, the former prime minister of the government-in-exile, as its head. He garnered support mainly from rural communities and intellectuals. Other independent politicians were systematically isolated. Many were put to death.

For official purposes, the Communists gave the impression that a democratisation process was taking place. Soviet advisers urged their Polish counterparts to promise the end of

poverty and fear, the prospect of a bright future and a new beginning after the harrowing years of German Occupation.

On 19 January 1947, the long-promised general elections were held. While foreign observers recorded a 60 percent vote in favour of the PSL, the Communist-led "Democratic

Block" were awarded 394 of the 444 parliamentary seats. There followed a wave of mass arrests among the PSL members and Mikołajczyk fled abroad.

Rebuilding the economy

In 1945, the Polish economy lay in ruins. Although the people found themselves living in a new state with geographically favourable and historically acceptable borders, some six million Poles had lost their lives since 1939. A third of the national wealth had gone and two-thirds of its industrial potential had been destroyed. Those areas in the north and west that had seen the expulsion of some 3.5 million

LEFT: *Manifest,* a depiction of the issuing of the Polish communist manifesto, by Wojciech Weiss.
RIGHT: an example of Socialist Realist art.

Germans were optimistic about the future, as new arrivals from eastern Polish provinces moved in to take the Germans' places. But here, too, the war had left a bitter legacy: the Russians had dismantled any surviving industrial plants and transported them back to the motherland.

In 1946 all companies were nationalised. As compensation for Poland's properties abroad, the state received some 200 million dollars. But under pressure from Moscow, Poland was not allowed to take advantage of the Marshal Plan

JOINING FORCES

In 1955 Poland became a member of the Warsaw Pact, intended to be the reply to NATO. In 1949 it became a member of COMECON, the Union of Mutual Economic Aid.

tions from Moscow to establish a governing unity party. This was to include the remnants of the Polish Socialist Party (PPS) and the Polish Workers Party (PPR). The pre-Communist Peasant Faction, the United Peasant Party (ZSL) and the Democratic Faction (SD) were allowed to remain independent but under the auspices of the Communists.

In June 1948, the head of the Polish Communists, Władysław Gomułka, was accused of right-wing nationalist tendencies and spent from 1951 to 1954 in prison. He was

money; the Communists imposed a centralised economy on the country. Private industry and services were abolished in 1947 but, as the new bureaucracy was unable to replace the private sector, the black market flourished. By dint of hard work, the targets set in the 1947 Three Year Plan were met and Poland quickly reached its pre-war per capita income.

The Stalinist era (1948–56)

In 1948 Europe entered the long dark tunnel in its history known as the Cold War. With the blockade of Berlin, the era of Stalinism also began for Poland. In March 1948 the prime minister, Józef Cyrankiewicz, received instruc-

in favour of a "Polish route" to socialism and advocated the maintenance of private property. Some months later, the PPS was incorporated into the Polish United Workers' Party (PZPR). With the approval of Stalin, power passed to the loyal, but incompetent figure of Bolesław Bierut, formerly a member of Comintern.

In the December of 1948 the congress of the PZPR was formed and Beirut was appointed as first secretary. With the embodiment of the pre-eminent role of the PZPR in the new constitution of 22 July 1952, the last chance to establish a democratic society in Poland passed.

Along with the tyranny of PZPR and its front organisation, the hallmarks of Stalinism in

Poland were: the adoption of Marxism-Leninism as an infallible ideology; the amassing of armed forces on a huge scale; centralised economic planning; and concentration on heavy industry. This model was transferred directly from the Soviet Union to all countries of the Eastern bloc and was retained, virtually unchanged, until the end of the 1980s.

Officially the constitution was quite democratic: it guaranteed civil rights and a so-called democratic government elected by parliament with a president and a state's council. The parliament itself, the *Sejm*, was voted in by general election. In reality, however, it was little more than a front. The "working people in the city and in rural areas", according to the letter of the constitution nothing less than the true rulers of the country, were only helpless victims of the state. The party alone, the Politburo, the first secretary and the privileged élite of the nomenclature, really wielded all the power. In effect, it was a dictatorship of the party over the people.

The conviction of Stalin and his minions that the Soviet bloc was constantly threatened by an invasion from the "powers of American imperialism" led to the recruitment of an enormous Polish army (400,000 troops). The officers were trained in a Political Military Academy (WAP, founded in 1951).

Top priority was accorded to building up the steel, coal, iron and armaments industries. In order to accommodate the flood of migrant workers from rural areas who were now required to take their places on the production lines, whole new cities and suburbs were built virtually overnight. On the outskirts of Warsaw and in Nowa Huta near Kraków these municipal, architectural monstrosities can still be seen in all their ghastliness. The supply of foodstuffs was largely handed over to the newly established PGRS (national farmsteads – the Polish version of the Russian state farms), whose gross inefficiency resulted in disastrous consequences for both productivity and quality.

The system's intention was to fashion new, socialist man: in effect that meant the abolition of humanitarian ideals. Political terror and repression reached a climax in 1951. Everyday life became a nightmare. All contacts with the outside world were immediately denounced; in bogus trials innocent people were arbitrarily accused of being spies and sentenced to internment or death. There were also executions without trial (in 1990 mass graves were found dating from this time). Many people were deported to the Soviet Union and simply vanished without trace. A dense network of informers infiltrated factories and offices, the schools and the universities.

The propaganda, of course, told a different story. The news was full of stories about the construction of gigantic collective combines, factories and other buildings, and tales of rising

CATHOLIC RESISTANCE

The Roman Catholic church was one of the few "organisations" that retained a level of independence against the new Communist regime. It was generally regarded as a reactionary relic of the pre-war system. However, priests and laymen alike were openly attacked and constantly threatened with arrest by the governing forces and by 1950 the financial assets of the church had been confiscated. In 1952, one of the heroes of this frightening era, was Cardinal Stefan Wyszyński, the primate of Poland, who was arrested for his "anti-state" attitudes and was exiled to a monastery where he was kept prisoner for three years.

LEFT: workers' May Day demonstrations in the 1940's.
RIGHT: Soviet badges and medals for sale.

work quotas. The ever-increasing number of success stories perpetuated the course that Stalinism had planned for the country. Monumental sculptures in the style of socialist realism provided visible proof of the superiority of the new system and its ideology to all who saw them.

And yet in Poland the omnipotence of Stalinism never quite reached the level that it did in other Eastern bloc states. The political trials never developed into a series of propaganda trials. It proved impossible to eradicate the bourgeois and intellectual milieu. The collectivisation of agriculture was carried out slowly and incompletely. Nevertheless, the memory of the Stalinist years was engraved upon the mind of the nation.

Josef Stalin died in March 1953. Within two years the liberalising effect of his death was felt in Poland. In December 1954 the despised Ministry of Public Security was disbanded and the censorship laws relaxed. Władysław Gomułka was released from prison. There was no further talk of collectivisation. The political thaw commenced. In June 1956 worker protests in Poznań, which started with the slogan "bread and liberty", showed that the country needed a new pragmatic party leader whom the people

SOCREALISM

Social Realism – socrealism for short – was the form of visual art allowed by the Communist regime. The object was the veneration of the working class and of its self-appointed leaders. In its pure form, it was characterised by an almost photographic realism, a style which was at odds with the idealism of its message. Typical subjects were workers, happy in their work and communist leaders in Heroic poses heralding the utopia to come – aspirations which were far removed from the brutal realities of the day. The most imposing manifestation of socrealism was in architecture, much of which remains to this day – the Palace of Culture in Warsaw being the supreme example.

This gift of the Soviet Union to Communist Poland is an incongruous mix of concrete tower block and Baroque decoration. Because of its size and the strength of its construction, it is extremely difficult and costly to demolish. It will therefore spoil Warsaw's skyline for some time to come. Houses along the central Marszałkowska street are decorated with large concrete figures of workers. They lead to one of the ugliest modern squares, Plac Konstytucji (Constitution Square), with its pretentious "candelabra" for street lamps. Fortunately, apart from the monstrosity of the Palace of Culture, these excesses of bad taste are too few to spoil the overall beauty of Warsaw.

could trust. This man turned out to be Władysław Gomułka. After Khrushchev had assured himself of his loyalty, the Stalinist era came to an end in Poland.

National Communism (1956–80)

In October 1956 Gomułka managed to free Poland from total control of the Soviet Union, which determined the political life of the nation for the next 25 years. Gomułka was of the opinion that there were "various ways to socialism" and he managed to prove that Polish Communists could look after the affairs of their country on their own account, without having to take

run its priest seminars, its own social and intellectual societies and its own university. It thus became the only really independent church in the whole of the Eastern bloc.

Sociologists who adhered to the party doctrine had prophesied that industrialisation and urbanisation would change the cultural patterns of traditional society and would sever the ties between the people and church. They couldn't have been more wrong. The Polish church did not lose its adherents – on the contrary it turned out to be a place of refuge and the driving force behind the Polish opposition. The same kind of fate befell the collectivisation plans of the agri-

constant instructions from Moscow (Imre Nagy in Hungary was not so lucky).

Gomułka managed to achieve three vital concessions: an independent church, free agriculture and an open political forum. These concessions were designed to be transitional only, until the party had found a firm footing, but matters turned out differently. The church was stronger than ever before. Within the framework of its self-administration, it continued to

LEFT: Khrushchev being greeted at Warsaw Airport by Władysław Gomułka.
ABOVE: Edward Gierek (in centre) removed from power in 1980.

cultural programme. Gomułka had no intention of committing the same errors that had led to the death by starvation of millions of people in the Ukraine 30 years previously. More than 70 percent of the arable land thus remained in private hands, while collective farming was only retained in the areas where it had already been introduced (for example on the huge, former German estates in the west of Poland). The experts did not regard that as a problem. In time, the small, private farms would disappear of their own accord, as the state had other means of making it plain to the farmers that private industry was not worthwhile. In practice that meant granting privileges to the collective sector and neglecting the private sector, measures that ultimately ended in unmitigated disaster for the whole nation.

Within 40 years the government managed to lead the country to the very brink of starvation. Poland, traditionally an agricultural country, was ruined, despite its fertile soil. The population was plagued with food rationing and queuing outside grocers' shops. Nevertheless, private agriculture survived.

As for demands for pluralism, the leadership accommodated those by licensing several political organisations. However, the fact that these were all united under the one roof of the National Union Front – under the patronage of the party – meant that any ideas of pluralism were pure illusion. It soon became clear that neither Gomułka nor his successor, Edward Gierek, backed as they were by a total lack of any constitutionality, were prepared to adhere to the promised concessions. Civil liberties were severely curtailed. Again and again (1968, 1970, 1976 and 1980) dissent broke out. The slogan of the protesters was "bread and liberty". The protests were organised either by labourers or students and intellectuals. They had to be put down forcibly by the government and there were frequent casualties. By this time there

BREAKING DOWN THE BARRIER OF FEAR

The protests of March 1968 not only mobilised the students, but also the whole intelligentsia. For the first time the names of several dissidents became well known, including Adam Michnik, Jacek Kuroń and Karol Modzelewski.

Unrest in December 1970 in Gdańsk and Szczecin succeeded in moulding a generation of intransigent and embittered workers. Between 1975 and 1976 the changes in the constitution, which resulted in even greater dependency on the Soviet Union, contributed to the organisation of a national dissident group, the Polish League for Independence (PPN) in 1976, by Zdzisław Najder.

In June 1976, when workers in the tractor plant in Ursus and the armaments factory in Radom were punished for their participation in a protest action, intellectuals founded the KOR (Workers' Defence Committee). For the first time intellectuals and workers were unanimous in pursuing a common goal and from this moment on one could talk of an organised, supranational opposition. The committee worked quite openly (although not legally) as an information and co-ordination centre for the whole country. With the investiture of the cardinal of Kraków, Karol Wojtyła, as Pope in 1978 and his visit to Poland in 1979, the psychological barrier of fear was also destroyed.

could no longer be any doubt that the government had lost the confidence of the Polish people.

August 1980–December 1981

The organised opposition that emerged in 1980 had a long history that had begun with the student protests of 1968.

In summer 1980 government attempts to implement drastic price increases for foodstuffs and consumer goods caused a wave of public strikes. The epicentre of the protest was in Gdańsk, in the Lenin Shipyard (*see page 335*), whose tradition of resistance went back to

The founding of *Solidarność*

An agreement between the workers and the government was eventually signed on 31 August 1980. As an immediate consequence of this event, representatives of the strike committee from all the provinces of the country formed the national co-ordination committee of the independent, self-administered trade union *Solidarność* known in the west as Solidarity. The 37-year-old Lech Wałęsa was elected chairman. Just a few months later the Farmers' Solidarity (*Solidarność Wiejska*) was permitted as an official organisation.

In the 15 months of its activity Solidarity

December 1970, when workers had been killed during protest action. The KOR members were involved right from the start of the political agitation. Included on the list of 21 demands posed by the strike committee were the right to strike, the right to form independent trade unions and the permission to erect a monument for colleagues who had died in the 1970 uprising. In return the workers declared themselves willing to accept the leading role of the party.

LEFT: with Tadeusz Mazowiecki at his side, Lech Wałęsa holds the first Solidarity press conference in October 1980.
ABOVE: Solidarity in the streets of Warsaw.

proved to be a peaceful reform movement which, with its 10 million members, represented a broad section of the whole nation. It could only defend itself with its own ideals.

Martial law

The rise of Solidarity was viewed with great misgivings in the Soviet Union. However, the leaders of the Kremlin rejected the idea of military intervention. Unlike in the case of Czechoslovakia, it was feared that part of the Polish army, supported by the majority of the population, would actively resist the invasion, embroiling the Soviet Union in a war in Europe, while the Afghan war was still in progress.

In addition, also unlike the Soviet invasion of Czechoslovakia, NATO powers did not declare their total indifference. Taking into account the well proven fighting qualities of the Poles, the risk was too great. Instead, the Head of the Communist Party and the Commander-in-Chief, General Jaruzelski, was ordered to crush Solidarity.

On 13 December 1981, he proclaimed martial law and ordered the army to virtually occupy the country. Solidarity was officially abolished and all its leaders, including Lech

PAPAL INFLUENCE

Martial law was only lifted in 1983, triggered by the second visit to his homeland by Pope John Paul II.

Wałęsa, were imprisoned. A wave of repression was put in motion and all remnants of constitutional rights disappeared. The success of martial law in suppressing Solidarity was, however, very short-lived. Its organisation simply went underground.

The entire population now clearly understood that the time for compromises had come and gone. From then on, the only true political division among Poles became between that of "us" (which meant every Pole) and "them" (the Communists in power).

The next few years were characterised by an ever more acute economic crisis. With Solidarity banned, the opposition centred around the Church. It became the only truly independent institution that could afford protection to anyone requiring it. The Church was at the same time a forum for political discussion, meetings, lectures, tuition and the dissemination of illegal literature, publicity and magazines. For all this, its members often paid a heavy price. Fearless Father Popiełuszko was tortured and murdered by members of the security police in 1984.

Life was, for the majority of the population, now divided into two spheres: the official, legal, everyday routine and the clandestine, illegal underground. The government proved entirely incapable of coping with the political and economic crisis.

Signs of a deep political crisis were also to be seen in Russia. The new leader in power, Mikhail Gorbachev, who came to the Kremlin during 1985, was only too aware of a progressive weakening of the Soviet grip on Poland but

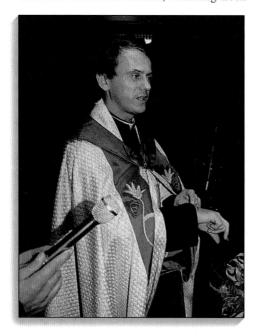

THE FACE OF SOLIDARITY

Like the TV images of the fall of the Berlin Wall in November 1989, Lech Wałęsa's personality and the Solidarity movement has come to symbolise popular demands for the end of East European communism in the late 1980s.

Awarded the Noble Peace Prize in 1983 for his work on human rights, Wałęsa's political career had humble beginnings. Born in 1943 in Popow, Poland, in the mid-1960s he worked as an electrician in the Lenin Shipyard in Gdańsk. In 1976 he was sacked for anti-government activities but he returned to the shipyard in 1980 to lead a workers' strike demanding better working conditions, the

right to form a trades' union and the right to strike. After most of the 21 demands were met, Solidarity began to represent the national consciousness. New members were drawn from across Polish society and more than 10 million people joined the movement over a year and a half.

When Solidarity won a landslide election victory in 1989 it declared "History has taught us that there is no bread without freedom." When Wałęsa was elected president in 1990, Solidarity stated "What we had in mind was not only bread, butter and sausage but also justice, democracy, truth, legality, human dignity, freedom of convictions, and the repair of the republic."

was no longer able to strengthen it. The Soviet Union for the first time no longer showed any imperialistic tendencies. An invasion, such as had been feared in December 1981, was therefore no longer a realistic possibility by the latter half of the decade.

The collapse of communism

After waves of strikes in the spring and autumn of 1988, the Communist Party agreed to share political power. After "round table" talks were held to discuss basic political, social and economic reforms and an agreement was signed on 5 April 1989, in which party and represen-

any attempt to do so would have failed. The Solidarity movement won almost every seat it contested. Ultimately, Tadeusz Mazowiecki was entrusted with the task of forming the new government. A journalist by profession, he had already acquired authority as the editor-in-chief of the *Tygodnik Solidarność* in 1980–81 and, later, during his imprisonment, he had enjoyed popular esteem. The PZPR dissolved in January 1990 and Polish Communism was on the wane.

The events in Poland led to the collapse of Communism in Europe as a whole. What had begun with a wave of strikes in the spring of 1988 had resulted in general unrest; the Communist

tatives from the Solidarity movement specified their conditions. These included legalisation of Solidarity, the right to a free press and elected seats in parliament. The path towards democracy had finally been laid.

For the elections, Solidarity founded citizen committees to represent the opposition. Even during the "round table" talks, the Communist Party had reserved the right to form the government. But in the election of June 1989 the Communists were so soundly thrashed that

LEFT TO RIGHT: key players in the Solidarity movement: Father Jerzy Popiełuszko; Lech Wałęsa and General W. Jaruzelski.

party had lost its power and was soon to disappear altogether. Other Eastern bloc countries were quick to follow the example set by Solidarity and the process became unstoppable. It eventually led to the fall of Communism in the Soviet Union.

Ten years later on, in 1999, Poland became a member of NATO. By this act, Poland returned to its 1,000-year-old historical role. In this role, the country provided a shield to Europe, defending it from Tatars, Turks, Cossacks and from invasions of the semi-barbaric Grand Duchy of Muscovy. The shield was broken in the 18th century, with calamitous consequences, not only to Poland, but to many other nations. ❏

POST-COMMUNIST POLAND

While Poland has adapted to the free market and economy, two decades on there remains a huge gap between living standards in town and country

Post-communist investment in Poland did not take long to materialise. While the early years were chaotic to say the least, the sheer size of the Polish market, and of the potential returns, were enough to allay any fears of political instability – and there was plenty of that. Now a member of both NATO and the EU, Poland is a modern parliamentary democracy unrecognisable from the country that had to be dragged quite literally kicking and screaming into the 1990s.

The road to a market economy

At the beginning of the 1990s, visitors to Poland were greeted by a bizarre sight: between the city's three largest department stores (built in the 1970s as symbols of a new attitude towards consumerism) and outside the vast Palace of Culture, thousands of people were out on the streets buying and selling consumer articles of every conceivable kind. People wanted not the goods on the shelves in the shops, but those laid out on the pavements. The atmosphere amid the drab landscape of central Warsaw was more akin to that of an Oriental bazaar.

From cassettes and bananas to ladies' underwear and Lacoste tops, the booty from weekends in Berlin or trips to Turkey – anything that would sell – was spread out on blankets, if not on the ground then on the bonnet of the ubiquitous Polski Fiat 126P. The Poles were doing what they have often had to do at times of crisis: putting into practice the skills of survival, essential during this difficult period of transition to a market economy.

Prices of basic goods were rising faster than wages. In August 1989, the government lifted price restrictions and the price of a kilo of butter rose within a year from 1,000 to an astonishing 10,000 złoty. Poland found itself without state support and production plummeted. Unprofitable companies were closed down, and unemployment increased dramatically, putting

thousands of people out of work almost overnight and presenting families with severe financial difficulties.

For many, street trading of almost any goods they had access to was the only way of obtaining income to continue to feed their families and pay the rent on their homes.

Root and branch reform

The country has undergone a dramatic transformation within only a few years, as a quick look back at history will reveal. The new government, the first freely elected non-Communist leadership in a Warsaw Pact state, took office on 12 September 1989.

The cabinet, consisting of both Communists and democrats, had to face up to some extremely serious problems: the political reorganisation of the state, a revival of democracy and political and social pluralism, armed defences, not to mention the avoidance of an impending economic collapse. Their solution was not helped by the absence of people used to high

LEFT: a farmer's market in Kazimierz Dolny.
RIGHT: first steps towards a market economy.

office of government. Those who governed the Peoples' Republic had simply been carrying out orders from Moscow. Since they also took part in the government of Free Poland, the attitude of the population remained highly suspicious and reserved, which manifested itself in low turnouts for elections. The first elected prime minister, Tadeusz Mazowiecki, took great pride in the fact that the revolution in Poland had been bloodless, unlike in other countries of the Soviet block. Whatever the merits or demerits of this kind of revolution, the retention of former Communists in government bodies did not add to public confidence in the new ruling party.

led governments – all of which had difficulty implementing their policies when there were as many as 29 different parties represented in the *Sejm* – many voters chose to elect the reformed Communists (SLD), the successors to the reviled Communist Party. They increased their number of parliamentary seats from 60 (in 1991) to 171.

There are many reasons why this party became the strongest faction within the *Sejm*. Given the great economic changes, many Poles simply forgot about the political patronage and economic misery that the Polish Communist Party had presided over. Many looked back wistfully to the days of state-guaranteed em-

However, the first coalition government was quite clear in its goals and plans for reform. It also saw its principal foreign policy goal as making approaches towards integration with the west. It wanted Poland to withdraw from the Soviet-oriented group of Communist nations known as COMECON (Council for Mutual Economic Aid) and the Warsaw Pact and to become an associate member of the EU.

Domestic politics

For many, the victory of the old cadres in the elections of September 1993 was an unexpected and worrying development. As in other former Eastern Bloc states, after four Solidarity-

ployment and the harmonious interpersonal relations that they as workers once enjoyed. In September, the last troops of the Russian army, instumental in bringing the communists to power after World War II, left Poland.

The coalition government of 1995

The government formed in October 1993 by Waldemar Pawlak was an alliance between the Democratic Left Alliance (SLD) and the Polish Peasants' Party (PSL). On 1 March 1995, Jósef Oleksy, a former senior Communist Party official was elected prime minister after a crisis within the ruling coalition. The dominance of the Communist old guard was further reinforced by the narrow victory in the 1995 presidential elections of Aleksander Kwaśniewski, a former Communist minister (but now no longer affiliated to any party), after a hard-fought battle with the previous president, Lech Wałęsa.

The Polish Peasant Party, the SLD's coalition partner, a satellite of the ruling Communist party in the pre-1989 era, draws its strength from the fact that 30 percent of the Polish population still live from the land. The new government was able to benefit from the achievements of the previous administration,

OUT OF POLITICS

After failing to win any seats in 2001's General Election, the AWS, the political arm of Solidarity, disbanded.

certificate for 20 złoty in the privatised enterprises. Poland became a member of OECD. The government's slow and ineffective response to devastating flooding in Southern and Western Poland in 1997 was the death knell for the coalition, which performed badly in that year's elections. Indeed, it was the newly formed Solidarity Electoral Alliance (AWS; the political wing of the Solidarity Movement) which procured most votes, its ebullient leader Jerzy Buzek becoming prime minister.

which between 1989 and 1993 had pointed the country firmly in the direction of democracy and market economics. The economy, which by now had virtually freed itself from political interference, had been boosted by a six percent growth in Gross Domestic Product.

In December, prime minister Oleksy was accused of spying for Russia and resigned in January 1996. His successor, also a former communist, Włodzimierz Cimoszewicz, continued the mass privatisation programme under which every adult Pole was able to buy a share

EMIGRATION

The biggest effect of EU membership has been emigration. From Eastern Poland especially, as many as 1.5 million Poles – mostly young males – have emigrated to the rest of the EU since 2004. As many as two million have left in all since 1989. The majority have made new homes in the UK and Ireland, where they may freely live and work.

So widespread has emigration been that many Polish industries now face labour shortages: the construction sector has been especially badly hit. Workers are being brought in from Belarus, Ukraine and even China to fill the gaps.

LEFT: the traditional form of the market economy.
ABOVE: the *Sejm*, Polish Parliament, in session.

Buzek's first task was to oversee the rewriting of Poland's communist-era constitution. The new version made sweeping changes to the way Poland was governed, decentralising the administration, though its ultimate aim of bringing government closer to the population did little more than create new levels of bureaucracy. It also created a new kind of bureaucrat to fill the many vacancies created: in the main these posts were filled by Solidarity members. Many Poles began to feel that a new party-state was being created.

NEIGHBOURLY RELATIONS

With the recognition of the Oder-Neisse line – awaited for 45 years – a new chapter has opened in the history of German-Polish relations. It is hoped that this will lead to an amicable co-existence.

Solidarity – whose base had always been in the cities – also made the fatal error of neglecting the countryside.

As quickly as skyscrapers were going up in Warsaw so living standards were falling for most agricultural workers, almost a third of the country's workforce. Solidarity's support collapsed and many of its members deserted for other parties. By 2001, when a general election was held, what was left of the AWS was so unpopular it failed to win a single seat in parliament. Instead, the former communists (SLD) were returned to office, with the Polish Peasant party as coalition partner. Kwaśniewski, who had tilled a steady course through the turbulent

AWS period, easily won a second term as president. The AWS disbanded a year later, Solidarity becoming once again solely a trade union.

21st Century Poland

Poland entered the 21st century with a single issue on its mind, membership of the EU. Broadly backed by all political parties the SLD-led coalition set about ensuring that Poland met all of its targets to ensure entry to the EU on schedule in 2004. In order to do so it had to deal very visibly with high-level corruption, and to set about finally reforming its under-performing agricultural sector. The former proved surprisingly easier than the latter. Nevertheless, the EU was happy to conclude entry negotiations with Poland in 2002, the country duly became a full EU member on May 1st, 2004.

The economy continues to boom – a visit to any major Polish city is evidence of that. Warsaw especially, with its increasingly New York-esque skyline, is a city that both looks and feels the major international centre of business it has quickly become, almost in spite of the governments which have come and gone with alarming regularity over the past two decades. In 2005 the slightly bizarre Kaczyński twins – Lech and Jarosław – took the reigns, Lech as president and Jarosław as prime minister. Their Law and Justice party was beset by infighting however and Jarosław was forced to resign in 2007. New elections brought the Civic Platform of moderniser Donald Tusk to the fore, Tusk becoming Poland's youngest prime minister for a generation. He has made convincing migrant Poles – as many as two million have departed since the fall of communism – to return home a priority.

Those who do will find a country that despite setbacks retains the bullish mood that set in during 1989. Poland's often stunning growth over the past two decades has been a result not of government policy but of the sheer ebullience of the market and of that rare Polish work ethic. Though certain sectors of society have unquestionably been left behind – pensioners in particular – Poland is unrecognisable from the place it was 20 years ago. ❑

LEFT: girls out shopping in Lublin.
RIGHT: a reflection of old and new in Warsaw.

THE POLISH PEOPLE

Despite the centuries of foreign rule, the Polish people have maintained a strong identity and welcome visitors with lavish hospitality

*How long, O God, shall men be ridden down,
And trampled under by the last and least
Of men? The heart of Poland hath not ceased
To quiver, tho' her sacred blood doth drown
The fields, and out of every smouldering town
Cries to Thee, lest brute Power be increased
Till that o'ergrown Barbarian in the East
Transgress his ample bound to some new crown: –
Cries to Thee, "Lord, how long shall these things be?
How long this icy-hearted Muscovite
Oppress the region? Us, O Just and Good,
Forgive, who smiled when she was torn in three;
Us, who stand now, when we should aid the right –
A matter to be wept with tears of blood!"*

These lines by Alfred Lord Tennyson, written in 1833 after the Russians had invaded Poland, eloquently express a theme that runs through Polish history. In 1774 the English statesman Edmund Burke referred to Russia's aggressive designs by saying: "Poland was but a breakfast." And in 1794 the poet Samuel Taylor Coleridge wrote: "Poor Poland! They go on sadly there."

Although few people would doubt that Poland's geography is the main reason for its historical problems, a close analysis of the location of Polish land would indicate that the open plain from the east to the west was a perfect platform for the migrations of different groups of people. This resulted in an exchange of cultures, rapid progress and an equal amount of trouble.

On the other hand, rivers flowing to the Baltic Sea would become, in the history of the country, the main factor speeding the cultural, economical and political development of this first democracy in modern Europe.

PRECEDING PAGES: Łazienki Park, Warsaw.
LEFT: sitting for a portrait in Gdańsk.
RIGHT: feeding the pigeons in Gdańsk.

The history of the people

The first written information about Poland survives from AD 965, from letters of a Moorish Jew from Spain, Ibrahim–Ibn-Jakub. They talk of very fertile land ruled by Duke Mieszko I. Ethnographers and archaeologists have since found on this land signs of the presence of

Scythians and Celtic tribes, which established the foundations for the city of Kraków. One of the first of the major aggressors to Polish territory came from the southeast, from Huns, who in the 5th century AD plundered the land.

Mieszko I baptised the country in AD 966, more as a political than a religious act, which brought Poland to the Christendom of western Europe. His son Bolesław I went further in this incorporation and became the first king of Poland in 1025, to the great irritation of his German neighbours (*see page 21*). Polish land was fertile and rich, with its rivers flowing into the Baltic full of yellow "gold of the north" – amber – and, even more important in the years to come, wheat. Consequently, the country was the object of occasional attacks from its western neighbours, the Germans. The first capital city, Gniezno, was established in the western province of the country, Greater Poland, but as of the 11th century, Kraków's role as a capital city began to grow (*see page 22*).

Tragic in its consequences had been the act of inviting the Order of the Teutonic Knights to establish themselves in Poland, issued by the Duke Konrad of Mazowsze (*see page 22*). The militant order brought for two centuries destruction and misery to the whole country. The Piast family, who ruled the country for the whole of the early period of its formation, never managed to combat the German Order. Nor did Casmir the Great, the last of the Piasts and the first to build solid foundations to the Polish legislation and give freedom and privileges to minorities. "He found Poland made of wood," the saying goes, "and left it made of stone".

Especially prosperous was the period of the Jagiellonian dynasty, beginning with Władsław Jagiełło, a Lithuanian Prince who became Polish King in 1386. He refounded Jagiellonian University in 1400 and won the battle of Grunwald in 1410 that eventually led to the end of Teutonic era in Poland (*see page 22*).

LAND OF RELIGIOUS TOLERANCE

Poland in the Middle Ages has a far less brutal history than many other European countries. When Polish Jews were obtaining their Statute of Jewish Liberties at Kalish in 1264, the rest of Europe was engulfed in religious wars and later in the Holy Inquisition. Monks from all over Europe came here to practise their religion; the Convent of Cistercian Brothers had a tremendous input into the growth of Poland's wealth. From countries torn by religious wars and reformation, waves of Huguenots, Protestants, Jews, Hussites, and members of the Orthodox church all came to Poland, where they lived in unison under the watchful eye of the Polish rulers.

Fertile land, the economic wealth of its citizens, especially from the 14th–17th centuries and religious tolerance appealed to the greedy neighbours as much as to the oppressed religious and ethnic minorities from all over Europe. The thriving economy and liberal attitudes, unique in Europe, also made Poland and its 16th-century democracy very attractive to the royal courts of Europe. They longed to have their sons elected as kings and to have them on the Polish throne.

However, the power and untamed prosperity of the Polish nobility and aristocrats, and the abuse of democracy through "Liberum Veto", severely undermined the strength of the country. The 18th century saw the decline of Poland's political strength and in 1772, the first partition took place when the Austro-Hungarian Empire, Prussia and Russia divided the country among themselves (*see page 30*). They did so in 1793 and again in 1795. For 125 years, Poland was deprived of full sovereignty.

Patriotic nation

But the indefatigable spirit of Polish national feeling has been ever present and has led to exceptional accomplishments in arts, music, science, culture, the civilisation of Europe and indeed the world. These many achievements

leaders and heroes over the past two centuries.

Tadeusz Kościuszko, who fought against the English as a general of George Washington and later led the uprising of his people against the Russians, used these words (*see page 31*). They turn up again in the speeches of Józef Piłsudski, who commanded the forces of the young country at the "Miracle of the Vistula".

This so-called "miracle" occurred when the Soviet army was defeated and forced to abandon its attempt to advance into central European territory through the open Polish plains, which for centuries had been the route of Western expansion of Russian regimes (*see*

prevailed for the 125 years of political and formal nonexistence of the country. Names such as Frédéric Chopin (composer), Adam Mickiewicz (poet), Maria Skłodowska (Curie scientist), Henryk Sienkiewicz and Joseph Conrad (writers) and many others are connected with this period of Polish history. Patriotism was always very present in their lives.

The Poles, when attacked, have always stood up to their aggressors. The sentence "*Nie damy sie!*" ("We will not give in!") has been repeated in countless great speeches by the country's

page 29). The battle and the whole war of 1920 is now generally considered as one of the most historically significant of all European wars, for it stopped the Soviet expansion in its tracks and changed the course of history.

Finally, these same words are inseparably linked with the figure of Lech Wałęsa, the workers' leader from Gdańsk who played a crucial part in the defeat of the Communist regime in the Solidarity Movement of the 1980s (*see page 63*). "We will not give in!" The Poles have always had plenty of reason to express their defiance with this rousing declaration. It has lost none of its significance today, nor is it likely to do so in the future.

LEFT: horses and carriage in Kraków.
ABOVE: violin player in traditional costume.

Troublesome neighbours

The geographical position of Poland has often caused political problems: to the west they have the Germans as neighbours, to the east the Russians. In their relationship to both countries, military conflict has historically played a much more prominent part than peaceful coexistence. And, as a result, the three countries have seldom a good word to say about one another. The Russians generally find their neighbours unreliable and much too happy-go-lucky for their liking. In

> **MILITARY DISDAIN**
>
> Bismarck's opinion of Poland "The Pole has to be beaten until he loses heart" was as uncompromising as its other neighbours'.

disarming of the German army in Warsaw under the leadership of Józef Piłsudski *(see page 38)*, who on that day assumed control over the re-emerging Polish military. Poland in the early 20th century cultivated a class of intellectuals unique for Europe at the time, which was given the task of rebuilding the country after more than 120 years of oppression. This intellectual force was used by Allied forces in World War II, when Polish mathematicians cracked the German encoder Enigma. However, the internal stability

German "Polish economy" is an expression denoting a shambles. To the Prussians in particular, with their authoritarian state, their dynamism and their moral code which frowned on every kind of instinctive behaviour, Poland was not merely a mystery, but a positive horror. In 1814, a Prussian field marshal wrote to Baron Von Stein: "Disorder and a life of chaos is the Pole's element. No – these people deserve to be trodden underfoot!"

The Treaty of Versailles in 1919 included a Polish delegation in peace talks as a representation of a sovereign state; 11 November became and still is Polish Independence Day, commemorating the end of World War I and the

of the state was constantly under threat from Greater Poland's nationalism on one hand and separatist resistance on the other.

Caught in the middle

The liberal attitude of past governments of Poland was tarnished during this era of nationalistic movements in Europe by the Polish National Democratic party, who believed in the Jews' collaboration with the Soviet Union against the interest of Poland. Weak Poland was again a target to the expansion policy, this time of Hitler's Germany and Stalin's Russia. After a secret agreement with Soviets in August 1939, Hitler attacked Poland on 1st September.

Left to her own devices, abandoned by France and England, the Polish Army fought the war until 2 October when the last of the Polish strongpoints succumbed to German power.

The long five years of war still evoke very strong emotions and opinions in Poland today. The Nazis applied without mercy their propaganda and philosophy of prejudices and racism to Poland. When they occupied the country, they established a reign of brutality and cruelty that cannot be forgotten.

STRANGER THAN FICTION

The Polish underground informed the Americans and British about the Holocaust, but the report of Jan Karski was thought to be too horrific to be believable.

The nation was fighting. Several thousand Polish soldiers and officers through Hungary and Romania, under General Sikorski, re-created the Polish Forces, which fought throughout the war together with the British Army, the Royal Air Force and the Royal Navy. Polish pilots fought in the Battle for Britain and their courage became legendary. In Poland itself, the Home Army (*Armia Krajowa*) fought an underground war with the occupants.

The Polish government-in-exile in London was the co-ordinator and the organiser of the Polish Resistance. Crucial information such as facts of existence of Holocaust, V-1 and V-2 missiles and information about the German defence of Atlantic, were obtained and passed on to London by the AK.

One cannot forget that Poland at the beginning of the war was also occupied by Russians. Massive deportations to Siberia of Polish soldiers and civilians took place, especially in 1940 – about 300,000 people were sent to camps and 10,000 imprisoned Polish officers were among the many Poles murdered, each with a single gunshot. Between 1939 and 1945 a total of nearly 2 million Polish citizens were deported to the Soviet Union. When Stalin changed Allies, he permitted the creation of a Polish army in the Soviet Union and allowed her to leave Soviet territory. Through the Middle East this army, under the command of General Anders, fought in the battle of Tobrouque. In 1944 in Italy they conquered the monastery of Monte Cassino, converted by the Germans into a fortress.

Warsaw particularly remembers the two

uprisings that took place during the years of the German Occupation. One in 1943 in Warsaw's ghetto, where the Germans had barricaded within just a few streets hundreds of thousands of Jews, condemning them to death if not from brutal killing then from hunger and disease (*see page 40*). From here and from all over Europe, Jews were transported to concentration camps. The most horrific of them all was Auschwitz– Birkenau, in which Poles, gypsies, but mostly Jews were murdered in specially

designed gas chambers (*see page 54*). Reprisals against the Poles for helping the Jews were the worst in Europe, with whole families being wiped out. In Yad Vashem memorial park in Jerusalem, many trees planted have been planted by Polish heroes who helped save Polish Jews, in memory of those who did not survive. In 1944, as the Soviet Army approached Warsaw and the end of war was inevitable, the Polish resistance began the Warsaw uprising. It lasted 63 days, and the Soviets watched the flower of Polish youth and the whole of Warsaw bleed in order to state Polish will and their right of self-determination and sovereignty (*see page 52*).

LEFT: World War II veterans in Gdańsk.
RIGHT: synagogue in Kraków.

During the 50 years of Soviet domination after the war, the fear of this same attitude prevented the Kremlin from implementing military interventions in 1956 and 1981, when Poland again stood up against the foreign presence on its soil.

The final Soviet offensive against the German army started from Wisła valley in January 1945. The new partitioning of Poland was begun, this time with only Russian participation. What the Germans and war did not destroy, the

> **PROPAGANDA TACTICS**
>
> Propaganda directed by the NKVD, the Soviet secret service, began its reign in Poland after World War II. Using NKVD (later KGB) methods, the regime imposed Soviet ideals.

whom there were an estimated five to seven million. They were followed by the Jews, who numbered 3.3 million, the Belorussians, of whom there were 1½ million, and a total of 500,000 Lithuanians and Germans.

With such a mixed ethnic structure, potential conflicts could have arisen, but the government managed to avoid serious antagonisms. Demographic boom, agricultural reform, idealism of popular democracy carried Poland through the post-war years.

Soviets annihilated by robbing and burning.

Western regions and Upper Silesia were returned to Poland due of the agreements with Stalin and western governments. The Soviets spared this territory, counting on it being a future supply centre for steel and coal. As Polish borders shifted, Poland lost important centres of culture such as Wilno in Lithuania and Lwów in Ukraine (*see page 43*).

Multinational state

The Second Republic of Poland (1918–39) was a multinational state: out of 35 million inhabitants, only 24 million were of Polish origin. After the Poles came the Ukrainians, of

The new Poland within the borders established at the conferences of Yalta and Potsdam was to be an ethnically homogeneous state free from conflict between different nationalities. Its borders were pushed westwards and the non-Polish inhabitants inside these new boundaries were to be resettled. It soon became apparent, however, that the alteration of the borders and the mass resettlements under the pompous name of repatriation did not heal old wounds, but inflicted newer, more painful ones.

Added to this was an atmosphere of hostility between the individual nationalities that were all reproaching each other for their behaviour during the war. The Ukrainians were accused of having collaborated with the Gestapo, the Belorussians of having sympathised with Stalin's secret service, and the Poles of having blackmailed the Jews and denounced them to the Germans. There was no mention of the fact that it was often only individuals who had been guilty of such behaviour and the prejudices were merely fuelled by the propaganda of the nationalists from each group.

Ukrainians

Although the Polish eastern border had been moved westwards, some 700,000 Ukrainians remained in Poland. Most of them moved to

were still unoccupied farms, abandoned by the Germans. The paradoxical result is that the administrative regions of Wrocław, Szczecin, Koszalin and Olsztyn are now the main centres of the Ukrainian population in Poland.

Today there are around 300,000 Ukrainians living in Poland. They have only one primary school (in Biały Bór/Koszalin), where the children are taught in the Ukrainian language, and two high schools (in Legnica and Goró“w Iławecki), where, although the children are taught in Polish, Ukrainian is also incorporated into the timetable. The Department of Ukrainian Studies at Warsaw University enrols only a

the Ukrainian Socialist Soviet Republic, but many refused to leave their homeland. In southeast Poland, a war broke out between the Polish government forces and the nationalist UPA (Ukrainian Insurrectionary Army). In 1947, the Polish authorities decided to distribute the remaining 200,000 Ukrainians over the whole country. What this meant in practice, however, was resettlement in that part of the country that had formerly been eastern Germany, since it was the only area where there

few students each year. The only museum dedicated to Ukrainian culture, in a wooden hut in the small village of Zyndranowa near Dukla, was founded by a private individual, Teodor Gocz, although it was officially prohibited. The Ukrainian churches around Przemyśl and Krosno were either handed over to the Catholic Church, and in the process stripped of all signs of their past, or they were allowed to fall into a state of disrepair.

There is one Ukrainian language newspaper, *Nasze Slowo*. One established event is the Festival of Ukrainian Culture which takes place in alternate years in Sopot and brings together Ukrainian choirs, music ensembles and dance

LEFT: musicians making music in a traditional music festival.
ABOVE: children in colourful folk costumes.

groups. The most famous of these are Żurawie, composed of Ukrainians from all over Poland, Połoniny from Legnica and Łemkowie from Bielanka near Gorlice.

Lithuanians and Belorussians

Fate was kinder to the Lithuanians and the Belorussians. The several thousand Lithuanians who lived around Suwałki on the Lithuanian border were left more or less alone after World War II. In Puńsk there is a primary school and a high school, several folk ensembles and an ethnographical museum, and the Lithuanian Social and Cultural Society has its national head-

to represent an ethnic minority, is now attempting to counteract this development. The Ortho-dox Church assists it in this aim. The Holy Mount of Grabarka near Siemiatycze has again become very important as a shrine for Belorus-sians and other Orthodox believers.

At the festival of Corpus Christi the Belorus-sians make a pilgrimage to the summit of the mountain with penitential crosses on their backs. These are later set in the ground next to the church; there are already tens of thousand of crosses there. In June 1990, however, the church was plundered and set on fire, but the perpetra-tors were never identified.

quarters in Sejny. Of the over 200,000 Belorus-sians who were still in Poland after the war, 36,000 had resettlement forced on them. Those who remained in the country lived in concen-trated groups in their home villages and towns in the area of Białystok, Bielsk Podlaski and Hajnówka.

In spite of this, the Belorussians are one of the best integrated of Polish minorities. As they have a relatively good social position, partici-pate in local government, and the number of Belorussian schools is on the decrease, their national consciousness is weakening. The Belorussian Democratic Union, which was founded in 1990 and is the first political party

Germans

The situation on the western border of Poland has always been quite different from that in the east. At the Potsdam Conference it was decided that the Germans should be resettled. Some had already fled from the advancing Red Army and a Polish army eager for vengeance, but about 5 million remained. They were systematically dri-ven out of their houses and marched in columns to the border. The transfers to Germany were made by train or boat.

On 13 November 1945, a Ministry for Recovered Territories was established by the Polish government and this set up a citizen's militia which had the power to carry out arrests, transported Germans to labour camps, confiscated property and handed over German homes to Polish people. In 1970, the signing of the Warsaw Treaty heralded a return to normal relations between Poland and the Federal Republic, and five years later an emigration agreement came into force. In return for the payment of DM2.3 billion, at least 125,000 Germans were officially allowed to leave Poland. In fact, between 1976 and 1989 some 770,000 Germans were granted visas to leave.

BURYING DIFFERENCES

Sympathy from the Germans towards the Poles emerged after the imposition of military rule at the end of 1981, when the West Germans sent millions of aid packages to the crippled country.

ment officially recognised the Oder-Neisse line, which helped to dissipate the Polish sense of insecurity. The German-Polish Co-operation Treaty, signed in 1991, consolidated the rights of the German minority in Poland.

On Annaberg, a mountain that is considered holy by both Poles and Germans, mass is now also read in German; it is now perfectly legal to attend German classes and new music ensembles and choirs have been founded. The Social and Cultural Association of the German minor-

In 1989 after the fall of the Communist regime, nationalistic prejudices flourished, mainly on the part of the Poles, who had undergone years of indoctrination and been presented with countless distorted versions of history, but also on the part of the German minority. The government of Tadeusz Mazowiecki sought to strike a balance. Soon after coming to office, he introduced legislation that abolished any discriminatory rules and regulations and sought to educate the population.

In 1990, the new, unified German govern-

ity has established its headquarters in Gogolin and in Katowice the regional television programmes are broadcast in German. In Kemielnica/Himmelwitz the first sign in German has appeared in a bar, and the letterbox also bears a German sign. The German minority is concentrated around Strzelce Opolskie/Gross-Strehlitz, Głogówek/Oberglogau, Gogolin and Krapkowice/Krappitz. Krapkowice is the home of Henryk Król, the leader of the German minority party which now has two deputies in Warsaw parliament. His party is guaranteed a seat in the Sejm, even if it does not achieve the five percent share of the vote that the other smaller, countrywide parties must obtain.

LEFT: children after church mass.
ABOVE: sharing festival food.

A question of identity

When the Soviet Union fell apart in the early 1990s, the old argument was resumed about whether Poland belonged culturally and politically to the east or the west. What the Poles have in common with the east – the Russians, the Belorussians and Ukrainians – is that they are also a Slavic people. What has bound them to the west throughout their history and still keeps them firmly linked to this half of Europe is western culture – the Renaissance and the Enlightenment, and religious faith, which they share with many western European countries.

The Lithuanians demanded a guarantee that their capital city Vilnius would not be annexed again as it had been in 1920 under Marshal Piłsudski, who had pushed the border of Poland further east to absorb chunks of Belorussian and Ukrainian territory. And the Ukrainians asked what justification Piłsudski, a figure who is incidentally greatly admired by the workers' leader Lech Wałęsa, had had when he led a Polish army of invasion into their capital, Kiev, in 1920.

In Czechoslovakia the people had not forgotten that after the Munich Dictate that gave Hitler Sudetenland, the Poles took advantage

When the debris of the Communist system had been cleared away, however, the old hostilities between the Poles and their neighbours were shown to be still very much alive. It was not only the relationship between the Poles and the Germans that was troubled again by the emotions of the past: Lithuania, Belorussia, the Ukraine and Czechoslovakia also brought up old grudges they had against the country.

Some of the issues are not that old. At last, it was possible to talk not only about past German dealings with Silesia, Pomerania, West and East Prussia, but also the expulsion of the Germans from Poland after the war and the fate of the German minority.

of the situation to get a share of the land themselves and invaded a part of Bohemia.

The Poles were confronted with the fact that they still had to come to terms with much of their past, and were eventually forced into acknowledging that in their conflicts with their neighbours, even those that had taken place this century, they had not always been the victims.

Looking forward

With respect to minorities, the Polish government has adopted camouflage tactics right from the beginning in the post-war period. It was as if, failing to grasp the true facts of the situation, the government was taken in by its own propaganda that glorified a "homogeneous Poland". The annual statistics contained no information about minorities, since the powers-that-be proceeded according to the assumption that if something is not mentioned then it does not exist.

The minorities themselves, whose insecurity was compounded by the ambivalent attitude of the Catholic Church, could only take this as a declaration of war and thus refused to co-operate with a state that was highly suspicious of independent cultural activities of any kind. The constitution of 1952 – on paper perfectly democratic – guaranteed the minorities equal

forced for decades was one of the reasons why, after the change of government in 1989, only the German minority showed any interest in putting forward candidates for election and the minorities in general did not take the opportunity to secure representation in local government. There are already signs that this was a big mistake, since, as has often happened during crises in the past, strong nationalistic tendencies are again making their appearance in parts of Poland.

This time, however, they are not the result of encouragement from above, but are being generated by the discontent of the middle classes.

rights in every respect. In practice, however, the aim of this totalitarian state was "polonisation" and the uprooting of the other nationalities. The state executive bodies interpreted the constitution to suit themselves. In the face of such despotism every attempt on the part of a minority group to preserve and develop its culture naturally came up against numerous bureaucratic obstacles.

The mutual mistrust that had been thus rein-

LEFT: accessory shopping for beads and bracelets in the market square.
ABOVE: enjoying milk shakes on a bench in the centre of Kraków.

In his inaugural speech in September 1989 the first Prime Minister of a democratic Poland, Tadeusz Mazowiecki, said: "Poland is our homeland, but it does not belong only to Poles. We share this country with people of other nationalities. It is our wish that they should feel at home here, keep their own languages alive and enrich our community with their culture."

However, like people of their age everywhere else in the world, Poland's younger generation is not interested in carrying on the conflicts and arguments of yesterday. For years, both the culture and political values of the west have become increasingly familiar to Poles, and increasingly attractive. ❏

LIFE IN RURAL POLAND

More than a quarter of the population works on the land and many people maintain their traditional customs and way of life

The airline stewardess announces: "We have just flown over the Polish border," and all heads turn to look out of the window. Far below, the landscape is gradually turning into a colourful mosaic and the first impression is of a country totally different in appearance from its western neighbours.

The fantastic, brightly coloured carpet of small fields and meadows is what the new visitor to Poland notices first. If a weaver had taken all the colours available and put them together at random to make a rug, the effect would not be very different: there is the yellow of the rape crop, the ochre-coloured fields of wheat and rye, and dark green squares of bushy-topped potatoes. Narrow strips of land are separated from one another, and hardly any of the farmers have more than one diminutive field to till.

A further surprise is the number of trees lining the roads. Such avenues are all too rare elsewhere in Europe, where "efficient" agriculture has had them felled; here they have been preserved, providing a bright green border along the way.

The rural landscape

Poland's landscape is one of almost endless greenery, with many shades of forests, woods, fields and meadows. There are six different determined types of landscapes in Poland which fall into six parallel belts: the Baltic lowlands, the lake district, the central lowlands, uplands, the sub-Carpathian depression and mountain regions. The central Polish plains are the most agricultural area of the country, with a specific charm of their own. The landscape here is enlivened by isolated hills, dune embankments and the wide valleys of the largest Polish rivers, the Vistula, Oder, Warta and Bug.

Rural Poland, however, now has a modern appearance in some places, with large, mech-

anised farms, yet in other areas it still recalls the 19th century. The west and northwest regions (Wielkopolska, Pomerania, Kashubia) in particular bear the imprint of the German and Prussian presence *(see page 30)*.

The villages vary in appearance as well. In the west the houses are large, wide and built

from stone. In Mazuria they are smaller and sometimes thatched. The eastern provinces still sport thatched wooden cottages. In the mountains they are built of wood with stone foundations and a pointed roof to deal with heavy snowfalls. Zakopane is famous for its particular wooden architecture and interior decoration *(see page 243)*.

The economy of Poland's agricultural regions has also altered since the Communist days. The houses are better built and the surrounding areas are far cleaner and well tended by the farmers. Today, large private farms have developed, financed by credit from banks and better equipped with modern machinery.

LEFT: setting off for a day's work.
RIGHT: storks are common in the Mazurian region and nest in available chimneys and roofs.

Folk traditions

Polish village life and old traditions have successfully survived down the years. Catholic traditions and family ties have remained intact and the church is still present at every important occasion: christenings, weddings and funerals. The local church, shop, restaurant and administrative office are the focal points of village life.

Polish country villages, are still home to talented embroiderers who continue to copy the designs passed down from their great-grandmothers. Folk artists specialising in paper cut-out decorations (particularly in the Kurpie region), self-taught craftsmen capable of turning out the most wondrous shapes at the potter's wheel or using the most primitive penknife to carve mournful religious figures out of wood from pear or linden trees are also strong in numbers.

Christmas has its own set of very specific traditions. Hay is placed under the white tablecloth when families eat their Christmas meal (*see page 125*). Afterwards they predict their health and fortune based on the length and quality of the stalks. On Christmas Eve many country people still share their food and homes with their animals, because it is believed on this

TRADITIONAL COSTUMES

In regions such as Kashubia, people still wear traditional coloured aprons and headscarves, particularly when going to mass or a church fair. Picturesque peasant dress, dances and customs are also still very much alive in Łowicz, the biggest feast of Corpus Christi.

In the Tatras villages, men wear low rounded black hats, embroidered cloth jackets, white cloth trousers and mocassins made from one piece of leather, holding a "*ciupaga*" (walking stick) in one hand with an axe-shaped handle, the shaft decorated with brass studs. The women sport flowery kerchiefs, colourful jackets and aprons, beads round their necks and leather mocassins.

night all creatures should share each other's fate; the animals are said to understand what the people say.

Christmas is also associated with the preparation of nativity crèches – miniature models of the kind of small stable once found on every Polish farm and considered to be the birthplace of Christ in Polish folk tradition. Each crèche has models of the infant Jesus and Joseph beside each other, together with a group of animals who, according to legend, are capable of speaking in human voice once a year on Christmas Eve.

The feast of Christmas has for centuries been the most important in the Polish calendar. One of the old customs is *"Jaselka"*. A group of youngsters, called "herods", go from door to door asking for money and in each group there is always one youngster dressed up as a winged angel, one as the Grim Reaper, complete with scythe, and one as the wicked King Herod. Buying off the young actors is said to bring good luck in the New Year.

At Easter, brightly painted eggs are knocked against each other as in the English game of conkers. The person whose egg proves most resistant wins the next Easter egg. The tradi-

MIDSUMMER TRIBUTE

To celebrate Midsummer's Night wreaths of flowers are cast into the Vistula with burning candles on St John's Night (24 June).

for emotional demonstrations and patriotic and religious ceremonies, performed in smoky cemeteries among burning candles, resembling pagan rituals.

Town meets country

Social changes in the 20th century have brought the rural population into the towns. This migration has greatly benefited the country as a whole. For individual rural families it brought an improvement in living standards and opened up new opportunities. But this migration was selective – it was the

tion of sprinkling people with water is on Easter Monday (*see page 89*).

An equally ancient custom is the drowning of the "Marzanna", an ugly scarecrow figure symbolic of winter, on the first day of spring.

For the Catholic feast of Palm Sunday, commemorating the Biblical account of Christ's entry into Jerusalem on a donkey, symbolic palms are prepared, often several metres high, from dried flowers and coloured paper, to be carried in the procession to church. All Saint's Day has never ceased to be an occasion

more enterprising individuals, better educated and with greater aspirations, who moved.

Once in the towns, children from the country often cease to identify with their own village, especially after having made a considerable effort to shed the rural elements of their language, traditions and everyday culture.

However, not all the ties are broken: some rustic traditions and rituals are still common in the big cities. In Katowice, in the mining region of Silesia, for example, the most visible elements are probably the grand costumes worn by the miners on such ceremonial occasions as the veneration of St Barbara, patron saint of all miners, which is universally evident all over

LEFT: farm workers enjoying lunch.
ABOVE: ploughman at work in an orchard.

the region on her feast day, 4 December. An interesting urban folklore is also maintained in Kraków to commemorate the Tartar invasions in the 13th century by the bugle call at midday from the tower of the Church of St Mary. During Kraków festivals, the "*Lajkonik*", an Orientally-clad rider on a hobbyhorse cavorts round the Market Square.

Country people

Country people in Poland have a highly developed sense of honour. Business agree-

PURITAN ATTITUDES

Modern attitudes to sex meet with conflict in rural Poland, where puritanism and intolerance on the part of parents and the priest conflict with risqué images seen in the cinema and on television.

blooded temperament. When they take to someone they will do anything for them, but if someone falls foul of them, he would be better to keep his distance. On summer evenings, farmers often still sit on the benches in front of their homes and tell stories about the mysteries of nearby forests and marshlands.

Poles like a big family occasion, when several dozen members of the family can get together and eat and drink for two or three days. This includes the imbibing of large quantities of

ments in the marketplace are often sealed with a handshake. The code of honour also includes completing military service and appearing at celebrations in uniform.

Poles, be it in the cities or in the remote countryside, generally have a friendly disposition towards their fellow human beings – they raise their hats to greet them and gladly show them the way. Polish men also follow the code of chivalry – they still kiss a lady's hand and let her pass through a doorway first. They are friendly and hospitable towards foreigners. They laugh and chat naturally, and speak their mind openly without hesitation. Highlanders in particular, combine this friendliness with a hot-

hard vodka. A celebration without vodka would be interpreted as an act of inhospitality, or even a sign of poverty on the part of the host. When weddings take place, tradition dictates that the festivities must last at least three days.

Agrotourism

Whereas for so many years it was the country people who sought out urban life, now some people suffering from the pressures of big city life wish to own a second home in rural villages. Weekends spent in a rural setting have become increasingly popular, but people generally crave a high standard of luxury despite wanting to rest on an actual farm in a typically rural environment. Polish agrotourism is becoming increasingly fashionable. A lot of tourists from the west and from urban Poland prefer rural holidays with unspoiled countryside, a beautiful landscape and interesting flora and fauna. It also allows long-standing city dwellers to learn about the traditional way of life in the country.

Host families serve as tour guides for visitors, using their knowledge of the neighbourhood, parks and nature reserves, local history, culture and historic monuments. All attractions and recreation can be tailored to the wishes of individual guests. Possibilities

addresses of all associations and the 180 farms nationwide which offer accommodation.

Open-air museums

Every historic region of Poland today has an open-air folk museum, called a "*skansen*", in which the tourist can often view within a few acres of land traditional buildings such as a wealthy country manor house made of valuable larch wood, prosperous farm buildings, a poor peasant's hut thatched with straw and a small country chapel. In addition, there may well also be a village inn, watermill and windmill. Inside these buildings are usually authentic wooden,

include hiking, cycling, horse riding, cooking over open fires and camping out and walks in the forest. Some farmers also offer fresh milk, home-made cottage cheese and genuine country broth made from the cockerel that was strutting around the farmyard the day before.

The Federation of Country Tourism (www.agritourism.pl) now publishes a catalogue in several languages entitled "Host Farms", which includes detailed descriptions, photographs and

LEFT: ploughing fields in rural Poland.
ABOVE: *skansens* (open-air museums) preserve traditional rural architecture and crafts and can be found all over Poland.

metal or clay implements and utensils and sometimes demonstrations of traditional crafts and skills such as thatching and weaving.

Moreover, every region, no matter how small, also has presentations in its folklore museums – permanent ethnographic exhibitions exist in more than 120 Polish museums.

But despite the popularity of *skansens*, nothing competes with the real thing. Many villages in Poland may resemble outdoor museums but are in fact genuine communities, where the wells still creak, pots and jugs are hung on the fences to dry, and on the roofs of many houses storks in their nests prepare their off-springs for a long flight over the oceans. ❏

THE JEWS

*The history of Polish Jewry is one of the most tragic of the last century. Today, the
Jewish community is slowly coming to terms with the past and building a future*

According to the earliest reliable records, Jewish exiles arrived from Prague towards the end of the 11th century. For centuries, Jews then converged on Poland from all over Europe, fleeing political or economic persecution in their home countries. However, there were also many who came, not because of any external threats, but because they were drawn by the opportunities in the most tolerant country of the continent. It was not without justification that Poland was known as "a paradise for the aristocracy, heaven for the Jews and hell for the peasants".

A safe nation

The Jews called Poland "Polin" ("po" means "here" and "lin" means "rest") because they felt safe there. Poland's masters needed Jewish traders and craftsmen and their knowledge of commerce. Jews were subject only to the king's own courts or those of his representatives; the murder of a Jew was punishable by death, and even failure to help a Jew who was attacked was punished with a fine. Towns that did not step in quickly enough to quell anti-Jewish riots were also fined, ritual murders could be brought to court, the distribution of anti-Jewish literature was forbidden, and so on.

In 1264, by the decree of the Statute of Jewish Liberties issued in Kalish, the Polish King established a Jewish social class, an unprecedented attitude at that time in Europe which was engulfed by the Holy Inquisition.

The Jewish Council of Four Lands, founded in 1581, was another political institution unique in Europe. It was responsible for Great Poland, Little Poland, Lithuania and Russia, the four main territories within the Polish-Lithuanian kingdom. It was concerned mainly with internal Jewish affairs and kept in close contact with the authorities. The Jews' main occupation was banking, money-lending and financial activity, often leading to conflicts with nobility deprived

of the rights of financial operations. But these disagreements were acted on the individual not on an ethnic or religious level.

During the First Republic (1569–1795) there were relatively few anti-Jewish excesses in comparison with the rest of Europe. This is partly explained by the financial status of the

state and the pragmatism of the Polish aristocracy: in Poland, there was simply no general hatred of the Jews, and the aristocracy was not inclined to harass the Jewish communities.

In contrast, in the violent uprising of Bohdan Chmielnicki in the Ukraine (1648–57), which was actually directed against the Polish rulers, the Jews were massacred in their thousands as suspected allies of the Poles. The tragedy was repeated during the popular uprising in the Ukraine and Podolia in 1768, when thousands of Polish aristocrats as well as Jews suffered terrible deaths.

The Catholic Church in Poland was ambivalent towards the Jews. While on the one hand

LEFT: remembering the victims of the Warsaw ghetto.
RIGHT: the Zionist Dov Ber Borochov and friends in Płońsk.

they were regarded as "the chosen people", on the other they were also "the murderers of Jesus". The church accordingly announced that they should not therefore be persecuted, but that they should live together in a separate community. This attitude fell upon fertile ground with Polish peasant communities, where Jews ran inns and mills. Peasants, oppressed by the nobility found themselves often indebted to the landowners and their rich Jewish advisors alike. Their animosity towards both grew with the level of oppression.

POLAND'S FIRST VOICE

Notably, it was a Jew who made the first mention of Poland in print – Ibrahim-Ibn Jacob, a Moor from Spain, visited Poland in AD 965.

dom as farmers. They were often wealthy. The basic unit of Jewish autonomy was the community, governed by the *kahal*, a body responsible for the judicial system, administration, religion and welfare, where all were responsible for one towards the outside world.

During the 17th century, however, the Jews were badly affected by the weakening of Poland because of wars and internal anarchy. Gradually their economic and political situation deteriorated. In 1764 the Polish parliament, the *Sejm*, dissolved the Council of Four Lands

The unique position of the Jews in Poland is illustrated by the fact that a Jew who had been converted to Catholicism could even be elevated to the nobility.

Wealth and poverty

Because most Jews remained true to their faith, for centuries Polish culture was enriched by specific Jewish characteristics. They made major contributions to scientific development and frequently occupied leading positions in medicine, mathematics and astronomy as well as in architecture, painting and goldsmithing.

Jews were industrious and usually worked as craftsmen, merchants, doctors and bankers, sel-

for economic reasons, but it did not touch the communities. Although the government was aware that the status of the Jews in Poland was in need of fundamental reform, no changes were made before Poland finally lost its independence. In 1795 some 900,000 Polish Jews automatically became citizens of one of the three occupying countries.

In the 19th century the occupying powers abolished many of the laws that protected the Jews, but patriotic feelings towards Poland prevailed and they supported the struggle for independence, fighting alongside them in the Kościuszko uprising (1794), the November uprising (1831) and the People's Spring (1848–49).

But as nationalism swept Europe at the turn of the 20th century, the Jewish community turned increasingly to Zionism. The worsening economy, the politics of the occupying powers and growing signs of anti-Semitism led many Jews to emigrate, many to the United States.

The growth of anti-Semitism

During the Second Republic (1918–39), the National Democracy Party, which had strong right-wing leanings, became increasingly radical in its attitudes towards the Jews. The party had placed a high value on the "national cultural community". From this perspective,

Jews responsible for every social evil. They were accused of Communism, association with the Freemasons, economic parasitism and of an inability to assimilate themselves into Polish society. There were pogroms, harassment at the universities and an economic boycott.

The sections of society that supported Marshal Piłsudski (in power from 1926) did not share these attitudes. Many Jews had fought for the independence of Poland under his leadership and their loyalty to the state was more important to the political realist Piłsudski than their forced assimilation. After his death in 1935, however, his followers' programme grad-

the fact that the Jews used a language similar to that used by Poland's enemies, Germany and Austria was perceived as a threat and an attempt to maintain an separate cultural identity. Also, in a country devastated by wars and partitioning the financial strength of the Jewish community and the unwillingness of some of its members to invest in the country, could be interpreted as deliberate alienation from Poland.

Again, it became fashionable to make the

LEFT: the standard of living was high for most Jewish families before the growth of anti-Semitism.
ABOVE: the age of many Jewish graveyards indicate the strong roots of the community.

JEWISH SECTS

The Jewish way of life in Poland remained by no means unaffected by the religious and social trends of the times. As well as Sabbatarianism with its strict observance of the Sabbath, there was Frankism, a mystical cabbalistic sect that emerged in Podolia in 1755, and the haskalah of the Enlightenment, Hasidism, a popular movement of both a religious and mystic nature based on the cabbala and Judaism, also had its origins in Podolia in the 18th century; its founder, Baal Schev Tov, was born in Poland, and the movement, within the Jewish population till today is regarded as Polish with its characteristic philosophy, traditional dress, music, dance and warm joy of life.

ually grew closer to that of the nationalistic right. Although the state condemned the use of force, various politicians seemed to support an economic boycott of the Jews.

The Zionists had a good relationship with the government of Poland. The left wing of the Zionist movement, under the leadership of Włodzimierz Zabotyński, was even supplied with weapons and money, and offered military training. The first "Kibbutz " communities were established in Poland.

The Orthodox Jews, represented by the party Agudat Israel, were also on perfectly normal terms with the state administration. The Jew-

ish socialists, on the other hand, acknowledged only one homeland: Poland. Understandably, however, the right-wing rulers did not approve of some of their political programmes, which sympathised with the Soviet programme of Communist ideologies.

Poles and the Holocaust

Of the 3.5 million Polish Jews, only 250,000 survived the war, mostly because they were able to escape from the Nazis. Opinions differ greatly when it comes to evaluating the attitude of the Poles to the Jews and the concentration camps during the Occupation. Nevertheless,

THE JEWISH STETL

The contributions made by Polish Jews to the country's culture and the major part they played in shaping its renaissance are undisputed. The wealth of literature produced by this community is a good example of its cultural involvement. Yet the Polish Jews always retained their cultural independence. It was a separateness that made them vulnerable to racist and religious harassment, a problem nowhere more obvious than in the *stetl*, the Jewish quarter that existed in almost every Polish town. This Jewish world in miniature was one of characteristic architecture and a dense network of cultural relationships and deep-rooted religious tradition.

many Poles took the risk of helping Jews. Often, in this changing climate, people even overcame their own pronounced anti-Semitic prejudices. It is known that Jews were hidden and saved from the Nazis by National Democrats. The Christian community was also very much involved in rescue operations, above all the clergy themselves; nunneries were particularly active and saved many Jewish children. An important part was played by the Council for Jewish Assistance, ŻEGOTA, an organisation which the government-in-exile helped finance.

The risks cannot be overstated – helping Jews was punishable by death of not only the "guilty" but also his family. There were, of course, many cases of denunciation and some Poles enriched themselves unscrupulously by appropriating Jewish possessions. In what were desperate times, many are known to have handed Jews over to the Nazis in exchange for a kilo of sugar. On July 10, 1941 in the small town of Jedwabne, in today's Podlaskie voivodship, several hundred Jews were burned alive by the local Poles, probably at the instigation of the German police. It is, however, known that Jews

IN MEMORIAM

In the memorial park Yad Vashem in Jerusalem, many trees have been planted by Polish heroes who helped save Jews, in memory of those who did not survive.

uprising, the Germans used tanks and soldiers. The Jewish fighters either died of bullet wounds or took their own lives. A very few of them escaped through the sewer canals network to bear witness to the terrible crimes committed on their race in the Warsaw Ghetto (*see page 169*).

Of all the extermination camps in the whole of Poland Auschwitz-Birkenau is the most horrific. Built in 1940 it became one of the most sinister creations of humanity. According to their "final solution", the Nazis in this

themselves were not always loyal to their fellow men. War and fear of death evoked all sorts of emotions and behaviour.

One of the most tragic moments in the history of the Jewish nation is connected with the Polish capital Warsaw. During the occupation of the city by Germans, they locked part of the city and brought into it Jews from all over Poland. Cramped and oppressed, hungered and persecuted, in desperation the Jews took to using guns in April 1943. For about one month a desperate fight took place. To combat the

camp exterminated Jews in gas chambers and in death blocks. It is now estimated that 1.5 million people died in Auschwitz-Birkenau, 1.1 million of them Jews. Others were gypsies, and Poles, Czechs, Austrians, Danes, French, Dutch and Germans who opposed the Nazi regime. It remains a place of great sorrow for people from all over the world, regardless of their faith (*see page 54*).

Auschwitz was also a place of great sacrifices and the noblest of human behaviour, as people risked their lives to help others. One such prisoner, Gertruda Stein, a nun of Jewish origin who helped and tended other prisoners, was recently beatified.

LEFT: memorial to child victims of the Holocaust.
ABOVE: the camp motto, "Work Makes You Free".

Great hopes for Israel

In the first half of 1946, some 137,000 Jews who had either fled or been deported returned from the Soviet Union to Poland. The new government was anything but charitable towards the survivors of the Holocaust and often actively prevented the Jews from reconstructing their communities. There were even isolated cases of anti-Semitic riots, culminating in the Kielce pogrom of 1946, when Poles killed 46 Jews. Because of this climate, many Jews finally decided to emigrate to Palestine to make a new life for themselves.

Immediately after the war the Communist

leadership of Poland was still hoping that the new state of Israel that was just coming into being would be socialist-orientated, or would at least sympathise with the countries within Moscow's sphere of influence. For this reason, a military camp was set up to offer training to volunteers who belonged to the Zionist Haganah movement.

However, these friendly feelings soon evaporated when it became evident that Israel was developing along the lines of a western democratic society. The Jewish exodus reached record levels during the political crises of 1956–57 and 1968–69, which were often accompanied by anti-Semitic propaganda.

Soviets now needed good relations with the Arabs and enticed this attitude which was not always in tune with the general feeling of the people. This all took place against the background of the Arab-Israeli war, when the whole of the Eastern Bloc was vociferous in its condemnation of the Israelis.

Many artists, scientists and students were of Jewish origin, and the Polish rulers found that the simplest thing to do was to make the Jews the scapegoat, since they were likely to offer the least resistance. To the country, however, it was a tremendous loss of much of its intellectual capital.

In order to stir up the population against them, the Polish rulers drew attention to the inglorious part some of the Jews had played during Stalin's reign of terror. The campaign forced at least 20,000 Poles of Jewish origin to turn their backs on the country of their birth and which they considered to be their homeland to seek a new life in Israel or the USA.

Jewish renaissance

The reduction of the Jewish population from 3.5 million to 5,000 was an irreplaceable loss to Polish society. As a result of a shortage of pupils, the three Jewish high schools had to be closed and rabbis brought over from the USA. It is even more startling that, at election time, old demagogic formulas have been revived and the "Polishness" of Jewish candidates is often questioned. In recent years, however, attitudes are changing again. Post-war, Jewish minority has had its own cultural, religious and scientific institutions, folklore, magazines, a theatre, and a Jewish Historical Institute with a library and a museum in Warsaw. Poland also now has a Chief Rabbi and Kosher restaurants are in great demand. There appears to be a strong revival of interest in Jewish tradition and folklore among the young generation of Poles who want to grow up without the label of prejudice their parents had. Many liberal forces still remember the tolerance for which, hundreds of years ago, the Poles were renowned.

Moreover, Poland is now a destination favoured by Jews from all over the world who come in search of their roots and traditions. ❏

LEFT: Jewish cemetery in Kazimerz, Warsaw.
RIGHT: the Monument to the Heroes of the Ghetto Uprising, Warsaw.

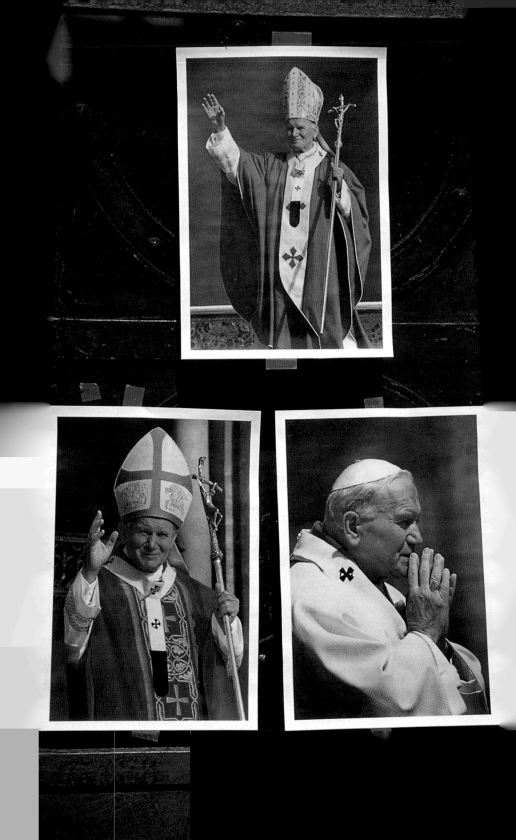

THE CATHOLICS

Until recently the Catholic church played a hugely significant role in the country's politics. Today its cultural and social role is dominant

If on a Sunday you are anywhere near a church it is as well not to be in a hurry. The roads and squares are full of families dressed in their Sunday best making their way to mass. And on special religious holidays the procession of brightly coloured flags extends for miles as the miraculous picture of the Madonna of Częstochowa is carried for several hours from house to house. In the home of every family a picture of the Virgin Mary or a portrait of Pope John Paul II occupies pride of place.

Religious origins

Christianity was introduced to Poland in the 10th century. It was primarily for political reasons that the first ruler of the land Mieszko I, the Polish Duke, had himself baptised and took the country from the Pope as a fiefdom. He did not consult all of his subjects and followers, members of the Slavic tribes and adherents of a very different religion based on ancestor- and nature worship, and resistance to Christianity continued for two centuries.

In spite of this, at around the turn of the first millennium the archdiocese of Gniezno proceeded to expand its influence. In AD 1000 it became the Archdiocese of Poland with subordinate dioceses of Kraków, Wrocław, Kołobrzeg and Poznań. Missionary-style groups left from here with the purpose of converting neighbouring tribes. The first Christian missionaries did not have it easy and many, like Bishop Wojciech of Prague, who sought to convert the Prussians, met a martyr's death: he became the first Polish saint, St Adalbert. His brother Gaudenty became first Archbishop of Poland.

Gradually the rulers imposed their will. Polygamy and working on religious holidays were prohibited, times of fasting and contributions to the church were made compulsory. The Cistercians established the new religion in the towns as well as the new economy system in the country. Religion brought with it a rich cul-

tural tradition and skilled craftsmen from all over Europe worked on the construction of places of worship. By the middle of the 12th century all babies were christened and the old faith merged with the new without conflict.

The church in Poland, as it has in most of Europe, made concessions to tradition by

allowing memorials to be built to ancestors, tolerating ancient customs and introducing festivals involving intercessions for good weather and rich harvests. But with the breakdown of central secular power in the 13th century the church was able to escape secular domination. From then on it followed the doctrine of St Thomas of Aquinas, according to which it was the duty of the church to admonish tyrants and protect the rights of the faithful.

As early as the 11th century, the Kraków bishop Stanisław had publicly opposed a king. The conflict resulted in the fall of the ruler, which strengthened the authority of the clergy as defenders of justice, and the Polish church

LEFT: postcard portraits of Pope John Paul II.
RIGHT: a roadside shrine.

has taken this role seriously ever since. At the beginning of the Reformation the Catholics lived in the western half of the enormous Polish-Lithuanian state and the adherents of the Orthodox church in the eastern half. In order to establish a counterweight to an increasingly powerful Moscow and to the patriarch of Constantinople, some Orthodox bishops joined the Roman Catholic church at the synod of Brest (Brześć) in 1596, creating an act of union between the two traditions (Unia Brzeska). The "Uniates" or Unici kept their Slavonic rites but recognised the supremacy of the Pope.

In later years, with misfortunes falling upon the country from Protestant Germany and Orthodox Russia, the maxim "to be a Pole is to be a Catholic" overruled all else.

The church and the people

The church in Poland was always tuned to the worship of saints. In the 17th century the Mother of God, the mother and queen of Poland, was the chief object of veneration, especially after the attack by the Swedish army on Jasna Góra monastery in Częstochowa (*see page 256*). Success in the uneven defence was accredited to her divine protection.

While the state fell apart, religion flourished.

LAND OF RELIGIOUS TOLERANCE

Although Poland is a Roman Catholic country, religious tolerance has always gone hand in hand with national belief. There has never been widespread religious persecution in Poland. Protestant Scots, fleeing the Counter-Reformation in Scotland, Huguenots and followers of Jan Hus, and Jews fleeing the Inquisition all found in Poland a safe haven.

Calvinism and Lutheranism had their followers, especially in Pomerania, Gdańsk, and a radical group the Aryans or Polish Brothers, separated from the Calvinists. Despite activity by the Jesuits, the Counter-Reformation in Poland did not fully develop.

Superstitious beliefs were also popular. There were over 400 local cults based on miraculous manifestations and pictures that were supposed to save people from having unpure thoughts. It was at this time that the idea of "Catholicism under siege" became part of the church's ideology, the idea of the one true faith in a heretical world.

Historic events such as the wars against Swedish and Turkish infidels, whom the Poles resisted at Częstochowa and Vienna respectively, reinforced their belief that they and their nation were a bulwark of true Christianity. Some members of the high-ranking clergy – who were, after all, principally aristocrats from the ruling Polish families then fighting for power and influence – were not entirely blameless when Poland was split up in 1772, and frequently made deals with the occupying powers. But the bond between the church and the people was never destroyed. Aided by the uprising against Russia and the Vatican's defence of Polish independence, the church was able to win back the trust of the nation. It became a stronghold of what the nation stood for; it educated, often in conspiracy conditions; it taught patriotism and, above all, it gave hope to the majority of people.

Numerous monastic orders also settled in Poland and established the image of the church through their ministering work. At the dawn of Polish Christianity monks taught the art of writing and copied books. The Cistercian Order, established in the 12th century was noted for its role in the development of education, culture and economy. The Dominican Friars opened schools. The Franciscans taught how to construct brick buildings. The Bernardine Order built monasteries and churches. The monks of the Pauline Order built the most famous of Polish sanctuaries, Jasna Góra, with its icon of the Black Madonna. The Piarists and Jesuits opened colleges. Ursuline Nuns opened orphanages and worked as nurses in hospitals.

A momentum developed of its own and became something for the people to hold on to; the idea that the cultural identity of Poland, including its freedom and religious tolerance, was guaranteed as long as the Catholic church continued to exist – even if state sovereignty was a long way off. The church went along with this, at first tentatively then more actively. Throughout the occupation by Nazi Germany and the terrors of the Stalinist regime, as well as the persistent endeavours of the Communist leaders, the church held firm.

Two men stand out among the countless heroes who confronted these troubled times. The Franciscan friar Maksymilian (Rajmund) Kolbe went voluntarily in 1941 to the hunger block to be killed with a phenol injection through the heart to save the life of an unknown man. He was later canonised. In October 1984, Father Jerzy Popiełuszko, a young Warsaw priest, was abducted by the secret police and brutally murdered for his defence of his community and the political goals of Solidarity which he supported.

Spokesman of the nation

When in 1976 the Polish conference of bishops published a pastoral in which the Catholic church was portrayed as the legitimate representative of the people and the nation, it received the people's unanimous approval. The election of Cardinal Karol Wojtyła as Pope in 1978 strengthened this claim still further. In 1979, on his first journey home, he encouraged millions of his countrymen with the words "Do not be afraid!" John Paul II

visited his homeland on seven occasions: in 1979; in 1983 after the marshal law was lifted; in 1987 to help Poles cope with the communist stronghold and in 1991 (twice) to celebrate a free Poland. He returned again for short visits in 1997 and again in 1999. In 2005, Pope John Paul II died and was buried in the vatican.

Today Poland is still synonymous with Catholicism, but whether the people's faith will suffer as political liberalisation advances is debatable. Democracy has forced the church to reconsider its role in Polish society. In 1998 the Catholic hierarchy announced its withdrawal from politics. Yet the Catholic "Radio Maryja" still has more than its fair share of listeners. ❑

LEFT: finding solace in the church.
RIGHT: a Catholic nun.

„MAŁA KOMEDIA"
(II scena Państwowego Teatru Komedia)

Krakowskie Przedmieście 21/23

Felicien Marceau

JAJKO

PRAPREMIERA STYCZEŃ 1958 R.

THE ARTS

Poland has always had a high profile in the international arts scene because of the deep cultural awareness of its population and its artistic traditions

Although Poland's historical presence in Christian Europe dates from the 10th century, Polish literature was late in emerging. Medieval Poland was frequently attacked by foreign invaders and weakened by division into small principalities. Additionally, as in other European countries, Latin was the only literary language. Early medieval writings are confined to the lives of the saints and historical annals and chronicles.

Poetry and drama

Even though the Renaissance reached Poland late and lasted for a comparatively short period, the country flourished during that time and the name "golden age" was attributed to it. The leading personality of the period is Jan Kochanowski (1530–84) whose influence on future generations of poets gained him the title "Father of Polish poetry". His masterpiece *Treny* (*Laments*, 1580) speaks of the death of his infant daughter and of his subsequent recovery of spiritual harmony. The poems put him among the great European poets of that era.

In contrast with the Renaissance, the Baroque period appeared in Poland very early, almost at the same time as in Italy. The 17th century was dominated by constant military conflict with Russia, Sweden and Turkey and by internal unrest and disputes over constitutional reforms. The masterpiece of Baroque lyrics is the poetry of Jan Andrzej Morsztyn (1613–93) who supplied the royal theatre with superb translations of Corneille's tragedies.

After the decadent period of the Saxon reign in Poland, the Enlightenment literature was genuinely preoccupied with building political awareness and recreating Polish national culture in order to save the weakened country from its inevitable collapse. The notable event was the inauguration in 1765, on the king's initiative, of the first public theatre. The comedies

by Franciszek Zabłocki (1754–1821) and Aleksander Fredro (1793–1876) successfully combine the foreign plots borrowed from Molière and Goldoni with typical Polish archetypes and their anxieties. The period was mainly didactic in character yet it saw the emergence of the first professional periodicals, the first *Dictionary of*

the Polish Language (1807–14), the introduction of the sentimental novel and, in poetry, of western genres, all of which were practiced with high artistic standards.

Romanticism coincided with the most tragic moments in Polish history. The juxtaposition of the loss of national independence with the uplifted Romantic ideology led to the emergence of some extraordinary poetic output which makes Polish Romanticism one of the most distinctive literary periods in Europe. On the one hand there was the poet's duty to keep the spirit of Polishness alive, on the other there was the fascination with Byron and Shelley's Promethean myth. According to the formula, the evil Gods were

---

PRECEDING PAGES: examples of Polish poster art.
LEFT: a painting by Polish artist Leon Tarasewicz.
RIGHT: the late theatre director Tadeusz Kantor.

either the oppressors or the Christian God who let them reduce the nation's position to mere martyrdom. The human being was the poet who "suffers for millions". The rebellion was of course the fight against the tyrants often in a truly Promethean situation, as the genius trio of Polish Romantic poets went into exile. Had they stayed they would have been deported to Siberia with the most luminous people of their generation.

The star trio are Adam Mickiewicz (1798–1855), Juliusz Słowacki (1809–49) and

EARLIEST TEXT

The oldest Polish literary text is a song in honour of the Virgin Mary, the *Bogurodzica*. The first copy dates from the 14th century but it was probably written earlier.

nation was severely punished for rebelling against the Russian oppressors, all hopes were abandoned and the period that followed is now called Positivism. It was a mood of practical thinking which expressed a rationalist reaction against Romanticism and the domination of literature over life. "Work from the foundations" was the new realistic slogan, implying the renunciation of armed resistance and the concentration on the preservation of the ideological and cultural assets of the nation. The period produced

Zygmunt Krasiński (1812–59). Mickiewicz is the most popular and accessible of them all. His works have been translated into many languages and among the highlights are *Dziady* (*The Forefathers' Eve*, 1823) a Messianic drama presenting Poland suppressed by foreign powers as the Christ among the peoples destined to rise in glory. His poetic tour de force is *Pan Tadeusz* (1834) presenting the Polish landed gentry in the context of Napoleon's expedition to Moscow in 1812.

Practicality and realism

The Romantic vein continued until 1863 when another unsuccessful uprising began. After the

two extraordinary novelists Bolesław Prus (1847– 1912) and Henryk Sienkiewicz (1846–1916). The latter was the first Polish winner of the literary Nobel Prize in 1905. Recently published in England, Prus's *Lalka* (*The Doll*, 1890) is an accomplished and vivid picture of contemporary Warsaw with an intricate plot and a collection of unforgettable characters. *Trilogy* (1884–88) by Sienkiewicz is a picture of Poland's struggles against its 17th-century enemies and the Nobel Prize winning *Quo Vadis* (1896) is a historical novel of Rome under Nero. Historians argue over their factual value but their literary qualities are undeniable.

While positivism flourished in Warsaw,

Kraków saw an emergence of the Young Poland movement which proclaimed the return to the expression of feelings and to imaginative writing. The most outstanding figure of the movement was Stanisław Wyspiański (1869–1907) (*see page 112*). In his play *Wesele* (*The Wedding*, 1901), based on the foundations of primitive folk theatre, he created a visionary drama which he used as a vehicle to criticise the problems of his age.

The newly found freedom in 1918 turned the artists' attention to subject matters other than

RURAL SUCCESS
The epic *Chłopi* (*The Peasants*, 1909) by Władysław Reymont (1868–1925) was translated into every European language and was awarded the Nobel Prize in 1924.

known as Witkacy (*see page 247*) and later Sławomir Mrożek (born 1930), both translated into many languages and given numerous international performances.

The reconstruction of an independent Polish state was harshly interrupted by the invasion of the Germans and the Soviet Russians in 1939. The rich literary harvest of these years was only fully revealed after the end of the war. One of the most devastating works of this period is Tadeusz Borowski's *Proszę Państwa do Gazu* (*Would

independence, which had dominated Polish literature for over 120 years. Between the two World Wars Polish writers produced a wide range of distinguished literary works. One of the most interesting writers of that time was Witold Gombrowicz (1905–1969) whose satiric prose has influenced the birth of the Theatre of the Absurd on an international scale. Other playwrights who exercised the genre were Stanisław Ignacy Witkiewicz (1885–1939),

FAR LEFT: writer Barbara Wachowicz. **LEFT:** Wisława Szymborska won the Nobel Prize for Literature in 1996. **ABOVE:** film director Andrzej Wajda (right), a leading light of the Polish Film School (1955–63).

You Please Proceed to the Gas Chamber, 1949) based on the author's personal experiences in the concentration camp at Auschwitz-Birkenau (*see page 54*).

From 1945 until the political "thaw" after Stalin's death, literary life in Poland was dominated by Socialist Realism. The factory worker or collective farmer was now to become a literary hero. After 1956 Polish literature concentrated on the nuances and contradiction of life in a communist country. The most important authors of this epoch are Tadeusz Konwicki, Sławomir Mrożek, Zbigniew Herbert, Stanisław Barańczak, Tadeusz Różewicz, Andrzej Szczypiorski and the two Nobel Prize winners Czesław Miłosz and Wisława Szymborska. Ryszard Kapuściński gained international acclaim with his books on dictatorships in Africa and Asia, exposing parallels with communist rule in Poland.

Since the collapse of Communism, the Polish literary scene is enjoying all the privileges of democracy. Along with the discovery of the writers whose works were banned under the Communist regime, the young generation of writers is preoccupied with such phenomena

> ### MUSIC FESTIVALS
>
> Many musical festivals are held in Poland: the annual Warsaw Autumn Festival of modern music and every four years the Chopin Competition in Warsaw and the Wieniawski in Poznań.

national success was probably the polo-naise, a lofty court dance in simple triple time. It became fashionable in the 18th century onwards and features in the works of Bach, Mozart, Beethoven, Schubert and Liszt, and of course the famous piano polonaises by Chopin. The most famous Polish polonaise is Oginski's *Pożegnanie ojczyzny* (*Farewell to the Homeland*) written soon after the country disappeared from the map of Europe in 1795. For the following 120 years Polish music, like literature

as feminism, sexual revolution and the discovery of the national identity under the new political system. There remains a literary bequest; a moral issue of a dichotomised nation, split over the last 50 years into oppressors and oppressed. The contemporary literary climate that facilitated the extraordinary success of Paweł Huelle's novel *Weiser Dawidek*, looks set to resolve this.

A national rhythm

Frederick Chopin (*see page 196*) is not the only Polish contribution to world music, although he is undoubtedly the most important composer to represent Polish music abroad. The first inter-

and fine arts, was an expression of national spirit full of allusiveness and political message. Chopin (1810–1849) and his contemporaries were putting elements of folk music into their works – elements that achieved the status of a national Polish musical style in the words and music of the "father of Polish national opera", Stanisław Moniuszko (1819– 1872). They allude to the heroic era of Polish nobility in works such as *Straszny Dwór* (*The Haunted House*, 1864) and introduce common people as victims (*Halka*, 1858). The patriotic plots along with a great use of Polish dance rhythms such as the mazurka and polonaise were to foster deep patriotic feelings.

Henryk Wieniawski (1835–1880) was both a patriotic composer and one of the most important violinists of the generation after Paganini. He combined the technical advances of the great Italian virtuoso with Romantic imagination and Slavonic spirit.

After the country regained its independence in 1918 folk tradition was still present in music. The most distinguished composer of the entre-guerre period was Karol Szymanowski (1882–1937) who took the challenge of translating folk music into the symphonic spirit of Modernism. He spent half of his life in the Tatra Mountains resort of Zakopane (*see page 243*),

tory. On the one hand they were influenced by the horrors of World War II and on the other were dependent on the political situation in Communist Poland. Lutosławski's early works were composed under official restraints insisting on a style based on folk-song. When the political repression lifted, he became internationally active as a teacher and conductor of his own music. Baird also started out toeing the party line but the cultural thaw of 1956 enabled him to pursue his own artistic vision. Penderecki gained international acclaim with *Threnody for the Victims of Hiroshima* (1961), *St Luke Passion* (1965) and his dynamic operas.

where he studied the songs and dances of the mountaineers which led to the composition of an exotic ballet *Harnasie* (1935). His other major works are the opera *King Roger* (1924) and the choral orchestral *Stabat Mater* (1926), both outstanding examples of modern Romanticism. Szymanowski's villa in Zakopane is now a museum and a popular tourist attraction.

Post-war music is represented by Witold Lutosławski (1913–1994), Tadeusz Baird (1928–1981) and Krzysztof Penderecki (born 1933). Their works are closely linked with his-

LEFT: dancing the polonaise in the late 18th century.
ABOVE: Krzysztof Penderecki conducts.

MUSIC AND POLITICS

The combination of music and patriotism found its best expression in the life of Ignacy Paderewski (1860–1941) who was not only an outstanding composer and a world-class pianist but also an important politician. His works are deeply rooted in the Romantic Polish national school among which the opera *Manru* and the *Fantasie polonaise* are most noteworthy. During World War I Paderewski represented the Polish nation abroad, making speeches and assisting victims of oppression, and eventually becoming Prime Minister in 1919. Paderewski lived much of his life in exile, but in 1992 his remains were returned for burial in Warsaw.

Fine Arts

As with literature and music, it is impossible to appreciate Polish art without an understanding of their references to the historical situation. Polish artists worked either in exile or in the partitioned country trying to convey some implicit political message.

One of the most outstanding figures of the first half of the 19th century was Piotr Michałowski (1800–55) who settled in Paris and produced works that were on a level with those of Géricault and Delacroix. His patriotic scenes of horsemen from the Kościuszko Uprising and the Napoleonic wars (now in the

Kraków Museum) demonstrate a more lively and explosive temperament than the Paris artists trained in the tame classical tradition.

Michalowski's successors in allegorical and historical art were Juliusz Kossak (1824–99), Artur Grottger (1837–67) and Jan Matejko (1838–93). Their works portray the nation's grand historic events with patriotic emotiveness. The depiction of the nation's fate and the fight for independence fulfilled the criteria of the patriotic mission being enthusiastically received by large sections of the population. Matejko's pupil, Stanisław Wyspiański (1869–1907) was a versatile painter, poet, playwright, architect and man of letters who

translated historic Romanticism into eerie visions of Symbolism. His paintings revealed a genius for dramatic construction, but the loss of the use of his hand forced him to turn to designing and writing.

Most of Wyspiański's architectural designs still exist on paper. Notably, he turned the attention of his generation to the wooden homesteads and churches built by the Polish peasants, wishing to apply the rural forms to monumental buildings in order to create a national style. Wyspiański was one of the first artists to choose Zakopane as his home, which was to later become an artistic centre.

Another outstanding artist of early 20th-century Polish Symbolism was Jacek Malczewski (1854–1929), who combined the dreamlike visions of the past with a psychoanalytical perception of humanity.

After Poland achieved independence, Leon Wyczółkowski (1852–1936) and Julian Fałat (1853–1929) were the major creators of Polish Impressionism. In Poland the younger generation was no longer prepared to convey patriotic duty and new artistic groups emerged. The Futurists and late Expressionists made a break from all that had gone before.

After the war artists had to conform for over a decade to painting in the style of Socialist Realism in order to gain any recognition. One of the most interesting alternative movements was the group Blok, which introduced its own interpretation of constructivism. Its reference points were architecture, sociology and the new technical civilisation. Władysław Strzemiński (1893–1952) and Henryk Stażewski (1894–1988) gave their particular approach to arts the name "unism". The movement had a charismatic influence on the constructivist avant garde. Recently Stażewski has become the central figure of the younger generation of art analysts and representatives of concrete art.

Contemporary aesthetics embrace installment art: instead of pictures there are now "environments". The showing of slides and films is being used to supplement the traditional media. The opening up of the Eastern Bloc and the consequent free-flow of ideas across Europe means that Polish art now participates within a universal framework as opposed to the isolated national movements of before. ❑

LEFT: *Self-portrait* by Jacek Malczewski.

Film School of Łódź

In his autobiography, Roman Polański writes: "It was through a mere whim of history that Łódź became the film capital of Poland... after the war the capital, Warsaw, lay in ruins and... the government chose the nearest suitable town when looking for a place to establish a centre of cinematography." Two years after World War II the Kraków film course was also transferred to Łódź and from then on it was here that film-makers received their training. The Communist authorities appropriated a small palace belonging to an industrialist, and by 1948 they had already promoted the school to the status of a college. From the beginning the school was orientated towards the production of an élite. Despite the war devastation, it was well equipped and had excellent teachers, no expense spared. The reason why they went to so much trouble is summed up in the quote by Lenin carved in marble in the main hall: "Of all the forms of art we have, film is the most important."

In the 1950s Polish film-makers were bound by the Socialist style and there was no room for originality. Only after Stalin's death did it become possible to make films that did not reflect the propaganda clichés of the Communists. There emerged what came to be known as the Polish Film School and its founders portrayed the war and the heroism of that period in a new light. For the first time they were able to concentrate on the problem of human loneliness. *Kanal* (Silver Palm winner in Cannes, 1957) and *Ashes and Diamonds* by Andrzej Wajda (FIPRESCI in Venice, 1959) and *Eroica* by Andrzej Munk – the best-known postwar productions – all date from this period. A few years later Jerzy Kawalerowicz made *Mother Joanne of the Angels* (Silver Palm in Cannes, 1961) and Roman Polański made the Academy Award nominated *Knife in the Water* (FIPRESCI, 1962).

Almost all contemporary Polish directors are graduates of the Łódź film school, among them Andrzej Wajda and Roman Polański, both now world-famous. Wajda (born 1926) has been heaped with prizes: for *The Promised Land* (Moscow 1975; Valladolid 1976; Cartagena 1978; Academy Award nomination), *The Iron Man* (Grand Prix Cannes 1981), *Danton* (Prix Delluc 1983; Cezar 1983) and an Oscar (honorary award) in 2000, to name but a few. Today Wajda is the undisputed authority among young directors. In 1989, in the first free elections in Poland, he also became a member of the Senate. Polański, in contrast, left Poland at an earlier stage and made films abroad that enjoyed huge international success, including *Rosemary's Baby*, *Repulsion*, *Cul-de-Sac*, *Chinatown*, *The Tenant* and *Dance of the Vampires*.

Towards the end of the 1980s the films being produced by young directors dwelt with painful precision on the social realities of the decade while attempting to establish a new manifestation of solidarity. Krzysztof Kieślowski's 10-part television series *Dekalog* about the Ten Commandments is a good example of this development. While his

works, such as *Film about Love* and *The Double Life of Veronique*, received more acclaim abroad than at home, his trilogy *Three Colours: Blue, White, Red* did bring greater recognition among his compatriots. He died in 1996 at the age of 55. Another Łódź graduate, Sławomir Idziak, was nominated in 2002 for an Oscar for Best Photography for Ridley Scott's *Black Hawk Down*.

Today, the school continues to train directors and cameramen. Its curriculum includes humanities and practical training, combining the qualities of a university, polytechnic and academy of fine arts. It has its own studios where students make short films, and full-length feature films are made in conjunction with professional film institutes. ❏

RIGHT: Roman Polański, a leading Polish film maker.

MAINTAINING TRADITIONAL CULTURE

Numerous ethnographic museums showcase regional folk arts, crafts and architectural styles and illustrate the life of rural communities

Skansens (open air museums) comprise different types of buildings, brought together within a park to recreate a village community. The range of buildings show how peasants as well as owners of small-holdings lived and worked, with these houses decorated in period style, while other buildings such as a windmill or blacksmith's forge show how these rural crafts were operated. One of the earliest *skansens* was established in 1906 at Wdzydze Kiszewskie. A vast park features cottages, farmhouses and barns dating from the 18th and 19th centuries, together with a Kashubian school house, a wooden church and a centre of folk arts and crafts. *Skansens* can also be found in city centres, with Toruń for instance having a *skansen* occupying a central park containing farmsteads, a windmill, forge, and even a fisherman's barge moored on the river Vistula. There are also museums with collections of folk arts and crafts in many major cities, such as the Museum of Mankind in Warsaw, and in Kazimierz, the historic Jewish district of Kraków, where an extensive collection is housed in the former town hall.

▷ **OLSZTYNEK**
The *skansen* at Olsztynek includes a 19th-century inn and this half-timbered, arcaded building.

▷ **BEE KEEPING**
Bee keeping is an ancient rural occupation, with honey also made into alcoholic mead. *Skansens* such as Biskupin display historic bee hives.

△ **WIND POWER**
Windmills were essential to every rural community. This one is from the Olsztynek *skansen* near the town of Olsztyn in the Mazurian lake district.

▷ **SACRAL BUILDINGS**
S*kansens* contain a wide range of wooden Russian orthodox churches, mosques and Roman Catholic churches.

▽ **CHOCHOŁÓW** *SKANSEN*
This *skansen* includes 18th- and 19th-century houses with their characteristic small front gardens collected from the Tatra mountains.

GÓRAL CULTURAL STYLE

One thriving ethnic community culture is the Górals, who live in the Podhale and Pieniny regions of southern Poland. Traditionally they are shepherds and farmers, have their own dialect and maintain traditional customs and regional costumes. Góral style can be seen in the local architecture with ornately carved wooden houses and churches still remaining in Tatra villages, as well as in Zakopane. There is also an important collection of Góral folk art in Zakopane's Tatra Museum. In addition to architecture, music and folk dancing are essential elements of the culture. Among a varied programme of cultural events, Zakopane hosts the annual international Festival of Highland Folklore in September.

◁ **TRADITIONAL SKILLS**
Skansen buildings are maintained in using traditional skills. This scene shows thatchers at work repairing the roof at the Olsztynek *skansen*.

▽ **FOLK COSTUMES**
Krakowiacy, wearing the traditional folk costumes of the Kraków region can be seen singing folk songs in Kraków's Main Market Square on a daily basis.

FOOD AND DRINK

Polish food is a delicious mixture of influences drawn from Russia to Ukraine,
served in up in hearty portions and accompanied by freely flowing drinks

Poland has always been better known for politics rather than cuisine, and when the cuisine is thought of it is usually in terms of clichés, such as herrings, stuffed cabbage leaves and various other rich, stodgy dishes. These elements do of course exist, as they do in virtually every national cuisine, but Polish food also offers a wealth of light, elegant dishes. Specialities include Baltic salmon, ceps and truffles, a wide range of game led by venison and wild boar – typically flavoured with juniper berries, while various dishes are garnished with dill (the national herb). Terminology also shows how powerful associations can be: if you translated soured cream into crème fraiche, which is the same thing, then it automatically receives approbation simply for being French.

Polish cuisine was constantly evolving as new ingredients and techniques became known to cooks. From the 12th century Poland was already on the spice route from the East to Europe and Scandinavia, with the salt mines at Wieliczka just outside Kraków also mined from the 12th century.

In the 16th century the Italian Princess Bona Sforza married King Zygmunt Stary and introduced Italian favourites such as tomatoes, chicory, asparagus, artichokes and, of course, pasta. King Jan III Sobieski, who reigned in the 17th century, had a French wife who brought the omelette and various French specialities with her, while Jan Sobieski's defeat of the Turks at Vienna in 1683 resulted in him bringing back coffee, which was booty taken from pavilions which the Turks had abandoned. The Austrian emperor also gave the king some potato plants, which were initially planted at Wilanów, the royal summer residence outside Warsaw, and were considered an "exotic" novelty. In the 17th century the Polish and Lithuanian commonwealth was Europe's largest country, except for Russia, reaching from the Baltic to the Black Sea, with Lithuan-

ian dishes like boiled meat dumplings being integrated. A large Jewish community also contributed various dishes.

Soup and dumplings

Polish hospitality is warm and generous, summed up by a popular saying: "a guest in the

house, God in the house." Breakfast is typically a selection of sliced charcuterie, tomatoes and cheese, rye bread and plenty of strong coffee. A late lunch is usually the day's main three-course meal, with a light buffet-style supper typically comprising cold cuts, vegetables such as tomatoes and pickled cucumbers, with rye bread.

Soup is a popular starter. Poland's more than 30 types of mushrooms are put to good use in numerous versions of mushroom soup, while *kapuśniak* is a hearty winter warmer of boiled cabbage. The most popular soup is *barszcz* (beetroot soup), served either "clear" or with chopped beetroot and boiled potatoes added. Ukranian *barszcz* means extra chopped

LEFT: beer and bread at a food festival in Warsaw.
RIGHT: Polish sausage for sale.

vegetables including cabbage. *Chłodnik* is the summer version, served cold garnished with a freshly boiled egg, chopped dill and soured cream, which turns the soup a shade of lilac.

Pierogi are variously translated as dumplings or ravioli, but this makes them sound like a derivative rather than a speciality in their own right. Where they originated is unclear – they may have arrived during the 12th century from Russia or they may already have been an original Slavic folk dish. *Pierogi* are prepared by placing a small amount of stuffing in a circle of dough, which is then folded over the stuffing and sealed with a scalloped edge, mak-

cream. Sweet *pierogi* are also served, stuffed with curd cheese mixed with candied zest and raisins, or various fruits such as blueberries, diced apples or thick preserves, which are served with caster sugar and soured cream.

Meat and vegetables

Bigos ("hunter's stew") is a classic example of a one-pot dish, originally prepared with whatever game a hunter (or poacher) could get. The line-up of extras is also variable, though the usual basis of *bigos* is chopped white cabbage, sauerkraut and dried mushrooms, cooked with pork, bacon and *żywiecka* (Polish sausage).

ing them look rather like large ears. The most popular filling "*z serem*" ("with cheese"), also known as "*ruskie*" ("Russian"), means a combination of curd cheese, mashed potato and chopped fried onion.

Another popular style "*z kapsutą*" ("with cabbage") means either cabbage or sauerkraut (or a combination of both) mixed with chopped sautéed mushrooms; while "*z mięsem*" ("with meat") is minced beef mixed with breadcrumbs and onion. Buckwheat, a staple of the Slav diet, is the most historic style. Once boiled, the typical garnish is breadcrumbs fried in butter. Alternatively, the *pierogi* can be lightly sautéed to give a crispy texture, and served with soured

Adding a little lard is traditional and gives a wonderful depth of flavour, whereas the question of whether or not to add a few tablespoons of tomato purée is a great talking point among serious cooks.

Meat essentially means pork in Poland, whether a fried breaded cutlet, roasted with prunes or served with stewed cabbage. Chicken (not usually considered to be "real meat") is typically served as *de volaille* (stuffed with butter and garlic). Beef is also less popular, unless it is served as the ultra-popular *zrazy*, established in the 14th century by King Władysław himself. Pieces of beaten, seasoned sirloin of beef are rolled around a filling of chopped fried bacon, breadcrumbs, dill cucumber and mushrooms, and then fried or grilled.

The usual accompaniment of *zrazy* – and indeed other meat dishes (but never fish) – is buckwheat. This is also the most traditional stuffing for favourites such as *gołąbki*, literally "little pigeons", which are stuffed cabbage leaves and roast suckling pig. Another favourite side dish with various roast meats is a cucumber salad named *mizeria* (literally "misery"). The name is no indication of the wonderfully refreshing flavours, with wafer thin slices of cucumber dressed in a combination of soured cream, lemon juice, a dash of caster sugar and

most historic, made with baked or cooked beetroots, sliced and layered with a dressing of vinegar, caraway seeds, horseradish and lemon juice. Beetroot is also popular puréed, sliced and fried in batter, or grated and combined with a little soured cream or minced onion.

Modern Polish cuisine

Under Communism Polish cuisine virtually disappeared, with rationing and frequent shortages a daily reality. Even having a ration book entitling you to a certain amount of butter, meat, and so on was no guarantee, as it still meant having to find a shop that actually had those

salt, garnished with minced dill or spring onion, and chilled before serving. The origins of *mizeria* are attributed to Queen Bona Sforza, but the reasons vary. The name may have stemmed from her weeping nostalgically for Italy whenever she ate it (before settling in and living happily in Poland). Alternatively, she may have eaten *mizeria* in such quantities that the consequent pain of indigestion made her ask for a misericord (a dagger for committing suicide).

Meat dishes are also frequently accompanied by various beetroot dishes. *Ćwikła* is one of the

LEFT: a plate of *pierogi*.
ABOVE: buying pretzels.

POLISH SWEETS AND CAKES

Many Polish cakes and pastries originally arrived from France, such as *napoleonki* (millefeuille) and *eklerka* (eclair). Among the classic Polish cakes are *sernik* (cheesecake) prepared with either curd or cream cheese (or a combination of both) and always baked. Variations include adding cream to the cheese (for greater moistness), raisins (Viennese-style), and with a surface layer of either icing sugar or dark chocolate and crushed nuts. *Makowiec* is prepared like a sponge cake and rolled around a filling of poppyseeds or a "poppyseed cream". At Christmas, doughnuts filled with rose petal jam and *chrusty*, also known as *faworki* (little flavours), are eaten.

items in stock. Consequently, Poles refer to the cooking of this era as "Communist food".

Not surprisingly, restaurants offered a very erratic menu, while chefs also had to endure various other restrictions. The government issued every restaurant with a compulsory menu (the ultimate "set menu"), which never changed, seasonally or even annually, and no deviation was allowed. Chefs also had to follow government cookery manuals which not only stipulated the cooking method, but also the exact amount (in grams) and number of ingredients in each dish. Vigilant controllers would subsequently cross-reference the num-

ber of dishes served with the remaining amount of stock in the kitchen.

It is only since privatisation that chefs have become liberated and able to use their own ideas, and of course have the advantage of regular supplies. Not only was real Polish food back on the menu, but Polish chefs also began returning from having worked abroad, bringing with them a modern European perspective. As chefs began to re-interpret their national dishes, so Modern Polish cuisine began to emerge in a few key Warsaw restaurants during the mid-1990s. The Malinowa within the Hotel Bristol, Fukier, and the Hotel Jan III Sobieski were among the key pioneers.

Modern Polish cuisine is, fortunately, retaining the authentic character of classic dishes, but producing lighter, more subtle and interesting versions. A new style *barszcz*, for instance, comprises delicate jellied consommé with soured cream and a beetroot julienne; herring appears as a tartare, *pierogi* may feature brains or Baltic seaweed, while *bigos* benefits from a wider repertoire of choice cuts such as smoked duck and venison.

Communism also sought to wipe out regionalism, which is now beginning to return. Poznań, for instance, is known for *pyzy* (steamed yeast dumplings), Warsaw thrives on tripe soup, while *polewka Gdańska*, is a goulash soup flavoured with pickled cucumbers, olives and capers.

Vodka

"Vodka doesn't taste of anything", and the subsequent conclusion that "all vodkas taste the same", are two popular clichés – but they are very far from the whole story. The traditional style of vodka in the UK and USA doesn't, in fact, taste of anything, being entirely neutral and only intended as a means of adding alcohol to a mixer such as tonic water, or a cocktail, without adding any flavour. Polish vodka, however, offers "character", drawn from the raw material, which is either rye or potatoes.

Wyborowa vodka, for instance, provides distinct rye aromas, while the flavour combines wonderfully mellow rye and nutty notes with a natural, elegant sweetness.

Potato vodka may seem as though it's produced from a "second class" source, but not only are some of the most popular brands produced from potatoes, but potatoes have in fact been elevated into a speciality, being more expensive to cultivate and distil than rye. A special variety of potatoes is used, cultivated in specific microclimates by the River Vistula and on the Baltic Coast. Vodkas such as Luksusowa and Cracovia yield fresh potato aromas, while the palate thrives on a subtle sweetness, with hints of creamy mashed potatoes.

There has been a long-standing dispute between the Poles and Russians about the origins of vodka. After all, who wouldn't want to take the credit for inventing such a drink. While there is no definitive evidence, circumstantial evidence points to Poland. Knowledge of distillation spread from France across Europe around the 14th century, and is likely to have reached Poland before going on to Russia via Lithuania and the Ukraine. Moreover, the earliest recorded use of the word "vodka" in Eastern Europe is on a Polish document, dated 1405. The Russians, however, claim vodka was first distilled in a monastery outside Moscow in the 14th century.

NATIONAL TIPPLE

As early as the end of the 16th century vodka was established as the Polish national drink.

At least the Poles and Russians agreed on the name for this drink, with vodka being the diminutive of *woda*, meaning water (so vodka literally means "little water".) When this term was coined using the diminutive it indicated that it was an improved version of the original. The earliest centres of commercial distillation, during the 16th century, were Kraków, Poznań and Gdańsk. By then vodka had developed from being purely medicinal into a social drink.

Commercial distillation was originally limited to the aristocracy (providing plenty of tax revenue), though early distillation methods were inevitably rudimentary, as it was impossible to rectify (purify) the spirit. This meant that the resulting vodka was marred by unpleasant flavours and aromas. The answer was to disguise these imperfections by adding aromatic oils, fruit, herbs and spices, and to sweeten it with honey. When rectification was developed during the 19th century, flavourings were added for their own sake, as there was nothing left to hide.

During the 19th century around 100 flavoured styles were available, and Poland continues to produce the world's largest range of flavoured vodka. Flavourings can be used in a "minimalist" way, solely to enhance the flavour of the grain, with a hint of aromatic

fruit and apple spirit maximising the rye flavours of Extra Żytnia. At the other extreme is Gnesnania Boonekamp, flavoured with 23 herbs and spices, which originated from Gniezno, briefly the capital of Poland during the 10th–11th century.

A classic style dating from the 16th century, and still going strong is Żubrowka, which includes the simpler reference of "Bison Vodka" on the label. The flavour is derived entirely from bison grass, and not from any part of a bison, with this wild herb growing only in the Białowieża Forest, a national park in eastern Poland (*see page 186*). A blade of grass features in each bottle of Zubrowka, but that is merely a

LEFT: ready to order at Szara na Kazimierz.
ABOVE: café-bars in Zamość.

decorative accessory, as it takes far more bison grass to create this complex, aromatic vodka with herbaceous, fresh grass/hay aromas, and beautifully balanced herbaceous flavours of thyme and lavender, together with lemon, tobacco and chocolatey hints. The most popular way of serving Zubrowka today is known as "Tatanka", which means a measure of vodka topped up with apple juice, creating a refreshing but dry combination.

The name Tatanka was coined after the release of the 1995 film *Dances With Wolves* in Poland, because this was how the Native Americans referred to bison.

After enjoying vodka with *zakąski* there's no need to stop there, and indeed vodka is often served with a meal in Poland, after which a choice of digestif-style vodkas take over. Goldwasser ("Gold Water"), which originated in Gdańsk during the 16th century, is based on an aniseed-flavoured vodka infused with various flavourings such as gypsy rose, valerian root, sandalwood and rosewood, before adding the final touch: 23-carat gold leaf.

This twinkles beautifully within the vodka, and is of course an automatic talking point, though the original rationale was the alleged medicinal benefits of gold leaf. Whether gold

VODKA PARTIES

A great benefit of having a vodka session in true Polish style is that it's an instant party, because Poles always serve food with vodka. There is actually a specific range of specialities called "*zakąski*" (literally "a nibble") all of which have a genuine rapport with vodka. This is typically salted herring fillets and *blinis* with soured cream, pickled cucumbers, pickled mushrooms, sausage, ham, rye bread and curd cheese. These flavours are substantial enough to stand up to the vodka, while vodka tames the saltiness of herring fillets, and melting soured cream. Moreover, rich, salty, spicy flavours naturally encourage another glass of vodka, so it's a perfect relationship.

leaf actually contributes to the flavour is debatable, and actually irrelevant, because there's already plenty to enjoy with rich flavours spanning aniseed, liquorice, cooked fruit (particularly rhubarb and oranges), culminating in an elegant, dry finish.

Another rarity is Starka (meaning "old"), a style that dates from the late 14th century. Aristocrats traditionally celebrated the birth of a daughter by filling empty wine casks with vodka, which were aged in a cellar until the daughter's wedding day and served at the wedding banquet. The intervening years saw the vodka gently mature into an elegant, aromatic style. Starka is still produced, and aged for ten years in oak barrels, yielding an indulgent rye flavour.

High strength vodkas extend the range of choice, with Polish Pure Spirit at either 57 per cent or 79 per cent abv, while Rectified Spirit (*Spirytus Rektyfikowany*) at 95 percent abv, the world's strongest spirit, is distillation strength vodka. These styles are usually a base for home-flavouring, with a favourite combination being Rectified Spirit and cherry cordial, resulting in *wiśniówka*, while *karmel-*

> ## WORDS OF WISDOM
>
> Numerous "vodka sayings" have evolved in Poland, such as *"wodka grzeje, wodka chlodzi, wodka nigdy nie zaskodzi"*, meaning "vodka cools and vodka warms, but vodka never harms."

Beer and wine

Beer and mead were the earliest alcoholic drinks prepared by the Slavs, with major cities such as Warsaw and Wrocław still featuring mead bars. Mead is kept hot by serving it in ceramic beakers that stand on a tray heated by a small candle.

Additionally, a range of fruit wines are very popular and make the most of readily available favourites such as cherries, strawberries, redcurrants, blackcurrants, gooseberries, apples and blackberries.

ówka means adding a sugar syrup to Rectified Spirit for an instant caramel vodka.

The Polish toast "*na zdrowie*" (meaning "to your health") is not simply a polite line. Vodka is renowned for purity, and actually contains a lower level of congeners (impurities responsible for hangovers) than other spirits. While devotees claim that drinking vodka is a guarantee against hangovers, this also depends on the quantity of vodka consumed, particularly as an enthusiastic refrain in Poland is "*do dna*", meaning "to the bottom" (of the glass).

Polish beer is generally lager, though porter, stout and other dark beers are also brewed in some parts of the country. Some of the most famous brands come from the south, including Żywiec and Okocim, both produced at the brewery and town of the same name.

Coincidentally, the north of Poland is also the source of some excellent beers, with Gdańsk the source of Hevelius (originally brewed by the family of Jan Heweliusz, the renowned 17th-century astronomer, who boosted his income from brewing).

One of the leading brands, EB is produced in nearby Elbląg, where beer has been brewed since 1309, when the Teutonic Knights who

LEFT: a drop of *Krupnik* – honey vodka.
ABOVE: an imaginative place to stop for refreshment.

then controlled the region *(see page 263)* granted the first brewing licence to Siegfried von Feuchtwanger. By 1336 the town had a brewers' guild with more than 160 members. Moreover, there is a fascinating link between Elbląg and Great Britain, as from 1580 English merchants who were then trading with Baltic ports purchased land around the area, which includes the site of the current Elbląg brewery. The land provided a recreational area from which the English merchants could watch

> ### HAIR OF THE DOG
>
> If, after all this vodka and alcohol, you have a hangover, you can try a classic Polish remedy – drinking the juice drained from a glass of sauerkraut. Failing that it's back to the drink that caused the problem.

Soft drinks

Poland's vast amount of spas also means a comprehensive selection of mineral waters, all with varying taste profiles, as spas across the country increasingly commercialise their finest liquid assets. Krystynka, for instance, is bottled at the Ciechocinek spa, while Perła Bałtyku ("Pearl of the Baltic") hails from the spa in Kołobrzeg on the coast *(see page 330)*.

Among a wide range of fresh juices produced from indigenous fruits, the clear leader in pop-

their ships and simply relax and gossip. The locals referred to the area as *"Angielski Zdrój"* ("The English Springs"), after the springs of pure water which flowed there at a very low temperature.

Not surprisingly, these springs now provide the water used in the production of EB beer. As one of the world's few beers that is actually triple filtered, with an alcoholic strength of 5.4 percent abv, it has an unusually clean, crisp taste. Polish brewers and fans of EB will try to convince you that however much EB you drink, you won't get a hangover. If only. Draft beer is not common in Poland although it can be found in small villages in the south.

ularity must be *sok z czarnej porzeczki* (blackcurrant juice), deliciously ripe and rich, but with a dry finish. Bottled fruit juices mixed with mineral water are refreshing, with strawberry and apple being the most popular flavours.

Coffee *(kawa)* is typically served *cappuccino* style, strong and full-bodied with a dash of milk, while tea *(herbata)* is served without milk but with a slice of lemon and in tall glasses. In a café or restaurant this usually means a glass of boiling water and a tea bag on the saucer will arrive at the table for customers to brew the tea according to their own preference. ❑

ABOVE: the restaurant at the Hotel Stary, Kraków.

Festive Food

The religious and gastronomic focus of Christmas is Christmas Eve rather than Christmas Day. However, until the Christmas Eve dinner (traditionally comprising 12 dishes, one for each apostle) a semi-fast is observed, involving a small helping of rye bread and salted herring fillets.

There is no set time to assemble for Christmas Eve dinner, known as Wigilia – it depends on when the first star appears, symbolising the star that guided the Three Kings to Bethlehem. The table is laid with a white tablecloth, under which a small amount of hay is placed, recalling the hay of the crib. Traditionally an extra place is set, so that no unexpected visitor will be turned away and experience the same treatment that inns in Bethlehem extended to the Holy family. Christmas greetings are then exchanged and food is served.

Everyone has a small wafer, blessed by a priest, and small pieces of wafer are exchanged. As this is a Holy day, the entire meal excludes meat products of any kind, even animal fat. Consequently, the Christmas Eve *barszcz* (soup) is based on vegetable stock. The soup can be garnished with "*uszka*" (literally "little ears") which are scaled-down *pierogi* filled with sliced mushrooms. Several types of fish, prepared in various ways, provide the subsequent dishes. Salted herring fillets, for example, are served with a garnish of chopped onion and soured cream or apple. Baltic salmon and pike are popular, though the archetypal choice is carp, either fried or served with "*szary sos*" ("grey sauce") prepared from ground honeycake, raisins and almonds. An old superstition states that saving a scale from the carp and keeping it in your wallet ensures prosperity in the new year. Fish is followed by a selection of *pierogi* including curd cheese and potato, and mushroom with sauerkraut or cabbage. Fruit compote is the classic dessert, prepared by stewing dried fruits flavoured with a vanilla pod, followed by *makowiec* and various other cakes with lemon tea. Then it's off to church for midnight mass.

Roast goose is the main event on Christmas Day, with the festive period known as Carnival lasting until Shrove Tuesday. This is the season when people go from house to house celebrating. Hot honey vodka is the usual tipple, accompanied by

doughnuts filled with rose petal jam and *chrusty* (literally "brushwood"), also known as *faworki* ("little favours"). These light, deep-fried pastry twists are served with a sprinkling of icing sugar.

Easter celebrations begin with a semi-fast on Good Friday, usually herrings and rye bread, prior to the Easter Sunday breakfast served after an early morning mass. A basket of hardboiled eggs decorated with rustic motifs forms the centrepiece of the table, with the host and hostess exchanging an Easter greeting by passing everyone a small piece of egg. The breakfast fare represents daily staples, which are taken to church to be blessed on Easter Saturday in baskets decorated with

colourful napkins and greenery. These foodstuffs, known as *święcone* ("blessed") include various types of Polish sausage, hardboiled eggs, rye bread, salt and horseradish. There are also cakes, including Easter Babka, a yeast cake flavoured with chocolate and vanilla, baked in a tall fluted tin. Egg shells and sausage skins are burned, as anything that has been blessed must be eaten or burned.

Easter Monday sees a ritual known as "*śmigus dyngus*". Until noon everyone has the "right" to splash people with water. The victim is not supposed to retaliate. Traditionally young boys sought out unsuspecting girls. A sprinkling of cologne water is more gentlemanly, though jugs of cold water are not uncommon. ❏

RIGHT: traditional *bryndza* (smoked cheeses) are a speciality of the southern highlands.

POLAND'S NATIONAL PARKS

The country's national parks have excellent hiking, cycling and horse riding trails
and exceptional opportunities for anglers, climbers and skiers

Nature lovers will find few other countries in Europe that can offer such a diverse range of natural landscapes and rare fauna and flora as Poland. The woods, marshland and valleys are not the only places where walkers will find plants and animals that are now extremely rare elsewhere in Europe. Even areas of land that are used for agricultural purposes, fields, meadows and forests, remain that are still farmed and managed using the traditional methods, preserving the natural habitat. The most valuable areas are now designated as national parks and are generally open to the public. There are currently 23 national parks in Poland, covering a total area of approximately 312,000 hectares (770,000 acres). Six of them, the Babiogórski, Białowieski, Bieszczadzki, Karkonoski, Słowiński and Tatrzański National Parks have been registered on the UNESCO list of World Biosphere Reserves; additionally, the Białowieski National Park has been included in UNESCO's list of Humanity's World Heritage, and two – Biebrzański and Słowiński – have been made a part of the International Ramsar Convention of protection of waterways.

All aspects of the Polish natural world are preserved here: from the rocky, almost alpine Tatra Mountains to the wooded Pieniny and Bieszczady, from the shifting dunes in the mini-desert beside the Baltic to the lakes and rivers hidden among the forests of the Suwalskie region and the Roztocze Heights.

Although standards are modest in comparison with western Europe, accommodation and restaurants can be found in or near to all the 23 national parks. Tourist trails and educational paths leading through the parks also make getting acquainted with nature much easier. Way-marked footpaths and nature trails help visitors to explore deep into the parks and the nearby natural history museums invariably

PRECEDING PAGES: a European bison.
LEFT: the Karkonosze Mountains.
RIGHT: the Dunajec Gorge in the Pieniński National Park.

have interesting collections. Services offered by professional guides and specialist travel agencies are available to those who wish practise different forms of nature tourism.

The most productive region for nature-loving tourists is the Nizina Polnocnopodlaska lowland plain (Bialystok and Lomza provinces)

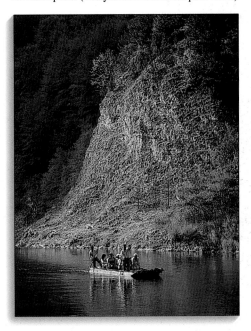

with the Puszcza Białowieska primeval forest and the marshes of the Biebrza and Narew river valleys. This area, together with a section of the Suwalki-Augustów Lakes and the Great Mazurian Lakes, is often described as Poland's "Green Lung".

Białowieski National Park

The preservation of this area as a park goes back to 1921, when the forestry " Reservation" was created. In 1932 it was transformed into the "National Park in Białowieża" and restored in 1947 as Białowieża National Park; the area was enlarged again in 1996. It is the oldest national park in Poland and one of the most precious natural legacies to be found in this part of Europe. The Białowieża park is located in the central part of Białowieża Forest, in the eastern part of the Podlasie-Belorus Uplands, on Mazurian-Podlasie Land, in the natural forest region of the Białowieza Primeval Forest. According to biogeographical division, it lies in the boreonemoral province.

At first sight it seems an untidy place, with trees growing in strange ways and places. But this is the key to Białowieża – this is how nature intended and of Eastern Europe. Altogether the park is host to 600 types of flora – including many 300-year-old trees – and some 11,000 types of fauna, including 62 species of mammals and 120 bird species. Here one can come across, elk, fawn deer, wild lynx and wolves. But the park is probably most famous for its wild bison, now restored to their natural habitat.

There are many outstanding attractions in the park, but particularly recommended are the grounds surrounding the palace built by the Czar of

> **ANCIENT LAND**
>
> "The Białowieski National Park was formed and developed without influence of humans. It is in every sense a real, untouched primeval forest," says Bogdan Jaroszewicz, a forest ranger.

is much how forest would have looked in pre-historic times. The untidiness of the forest also allows an amazing range of flora and fauna to flourish freely. The most protected part of the forest is its central-northern region, where all types of human activity are strictly banned – even gathering berries or collecting dead leaves. Nature alone is king here.

The most common trees are oak, hornbeam, lime, maple and spruce. Much of the forest is covered with a mixture of trees and vegetation and there are two very distinct areas: one with leafy deciduous trees, with a distinctive Central European flavour; and another part which is full of spruce trees and much more reminiscent

Russia in the latter half of the 19th century (*see page 186*). In fact, all who know the park agree that it is almost impossible to capture its essence in words.

From water to desert

The Biebrzański National Park, which covers an area of 59,223 hectares (146,280 acres) is an eldorado for ornithologists. This, the largest and probably the most popular of Poland's national parks, extends along the River Biebrza and contains some marshland and peat bogs unique to Europe. The wide range of bird wildlife includes golden eagles, white-tail eagles, owls and ruff. The main attraction of

Słowiński National Park (*see page 331*), stretching for 33 kilometres (21 miles) along the Baltic coast, are probably the shifting dunes, some of which can reach 42 metres (140 ft) high. The most spectacular of these are found on the sandbar between the sea and the river Łeba. They can move at a speed of 10 metres (35 ft) per year, burying everything in their way. Nearby are attractive lakes, rich in birdlife, beaches and a mini-desert.

Tourism is rapidly gaining ground in the Pieniński National Park in the Pieniny Mountains in the southeast of Poland. The Dunajec Gorge is a spectacular stretch of river,

western Sudetens with Mount Snieżka (1,602 metres/5,254 ft) the highest point (*see page 282*). Characteristic of the Karkonosze are the *kotły* (cirques) – huge hollows carved by glaciers during the Ice Age. Kocioł Małego Stawu and Kościół Wielkiego Stawu near Mount Snieżka are the most spectacular. The climate in this region is notoriously unpredictable and yet it is popular with hikers. Warm, waterproof clothes are essential whatever the time of year.

The natural beauty of the West Carpathians is preserved by Bieszczady National Park, created in 1973 (*see page 237*). It is located in the southeast of the country, at the frontier with

which snakes for about 8 kilometres (5 miles) between steep cliffs, often over 300 metres (1,000 ft) high. Although raft rides have been an attraction since the 19th century, the modern versions, consisting of coffin-like canoes tied together with rope and navigated by local guides, attract 200,000 passengers every year.

Mountain country

A narrow belt running along the Czech frontier, the Karkonoski National Park includes the peaks of the Karkonosze Mountains in the

LEFT: tarpan in the Białowieża National Park.
ABOVE: waterfalls in the Karkonosze Mountains.

SAVING THE BISON

One of the species that may be encountered in Białowieża is the bison, Europe's largest animal. Once these were plentiful, numbering almost 2,000 in the mid-19th century, but by 1914 their numbers were reduced to around 700, and during the war the Germans killed them for food. By 1919 the last wild one died. The national park was set up to protect what was left and in 1929 wild bison were reintroduced into a closed area.

The bison population reached 211 by 1997 but bison remain an endangered species. The world population is around 3,000, of which almost 2,000 live in the wild in special reserves like Białowieża.

Ukraine and Slovakia, and covers 27.834 hectares (68,780 acres).

In the highest part of Polish upper West Bieszczady are "*połoniny*" (mountain pastures) – peaks which are free from forests and over the forest limit, such as Carynska and Wetlinska. These mountain meadows host a great number of rare, East Carpathian plant species. The forests, mostly beech with some fir and sycamore stands, cover 87 percent of the park. About 50 species of mammals are native to the area, including typical forest species: European bison, brown bears, wolves, red deer, the lynx and the wild cat. About 150 species of birds

have found a haven here. If visitors wish to spot the wild inhabitants of the park, they should walk quietly along the trails in small groups. The best time for wildlife watchers is the early morning – grazing red deers may be seen even from the roads in the valleys.

At Ustrzyki Dolne is the park's natural science museum and educational centre.

Tatrzański National Park surrounds and protects the whole Tatra mountain range on the Polish side. It is the only region of alpine character in Poland, with the highest peak being Mount Rysy, 2,499 metres (8,198 ft) above sea level. The 21,164-hectare (52,297-acre) park covers the whole area of the Polish Tatra moun-

tains, the youngest and highest mountains in the country. There are post-glacial pot-holes (Czarny Staw), Śnieżna cave which is 780 metres (2,560 ft) deep and an abundance of lakes – Morskie Oko, with an area of 34 hectares (84 acres) and Wielki Staw Polski, 79 metres (260 ft) deep. The foothill zone is dominated by spruce forests mixed with fir, larch, beech and sycamore. The highland zone is covered with spruce with a few stone pine stands. The dwarf pine layer gives way to alpine meadows and pastures, while over 2.300 metres (7,546 ft) above sea level stretch crags and peaks.

The flora and fauna of the Tatra range abounds in indigenous and alpine plant species as well as and marmot, chamois and a small population of bears. The Tatra range is also one of Poland's last refuges of the golden eagle.

The park has a natural history museum with many interesting objects and a scientific laboratory. The main tourist base is Zakopane, the winter capital of Poland (*see page 243*).

The Babiogórski National Park encompasses Mount Babia Góra, at 1,725 metres (5,660 ft) the highest peak of the Western Beskid Range. The woods here are very much like a primeval forest. The lower plant zone is dominated by fir and beech forest mixed with spruce and sycamore. Spruce, mountain-ash and dwarf mountain pine predominate in the upper zones. Next comes the alpine zone with its rare mountain plant species. Gullies filled with rubble can be found in the top rocky zone. The forests shelter a multitude of animals including bear, red deer, wolf and lynx; they are also a habitat for the rare wood grouse.

The Gorczański National Park comprises the central part of the Gorce Range, with the exception of its highest peak, Turbacz. This is a typical mountain forest park with storied layers of tree stands. The Carpathian beech and fir woods make up the lower layer, while the upper layer is dominated by spruce forest. Both alpine and endemic plants cover the numerous mountain glades. The park's fauna includes such typical forest animals and red deer, roe deer, wild boar, lynx, wildcat and wolf. Worth special note is the population of wood grouse and the spotted salamander.

The Góry Stołowe National Park envelops the Góry Stołowe (Table Mountain) massif. The main attraction is the original landscape of rocky plateaux with sheer ledges, which has developed due to the specific tabular geological structure of these mountains. Nature has formed labyrinthine passages among the rocks.

The most interesting clusters of rock formations may be seen in the " Błędne Skały" reserve and on Mount Szczeliniec Wielki (919 metres/3,015 ft). The slopes and foothills of the plateaux are covered with spruce and beech forests, while the high moors with marsh plants developed in places on the flat table-like tops.

MOUNTAIN STROLLS

One of the pleasures of Poland's mountain areas is its accessibility. Hiking trails are aimed more at leisurely walks than strenuous hard climbing.

and larch. The park's rich plant population includes many rare species of mountain and lowland plants. The king of the wildlife here is the red deer.

Forested landscapes

The Bory Tucholskie National Park protects the most valuable area of the Bory Tucholskie Forest. The sandy flat land is overgrown with pine woods, cut across with river valleys and dotted with lakes, nestling in deep ravines. In depressions and at the edges of some lakes are bogs which

The territory of Świętokrzyskie National Park includes the Łysogóry Mountains, with Mount Łysica reaching 612 metres (2,007 ft) above sea level, the highest range of the Świętokrzyskie Mountains and fragments of the adjoining valleys. The Świętokrzyskie Mountains, the oldest in Poland, were formed of paleozoic rocks. Worth particular attention are the small deforested areas (*gołoborza*), covered with quartzite boulders and stripped of green vegetation. The Łysogóry Range is covered with fir forests mixed with pine, beech

are the home of rare species of post-glacial plants. The wildlife includes trout found in the crystal-clear rivers, as well as water fowl, birds of prey, beaver and elk.

The Drawieński National Park, located in the Drawska Forest, contains parts of the Drawa river valley (one of the most beautiful rivers in Polish Pomerania), the Płociczna river, its tributary and 13 lakes.

Pine forests cover 78 percent of the park's total area, but there are also forests where pine is mixed with oak, beech, and alder. Of particular interest are the high moorlands in the Płociczna river basin, which abound in rare species of marsh plants and post-glacial remains. Var-

LEFT: a day out on the mountain trail.
ABOVE: undisturbed lake and surroundings.

ious species of fish inhabit the crystal-clear waters of the park. The park is also home to a colony of beavers, otter and osprey, a rare bird of prey.

The Kampinoski National Park is located in the vicinity of Warsaw and encompasses the Kampinoski Forest, spreading over the Vistula river pro-glacial valley. Belts of inland dunes, overgrown with pine woods, add to the attractiveness of the park's landscape. In the depressions between the dunes there are peat bogs, meadows and

CASTLE TRAIL

The Ojcowski National Park is popular with history lovers as well as nature lovers, located near the Eagles' Nest Trail of ancient castles and fortresses.

The flora of the park boasts many rare mountain species and protected plants. The park fauna is represented by bear, wolf, lynx, wild-cat, golden eagle and eagle owl.

Valleys and plateaux

The greatest natural asset of the Narwiański National Park is its well-preserved and unspoilt swampy River Narew valley which features a unique system of flood waters, meanders, old river beds, bulrushes and low-bogs, all of which are called "Polish Amazonia". It has particularly rich

marshes covered with a growth of alder. The park's flora abounds in rare protected species. Its wildlife includes such animals as elk, beaver, and lynx.

The Magurski National Park occupies the central part of the Lower Beskid Range, dominated by Mount Magura Watkowska (846 metres/2,775 ft). It covers areas typical for the Beskid Range landscape with forested dome-like hills separated from each other by rivers and brooks.

The river Wisłoka is born in the park and runs across its territory, forming numerous scenic gorges and meanders. The hills are overgrown with beech, fir and spruce forests.

birdlife with over 200 species, out of which 154 species have their nesting grounds in the park. Some species of the local waterbirds are difficult to spot elsewhere in Europe.

The Ojcowski National Park (19 sq km/7 sq miles) is situated near Kraków and occupies the southern part of the Krakowsko-Często-chowska Plateau and the valleys of the Prąd-nik and Saspówka rivers. Numerous caves, scenic ravines, rocky passes and spectacular rock formations, including the famous "Hercules Club", have been created by nature. Forest covers the majority of the park area.

The most characteristic species of the park's flora are those of stenothermal lichens. The insect population is extremely diversified (over 3,000 species) including 1,142 species of beetles and 520 species of butterflies. The caves are a shelter for a multitude of species of bats.

The Poleski National Park is located in the Łęczyńsko-Włodawskie Lake District (Lublin Polesie) and includes a unique flatland of extensive peat bogs and swamps, which in places is reminiscent of the tundra or the transitional zone between tundra and taiga. The peat bogs shelter many species of rare plants. The park is also a refuge to such animals as elk, wolves and the rare marsh turtle.

The Roztoczański National Park encompasses the central part of the Roztocze region. The eminences are divided by deep ravines; the Wieprz and Tanew rivers gently wind their way across the park. Forests, mainly beech and fir, cover 93 percent of the park's territory. The rich flora includes both lowland and highland species, as well as stenothermal species originating from southeastern Europe. There are also some 190 species of birds.

Lakes and islands

The Wielkopolski National Park near Poznań, in the Wielkopolskie Lake District, has all the characteristic elements of post-glacial landscape. Thus, there are hills 130 metres (426 ft) above sea level, subglacial channels and plenty of lakes. Pine and mixed forests cover the majority part of the park. The park's flora includes many rare and protected species and the forests are home to such animals as red deer, roe deer, wild boar, marten, badger, hare and numerous bird species.

Lake Wigry, one of the largest lakes in northeastern Poland, is an important element of Wigierski National Park. In addition, there are 25 lakes in the park interconnected by a network of rivers, the biggest being the Czarna Hańcza river. Small, marshy mid-forest lakes, surrounded by peat bogs are one of the special features of this park. The vegetation is dominated by pine and spruce forests, but there are also large colonies of moor, aquatic and meadow plants. Mammals living in the forest include elk, red deer, roe deer, wolf and beaver. There is a profusion of various species of water birds, and the park waterways teem with such

rare fish species as lavaret, European whitefish, bulltrout and European smelt.

The Woliński National Park occupies the western part of Wolin Island. It includes the morainic heights which end with a picturesque, steep 95-metre (312-ft) high cliff at the shore of the Baltic Sea and the Bay of Szczecin. Here the shore continuously retreats because of the destructive action of the waves. Almost the entire area of the park is covered with dense forests, the most valuable of which are the beech stands.

A group of lakes and sandy beaches is found in the southern part of the park. The diversified

plant cover is made up of many rare species of undergrowth, stenothermal and sand plants. Among the wildlife are such rare species as the white-tailed eagle, Aquila pomarina and numerous species of water birds. In the heart of the park there is a bison exhibition reserve (*see page 399*).

For visitors to Poland who wish to take full advantage of the many national parks, as well as learn about much of its unique flora and fauna, the addresses of the national park headquarters and the Polish tour operators specialising in tourism for naturalists can be found in the *Travel Tips* section (*see page 398*) at the end of this book. ❑

LEFT: lakes are the perfect environment for storks.
RIGHT: Woliński National Park.

THE ENVIRONMENT

During the communist era, Poland suffered years of environmental damage from heavy industry. Now regulations are in place and the clean-up has begun

Poland is a land of contrasts and that applies just as much to the country's politics and its society as it does to the culture and the different landscapes. When it comes to the demands of the environment and the conservation of the natural world, there are also some huge disparities.

Large parts of Poland have a reputation as refuges for rare fauna and flora, but many visitors are still shocked to discover how carelessly the Communist authorities treated the environment, particularly in the industrial regions. For years the damage that the natural surroundings were suffering was ignored by the people and covered up by the party; now, however, everyone is aware of the problems – and they are posing a major headache for the government.

Nature protection

Nearly one third of Poland's surface area (29 percent) represents natural attractions and is protected by law. This includes national parks, nature reserves, landscape parks and protected natural landscapes.

National parks are the highest form of nature protection in Poland (*see page 129*). They generally encompass a protected area distinguished by its singular scientific, natural, cultural and educational values. All nature and the characteristic features of a particular landscape are protected within the boundaries of 23 national parks throughout the country. These parks can be visited freely – nearly 1,700 km (1,050 miles) of tourist trails have been marked out within the parks' territories.

Apart from offering very popular hiking routes, the park areas are also available to skiers, mountain climbers and canoeists. Some trails for cycling have also been marked out recently within some of these national parks. Nature reserves are the second most

important form of nature protection and they embrace natural or only slightly changed ecosystems, selected species of plants and animals, and elements of still nature; all these of particular value from either scientific, natural or cultural viewpoints.

In 2000 there were 1,269 nature reserves in

Poland, with areas ranging from 0.5 to 5,000 hectares (1.25 to 12,355 acres); 634 reserves were assigned in forest areas.

Landscape parks and special protection zones occupy about 10 percent of the country's area. Landscape parks are created in areas which have not only natural but historical value as well. Unlike the national parks, they may be economically exploited under certain conditions, but no activities undertaken in the parks must ruin their landscape values: the beauty of the landscape should be preserved.

Certain zones are marked out and used for short-term holiday recreation, holiday stays and special interest tourism. Therefore, landscape

---

LEFT: a windfarm in rural Gdańsk.
RIGHT: many species of birds thrive in protected nature reserves.

parks often contain organised campsites with good facilities, bivouac fields, and even recreation and holiday centres.

Other areas of protected landscape include individual forms of nature surviving in clusters, which have either scientific, cultural, historical or landscape value, such as large, old trees, springs, waterfalls, rock formations, ravines, boulders and caves. The most fascinating caves are found in the Pieniński, Ojcowski and Karkonoski national parks.

All legal regulations in Poland concerning environment protection conform with the international conventions and agreements. Acting

in the spirit of the Bern convention the Minister of the Environment refused, in February 2002, the request by the authorities of the Podkarpackie voivodship to shoot wolves in that area. The minister pointed out that it is poachers and not the 110 wolves in Podkarpackie that kill wild animals.

Communist policy

For decades Polish industry used far too much water, and contaminated the air, the forests and the soil with toxins and discarded raw materials. As early as the 1950s, the government introduced laws and regulations that would, in theory, have protected the environment, but in the years that followed the pollutant emissions from manufacturing industries increased.

An Environment Ministry was established in 1972 and plans were drawn up for the closure of the worst industrial plants by 1990, but these measures were purely for the sake of propaganda and were never taken seriously by the government. If a party leader declared in a speech that the state of the environment was improving every year, it was hoped that eventually everyone would believe it, even though it was apparent that the fish "living" in the Vistula simply refused to swim in the normal way, floating instead with their bellies down, and many of the people, children in particular, who lived in areas close to the coalfields of Silesia were constantly ailing with respiratory disorders and other chronic diseases.

Nevertheless, the truly committed environmental campaigners were able to point to some small successes in their battles with the government. For example, Polish people

ENVIRONMENTAL DISASTER AREAS

Despite an apparent concern for the landscape shown in its many national parks and nature reserves, there are many regions in Poland that have suffered badly at the hands of an economic system that paid only lip service to environmental concerns.

There are areas such as the Upper Silesia-Kraków agglomeration, Turoszów and Konin brown coal-basins, Bełchatów Industrial District, Legnica-Głogów Copper-Basin and Tarnobrzeg Sulphur-Basin, all of whose natural resources are highly degraded as a result of the long-term influence of destructive factors. Possibly it is the region of Katowice, however, that has the worst problems. While this

local authority region comprises only two percent of the country in terms of land area, it is home to 10 percent of the entire population and approximately 20 percent of the inhabitants are employed within the country's heavy industries. As well as coal, zinc ore and lead ore mining, energy and steel production are the main sources of employment in this region. As a result of its industries, Katowice suffers from serious air pollution which puts the health of its inhabitants in jeopardy.

To this day, politicians tread warily in this part of the country, any major restructuring would inevitably have devastating consequences in social costs.

protested long and hard against the planned nuclear power station and the project was eventually abandoned by government environment officials.

But it was only when the Communist regime collapsed in 1989 that environmental policy really changed and was finally considered to be an important part of national policy.

Ecological optimism

The state of the natural environment has greatly improved in recent years, according to the State Inspectorate for Protecting the Environment. This was due to the decreased use of energy,

ish waters flowing into the Baltic. The emission of dusts and gases into the air also considerably diminished, as did the volume of liquid waste thrown into the country's waters and the mass of industrial wastes contaminating the natural environment.

As far as the investment in air protection is concerned, some devices, with a total annual capacity of 686 thousand tons, were put into operation, reducing the rate of dust pollution. Others, with the total annual capacity of 248 thousand tons, were also put into place to neutralise gas pollution. More and more used batteries are being recycled and in this way the

water and other resources by the government. A major part was also played by the reduction in output of heavy industry and the bankruptcy of many polluting enterprises.

A major success in the past decade is the almost 50 percent decrease in the emission of sulphur dioxide and the substantial lowering and subsequent stabilisation of emissions of nitrogen dioxide. In addition, the amount of untreated sewage has been reduced by over 35 percent, which decreased the pollution of Pol-

ecological threats they had posed will be lowered. In 2001 Poland adopted EU recycling standards ahead of membership in 2004. Polish taxes have been changed to provide greater tax relief for pro-ecological activities. Already relief on excise tax is in effect on lead-free petrol and petrol containing ethyl alcohol. There is also a lower tax in place to encourage the production and use of biodegradable packaging.

Foreign aid

Poland has not been forgotten by the international community and is receiving financial assistance for its work in cleaning up the

LEFT: visible signs of industrial pollution are just the tip of the iceberg.
RIGHT: environmental awareness is increasing.

environment. Between 1990 and 1998 €107 million were paid out from EU PHARE funds (the French acronym that originally stood for Assistance for Economic Reconstruction in Poland and Hungary). These funds were earmarked for expenditure on the introduction of environmentally friendly technologies – including technology transfer, the construction of a waste disposal system in Szczecin harbour, bio-diversity conservation in the Biebrzański National Park (the

CLEANING UP

The EU has accepted Polish requests for transitional periods to conform to EU standards on the environment covering such areas as air quality and water, waste management, industrial pollution and radioactivity.

for Environmental Protection and Water Management. The fund operates as agents for the Ministry of the Environment. In 1991, the Paris Club, an organisation made up of creditor countries, agreed to reduce Poland's debt by half providing that the remaining debt is paid off by 2010. The Polish government proposed a further 10 percent of the debt be allocated to address the most urgent environmental concerns. This initiative is usually referred to as the ecoconversion of debts or

marshlands in the northeast of Poland) and considerable improvements to the management of solid waste in various parts of the country.

After the serious flooding that occurred in Poland in July 2001, causing considerable loss of life and damage to infrastructure and housing, EU Commissioner Günter Verheugen, responsible for EU Enlargement, proposed the additional sum of €15 million from the EUPHARE pre-accession funds be used towards a flood damage reconstruction programme for the country.

Environmental projects are financed by aid from the EU, World Bank and foreign governments are administered by the National Fund

debt-for-environment swap. With the Paris Club accepting the proposal (up to 10 percent), in 1992 ECOFUND was established as an independent non-profit organisation to administer the available finances.

So far, on the basis of bilateral agreements with the USA, France, Switzerland, Sweden, Italy and Norway, Poland has received a total of US$571 million for environmental projects. ECOFUND's resources are utilised in the co-funding of projects of crucial importance. The organisation also participates in initiatives which contribute to achieving environmental objectives recognised as priorities on a European as well as a global level.

Cross-border projects

For several years now, Germany and Poland have worked together on environmental improvement schemes and there are several committees working on joint projects, for example water purification and sewage treatment plants situated near the border.

One of the spin-offs from these schemes has been an improvement in water quality in the Baltic Sea. The Oder, the Neisse and the Vistula rivers have for many years been the main carriers of domestic and industrial waste seaward. In 1996, the Czech Republic was invited to join Poland and Germany on the International Commission for the Protection of the Odra (Oder) River Against Pollution.

Environmental problems obviously do not respect man-made geographical borders and the former Communist states of East Germany and Czechoslovakia had a record on environmental pollution that was no better than that of Poland. The three parties to the Commission have agreed to a programme of immediate pollutant reduction for the River Oder and its catchment area. Measures to improve this corner of Poland where the three borders meet – often referred to as the Black Triangle because of the level of pollution – include the construction of several water treatment plants.

Bringing people together

Co-operation in the area of environmental protection has also led to agreements in other spheres which benefit all three countries and Europe as a whole. The number of points at which it is possible to cross the border has been increased; the roads to the Karkonosze Mountains, for example, have been improved to encourage tourism and regular meetings have been organised between local historians, sportsmen and women and cultural groups. It often turns out that, where problems can be sorted out in a co-operative atmosphere, the different factions can discover in the process that they have other things in common.

Returning to a local and regional level, multi-level co-ordination on environmental action is being attempted. The Green Lungs of Poland initiative is an experimental regional conserva-

tion strategy among five *voivodships* (counties) involving both local administration and international assistance.

The initiative includes policies on industrial development, conservation, forestry, organic farming and ecotourism. If the initiative proves to be successful, it may become the model for regional co-operation in other parts of Poland as well as across international borders.

In 2001 the EU Commission adopted three cross-border co-operation programmes between Poland and Germany within the initiative INTERREG III, comprising, on the Polish side the voivodships of Dolnośląskie, Lubuskie and

Zachodniopomorskie. The EU financial contribution towards environmental projects within the programmes amounts to €15.4 million.

The Ministry of the Environment has taken a more active role in recent years in international co-operation. The ministry is now actively co-operating with 20 other European nations, as well as with the United States and Canada. The Polish representatives participate in the work carried out by those authorities, drawing up international agreements to which Poland is a party, as well as taking part in negotiations for new multilateral agreements. Poland has now ratified approximately 20 international conventions and agreements. ❑

LEFT: preserving the eco-system requires vigilance.
RIGHT: the future looks brighter for the environment.

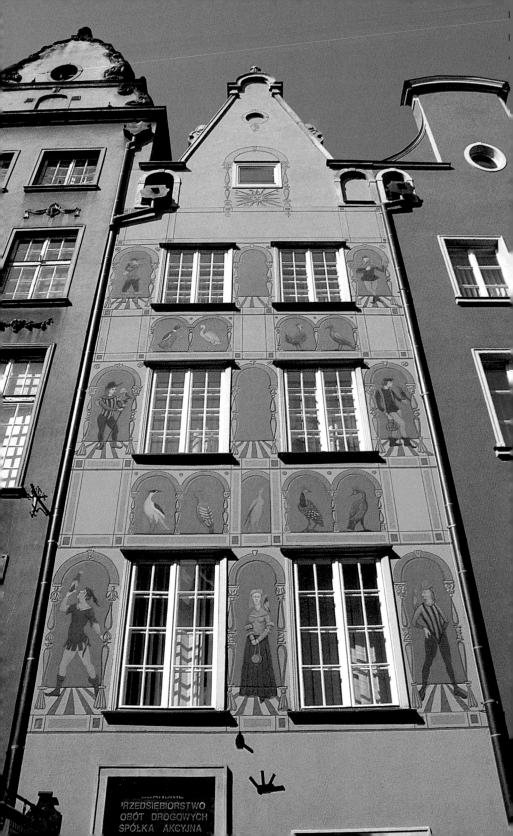

PLACES

*A detailed guide to the entire country, with principal sites
clearly cross-referenced by number to the maps*

Despite the world becoming a smaller place, Poland typically
remains an unknown quantity, even among seasoned travellers.
Moreover, not having visited Poland doesn't prevent people
from having definite views of "how it really is". The Communist
era gave rise to an image of cities comprising bleak concrete blocks,
inhabited by amorphous people who spent their lives either working,
or queueing outside shops which only had shortages on offer. As for
the countryside, the only landscapes were imagined to be industrial,
dwarfed by towering chimneys belching out toxic fumes.

The reality is that the Polish landscape offers a great variety of
immense natural beauty, protected by a large number of national
parks throughout the country. In the east, the Białowieża National
Park is a primeval forest, sheltering various rare species, including
herds of European bison. In the northeast the Masurian Lake district
comprises more than 1,000 lakes, many of which are linked by rivers
and canals, and bordered by vast areas of natural wetlands including
bogs and marshes. Meanwhile, the Carpathian mountains extend
across the southern border of Poland, offering skiers as well as hikers some magnificent terrain. In the north, the Baltic coast is characterised by secluded beaches fringed by pine trees and small cliffs.

Every architectural genre can be seen in Poland, with some extraordinary examples of Romanesque, Gothic, Renaissance, baroque,
neoclassical and Seccessionist buildings. Most Polish cities have
retained their medieval layouts, which means an "old town" district
with a central market square featuring a town hall and burgher's
houses. Having been a Roman Catholic country since the 10th century there are also numerous historic churches to see.

Joseph Conrad, the Polish-born novelist, referred to Poland as
"that advanced outpost of western civilisation". Having endured various oppressors, most recently 45 years of communism, Poles have
tremendous resilience and spirit. These characteristics were at the
heart of the Solidarity movement which defeated the communist
regime and, in turn, led to the liberation of the entire Eastern bloc. As
Poland rapidly acclimatises to a "western" lifestyle, Polish culture
and national identity are also stronger than ever. ❏

PRECEDING PAGES: the castle in Malbork on the Nogat; the old town, Warsaw;
the gables of the town hall in Wrocław.
LEFT: one of the tall houses Gdańsk Old Town.

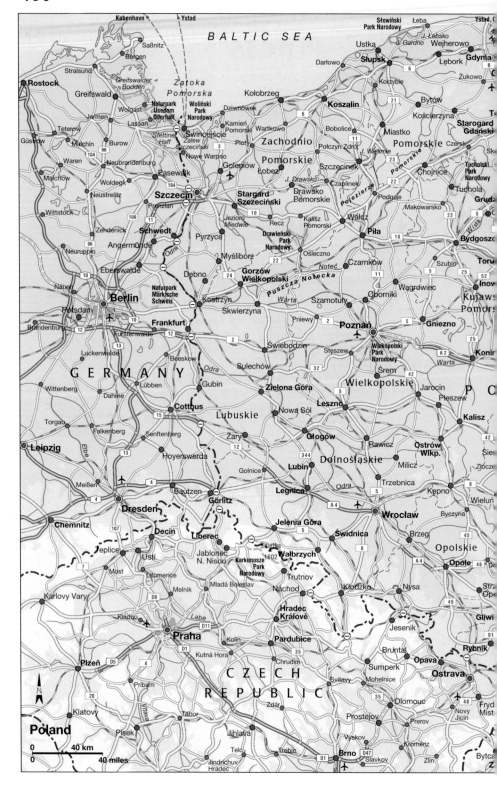

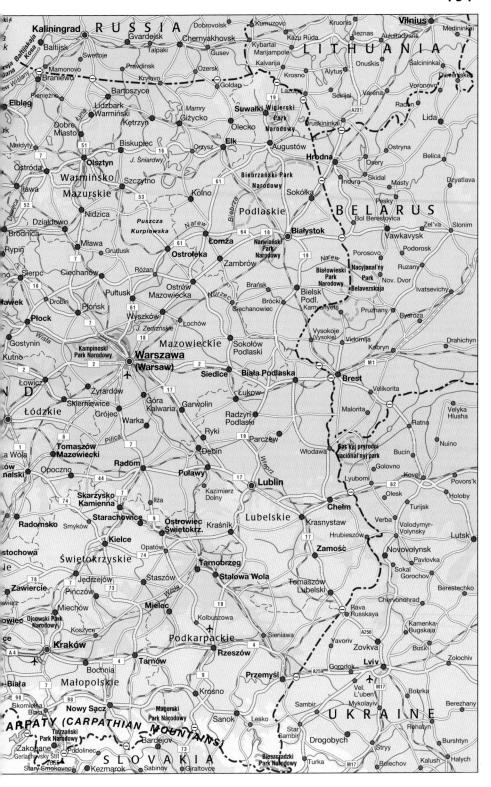

WARSAW AND MAZOVIA

*Warsaw's rejuvenation as it shakes off the legacy of
communism will draw more visitors both to the city
and to the surrounding region of Mazovia*

Warsaw encapsulates Poland's extraordinary history, with the
city subjected to a continual cycle of invasion, destruction,
rebuilding and resurrection. While much of the historic
centre was reconstructed, after the city was devastated by the Nazis,
the ensuing regime also established monuments to communism and
modernism. This helps to account for the city's diversity of architecture and atmosphere, which can take you from aesthetic highs to
bleak depths.

Warsaw also encapsulates a country in transition, as Poland
becomes fully integrated into Western Europe, while also nurturing
a distinct national identity. As Poland's most progressive city, Warsaw is a touchstone of modernity, yet also provides a direct link to the
past. The city's rapidly developing infrastructure means that visitors
can now enjoy a classic Polish experience, whether its shopping for
specialities such as amber, crystal and leathergoods, or dining on
modern or classic Polish cuisine, while also having the pick of international restaurants, brand names and services.

The following chapter includes a comprehensive tour of Warsaw,
spanning the city's historic, architectural and cultural extremes,
which could be completed within a day, although several museums
deserve leisurely visits.

Warsaw is also an ideal base for visiting the surrounding Mazovian region. The chapter entitled *Through Mazovia* (*see page 179*)
includes suggestions for day trips, as well as more extended tours, of
Mazovia's historic towns and villages. This includes Żelazowa Wola,
the manor house in which Frédéric Chopin was born, the enchanting
Nieboròw Palace (now a museum) and the deeply romantic landscaped park of Arkadia. Mazovia's low-lying, pastoral landscapes
also lead on to the Białowieski National Park, a vast primeval forest
extending to the border with Belarus, where European bison and
other rare species still roam.   ❑

LEFT: Warsaw's high-rise skyline.

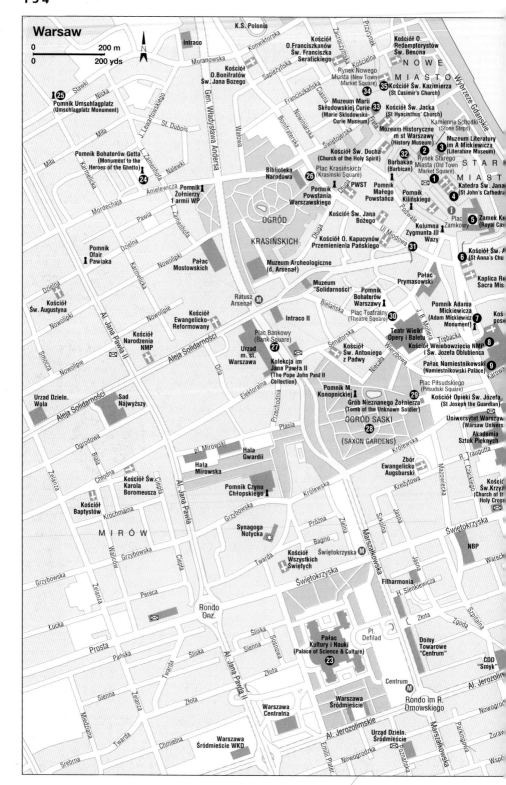

Warsaw

0 ——— 200 m
0 ——— 200 yds

K.S. Polonia

Intraco

Kościół O.Bonifratów Św. Jana Bożego

Kościół O.Franciszkanów Św. Franciszka Serafickiego

Kościół O. Redemptorystów Św. Benona

N O W E
M I A S T O

Rynek Nowego Miasta (New Town Market Square)

35 Kościół Św. Kazimierza (St Casimir's Church)

25 Pomnik Umschlagplatz (Umschlagplatz Monument)

34

Muzeum Marii Skłodowskiej Curie (Marie Skłodowska-Curie Museum) **33**

Kościół Św. Jacka (St Hyacinthus' Church)

Kamienne Schodki (Stone Steps)

Pomnik Bohaterów Getta (Monument to the Heroes of the Ghetto) **24**

Muzeum Historyczne m st Warszawy (History Museum) **3**

Muzeum Literatury im A Mickiewicza (Literature Museum)

S T A R E

Biblioteka Narodowa **26**

Kościół Św. Ducha (Church of the Holy Spirit)

Plac Krasińskich (Krasinski Square)

Barbakan (Barbican) **32**

Rynek Starego Miasta (Old Town Market Square) **1**

M I A S T O

Pomnik Żołnierzy 1 armii WP

Pomnik Powstania Warszawskiego

Pomnik Małego Powstańca

Pomnik Kilińskiego

Katedra Św. Jana (St John's Cathedral) **4**

OGRÓD

Kościół Św. Jana Bożego

Kolumna Zygmunta III Wazy

Plac Zamkowy **5** Zamek Kr (Royal Cas

Pomnik Ofiar Pawiaka

KRASIŃSKICH

Kościół O. Kapucynów Przemienienia Pańskiego **31**

Kościół Św. A (St Anna's Chu **6**

Pałac Mostowskich

Muzeum Archeologiczne (d. Arsenał)

Pałac Prymasowski

Kaplica Re Sacra Mis

Kościół Św. Augustyna

Ratusz Arsenał **M**

Muzeum "Solidarności"

Pomnik Bohaterów Warszawy

Pomnik Adama Mickiewicza (Adam Mickiewicz Monument) **7**

Kościół Narodzenia NMP

Kościół Ewangelicko-Reformowany

Intraco II

Plac Teatralny (Theatre Square) **30**

Teatr Wielki Opery i Baletu

Kościół Wniebowzięcia NMP i Św. Józefa Oblubienca **8**

Kościół pose

Urząd m. st. Warszawa

Kolekcja im Jana Pawła II (The Pope John Paul II Collection) **27**

Kościół Św. Antoniego z Padwy

Pałac Namiestnikowski (Namiestnikowski Palace) **9**

Plac Bankowy (Bank Square)

Urząd Dzieln. Wola

Sad Najwyższy

Pomnik M. Konopnickiej

Grób Nieznanego Żołnierza (Tomb of the Unknown Soldier) **29**

Plac Piłsudskiego (Pilsudski Square)

Kościół Opieki Św. Józefa (St Joseph the Guardian)

OGRÓD SASKI
28
(SAXON GARDENS)

Uniwersytet Warszaw (Warsaw Univers

Akademia Sztuk Pięknych

Hala Gwardii

Zbór Ewangelicko-Augsburski

Hala Mirowska

Kościół Św. Karola Boromeusza

Pomnik Czynu Chłopskiego

Kościół Św.Krzyż (Church of th Holy Cross

Kościół Baptystów

M I R Ó W

Synagoga Nożycka

Kościół Wszystkich Świętych

Świętokrzyska **M**

Świętokrzyska

NBP

Filharmonia

Rondo Onz.

Pl. Defilad

Pałac Kultury i Nauki (Palace of Science & Culture) **23**

Domy Towarowe "Centrum"

CDD "Smyk"

Warszawa Centralna

Warszawa Śródmieście

Centrum **M**

Rondo im R. Dmowskiego

Warszawa Śródmieście WKD

Urząd Dzieln. Śródmieście

Al. Jerozolimskie

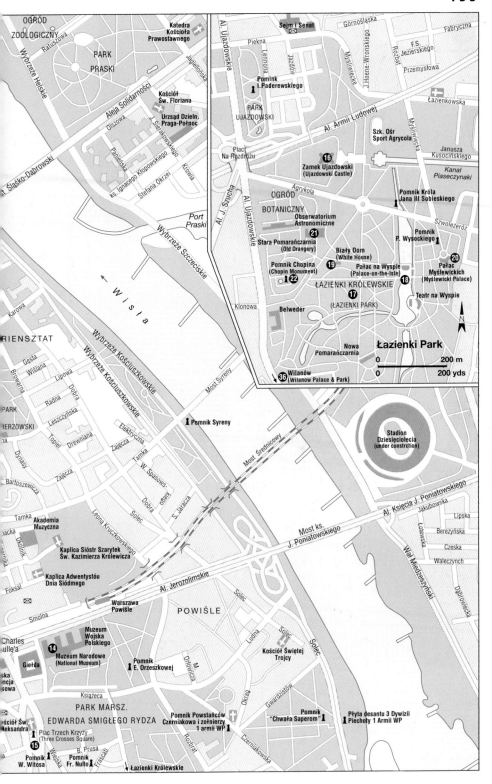

WARSAW

Warsaw's post-war reconstruction produced an eclectic mix of contrasting architectural styles, from the monolithic Palace of Culture and Science to the quaint streets of the Old Town

Map on page 154–5

Warsaw is a city full of extreme contrasts. "Depressing" is the verdict of some visitors, who are overexposed to the city's most brutal post-war redevelopment, and underexposed to the immense beauty which is also present throughout the city. As it is possible to go for long walks which can yield either unrelieved ugliness (in the mid-town area, for example), or spectacular architecture that exemplifies various genres (along the "Royal Route"), you need to know exactly where you're going and what the real options are. In fact, some of these contrasting "zones" are so rigidly defined that you can leave one and enter another simply by crossing the road.

Enormous changes since the 1989 democratic elections have turned Warsaw into a thoroughly European, metropolitan capital. Cafés are full of people enjoying a leisurely break of coffee and cakes, bars and restaurants are full of business people in power-suits brandishing mobile phones, and a growing number of shops stock everything from Cartier, Versace and exotic foodstuffs, to local specialities such as folk crafts. Of course the fact that everything is available doesn't mean it's accessible to all. Moreover, the "victims" of privatisation, left unemployed and homeless, beg on the streets – just as in any other major European city in the early 21st centry.

Warsaw (Warszawa) lies in the heart of the Mazovia region (Mazowsze) in central Poland, on the banks of the River Vistula (Wisła). As the capital and commercial centre of Poland, with a population of around 1.8 million, Warsaw is also a major cultural centre. Various institutions such as the Academy of Science, the National Library, National Museum and National Philharmonic are based here, while the city also hosts various international events such as the International Chopin Competition and the International Book Fair. Nevertheless, anyone from Kraków will tell you that their city is, and always has been, Poland's cultural centre. Throughout Poland, Varsovians are caricatured as being fast-talking, fast-driving, corporate climbers who consider themselves superior to the rest of the country.

Warsaw's history

While the exact origins of Warsaw have eluded historians, one legend states that an amalgamation of the names of two historic lovers, Wars and Sawa, who lived by the Vistula river, provided a name for the city. Another legend states that a mermaid swimming in the Vistula told Mazovian fishermen of an indestructible city which would be founded there. Warsaw has certainly fulfiled the mermaid's prophecy, with the city's history being a continual cycle of invasion, destruction, rebuilding and resurrection.

LEFT: typical street in the old town.
BELOW: memorial to the heros of the Warsaw rebellion.

The Old Town evolved around the residence of the Mazovian dukes, estab lished on the site of the present Royal Castle in 1281. The city's evolution con tinued on the basis of its key position on trade routes through Poland. Moreove Mazovia was also growing in importance as the central point between the tw capitals of the Polish-Lithuanian Commonwealth, Kraków and Vilnius.

Parliament first met in Warsaw in 1529, and from 1573 royal elections wer held here (the king being elected rather than hereditary). However, the kin continued to reside in Kraków, the capital of Poland since 1040, until Kin Zygmunt III Waza proclaimed Warsaw the capital city in 1596.

Between 1655–60 the Swedish invasion, known as "*Potop*" ("The Deluge" devastated Poland, and seriously depleted Warsaw's buildings and population Under King Jan III Sobieski, elected in 1674, the city enjoyed great prosperit with numerous buildings, palaces and principal thoroughfares dating from thi time, including the king's summer residence Wilanów on the outskirts of the cit

During the period of the Enlightenment, during the second half of the 18t century, commerce and culture evolved rapidly, which included the founding o the National Theatre and several periodicals, while the first constitution i Europe was ratified in Warsaw on 3 May 1791.

However, three successive partitions of Poland, beginning in 1772, saw th country progressively divided between Prussia, Austro-Hungary and Russia Initially under Prussian rule, Napoleon established the city as the capital of th Grand Duchy of Warsaw. Following the Congress of Vienna in 1815, Warsav was capital of the Congress Kingdom of Poland, ruled by the Tsar of Russia Warsaw was also the centre of numerous insurrections during this time, wit the uprisings of 1830 and 1863 the most significant.

BELOW: the roofs of the Old Town.

One of the most tragic periods in the city's turbulent history was World War II, ith more than 700,000 citizens killed during the German Occupation. After the /arsaw Uprising *(see page 51)*, Hitler ordered that the Poles be punished by raz-g Warsaw to the ground. The city was systematically destroyed and left virtually ninhabited, with the total wartime damage resulting in almost 85 percent of the ty being reduced to rubble. The recently opened **Warsaw Rising Museum** Muzeum Powstania Warszawskiego) details this historic rising.A massive post-war building programme recreated the Old Town and New Town districts, as well as merous palaces, churches and important civic buildings. Ironically, the Com-unists demolished 19th-century mansion blocks and tenement buildings in the ntre of Warsaw, which had survived the Nazi regime, and converted this area into "showpiece" of Socialist Realism architecture. The wartime legacy means that rious poignant sites are marked throughout the city. There are numerous plaques t on walls and pavements, stating when and how many Poles were executed on ch site by the Nazis, with candles and flowers still placed by many of these emorials. The Old Town and adjacent New Town took around 30 years to recon-ruct, which was done so authentically that both were awarded UNESCO World Her-ige status. If you didn't know the history you'd never guess they were "repro". rtunately they are not a case of "splendid isolation" either, as the surrounding eas are also historic and aesthetic.

Small wartime memorials to the dead of World War II are found around the city.

ld Town Market Square

he centre of the Old Town is **Old Town Market Square** ❶ (Rynek Starego iasta). It's always bustling with people visiting the square's numerous cafés, rs and restaurants, while street-traders and artists ply their wares outside the gal-

BELOW: dining out in the Old Town.

TIP

Some of the finest restaurants with authentic Polish character, are located in burghers' houses on Old Town Square. Fukier is decorated in a "folklore chic" manner. Gessler is a 19th-century Bohemian restaurant; its cellar houses a recreation of an 18th-century country inn, with a folk musicians trio adding to the atmosphere.

BELOW: carriage driver waits for a fare in the Old Town.

leries and shops. During the summer the square is covered with café tables, whi horse-drawn carriages clip-clop from here to the Old Town (which is closed t traffic). Beautifully recreated burghers' houses, dating from the 15th and 16th cer turies, line the square, each with individual architectural features. This includes late Gothic portal at Number 21, while the house "*Pod Bazyliszkiem*" ("Under tł Basilisk") at Number 5 features the mythical Old Town monster, whose sta apparently brought instant death. "*Pod Murzynkiem*" ("Under the Negro"), fe turing a Renaissance portal and carved head of a negro, is one of three burgher houses which were linked behind their façades to accommodate the **Warsa History Museum ❷** (Muzeum Historyczne Warszawy; Rynek Starego Mias 28; open Tues, Thurs 11am–6pm; Wed, Fri 10.30am–3.30pm; Sat, Su 10.30am–4.30pm; entrance fee except Sun; tel: 635 16 25). Numerous exhibi detail the city's history and evolution, while a film screened daily include footage taken by the Nazis documenting their systematic destruction of the cit

Also set within a burgher's house is the **Literature Museum dedicated to Mickiewicz ❸** (Muzeum Literatury im A. Mickiewicza; Rynek Starego Mias 20; tel: 831 76 91; open Mon, Tues, Fri 10am–3pm; Wed, Thurs 11am–6pm; Su 11am–5pm; entrance fee except Sun). Dedicated to Adam Mickiewic (1798–1855), Poland's greatest romantic poet (*see page 307*), the museum als provides insights into the life and work of various other Polish writers and ten porary exhibitions of authors of other nationalities. Beyond this museum, i the square's northeast corner, are the **Stone Steps** (Kamienne Schodki), a pi turesque thoroughfare leading from the Old Town to the Vistula.

Leaving the Old Town Square along Świętojańska leads to **St John's Cath dral ❹** (Katedra Św. Jana; Świętojańska 8; open daily 10am–1pm and 3–5.30p except Sun; entrance fee to crypt). Warsaw's olde church, and the largest church in the Old Town, tł cathedral was rebuilt after World War II in the origin 14th-century style known as "Vistulan Gothic defined by an austere but spiritual simplicity. The cry contains various Mazovian dukes and some c Poland's most renowned leaders and artists, includin Nobel Prize-winning novelist Henryk Sienkiewic (1846–1916), author of *Quo Vadis*, and the first pre ident of independent Poland, Gabriel Narutowicz. side altar contains the sarcophagus of Poland's forme primate, Cardinal Stefan Wyszyński.

Warsaw's Royal Castle

Świętojańska culminates at Castle Square (Pla Zamkowy), dominated by the **Royal Castle ❺** (Zame Królewski; Plac Zamkowy 4; open Tues– S 10am–6pm, Sun 11am–6pm, closes 4pm 1 Oct–mie Apr; entrance fee; tel: 657 21 70 ticket office at Pla Zamkowy 4). A castle was first established here in tł 13th century as the residence of the Mazovian duke From the end of the 16th century it became the roy residence, as well as the seat of the *Sejm* (Parliament). 1791 the 3rd of May Constitution was drawn up here, tł first of its kind in Europe. Between the two World Wa the castle was the president's official residence. Th Nazis' total destruction of the castle extended to drillin thousands of holes in the foundations for sticks of dyna

nite (a few holes can still be seen in parts of the crypt). The decision to reconstruct the castle was taken in 1971, funded by private subscriptions raised in
Poland and from émigré Poles around the world. The Communists did not con-
tribute, considering this to be too overt a symbol of Polish sovereignty. Opened
to the public in 1984, the surviving architectural fragments, including Baroque,
Gothic and rococo, were incorporated into a recreation of the 17th-century façade.

The interiors are largely 18th-century, with most of the works of art and furniture either original to the castle (some items were sent to Canada prior to the outbreak of war), or donated by museums and collectors. All the rooms have
individual characteristics. The pillared and gilded ballroom is in contrast to the
mausoleum-like character of the Marble Room, or the Picture Gallery devoted to
views of Warsaw painted by Bernardo Bellotto. (Known as the "Polish Canaletto",
he was the nephew of the renowned Venetian painter.) In the former chapel is an
urn containing the heart of the Polish hero Tadeusz Kościuszko (1746–1817). He
ed Polish troops against the Russians in a bid for freedom during the partitions,
and was also a hero of the American War of Independence. Adjoining the royal
castle, but also offering a different experience is **Pałac Pod Blachą** or Lubomirski
Palace (Plac Zamkowy 2; tel: 657 21 70; open Tues–Sun 10am–4pm; entrance
fee). This Baroque palace has a collection of rugs and carpets, with rare examples
from Persia, Turkey, and the world's largest collection of Caucasian rugs.

The Royal Route

Plac Zamkowy features Warsaw's oldest monument, **Zygmunt's Column**
(Kolumna Zygmunta). Erected in 1644, the king is depicted bearing a sword and
a large cross (reflecting his counter-reformatory stance). This square also marks

Map
on page
154–5

BELOW: the Royal
Castle and
Zygmunt's Column.

the beginning of the so-called Royal Route (Trakt Królewski), a favourite stroll for Varsovians and a good way to see numerous historic sights with almost no visual interference from modern buildings. Extending along Krakowskie Przedmieście, the Royal Route continues along Nowy Świat and Aleje Ujazdowskie past Łazienki Park and ends at Wilanów Palace. Walking all the way to Wilanów is unrealistic, but a leisurely stroll with café breaks en route should get you to Łazienki Park (*see page 166–8*).

The name Krakowskie Przedmieśćie (literally "Kraków Suburb") originated shortly after Warsaw replaced Kraków as the capital, as this street eventually leads south to Kraków. It was on this thoroughfare, and adjacent streets, that magnificent churches were established, while numerous aristocrats constructed palatial residences. At Krakowskie Przedmieście 68 is **St Anna's Church ❻** (Kościół Św. Anny; open 6.30am–7.30pm). The earliest sections are late 15th century Gothic, though the church was refashioned several times. Its current neoclassical incarnation includes a façade modelled on a Venetian church, Il Redentore, designed by the renowned 16th-century Italian architect Andrea Palladio. Ornate interiors, predominantly cream and gilt, create a sense of restrained flamboyance. Continuing along Krakowskie Przedmieście, decorative railings delineate a small square with lawns and flower beds featuring the **Adam Mickiewicz Monument ❼** (Pomnik Adama Mickiewicza). This monument dates from 1898, the centenary of the poet's birth. At Numbers 52–54 is the mid-17th century **Church of the Assumption of the Blessed Virgin Mary and St Joseph the Betrothed ❽** (Kościół Wniebowzięcia NMP i Św. Jozefa Oblubieńca; open daily). A neoclassical façade belies the dazzling Baroque interiors, culminating in a beautiful altar. Another grand neoclassical building is **Namiestnikowsk**

BELOW: the Adam Mickiewicz Monument.

Palace (Pałac Namiestnikowski; not open to the public) established as the residence of the Polish president in 1994. Formerly owned by various aristocratic families, it served as the residence of the Viceroy of the Kingdom of Poland, the Russian Tsar's official representative, during the partition of Poland. In 1955 the Warsaw Pact was signed at the palace (*see page 53*), and in 1989 the historic round-table talks between the Communist government and the Solidarity trade union movement were held here.

The neighbouring **Hotel Bristol** at Numbers 42–44, which re-opened as the city's premier de luxe hotel in 1992, is classified as a national monument, being a superb example of Seccessionist architecture and interiors. A coffee in the hotel's Viennese-style café is the least expensive way of enjoying its immense style. Opposite at Krakówskie Przedmieście 13 is the Europejski Hotel. Dating from 1855, this is Warsaw's oldest hotel, and features an impressive neo-Renaissance façade. The interior is currently being renovated. When the hotel reopens in 2010 it will be one of the best in the city.

One of the few churches to survive the Nazis, **St Joseph the Guardian**  (Kościół Opieki Św. Jozefa; open daily) has an elaborate façade. This artistry continues within, providing some of Warsaw's finest Baroque and rococo interiors. The church is also known as Church of the Nuns of the Visitation (Kościół Sióstr Wizytek), as this order has a convent adjacent to the church. At Krakowskie Przedmieście 26–28 is the entrance to **Warsaw University**  (Uniwersytet Warszawski; open daily). Several imposing buildings which serve as the university's lecture halls, set amid courtyards and greenery, have a distinguished provenance. This aesthetic enclave provides a delightful diversion, animated by the bustle of students arriving for lectures and meeting friends. The most impos-

Map on page 154–5

Guard on patrol outside Namiestnikowski Palace.

BELOW: Warsaw University gates.

Ironically, Sunday can be a good day for "church tourism". The city is much quieter as many Varsovians head off for the weekend to their "*dzialka*", small wooden houses set in a small plot, within about an hour's drive from Warsaw.

BELOW: standing in the bus queue on Nowy Świat.

ing building is the Kazimierzowski Palace (Pałac Kazimierzowski), originally the summer residence of King Władysław IV Vaza and the royal family during the 17th century. The neoclassical Tyszkiewicz Palace, the Baroque Uruski Palace, and other buildings were the residences of aristocratic families.

Opposite the university is the **Church of the Holy Cross** ⑫ (Kościół Św. Krzyża; open Mon–Sat 10am–4pm, Sun 2–4pm). This imposing twin-towered Baroque church, completed in 1760, also managed to survive the Nazis. By the entrance is an impressive double stairway, with a poignant figure of Christ carrying the cross. In a side pillar of the main nave are urns containing the hearts of Frédéric Chopin and the writer Władysław Reymont, who won the Nobel Prize for literature in 1924.

Nowy Świat to Ujazdowskie Avenue

A monument to the astronomer Nicholas Copernicus (Mikołaj Kopernik), also the work of Danish sculptor Bertel Thorvaldsen, stands in front of the early 19th-century neoclassical Staszic Palace, at the point where Krakowskie Przedmieście meets **Nowy Świat** ⑬ (literally "New World" Street). This has a totally different character, being much narrower and more uniform in style than Krakówskie Przedmieście. Rebuilt in its early 19th-century neoclassical style, both sides of the street feature attractive façades. As one of the city's smartest shopping venues, just as it was in the 1920s and 1930s, designer boutiques, jewellers and art galleries are neighboured by smart delicatessens, bakers and bookshops. All the street's cafés are eclipsed by **Blikle Café** at Number 35. This traditional rendezvous, with excellent patisseries, has an elegant pavement section screened by greenery, and *fin-de-siècle* Bohemian interiors. At Number 45 is an apartment in which novelist Joseph Conrad (born Józef Korzeniówski) spent his childhood, before leaving Warsaw for Marseille at the age of 17.

Continuing to the Rondo Charles de Gaulle, and turning left into Jerozolimskie Avenue, leads to the **National Museum** ⑭ (Muzeum Narodowe; Jerozolimskie 3; tel: 621 10 31; open 10am–7pm, closed Mon; entrance fee). The museum's "concrete block" appearance, the negation of aestheticism, belies an amazing collection, and the user-friendly layout which makes it easy to do either a grand tour or select your own highlights. The choice includes 16th- to 20th-century Polish paintings with works by Jan Matejko (1838–93), Poland's greatest historical painter, and various genres such as Romanticism, Realism and Impressionism.

Among the Polish decorative arts are china, leather, silver and gold artifacts, as well as furniture. Various Ancient Greek, Roman and Egyptian exhibits include early Christian frescos from Pharoahs in the Sudan, which were saved by Polish archaeologists from the waters of the Aswan dam. Nowy Świat then leads to **Three Crosses Square** ⑮ (Plac Trzech Krzyży). Despite the name, this square only features two crosses, each mounted on a column. On an island at the centre of the square is the neoclassical St Alexander's Church (Kościół Św. Aleksandra), dating from 1818. Beyond the square extends Ujazdowskie Avenue (Aleje Ujazdowskie), which marks another change of character. This avenue is considerably wider and busier than Nowy Świat, and showcases a different architectural genre, being lined with elegant *fin-de-siècle* Seccessionist villas and mansion blocks. Many of these are embassies, diplomatic buildings or headquarters for foreign legations. Nearby at Numbers 2–6 Wiejska is the seat of the *Sejm* (Polish Parliament) and the Senate of the Republic.

The Centrum Modern Art Centre (Sztuki Współczesnej) is housed within **Ujazdowski Castle** ⑯ (Zamek Ujazdowski; Aleje Ujazdowskie 6; tel: 628 12 71; www.csw.art.pl; open daily 11am–7pm, Fri 11am–9pm; entrance fee except Thurs). The site of the castle was the first residence of the 13th century Mazovian dukes, and subsequently became the summer residence of the Vaza royal family during the 17th century. Burned down during World War II, the remains of the castle were demolished in 1954. After careful reconstruction it is totally credible in its 17th-century Baroque incarnation, with this "modern-ancient" castle holding temporary modern art exhibitions. A terrace at the rear of the castle has extensive views over the Ujazdowski Park below and the castle has a superb post-modern style restaurant, Qchnia Artystyczna.

The **Botanical Gardens** (Ogród Botaniczny) were established in 1819 (Ujazdowskie 4; open April–Aug 9am–8pm, Sat, Sun 10am–8pm; Sept 10am–6pm; Oct 10am–5pm; admission fee; tel: 553 05 11; www.garden.uw.edu.pl). They have a comprehensive layout including flower beds, medicinal herbs and water plants, set around a fountain and pool. The beautiful grounds are not a complete "urban escape" as this is also the site of the neoclassical **Astronomical Observatory** (Obserwatorium Astonomiczne) dating from 1824, which is part of Warsaw University.

Coffee and cake at the Blikle Café, 35 Nowy Świat, established in 1869.

BELOW: food fare on Nowy Świat.

Łazienki Park and Palace

One of Europe's most beautiful palatio-park complexes, **Łazienki Park**  (Łazienki Królewskie; entrances along Ujazdowskie, or Agrykola; tel: 621 62 41; www.lazienki-krolewskie.com; open daily until dusk. Guided tours to the Palace on the Isle; the White House, Myślewicki Palace and the Old Orangerie) extends to 200 acres (81 hectares). Originally royal hunting grounds, the park's numerous avenues, woodlands and formal gardens were laid out by Johann Christian Schuch, who created both French- and English-style gardens during the late 18th century. He was commissioned by Stanisław August Poniatowski, Poland's last king, who was a great patron of the arts during the Polish Enlightenment. The park opened to the public in 1818, and continues to be a favourite promenade for Varsovians, particularly on a Sunday afternoon, with cafés in the park doing a roaring trade. While obviously peaking in the summer, the park is popular throughout the year for its escapism – here you can totally forget you are in the centre of a major city. Autumn is spectacular, with the densely wooded park assuming various hues.

A fine display in Łazienki Park.

Several palaces, pavilions and other buildings throughout the park were designed by the Italian architect Domenico Merlini, in conjunction with the king. This resulted in a combination of neoclassical and Baroque elements referred to as the "Stanislaus style", which is exemplified by **Palace-on-the-Isle** (Pałac na Wyspie; open Tues–Sun 9am–4pm; entrance fee). Romantically located in the centre of a lake, and approached by bridges, the palace was built in stages from 1784–93, on the site of earlier bathing pavilions. The Bacchus room, decorated with Delft tiles, was part of the original bath house. The palace also features a ballroom, portrait gallery with works by the court painter Marcello Bacciarelli, and the principal reception room, Solomon's Hall. While these

BELOW: a boat trip on the lake in Łazienki Park.

rooms were always intended to be showpieces, other rooms nevertheless provide a more personal insight into life at the palace. The king's bedroom, for instance, has a discreet little gallery from where he could keep an eye on proceedings in the ballroom below; in the dining room, the king held his celebrated "Thursday dinners", a salon for writers, artists and intellectuals. The bedroom of the king's valet also gives another perspective.

The neighbouring **Theatre on the Isle** (Teatr na Wyspie) dating from 1790, was modelled on an ancient amphitheatre. The stage is a "ruined temple", while a canal separates the auditorium, which can also be used as part of the stage. The park includes several other romantic neoclassical buildings within walking distance of each other: Temple of Sibyl (Świątynia Sybilli), Watertower (Wodozbiór) and Egyptian Temple (Świątynia Egipska). The compact Hermitage (Ermitaż) accommodated the king's fortune-teller, Madam Lhullier, who is said to have predicted his election to the throne.

The White House ⓳ (Biały Dom; open Tues–Sun 9am–4pm; entrance fee) does indeed have a white façade, and this small square villa was completed in 1774 as a residence for the king's sisters. Between 1801–5 the exiled Louis XVIII of France lived here. The dining room bears exquisite murals in the "grotesque" style (floral motifs in conjunction with human, animal and fantasy figures), while the drawing room and bedrooms are decorated with superior chinoiserie. **Myślewicki Palace ⓴** (Pałac Myślewicki; open Tues–Sun 9am–4pm; entrance fee) is early neoclassical with two semi-circular wings and took its name from a former Myślewice village nearby. This was the residence of the king's nephew, Prince Józef Poniatowski. In addition to paintings and furniture, the palace includes elements of chinoiserie, while murals in the dining

Map on page 154–5

BELOW: students painting by the lake in Łazienki Park.

TIP

If you are visiting Warsaw in summer, try to visit the Chopin Monument on a Sunday afternoon when concerts are held. Despite a hint of kitsch, the combination of the statue, lake and surrounding park create an ideal setting for the romanticism of Chopin's music.

BELOW: Złote Tarasy, Warsaw's futuristic shopping mall.

room depict views of Rome and Venice. The compact but fascinating museum creates a lasting impression; it has been so skillfully assembled that the aristocratic residence still feels as if it is occupied as it was in its heyday.

A sculpture gallery occupies one wing of the **Old Orangery** ㉑ (Stara Pomarańczarnia; open Tues–Sun 9am–4pm; entrance fee except Thurs), while another wing houses one of Europe's few remaining 18th-century court theatres. It is worth seeing for the extravagant Baroque interiors in what is otherwise an intimate setting. The New Orangery (Nowa Oranżeria) provides an atmospheric setting for the Belweder restaurant, one of Warsaw's finest. There are two dining rooms, one decorated in a neoclassical style, and one in the original glazed section of the orangery amid lush greenery. Nearby is the Chopin Monument ㉒ (Pomnik Chopina), a reconstruction of the original 1926 work by Secessionist sculptor Wacław Szymanowski.

Around the Palace of Culture and Science

Returning to the central district known as mid-town (Śródmieście) means another dramatic change of character, Socialist Realism and Modernism, exemplified by **Palace of Culture and Science** ㉓ (Pałac Kultury i Nauki; Plac Defilad 1; tel: 656 76 00; www.pkin.pl). Built on Warsaw's largest square, Plac Defilad, between 1952–5, it was officially a "gift" to the Poles from the Soviet Union. Needless to say, the palace of culture was universally loathed – as both a symbol of Communist oppression and for its uncompromising architecture. A traditional Polish joke poses the question: "where's the best place to live in Warsaw?" Answer: "In the Palace of Culture, because then you can't see it when you look out of the window."

Meanwhile, the statistics make interesting reading: 3,288 rooms on 30 floors

nd a total height of 235 metres (770 ft), with the palace playing an important ɔientific and cultural role, comprising scientific institutes, cinemas, theatres and multi-purpose Congressional Hall (Sala Kongresowa) seating 3,200. The bservation terrace on the 30th floor (open 9am–6pm; entrance fee) provides a ɪagnificent panorama of Warsaw and its suburbs. Maintaining such a colossus, owever, has become such a financial burden that office space within the palace as been let to businesses. Since the mid-1990s there have also been various lans to soften the impact of the palace, such as large "screening" structures at ɪch corner of the square.

Opposite the east side of the Palace of Culture is Marszałkowska, a principal ɪoroughfare on which numerous office buildings, fast food outlets and department ɔres are located. Some of the surrounding streets only provide more of the same, ith the **Central Railway Station** (Warszawa Centralna) an example of hideous ⅰ970s Modernist architecture. Nearby is Zlote Tarasy, an elaborately designed ɪopping mall (ul. Zlota; open Mon–Sat 10am–10pm Sun 10am–8pm).

Map on page 154–5

Statue on the façade of the Palace of Culture and Science.

ʰe Warsaw Ghetto

ɪorthwest of the Palace of Culture is the area of the former **Warsaw Ghetto**, ʰich has obviously lost some its pre-war Jewish character, though various ɪonuments and important buildings between Stawki and Świętokrzyska conɔy the tragic plight of Warsaw's Jews. The sufferings of the Jews in the ghetto ɪd their courageous uprising are commemorated in one of the most poignant ʳeas of the city, by Trakt Pamięci Męczeństwa i Walki Żydów (Memorial To ʰe Struggle and Martyrdom of the Jews) on Zamenhofa Street. Also on this ʳeet is the grass mound Bunker Monument (Pomnik Bunkra), from where

BELOW: the Palace of Culture and Science.

The Warsaw Ghetto was the largest in Nazi-occupied Europe. Jews were forced to identify themselves by wearing yellow stars.

BELOW:
Monument to the Heros of the Ghetto, built in 1948.

the ghetto uprising was led, raised to the level of the rubble that was left behind after the ghetto was destroyed.

The emotive **Monument to the Heroes of the Ghetto ㉔** (Pomnik Bohateró Getta) symbolises the Jews' bravery and eventual helplessness in the face of Nazi anti-Semitism; in 1970 the German Chancellor Willy Brandt knelt here as a gesture of reconciliation. Memorial stones mark the route to **Umschlagplat Monument ㉕** (Pomnik Umschlagplatz) in the adjoining street, Stawki. It was here that Jews were assembled before being transported in cattle trucks to concentration camps. There remains talk of plans to construct a museum in honour of the Polish Jews near the former ghetto, although nothing has yet been commissioned.

Krasiński Gardens to the New Town

Continuing to another historic area, Krasiński Gardens (Ogród Krasińskich) provides a nice stretch of greenery leading to **Krasiński Square ㉖** (Plac Krasińskich) where Krasiński Palace (Pałac Krasińskich) houses the **National Library** (Biblioteka Narodowa). The elegant façade was designed by Dutch architect Tylman van Gameren in 1677. Opposite the palace are the newly built Law Courts, and a Monument to the Heroes of the Warsaw Uprising. Unveiled in 1989, this moving monument includes figures emerging from the sewers which were a vital means of communication and escape during the uprising. Długa Street takes you towards the bustling, expansive metropolitan **Bank Square ㉗** (Plac Bankowy), with its multi-laned roaring traffic and multiple tram lines. A worthwhile detour from here will allow you to see two of Warsaw' darker sights. The first, a short walk north of Plac Bankowy is the former **Paw**

DESTRUCTION OF A RACE

Before World War II the Jewish community accounted for around one-third of Warsaw's population – the largest Jewish community in the world. In November 1940 the Nazis began rounding up and confining Jews to the ghetto, a district of about 4 sq km (1½ sq miles) – the largest of its kind in Nazi-occupied Europe. Ultimately around 500,000 Jews were enclosed within the ghetto where they endured inhumane conditions, suffering inevitably from overcrowding, disease and starvation.

Even the Nazis realised that the situation was untenable. In 1942 the Nazis began transporting Jews to the death camps of Auschwitz and Treblinka *(see page 54)* until only 60,000 Jews remained.

An underground resistance movement led by the Jewish Combat Organisation (ŻOB) culminated in the desperate month-long uprising of April 1943, but the ŻOB did not have the manpower or arms to defeat the Nazis *(see page 97)*. A few ŻOB commanders escaped through the network of sewer canals, but 7,000 fighters were shot and the rest deported to the camps, leading Himmler to declare "the Jewish quarter in Warsaw no longer exists."

Today many Jews from around the world come to Warsaw in search of their roots.

ak Prison (Więzienie Pawiak, ul. Dzielna 24–26; open Wed, Thurs, Sat am–5pm, Fri 10am–5pm, Sun 10am–4pm; tel: 022 831 92 89), a place of etention, torture and execution from 1830 – when it was built as a Tsarist rison – until 1944 when the retreating Germans blew it up. More than 100,000 eople were processed here during the Nazi occupation. The recreations of the ellish conditions in which prisoners were forced to live are chilling. South of awiak, one block from the enormous new Hilton Hotel, the **Warsaw Uprising Museum** (ul. Grzybowska 79; open Wed–Sun 10am–6pm, Thurs 10am–8pm; ntrance fee except Sun; tel: 022 539 79 33, www.1944.pl) is widely regarded as oland's best. Telling the complex story of the Warsaw Uprising of 1944 it ocuses on the role of civilians in the uprising, most movingly that of the many hildren who were killed running errands, or even taking part in battle.

Plac Bankowy leads to **Saxon Gardens** ㉘ (Ogród Saski), Warsaw's first pub- ic gardens, opened in 1727, where you immediately leave behind the roar of the raffic. Originally Baroque in design, the gardens were laid out in the style of an Inglish garden in 1827, and include a neoclassical watertower, decorative stat- ary and a fountain. At the edge of the gardens, on Plac Piłsudkiego is **Tomb of he Unknown Soldier** ㉙ (Grób Nieznanego Żołnierza). Consecrated in 1925, t includes urns from battlefields in which Polish troops fought, as well as from he graves of Polish officers murdered by the Red Army in Katyń (*see page 55*). The tomb is under a small section of a colonnade, which is all that remains of the ormer Saxon Palace (Pałac Saski) destroyed by the Nazis.

Every Sunday at noon a ceremonial changing of the guard takes place by the omb. Ul. Wierzbowa leads to **Theatre Square** ㉚ (Plac Teatralny), which is lominated by the Grand Theatre (Teatr Wielki), also known as National Theatre

Map on page 154–5

BELOW: the Tomb of the Unknown Soldier.

(Teatr Narodowy). Dating from 1833, the monumental neoclassical façade wa designed by the Italian architect Antonio Corazzi. With an auditorium of almo 2,000 seats, this is Poland's largest opera house. Opposite is the former Tow Hall building, recreated in 1997–8 in its original splendour.

Senatorska leads to the tranquil street **Miodowa** ❸, which features sever palaces (mainly used as government buildings and so inaccessible to the public and historic churches. From here Długa and Podwale streets lead to the **Bar bican** ❸ (Barbakan), fortress which dates from the 16th century as part of th Old Town's defensive wall, and now a popular haunt of street artists and enter tainers. Continuing along the elegant street **Freta** takes in the Baroque S Jacek's Church (Kościół Św. Jacka), opposite which stands Church of the Hol Spirit (Kościół Św. Ducha) founded in 1688 to commemorate King Jan I Sobieski's victory over the Turks at Vienna.

Marie Skłodowska-Curie Museum ❸ (Muzeum Marii Skłodowskie Curie) is set within her former home (Freta 16; tel: 831 80 92; open Tues–S 10am–4pm; Sun 10am–3pm; entrance fee). Twice winning the Nobel Priz Curie is best known for her experiments with radium, conducted with he husband Pierre Curie in Paris. The museum documents her life and work Freta leads on to **New Town Market Square** ❸ (Rynek Nowego Miasta Less formal than the Old Town Market Square (and not a perfect square shap either), it is also far less busy. Nevertheless, there are several cafés and restau rants from which to admire this beautifully re-created area, dominated by th domed **St Casimir's Church** ❸ (Kościół Św. Kazimierza; open daily designed by Tylman van Gameren, one of the most prominent Baroque archi tects in Poland.

BELOW:
the Barbican.

reater Warsaw

st to the south of Warsaw is King Jan III Sobieski's summer residence, ilanów ❸ (Ul. S. K. Potockiego 10/16; tel: 842 07 95; open May–mid-Sept on, Wed–Sat 9.30am–6.30pm, Tues, Fri 9.30am–4.30pm; Sun 10.30am– 30pm; mid-Sept–April 9.30am–4.30pm; entrance fee except Sun). Wilanów a popular day-out for many Varsovians, even if it's only for a stroll through e park rather than a full museum visit.

Dating from 1679, the palace was built on the site of a country manor house, th the new royal residence named "Villa Nova", literally the "New Villa". ich was "translated" into Wilanów. The architect was Augustino Locci, who bsequently designed some of Poland's most renowned Baroque buildings. ter the king's death (1696) the property changed hands, and in the following cades various extensions and annexes were added to accommodate galleries d towers, while pavilions were added in the grounds. Renovation work, lowing the Nazis ruination of the palace, also uncovered 17th- and 18th- ntury paintings which had been concealed by plasterwork applied in the th century. The Nazis also plundered the most valuable works of art.

Nevertheless, the palace has one of the largest collections of portraits by lish artists spanning the 16th to 19th centuries. This includes a portrait by cques-Louis David, of Stanisław Kostka Potocki, who acquired Wilanów in 99. As a connoisseur of fine art, Potocki established one of the first public useums in Poland at Wilanów in 1805, exhibiting *objets d'art* from the time King Jan III Sobieski, together with furniture, Chinese and Japanese art and cient ceramics. A tour of the palace includes royal apartments from the 17th the 19th centuries, decorated with period furniture and works of art.

Map on page 154–5

Wilanów Palace gardens, designed by astronomer Jan Hevelius.

LEFT: Wilanów Palace wing.
RIGHT: figure of Atlas, Wilanów Palace.

Map
on page
154–5

Two sculpted horses stand at the entrance to the mid-19th-century Rid
School, which now houses the **Poster Museum** (Muzeum Plakatu; op
Tues–Sun 10am–3pm; entrance fee). Established in 1968, this was the first
its kind in the world, housing a collection that acts as a vivid record of Polan
post-war history. The Orangery (Oranżeria) exhibits Polish arts and crafts.
the east side of the palace is an Italian Baroque garden, comprising seve
parterres, while the English-style garden was laid out between 1799–1821 a
includes a Chinese pavilion with a pagoda roof, dating from 1806. Also wit
the grounds are the Potocki family mausoleum built in the early 19th century
a neo-Gothic style, and the late 19th-century neo-Baroque St Anne's Chu
(Kośiół Św. Anny).

The city's oldest necropolis, **Powązki Cemetery** (Cmentarz Powązki) v
founded in 1790. Many of its gravestones are works of art in their own right,
a number of celebrated writers, artists and scientists are buried here, includ
Nobel-prize winning novelist Władysław Reymont and author Bolesław Pr
architects such as Domenico Merlini whose work included the palaces a
pavilions of Łazienki Park, various actors, the 20th-century opera singer .
Kiepura, musicians such as Henryk Wieniawski, and Chopin's parents.

Various other cemeteries within walking distance of Powązki include Co
munal Cemetery (Cmentarz Komunalny), which is effectively a milita
cemetery, serving as the final resting place for soldiers who lost their lives in
two world wars, many of them victims of the Nazi and Stalinist regimes. T
cemetery also contains the graves of scouts who lost their lives during the 19
Warsaw Uprising, and a symbolic tomb containing earth from the graves of P
ish officers murdered at Katyń. On 1 August, the anniversary of the first day
the 1944 Warsaw Uprising, many people bring flo
ers and light candles at the graves of relatives.

In **Żoliborz**, one of Warsaw's more exclus
residential areas and political hotbeds, is the Moder
church dedicated to St Stanisław Kostka, situated
Ul. Hozjuszaz. By the church is the grave of Fat
Jerzy Popiełuszko, a priest who was a prominent su
porter of Solidarity, murdered by the Commur
regime in 1984. His grave has now become a natio
memorial. A Stations of the Cross route in the chu
grounds pinpoints landmarks in modern Polish h
tory. Adjacent to the church there is a modern pilgrin
house with comfortable rooms and a restaurant.

The rightbank of the Wisła river includes the distr
of **Praga**, which became part of the city of Warsaw
1916 and was relatively undamaged during the w
Although this district is also where most of the cit
industrial and manufacturing plants are located, there
also plenty of *fin-de-siècle* architecture with charact
istic alleys and small courtyards to see, as well as t
Russian Orthodox Church of St Mary Magdalene.
Solidarności (Cerkiew Św. Marii Magdaleny) with
splendid interiors. A particularly local character thriv
at Różycki Market (Bazar Różyckiego), which a
offers a fine view of the Old Town across the Wi
River. Across from the Old Town is the Warsaw Z
(open daily 9am–4pm; entrance fee). Established
1928, it has animals from around the world.

BELOW:
remembrance of
victims of the
Warsaw Uprising at
Powązki Cemetery.
RIGHT:
Wilanów Palace.

THE BEAUTY OF ŁAZIENKI PARK

The extensive woodland of Łazienki Park features several palaces, pavilions, orangeries, and even an amphitheatre in the very heart of Warsaw

Łazienki Park is a delightful haven, with avenues lined by chestnut trees and beautiful formal gardens leading to several palaces, pavilions, orangeries, and other historic buildings. Visitors can enter the park free of charge until sunset every day.

Apart from the big attractions of the palaces and the Theatre on the Isle, contemporary art exhibitions are held in the Old Guardhouse which is on the edge of the lake to the north. Another interesting place to visit is the Ignacy Jan Paderewski and Polish Expatriates in America Museum, housed in the Great Outbuilding next to the Old Guardhouse. It was opened in 1992 to celebrate the life of the great Polish pianist and composer and the return of his body to Warsaw from America. It contains all kinds of personal memorabilia of the exiled composer along with exhibits relating to Polish emigration to America. Other attractions in the park include a circular neoclassical watertower which was used to store and pump water to the palace, an Egyptian temple, another small pavilion called the Hermitage and the early 19th-century Astronomical Observatory. The Belweder Palace, an official residence made available to visiting foreign dignitaries, is also within the grounds of Łazienki Park. The 18th-century building was redesigned for the governor of Warsaw in the 1820s and has not been used to house the Polish head of state since 1995 when the official residence was moved to the Namiestnikowski Palace by Lech Wałęsa. *(For more information on Łazienki Park see page 166.)*

▽ **WATER FEATURES**
Water features in the park include lakes, fountains set amid formal gardens, canals and water's edge paths which heighten the sense of tranquillity.

▽ **DREAMY BOATING**
Taking a boat on the park's lake provides a different perspective of the surrounding greenery as well as the buildings which overlook the lake.

◁ **ORNAMENTATION**
A detail showing a bas-relief above the entrance on the southern elevation of the Palace on the Isle.

▷ **BELWEDER PALACE**
The Belweder Palace is an elegant example of early 19th-century neoclassic architecture.

RELAXING IN THE PARK

Łazienki Park is a favourite place to relax and unwind for the people of Warsaw, and while visitor numbers obviously peak in the summer months, the park is popular all year round for its sheer beauty and escapism. Clusters of artists sell views of the park or offer their services as portrait painters while buskers provide a musical background as you leave the city far behind. Many visitors choose to sit at one of the two cafés in the park and watch the world go by. One café occupies a neo-classical pavilion neighbouring the Palace on the Isle, while another is within the Theatre on The Isle. If you're looking for a more formal setting, the botanical garden of the New Orangery provides a highly atmospheric setting for the Belweder Restaurant. Specialities of the house include roast fillet of beef with fois gras and truffles and hazelnut grouse.

△ **PALACE ON THE WATER**
The southern elevation of the palace was a bathing pavilion before being turned into a summer residence for the last Polish king.

◁ **NORTHERN ELEVATION**
The northern elevation of the Palace on the Water, as seen from the bridge featuring a monument of King Jan III Sobieski.

▽ **CHOPIN CONCERTS**
The park's lake provides the perfect setting for summer Chopin concerts, held on Sunday at noon by the Chopin statue.

THROUGH MAZOVIA

Day trips from Warsaw to the region of Mazovia can be made by public transport. Places to visit include dense forests, historical towns and Chopin's birthplace

Map on page 180

he region that surrounds **Warsaw** ❶ is known as **Mazovia** (Mazowsze). From the early Middle Ages to 1526 it was ruled by an independent branch of the Piast Dynasty, yet because of its geographical situation between the two capitals of the Polish-Lithuanian crown, Kraków and Vilnius, the region's bridging function made it inevitable that eventually the town in the middle, Warsaw, would be elevated to the capital of Poland. After the Third Partition, Mazovia was shared between Prussia and Austria, but in 1815 the Congress of Vienna set up the Congress Kingdom of Poland; effective power over the region passed to the Russian czar. Mazovia became part of independent Poland in 1918. The landscape of Mazovia was formed by Ice-Age moraines. Its broad river valleys, sandy plains and rolling hills are particularly beautiful. Visitors will discover fascinating national parks, national costumes and folk art in the Łowicz and Kurpie regions, two mosques and a stud farm for Arab horses. Mazovia is one of Poland's poorer regions.

On the outskirts of Warsaw

Immediately adjacent to Warsaw is **Kampinoski National Park** (Kampinoski Park Narodowy) ❷ which, with an area of 38,544 hectares (95,244 acres), is the second largest national park in Poland. Moors, dunes – some 20 metres (65 ft) tall – and large areas of broadleaf and conifer woodland between the Vistula and Bzura rivers are accessible via signposted footpaths. Rare black birches grow in the wetlands, while elks, boars, beavers and lynx have been reintroduced. In Truskaw the park authorities run a natural history museum which details local flora and fauna.

During World War II many Poles, including politicians, artists and scientists, were secretly brought to this wooded region and executed by Nazi firing squads. The most notorious location of such executions is **Palmiry** in the Puszcza Kampinowska at the northern edge of the park. After the war a proper cemetery was constructed, which contains the graves of 2,500 victims.

Not far from Palmiry, where the Bug and Narew rivers flow into the Vistula, stands the gigantic **Modlin Fortress**, made of earth bricks and constructed in 1806 under the orders of Napoleon. Later it was reinforced and extended by Russian troops; the barracks alone have a perimeter of 2,800 metres (8,650 ft) and it is the longest building in Europe. It accommodated the entire garrison of the fortress, with 20,000 men, and it remains in the hands of the military. East of Modlin lies the Zegrzyński Reservoir (Zalew Zegrzyński) that was created in 1964 by high water and the water pressure of the Narew.

LEFT: bison in the Białowieża National Park.
BELOW: sunset in Mazovia.

Market towns and woodlands

Further down the Narew is **Pułtusk ❸**, an old town situated on an island. Th[e] town has twice achieved world fame: in 1806 a battle was fought here betwee[n] the Napoleonic and Russian armies, and in 1868 the enormous Pułtusk meteori[te] landed nearby. The marketplace is the longest in Poland – a cobbled squa[re] dominated by a Gothic town hall, now home to a regional museum (Rynek tel: 023-692 51 32; open Tues–Sun 10am–4pm; entrance fee). The tower affor[ds] a fine view of the surrounding area that extends as far as the Collegiate Churc[h]. This dates from 1443, with a splendid Renaissance nave added in 1554. Pułtu[sk] also has a number of other attractive old churches that are worth visiting [as] well as parts of its original town wall. Pułtusk is also an academic centre, se[at] of the higher school of humanities (Wyższa Szkoła Humanistyczna).

The road that leads northwest out of Pułtusk passes next throu[gh] **Gołymin-Ośrodek**, which is also famous for its Gothic church. A further 40 k[m] (25 miles) from Pułtusk is **Ciechanów ❹**. Old Gothic buildings testify to t[he]

The former Bishop's Palace in Pułtusk is today the headquarters of Polonia, a non-profit-making organisation that looks after Poland's cultural heritage among émigrés.

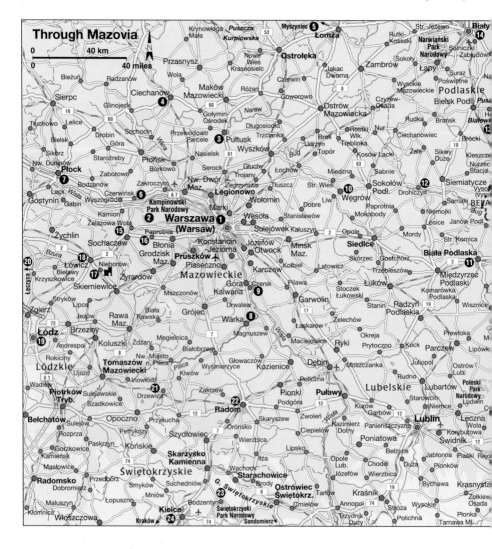

wn's long history; the impressively large castle and two churches are striking amples of Mazovian brick Gothic architecture. The **Museum of the Mazovian obility** (Ul. Warszawska 61a; tel: 023-672 53 46; open Tues–Sun 10am– 4pm; itrance fee) includes military exhibits as well as decorative arts. The country-de north of Ciechanów was the scene of a massive battle in September 1939, hen the Germans attempted to march straight through to Warsaw. The many mil-iry cemeteries in this area serve as a reminder of the conflict. Close to Ciechanów the little village of **Opinogóra**. In the crypt of the church is the tomb of one of e greatest Polish romantic poets, Zygmunt Krasinski. The town's neo-Gothic istle houses the **Museum of Romanticism** (Muzeum Romantyzmu, Ul. rasińskiego 9; tel: 023-671 70 25; open Tues–Sun 10am–4pm; entrance fee), id in the splendid park there is a monument to the poet.

Further to the east is an expanse of wooded countryside known as **Kurpie**. he wooden houses here are some of the most beautiful in all Poland. The best ace to stay and admire them is Nowogród where the River Pisa flows into the arew. The town has an attractive open-air museum.

Between Nowogród and Myszyniec lies the village of **Łyse**, where people con-egate each Palm Sunday to see a prize presented for the most beautiful Easter ulm. The palms are kept for a long time in the wooden church, the work of car-:nters from Kurpie, with an impressive interior decorated by local artists. From yse the road continues to the "capital" of Kurpie, **Myszyniec ❺**. Every year on e Thursday after Trinity Sunday the Corpus Christi procession sets out from e square in front of the neo-Gothic church. A similarly colourful procession n also be seen in nearby **Kadzidło**. This is the place to watch women skillfully itting traditional silhouettes from coloured paper. In the town's church there is i exhibition devoted solely to this form of folk art.

Continuing eastwards, Łomża on the River Narew, is an interesting permanent exhibition of amber, hich was once mined in Kurpie. Also in Łomża is an tractive Gothic cathedral with a beautiful interior.

n the banks of the Vistula

ie lower reaches of the Vistula north west of Warsaw are ied by many interesting towns with long histories. In zerwińsk ❻ a church displaying both Romanesque and othic features towers above the river valley. omanesque frescos in the east chapel are among the : treasures within. In the adjoining monastery an ethno-aphical museum houses many exhibits which were ought back by monks after doing missionary work road (open daily; entrance fee). The late Gothic bell-wer contains some of the oldest bells in the country. uring the summer it is possible to climb the bell-tower r a magnificent view of the town with its dilapidated ioden houses and its surroundings.

Further down in a pretty setting by the Vistula lies ock ❼, the "capital" of northern Mazovia. The ruins a castle, churches from all periods and styles and the dest grammar school in Poland (founded in 1180) are e dominant features of this historic town. In the crypt the impressive Romanesque cathedral are the tombs of o dukes of Poland, Władysław Herman (1040–1102) d Bolesław Krzywousty (1086–1138). The **Museum of**

Map on page 180

Płock Cathedral has copies of the Płock bronze doors made for the town in the 12th century in Magdeburg.

BELOW: the Narew haff (lagoon).

Mazovia (Muzeum Mazowieckie, Ul. Tumska 2; open mid-April–Sept Tues–S
10am–5pm; Oct–mid-April Tues 10am–3pm, Wed–Sun 10.30am–4pm; entran
fee; tel: 024-364 70 71) is well worth a visit. It houses one of the best Secession c
lections in Poland, including paintings and ceramics from the Młoda Polska mov
ment. North of Płock, near Sierpc, is an open-air museum with examples of t
traditional architecture of northern Mazovia. South of Warsaw, on the right bank
the Vistula, lies Maciejowice where, in 1794 Kościuszko led his troops into batt
against Russia: their defeat was to seal the fate of the Polish state.

Warka ❽, on the opposite bank, is best known as the birthplace of Gener
Kazimierz Pułaski, the freedom hero of Poland and the USA, and the town co
tains both a museum and two monuments named after him. Continuing in t
direction of Warsaw, you will come to **Góra Kalwaria**, which was modelled
the city of Jerusalem and is the destination of many Catholic pilgrims. Later
its history it also became a centre for Orthodox Jews.

Czersk ❾, with a medieval castle commanding a fine view over the banks
the Vistula, lies about 3 km (2 miles) from Góra Kalwaria. During the 14th a
15th centuries the town was home to the dukes of Mazovia. It lost much of
prominence due to the rise of Warsaw's importance and the reflowing of the Vi
tula, cutting if off from commercial trade. The Gothic castle (open Tues–Su
is still worth a visit, including its exhibition of regional art.

The Podlasie lowlands

Below: vernacular
architecture in
Podlasie.

The open countryside of the region known as **Podlasie** begins east of Warsaw a
extends right to the eastern border of Poland. In the early Middle Ages this ar
was first settled by Ruthenians, then Lithuanians and Poles; even today the

Map
on page
180

e places that contain both a Russian Orthodox and a Catholic church. Until
'39 every town in this region also had a synagogue, and in addition there were
any Protestant churches and even two mosques in the area. Podlasie was always
melting pot for many different cultures and peoples, a region where the Latin
aditions of western Europe met the Byzantine culture of eastern Europe.

The town of **Węgrów** ❿ is now within Mazowieckie voivodship (it was for-
erly in Siedleckie) and is typical of the Podlasie region. Next to the market
uare is a Gothic parish church, which was rebuilt in Baroque style and
corated with frescos by Michelangelo Palloni in the early 18th century. In the
cristy hangs the famous "Magic Mirror" dating from the 17th century. The
urch of the Reformation was built by the Polish architect of Dutch
igin, Tylman van Gameren. It also has frescos by Palloni and the splendid
mb of Jan Krasiński which dates from 1703. Among those buried in the
otestant cemetery are Scottish weavers who settled in this area. The Jewish
ttlement has long since vanished. The village of **Liw**, west of Węgrów and
thin the borders of Mazovia proper, is dominated by a massive castle. It was
ilt in the 15th century and after being destroyed twice by the Swedes was only
rtially reconstructed. A later building dating from the Baroque era, the
arostei, houses a museum of weaponry.

Siedlce, the administrative centre of the *powiat*, (district) is predominantly an
th-century town. The figure of Atlas crowns the Ratusz (Town Hall). The
rmer prison (1841–44) is now a regional museum (Ul. Piłsudskiego 1, tel:
5-632 74 70; open Tues–Sun 10am–4pm), and the town has many monu-
ents to the persecution of the community's Jews during World War II and the
vance of the Soviet army in 1944. **Biała Podlaska** ⓫, now within Lubelsuie

BELOW: rural scene
in Góra Kalwaria.

voivodship, is a town which, like Siedlce, is situated on the railway line betwee
Warsaw and Moscow. It was founded in the 15th century and for a long tim
belonged to the Radziwiłłs, one of the richest families in Poland. Radziw
Castle only partially survived the upheavals of Polish history. A pavilion wi
towers and a chapel, surrounded by a parapet, are all that remains. The castle
museum, however, illustrates just how impressive the original structure once w
(open Tues–Sun; entrance fee).

The churches of Biała Podlaska date from the 16th and 17th centurie
although the new Greek Orthodox church was consecrated only in 1989. Th
monument to Józef Ignacy Kraszewski (1812–87) recalls that this was where th
famous Polish writer went to school. The museum dedicated to his memory
located in **Romanów**, the picturesque village in which Kraszewski spent h
childhood, approximately 50 km (30 miles) southeast of Biała Podlaska.

Beside the River Bug

A few kilometres east of Romanów run the tranquil waters of the River Bu
which forms the border between Poland, Belarus and the Ukraine. **Jabłeczna**
the centre of the Greek Orthodox faith in Poland. The most important buildin
in the town are the Church of St Onufry (built in 1840) and the only Gree
Orthodox monastery and seminary for priests in Poland. Each June a country fa
is held here. Still further upriver is **Kodeń**, destination of many pilgrimag
because of the miraculous picture, the *Virgin of Kodeń*, in the town's chur
Kodeń has a special significance for the Catholics of Podlasie and Belar
similar to that of Częstochowa for the rest of Poland *(see page 256)*. On the s
of the former castle is a Gothic church that was once Greek Orthodox; it co

BELOW: the calm
waters of the
River Bug.

ins a wooden sculpture depicting the martyrdom of the Polish people and the ations of the cross. The most interesting town on the Bug, however, is **Dro- iczyn** . It was once the scene of a coronation when Prince Daniel Halicki 201–1264) crowned himself King of the Ukraine. The barrows in the area urrounding the town date from the 7th to the 9th centuries and the settlement self, with a history that goes back to the 7th century, was once the customs post ctween the Congress Kingdom of Poland and the Ukraine.

Archaeological excavations uncovered thousands of lead seals from all over urope, some of which are now on display in the town's museum. A dominant ature of the town is the castle hill, which towers over the river. Also of terest are the Orthodox church and the three Baroque churches, which were adly damaged in World War I.

Northwest of Drohiczyn is the little town of Ciechanowiec, with a scinating Agricultural Museum. The museum has an open-air section (*skansen*) ith a range of wooden buildings from Podlasie. On the other side of the Bug, ear Małkinia Górna is **Treblinka** (open 9am–7pm, until 5pm Nov–Mar). In e work camp Treblinka I (1941–44) and the extermination camp Treblinka II 942–43) nearly 800,000 people were murdered by the Nazis *(see page 55)*.

The **Puszcza Białowieska** , a vast forest that has been left untouched since the liddle Ages and the largest of its kind in Europe, runs along the eastern border of oland. Once the hunting ground of Lithuanian princes, Polish kings and Russian zars, this national park is now a world reserve under the special protection of NESCO. Around 1,000 bison roam free, and other species of animals and plants reatened with extinction are also protected. Wild horses (tarpans), bears, wolves, avers, lynx and rare species of bird, such as the black-headed eagle, live in the wild.

Map on page 180

TIP

Janów Podlaski, 20 km (12 miles) from Biała Podlaska, is famous as an equestrian centre and home to a stud farm that produces world-class Arab horses.

BELOW: Poland's stud farms are world famous.

In the village of **Białowieża** the former palace has been converted into hotel, next to which is an informative natural history museum with exhibi relating to species found in the forest (open Tues–Sun; entrance fee). On the wa to **Hajnówka** there is a reserve for bison and wild horses. In the town itself, o the western edge of the park, stands an imposing Greek Orthodox church, th combined work of artists from Poland, Greece and Bulgaria.

Palaces and mosques

The largest town in northeast Poland is **Białystok** , the administrative capital o the Podlaskie voivodship (Województwo) of the same name. In the 18th century th town was dominated by the Branicki aristocratic family, and their massive Baroqu palace is a particularly interesting piece of architecture, also called the Versailles o Podlasie. Today it houses the Medical Academy. The adjacent arsenal, built in 175 is used for exhibitions. Extensive gardens in French and English style surround th palace. In the Town Hall is an exhibition of 18th–20th-century Polish art (Ryne Kościuszki 10; tel: 085-742 74 73; open Tues–Sun 10am–5pm). The Orthodo cathedral of St Nicolas dates from the 19th century when Białystok was und Russian rule: the 1920s modernistic Church of St Roch provides an interestin contrast. The former summer palace of the Branickis in **Choroszcz** (Pl. Brodov icza 1; tel: 719 12 33; open Tues–Sun 10am–5pm), 12 km (7 miles) away, worth a detour for anyone with a keen interest in interior design.

Some 42 km (26 miles) northeast of Białystok is Sokółka. It was in this regic that Jan III Sobieski allowed Tartar prisoners-of-war to settle, and a whole sec tion of the local museum is given over to the arrival of this ethnic Musli group. The villages of **Bohoniki** and **Kruszyniany** have the only two remai ing mosques in Poland and there is an active Tart community here. Many of the characteristics of Po ish woodcarving can be seen in the architecture o these wooden Islamic buildings, which date from th 18th and 19th centuries. The *mizars*, as the Islam cemeteries are known, are also of interest, with grav stones inscribed in both Polish and Arabic.

Nearby, on the banks of the Biebrza river, the **Biebrz National Park** (Biebrzański Park Narodowy) is th largest marshy area in Poland, and almost certainly or of the largest unspoilt river landscapes in Europe to preserved in its original state. Beavers, wolves and thor sands of waterfowl, including sea eagles, sandpipe and herons, enjoy this protected environment of son 592 sq. km (228 sq. miles). The Biebrza is ideal fo watersports, and safaris are organised on the river and the surrounding area with guides who are expert Biebrzanski's natural history.

Between Warsaw and Łódź

There are two possible routes that can be taken we from Warsaw. The northern route runs along the edge o the Puszcza Kampinowska and passes through the vi lage of **Kampinos**. Here the little wooden church datir from the 18th century is a good example of how th craftsmen in the villages made use of the simple buil ing materials available to them to imitate the Baroqu stone churches in the towns. If you wish to explore th ampinoski National Park, horse-drawn carts and sleighs can be hired in the village. Further along this route is **Żelazowa Wola** ⓯, the birthplace of Frédéric hopin in 1810 *(see page 196)*. In his childhood home is a museum docu- enting his life and work (open Tues–Sun, 9.30am–5.30pm 1 May–30 Sept, oth- wise 10am–4pm; entrance fee). The house has been restored and the music oom has manuscripts of early works and a cast of Chopin's left hand on display. the summer, piano recitals are held almost every day in the park by interna- onally renowned performers. In **Brochów**, where Chopin's parents were mar- ed, Chopin's baptismal certificate is kept in the late medieval fortified church.

The second route along the E30 from Warsaw to the west runs south through **aprotnia** ⓰, which has a classic inn and a smithy, both at least 200 years old. apoleon is said to have once feasted in the restaurant, hence the name Kuźnia apoleońska. The Franciscan Niepokalanów monastery was built in 1927 by St laximilian Kolbe. Abbot of the monastery, Kolbe died to save the life of a fellow- risoner in Auschwitz in 1941 and was canonised in 1982. The church of iepokalanów was built between 1948–54; it also houses a Maximilian Kolbe emorial. In the vault is an exhibition: "One thousand years of Polish history".

The two routes leading west out of Warsaw meet in **Sochaczew**, which con- ins the ruins of the palace of the princes of Mazovia and a museum devoted the Battle of the Bzura. This was the biggest defensive battle fought by the oles in 1939. The Narrow Gauge Railway Museum sets a happier tone. From ochaczew there is a road branching off to the south to **Bolimów**. This com- unity has no buildings of architectural interest, but is well known as the place here, on 31 December 1915, the Germans first used chlorine gas as a weapon n the eastern front.

Map on page 180

BELOW: the grand façade of the Branicki Palace.

The ethnographic section of the regional museum (above) has a comprehensive collection of exhibits detailing the customs and traditional crafts of the region.

BELOW: the spire of Łowicz Cathedral.

Not far from Bolimów is **Nieborów** , one of Poland's most magnificen palaces and parks (open Mar–Apr Tues–Sun 10am–4pm; May–June Tues–Su 10am–6pm; July–Sept Mon–Fri 10am–4pm, Sat, Sun 10am–6pm; Oct Tues–Su 10am–3.30pm; entrance fee). The palace, designed by Tylman van Gameren ar built from 1690–96, today houses a museum with valuable exhibits, among the a Roman sculpture of Niobe, portraits of European monarchs and a huge Itali globe dating from the 17th century. These works of art were collected by the Radz witł family, who owned Nieborów until 1945. A second romantic park known a **Arkadia** (open daily 10am–dusk) is situated 5 km (3 miles) from Nieborów. It co tains almost everything you would expect to find in a park laid out at the end of th 18th century: a Gothic house, Greek temple, aqueduct, lakes and a ruined castl

The 12th century trading city of **Łowicz** forms the centre of the region ar was for several centuries the seat of the archbishops of Gniezno. Here, folk ar and crafts have not yet degenerated to the level of mass-production for th tourists. The wood carvings, paper silhouettes and colourful hand-wove materials of Łowicz are famous throughout Poland, and can be bought fro shops around the main square.

Anyone who is especially interested in traditions of this kind should pay a vis to the museum housed in a Baroque palace located right on the market squar (open Tues–Sun; entrance fee). The processions that take place at Corpus Chris in late May are particularly lively affairs.

The nearby Collegiate Church contains the tombs of the Polish primates, th princes of the church who took over leadership of the state between rulers, unt the new king was crowned. South of Łowicz, close to the railway line, is the vi lage of **Lipce**. The famous Polish writer and Nobel prize winner Władysła

eymont lived here from 1889–91, and set the story of his best-known novel *dopi (The Peasants)* in this village (*see pages 164 and 174*).

ódź

ith its 850,000 inhabitants **Łódź** ⓲ is today the second-largest town in Poland, ith light industry and 50 percent of the Polish textile industry located within boundaries. Łódź was granted a town charter as long ago as 1423, but in 20 still only had 800 inhabitants – a place of no significance whatsoever. ings began to change in 1823 with the building of Nowe Miasto, the first tex- e workers' estate. The removal of the customs barriers between Poland and ssia led to an enormous increase in the export of textiles to Russia, and in the cond half of the 19th century Łódź became one of the most important textile ntres in the world.

During World War II the Germans opened two large transit camps in Łódź for lish prisoners-of-war, as well as a camp for Russian airmen, a camp for 5,000 psies from Germany, Austria and the Balkans and also a camp for 4,000 lish children. Approximately 260,000 Jews were murdered in nearby ełmno nad Nerem, and the people of Łódź itself were also affected; of its 0,000 inhabitants only around half survived the war.

After the war new estates grew up around the original districts of the town. addition to the traditional textile industry, electrical engineering and chemi- l industries also came to Łódź. The first institutions of further education were unded, the most famous being the State College of Cinematic Art, Drama and elevision (*see page 113*). The University of Łódź now also has a Department of lish language for foreigners. Typical of Łódź are a group of buildings which

Map on page 180

TIP

The brightly coloured Mazovian national costume (*pasiaki*) hails from Łowicz and can be bought at many local souvenir shops.

LEFT: exterior of Poznański Palace in Łódź.
BELOW: the hallway and staircase.

Detail of intricate house façade along Piotrkowska.

BELOW: entrance to the Jewish cemetery in Łódź.

date from the 19th century: an industrialist's villa, a factory and the modest l tle houses of the textile workers. They were built in imitation of previous arch tectural styles, Gothic and Baroque in particular, as were the interesting tow residences in Piotrkowska and Moniuszko streets. At least 30 houses in the A Nouveau mode, *Secesja* in Polish, have also been preserved.

There are three museums in Łódź that are particularly worth visiting. Th **Art Museum**, in the palace once owned by the Poznański family, is where Po ish and international art from the 19th century onwards is exhibited. The ma emphasis is on modern art, including works by Chagall and Mondrian and Po ish artists such as Strzemiński and Witkowski (Więkowskiego 36; open Tu 10am–5pm, Wed, Fri 11am–5pm, Thurs noon–7pm, Sat–Sun 10am–4pr entrance fee). The **Historical Museum of Łódź** (Ogrodowa 15; tel: 042-654 (23; open Mon, Sat, Sun 10am–2pm; Tues–Thur 10am–4pm, closed Fri; entran fee except Sun) is accommodated in another of the Poznański family's palac which has a flamboyant interior. The museum documents the town's past, sho ing how it looked prior to World War II's devastation. The Historical Museu is today just one part of the enormous **Manufaktura** complex. Inside this seri of former textile mills is Poland's largest shopping centre, hundreds of cafes a restaurants, a cinema, art galleries and a huge public square which regular hosts concerts. The massive red brick building at the front of the complex on housed the mill's offices, and will open as a five-star hotel by the end of 201

The **Central Textile Museum** (Piotrkowska 282; open Tues–Wed, Fri 9an 5pm, Thurs 11am–7pm, Sat–Sun 11am–4pm; entrance fee) is set in the Whi Factory, in 1838 the first spinning mill in Łódź to be fitted with a steam-driv engine. There is a portrayal of the development of technology in the texti

CHAIM RUMKOWSKI

One of the most controversial figures in the who tragic history of Polish Jewry during World War II w Chaim Rumkowski.

A former textiles manager, Rumkowski was chosen the Nazis to lead the Łódź ghetto that they set up in t north of the city, a position that involved negotiating some say collaborating – between the Germans and t ghetto inhabitants as their spokesman and leader. T Łódź ghetto soon became one of the most productive Poland, but stories abound of Rumkowski's dictator manner and power-hungry motives, including offeri children up to the camps in place of healthy adults – believed that he would emerge as the head of a Jewi protectorate after the war. However, it cannot be deni that he reduced the numbers deported to the camps a that the ghetto was a place of culture and education, r simply slave labour.

In 1944, at the height of the Final Solution fren: Himmler ordered that the Łódź ghetto be liquidat despite its profitability, and Rumkowski volunteered to to Auschwitz, where he died soon after – possit murdered by vengeful fellow ghetto residents, althou this has never been proved.

Map
on page
180

...dustry and its social consequences in Poland, and the museum is rounded off ...th a collection of 16th- to 19th-century textiles from all over the world, along ...th impressive displays of modern textile work. Before the war over 30 per...nt of the inhabitants of Łódź were Jewish. The Jewish community, both syn...ogues and the old Jewish cemetery were destroyed during the war. Only the ...w **Jewish Cemetery** survived, with around 120,000 gravestones and the ...ael Poznański Mausoleum erected between 1893–1939. Today it is the largest ...wish cemetery in Europe and one of the largest in the world.

...North of the cemetery (on ul. Stalowa, around 20 minutes walk; there is no pub-... transport) is the moving **Radegast Station**, from where the Jews of the Łodz ...etto were deported to the extermination camps at Chełmno and Auschwitz. ...ree original Deutsche Bahn cattle trucks stand at the eerily empty platform.

...llages around Łódź

...rth of Łódź is **Łęczyca** ⓴, which, in the Middle Ages, was one of the most ...werful towns in Poland. It still has a number of monuments: a Gothic castle ...th an ethnographical museum, well-preserved town walls and a classical ...wn Hall. In the nearby village of Tum is a Romanesque church dating from ...41–45, and, adjacent to it, the ruins of an old castle. Not far from Kutno is ...porów, which has an attractive Gothic castle situated on a man-made island. ...To the southwest is the industrial town of **Piotrków Trybunalski**, which has ...well-known glassworks. The former Royal Palace, which was built between ...11–19, now houses a museum. Other historic sights in Piotrków include the ...mains of the town walls, some fascinating churches and the synagogue. The ...unicipal station dates from 1850, when the railway line was built from War-

BELOW: the
Poznański
Mausoleum in the
Jewish Cemetery,
Łódź.

saw to Vienna. Brick-built stations like this are typical of this particular area. favourite place for weekend excursions is the river **Pilica**, with its roman villages and medieval castles surrounded by water. In **Inowłódz** is Romanesque church founded by the duke of Poland, Władysław Hermann, wi a high stone tower that dominates the surrounding countryside. In the suburb Tomaszów Mazowiecki there is the **Niebieskie Źródła**. Literally meaning "bl springs", its name is a reference to the blue sheen of the water, which is caus by the minerals it contains. Further upriver, in **Sulejów**, is an old Cisterci monastery, one of Poland's most important architectural monuments. It w founded and financed by Duke Kazimierz the Just in 1177. The well-fortifi complex includes a church, the ruins of a monastery, defensive walls with ba tions and farm buildings. Today it houses a hotel.

Southwest of Łódź is **Zduńska Wola**, where, in 1894, the abbot and sai Maximilian Kolbe was born *(see page 103)*. As long ago as the 6th century settlement stood by the River Warta, not far from Sieradz. Churches dati from the 14th century and castle ruins are worth a detour. In **Wieluń** t fortified walls and the Kraków Gate have also been preserved; the classic Town Hall was built in 1842. The Pauline Church, which was originally Goth also has a splendid Baroque interior. There are 37 old wooden churches in t vicinity of Wieluń. One of them, the **Church of the Holy Spirit** which stan in Sieradz cemetery, was built after the victory over the Teutonic knights ne Grunwald in 1410. The church in **Grębień**, near Wieluń has interiors decorat with well-preserved Gothic-Renaissance wall paintings which date fro 1500–31. Also well worth seeing is the 14th-century walled manor in near **Trubadzin**.

BELOW: children on a horse-drawn wagon.

Between the Vistula and the Pilica

In the past this area was part of Little Poland (*see page 199*). In the north it is mainly flat, but towards the south it becomes more hilly. Between Radom and Puławy is **Czarnolas**, where Jan Kochanowski (1530–84) lived. This poet was one of the first to write in Polish rather than Latin, the usual written language in those days (*see page 108*). He is buried in the church of nearby Zwoleń.

Further to the west a monumental Gothic-Renaissance palace, now in ruins, towers above the town of **Drzewica ㉑**. This region was the scene of the fiercest partisan battles in Poland, and in the whole of Europe, during World War II. The commander of the Polish freedom fighters, Henryk Dobrzański, generally known as "Hubal", did not capitulate in 1939 but fought on with his uniformed division for another eight months. He fell not far from the village of Studzianna, which is well known for its Baroque church. In revenge for Hubal's resistance many of the surrounding villages were burned down by the Germans and all men over 15 years of age were murdered. The village that suffered the most was Skłoby, where 265 people lost their lives and 400 buildings were set on fire.

The area surrounding Drzewica and Studzianna is referred to by ethnologists as the **Opoczyński region**. Here traditional costumes are rather like those of Mazovia, with different striped patterns. Timber is still frequently used as a building material in this region and there are many folk artists dedicated to continuing the silhouette tradition.

The largest town in this region is **Radom ㉒**, an important centre with metal industry, leather and tobacco factories. The oldest monument is the Church of St Wacław. The medieval town centre has also been preserved, and there is an open-

Map on page 180

Milk is delivered straight from the churn in some places in the region.

BELOW: landscape near Radom.

air museum with examples of the various building styles of this area. There is also a display of old beehives of many shapes and sizes. A little further along road E77 in the local palace of Szydłowiec, is the **Folk Musical Instrument Museum**, the only one of its kind in Poland. Other features of Szydłowiec are a Renaissance Town Hall, a large Jewish cemetery and a well-known sandstone quarry.

An alternative route, the B9, leads from Radom to Sandomierz. Immediately after Radom you come to **Skaryszew**. The horse market held here on the sixth Monday after Easter attracts large numbers of gypsies, farmers and horse-lovers from all over Poland. It's an event well worth catching if you can.

Further along this road is **Iłża**, the scene of a major battle in 1939. The tower of the palace of the bishops of Kraków, a building that is now a ruin, was used as an observation point by the Polish army in the battle. A few kilometres from Ostrowiec Swiętokrzyski in **Krzemionki Opatowskie** there is a quartz mine which is known to have been in existence in the Neolithic period, when it was one of the largest in Europe. One section of it can be visited.

Between the industrial town of Skarżysko-Kamienna and Starachowice is **Wąchock**, which has a Romanesque-Gothic church and a Cistercian monastery dating from the beginning of the 13th century. The monastery contains the most beautiful examples of Romanesque art in the whole of Poland. Another famous partisan leader from World War II, Jan Piwnik "Ponury", is buried here.

The Holy Cross Mountains

BELOW: farmland and chapel in the mountains.

Further to the south runs a line of rocky mountains known as **Holy Cross Mountains** (Góry Swiętokrzyskie) ❷❸. This is the oldest Polish mountain range, an area of pine forests, exposed mountain peaks, quartz rock, a type of larch

Map on page 180

peculiar to the region, the remains of coral in the pre-Cambrian rock and a multitude of rare but protected fauna and flora. Amid the wild and romantic scenery there are many places worth taking the time to visit.

In **Samsonów** are the ruins of a metalworks dating from the beginning of the 19th century and now a technological monument. Nearby is "Bartek", one of the largest and oldest oak trees in Poland. The trunk has a circumference of over 9 metres (29 ft). Nearby **Oblęgorek** is where Henryk Sienkiewicz, the author of the novel *Quo Vadis*, lived until 1914.

The capital of this region is **Kielce ㉔**. Its bishop's palace was built in the 17th century, and now houses the National Museum: this includes a gallery of Polish art and a section dealing with the interior decor of palaces. Just opposite the palace is a Baroque cathedral with an interior preserved in its original style and a beautiful sculpture of the Virgin Mary made of galena, a lead ore (open Tues–Sun; entrance fee).

To the east of Kielce rises the Bare Mountain (Łysa Góra), with its forbidding scree slopes. Situated on this mountain is the **Holy Cross Monastery** (Święty Krzyż) belonging to the Benedictine order, where a relic of the Holy Cross is kept. Before the monastery came into existence there was a pre-Christian sanctuary on this spot. Today the countryside is sadly marred by a television broadcasting tower.

The whole area surrounding Łysa Góra is a **national park**, which extends over a total of 6,000 hectares (15,000 acres). The heath has splendid pine and larch woods and there are numerous clearings and deforested areas which are dotted with large boulders. At the foot of this range of mountains is the attractive village of **Nowa Słupia**. There was already an iron industry here in the second century and it is perfectly possible that iron was exported from this area to the Roman Empire. Remains of the old furnaces are on display in the local history museum.

All these mountains are composed of sandstone, and it is only north of Kielce that limestone begins to predominate. Here magnificent marble is also to be found, and even semi-precious stones such as malachite and azurite are relatively common. While on the way from Kielce to Chęciny along the E77 make a 10-km (6-mile) detour to see the most beautiful Polish grotto, known as **Raj** (Paradise). The cave is filled with beautiful stalactites and stalagmites (open May–Oct) and was discovered in 1964

The ruins of an old castle tower above the little town of **Chęciny**, once a place of considerable wealth. For centuries the town was the centre of the lead ore mining industry.

The next place of importance on the road towards Kraków is **Jędrzejów**. Its 13th-century Cistercian monastery was rebuilt in Baroque style. However, the town is best known for its museum, which is named after the local Przypkowski family and includes their fascinating collection of sundials (open May–Sept Tues–Sun 9am–4pm; entrance fee; guided tours obligatory). In the region east of Jędrzejów lies **Szyłdów**, a sleepy little village that once had a town charter. It's a pleasant place to stop for a wander; its town walls and church have survived the upheavals of the ages undamaged. ❑

South of Radom on the E77 road is the village of Oronsko, where a centre of Polish sculpture has been established at Heimstatt, the manor that once belonged to the painter Józef von Brandt (1841–1915). Stone and ceramic sculptures by modern artists are visible from the road.

BELOW: shrine.

THE SPIRIT OF POLISH ROMANTICISM

Frédéric Chopin's lyricism and unparalleled melodic genius has produced some of the most beautiful and spiritual music ever written

Chopin was born in 1810 in a country manor house in the village of Żelazowa Wola, outside Warsaw. His baptismal certificate is kept in the medieval church of the nearby village of Brochów, where his parents were married and his father, an emigrant from France, was engaged as a tutor at the nearby estate of Count Skarbek. He made his professional debut as a child prodigy, appearing at charity concerts organised by Warsaw's aristocratic circles. While Chopin was studying at the Warsaw School of Music he was captivated by Polish folk music and become familiar with various songs and dances in the villages surrounding Warsaw. In the autumn of 1830 Chopin left Warsaw and never returned to his beloved Poland. After performing in Dresden, Vienna, Salzburg and Munich, he finally arrived in Paris, where he initially gave numerous recitals before concentrating on composition. Chopin's social circle included many prominent musicians including Franz Liszt, and the love of his life, George Sand, the pseudonym of the French writer Aurore Dudevant. Their intense relationship resulted in her nursing Chopin for several years after he contracted tuberculosis. She finally left him in 1847, when he was seriously ill and virtually penniless. A desperate but highly successful visit to London briefly revived his fortunes, where he gave his final public concert in 1848. Returning to Paris, Chopin died in 1849 in his home in the Place Vendome.

▷ŁAZIENKI PARK SCULPTURE
This Art Nouveau sculpture of Chopin contemplating the beauty of nature was designed in 1926 by sculptor Wacław Szymanowski.

▷ ŻELAZOWA WOLA
Chopin's mother's room at the family home in Żelazowa Wola has been beautifully restored and combines elements of folk art with formal decoration.

△ BURIED HEART
Buried originally in the Pére-Lachaise cemetery in Paris, Chopin's heart was finally laid to rest within a central pillar of the Holy Cross Church in Warsaw.

▷ SUNDAY RECITALS
Summer concerts are held on the terrace at Żelazowa Wola, which is surrounded by delightful parkland containing a small lake.

△ POZNAŃ'S PIANO
The Musical Instrumen. Museum in Poznań has piano that Chopin playec and other mementos o composer's life.

CHOPIN'S MUSICAL LEGACY

Chopin's earliest compositions date from his childhood. He began composing seriously when he settled in Paris in the 1830s, and it was while convalescing in Majorca in 1838 that he composed the renowned Preludes, the Polonaise in A major, and the Sonata which includes the Funeral March. His music was as controversial as it was passionate, and his most vehement critics condemned its overt emotionalism as the ravings of a lunatic. Nearing the end of his life he wrote: "Where have my abilities gone, what has happened to my heart? I can hardly remember how they sing at home. The world is sinking round me in a strange fashion." At Chopin's funeral service, Mozart's Requiem was played according to his wishes and he was buried in the Pére-Lachaise Cemetery in Paris.

◁ **CHOPIN MUSEUM**
Chopin's restored 19th-century family home is now a museum, with a collection of various family possessions and early piano manuscripts.

▽ **OUTDOOR CONCERTS**
Łazienki Park's highly romantic atmosphere provides one of the best venues to listen to recitals of Chopin's music.

MAŁOPOLSKA – LITTLE POLAND

Małopolska is not small in either size or significance. From the historic city of Kraków to trekking in the Tatras, this region is packed with things to see and do

A region of immense natural beauty, which also includes some of Poland's most attractive and historic towns, Małopolska embraces the southern and southeastern corner of Poland, between the Ukraine and Slovakia.

To the south the Carpathian mountains and foothills extend along the border with Slovakia, while the centre of the region features the lowlying Koltina Sandomierska basin. To the north rises the Małopolska Upland (Wyżyna Małopolska), comprising a number of separate, low-lying ranges of hills, bordered by the Kraków Częstochowa Upland (Wyżyna Krakowsko Częstochowska). To the east the Lublin Uplands (Wyżyna Lubelska) jut out above the surrounding plains. The region is also traversed by important rivers such as the Vistula, Dunajec and San, as well as numerous picturesque streams and lakes, which continually add variety and heighten the appeal of the surrounding countryside.

The region's most important city is Kraków, the capital of Poland between the 11th and the 16th century. Although the city's political power subsequently diminished, it continues to be regarded as Poland's cultural and intellectual capital. Kraków is also one of Poland's most beautiful cities, with a wealth of museums including the Wawel Royal Castle and Cathedral, and a comprehensive range of architecture that includes definitive examples of Renaissance style.

The chapter entitled *Through Little Poland* (*see page 219*) highlights the vast number of attractions within easy reach of Kraków, including the salt mines at Wieliczka, dating from the 12th century, a network of ruined castles along the so-called Eagle's Lair on the border with Slovakia; Łańcut, one of Poland's most impressive palaces (now a museum) and the town of Zamość, a remarkable example of Renaissance architecture and town planning. ❑

LEFT: Corpus Cristi Church, Kazimierz.

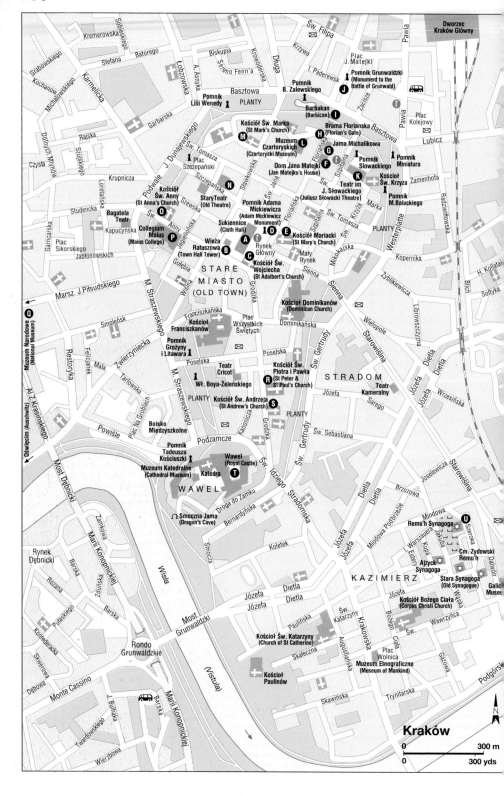

Kraków

0   300 m

0   300 yds

KRAKÓW

There's so much to do in Kraków that the city requires a week's stay to do it justice. It contains both low-brow and high-brow culture mixed with vitality and a sense of history

Map on page 200

ormerly the capital of Poland, Krakovians have always continued to think of their city as Poland's cultural and intellectual capital – despite the counterclaims of Varsovians. But no one can dispute the city's immense beauty, which is readily accessible within the pedestrianised Old Town. Hailed as European City of Culture in 1992 and 2000, Kraków (Cracow) is frequently termed an "al resco museum", with UNESCO's World Heritage Listing classifying 55 of the city's buildings and monuments as of the highest class. Meanwhile, 18 museums, containing more than two million works of art, span an amazing range of themes, including rarities such as the pharmacy museum and the insurance museum.

Alongside the sense of history, Kraków is also a vibrant, progressive city, with a full cultural programme of music (classical, jazz, alternative, whatever), film and theatre, including the country's foremost Helena Modrzejewska Theatre, as well as avant garde troupes. Numerous annual festivals include the Music of Old Kraków in August, with concerts held in atmospheric burghers' houses, churches and palaces throughout the Old Town. The International Festival of Short Feature Films at the end of May and beginning of June continues the city's heritage as the site of the first Polish film screening in 1896.

The Jagiellonian University (the "Oxbridge" of Poland) ensures a high youth quota, with the inevitable accompaniment of bohemian and various alternative sub-cultures. Even during the summer vacations there is an "academic" influx, as the university holds summer schools with courses on Polish language, culture and history for overseas students, particularly Polish émigrés.

The history of Kraków

According to legend, Krakus, the leader of a Slavic tribe called the Vislanes erected a fortified settlement on a hill known as Wawel. Being on key trade routes meant the settlement developed into a town, with the earliest recorded reference dated AD 965, when a merchant from Cordoba, Ibrahim ibn Jakub, wrote that Kraków was already a major town known throughout Europe.

The diocese of Kraków was founded in 1000, following the country's conversion to Christianity in 966. In 1040 King Casimir "The Restorer" made Kraków Poland's capital. In 1241 the town was destroyed by a Tartar invasion, although it was rapidly rebuilt, and blossomed again under the Jagiellonian dynasty (1386–1572), with commerce developing alongside art and culture. The Jagiellonian University was founded in 1364. The country's first university has retained its reputation as the country's premier educational institute. During the 15th century Kraków became a town of some 30,000 inhabitants, surrounded by fortified walls and turrets. Situated at the junction

BELOW: the Veit Stoss altar in the Church of St Mary.

of trade routes from western Europe to Byzantium, and from southern Europe to the Baltic, the city joined the Hanseatic League in 1430, which attracted many German craftsmen and merchants. The first half of the 16th century saw trade and handicrafts flourish, with as many as 60 different guilds. However, the union of Poland and Lithuania in 1569 decreased Kraków's status, as Mazovia and Warsaw emerged as the new "centre" of Poland, with King Zygmunt III making Warsaw the capital in 1596. Yet, as Polish kings continued to be crowned and buried in the Kraków's Wawel Cathedral, the city retained some of its importance.

The eagle of Kraków is also Poland's coat of arms.

Foreign rule

Under the Third Partition of Poland in 1795, Małopolska became a part of the Austrian Habsburg empire. After the Congress of Vienna, Kraków was a free city and capital of the so-called Kraków Republic from 1815 until, in 1846, the city was incorporated into the province of Galicia. The relatively liberal attitude of the Austrian authorities enabled Polish culture and science to progress; even the activities of the independence movement were tolerated. It was during this period that the painters Jan Matejko, Jacek Malczewski and Leon Wyczółkowski emerged as maestros. Subsequently, the forerunners of Secessionism (Polish Art Nouveau), Stanisław Wyspiański and Józef Mehofer, developed a movement called *Młoda Polska* (Young Poland) centred in the city. Austrian rule also transformed Kraków into a resilient "fortress" which even managed to withstand the Russian offensive of 1914.

BELOW: detail of the Renaissance-style Cloth Hall in the Main Market Square.

In November 1939 the Nazis established the headquarters of the General Government in the city, with the Governor General Hans Frank taking up residence in the Wawel royal palace. Having wiped out the Jewish population, as

well as the Polish intelligentsia, the Nazis mined the city for systematic destruction (which was the fate of Warsaw) in 1945. However, nothing was detonated as they retreated from a sudden advance by the Red Army, which liberated the city on 18 January 1945. In fact, this is one of the few Polish cities to have survived the war more or less intact (*see page 45*).

Kraków, the third largest city in Poland, now has a population of 745,000, with the post-war suburbs being purpose-built industrial centres, including engineering, metal processing, electronics, pharmaceuticals and foodstuffs. However, it was for political rather than economic reasons that the Lenin steelworks employed a vast proletarian labour-force. A horrific consequence was pollution from the factories, which attacked not only the inhabitants, but also the historic buildings. Fortunately, a tough policy of dealing with industrial waste has brought this under control.

The Main Market Square

The heart of the city, the **Main Market Square** (Rynek Główny) is always busy with locals and tourists, and during the summer this continues until late into the night. Measuring 200 metres (650 ft) on each side, it is one of Europe's largest medieval squares (only St Mark's Square in Venice is larger), with plenty of space for numerous restaurants and cafés, as well as flower stalls, pavement artists and street performers. Being such a cultured town, there are plenty of duos and trios playing exquisite classical refrains, with some buskers having a cheerful placard stating: "I'm healthy and happy, I'm just collecting money for beer."

The market square is surrounded by grand burghers' houses and palaces, with façades reflecting various architectural genres, while many of the rear courtyards

Map on page 200

BELOW: feeding the pigeons in the Main Market Square.

serve as *al fresco* cafés and restaurants. It's essential to dine at **Wierzynek** (Rynek Główny 15), which serves some of the city's finest dishes. This restau rant occupies three Renaissance houses, one of which belonged to the patri cian Wierzynek family. In 1364 King Kazimierz invited a number of Europea monarchs to a royal wedding in Kraków – a case of strategic political unior rather than true love – with the wedding feast hosted by the Wierzynek famil in one of these houses. One of the restaurant's dining rooms has a copy of 14th-century painting depicting this wedding feast. Other options include th Clock Room (featuring a wall full of antique clocks) and the Sala Rycersk (Knight's Hall); 14th-century sandstone Gothic arches are also a feature of th restaurant. The cellar is a wine bar specialising in Hungarian Tokay wines, con tinuing a vogue established by Hungarian-born Queen Jadwiga.

At the centre of the market square stands the **Cloth Hall** (Sukiennice; Mon–Fr 10am–7pm, Sat–Sun 10am–6pm) **Ⓐ**. Originally a covered market with stalls shops and warehouses, the current Renaissance façade was designed by Giovan nia Maria of Padua (known as Padovano) between 1556–60. The Italian sculpto Santi Gucci of Florence decorated the façade with mascarons, for which (appar ently) Kraków's most distinguished burghers posed.

The ground floor of the Sukiennice continues its commercial role, with stall selling folk arts and crafts, amber jewellery, leather goods and souvenirs, whicl are definitely a cut above the usual, while the arcades on either side house cafés

On the first floor of the Sukiennice is the **Gallery of Polish 19th-century Painting and Sculpture** (Galeria Sztuki Polskiej XIX Wieku). The name say it all, with this small but concentrated museum enabling you to see a lot in short time (Rynek Główny 1; tel: 422 11 66; closed for renovation). The col

BELOW: the arches of the Cloth Hall.

LIFE UNDERGROUND

The original medieval buildings of Kraków were not buil with cellars because of their shallow foundations Instead, they had three levels, the top level being used a the attic room. As the city became more wealthy anc expanded, new houses were built on top of the old and th street level was raised when new roads were added. The old houses consequently "developed" basements as th original ground floors now existed below street level Many basements were largely ignored by their owners fo hundreds of years and the situation was exacerbated b Communist property laws which controlled the use of a buildings. As a result, until recently, only two building around Rynek Główny had cellars that were accessible tc the public.

It has only been since the late 1980s and 1990s after change in the property law that these cellars, sc distinctive of the city's architecture, have been put to use and celebrated as a unique feature. Today, many of the cellars have been converted into atmospheric bars anc restaurants – even art galleries. The cosy ambience combined with unique medieval ceiling decoration ir many instances, make them an experience not to be missed by any visitor to the city.

ction includes Polish landscapes, portraits and historic scenes by Jan Matejko nd Adam Chmielowski, together with some works by late 18th-century artists ıch as Marcello Bacciarelli, the court artist of Stanisław August Poniatowski, oland's last king. The **Town Hall Tower** ❸ (Wieża Ratuszowa; open daily 0am–1pm, 1.45–4.30pm; closed second Sat–Sun of the month; entrance fee) rovides fine views of the immediate area. The tower also includes a museum ɔpen Wed–Sun; entrance fee) detailing the city's evolution.

The tiny Romanesque **St Adalbert's Church** ❻ (Kościół Św. Wojciecha; ɔen daily) dates from the 11th and 12th centuries, and features ornate interiors. he vaults include Romanesque and pre-Romanesque architectural fragments.

In front of the Cloth Hall is the **Adam Mickiewicz Monument** ❶ (Pomnik .dama Mickiewicza), commemorating Poland's greatest romantic poet, and ɪeeting "by the monument" is a favourite rendezvous for locals. The Main 1arket Square also hosts cultural events such as the colourful Lajkonik pageant, 'hich takes place shortly after Corpus Christi. This procession of Tartars march- ɪg through the streets, is led by the Lajkonik, a legendary Polish hero dis- ɹuised as a Tartar, "riding" a hobbyhorse which dances to the sound of drums. eing touched by the Lajkonik's wooden mace is considered good luck.

The imposing, twin-towered **St Mary's Church** ❸ (Kościół Mariacki; open 1on–Sat 11.30am–6pm, Sun 2–6pm) was built during the 14th–16th centuries. he triple-naved design features ornate interiors including an incredible late- ʰothic altar piece entitled "The lives of Our Lady and Her Son Jesus Christ". ɔmpleted between 1477–89 by the master carver of Nuremberg, Veit Stoss :nown in Poland as Wit Stwosz), it entailed carving around 2,000 realistic fig- ʳes and decorative elements in linden, which were given the features of con-

Map on page 200

TIP

If visiting Kraków in December, head for the Adam Mickiewicz monument to see the spectacular Christ Child Crib (Nativity Manger) competition which is held here.

BELOW: the Adam Mickiewicz Monument.

temporary Cracovians. The central panel, 13 metres (43 ft) high and 11 metres (3 ft) wide, depicts the death of the Virgin Mary, while side panels depict scene from the life of the Virgin Mary and Jesus. Stoss subsequently remained in the cit for 20 years fulfilling commissions for the king and other Polish aristocrats. Th interiors, including 19th-century murals by Jan Matejko, are so rich and cor centrated that it requires a leisurely visit to appreciate the various details. The are two entrances to the church, one for tourists (entrance fee) and another f those who wish to pray or attend a service. Tourists are not admitted during mas

Every hour on the hour a trumpeter plays the "*hejnał*" from the taller of th two church towers, which originally served as a warning against attack by th Tartars. One watchman who began the *hejnał* during an attack in the 12th cer tury was struck by an arrow after the first few notes and it took a few momen before a replacement continued: now there is always a pause after the first fe notes, in the watchman's honour. The *hejnał* now acts as a greeting for visitor

Around the Old Town

Taking Floriańska street from the market square leads to **Jan Matejko's Hous** **F** (Dom Jana Matejki; Floriańska 41; tel: 012-422 59 26; open Tues and Thu 9am–3pm; Wed and Fri 11am–5.30pm, weekend 10am–3pm; entrance fee excep Sun). The grandeur of the neoclassical façade and first floor wrought iron balcon immediately distinguish this house, where Poland's greatest historical painte Jan Matejko (1838–93), was born and subsequently worked. Retaining the sens of a private house, the original interiors include a salon with neo-Renaissance fur niture commissioned by Jan Matejko in Venice. The top floor studio, where hi linen jacket and walking stick hang on coat hooks, contains easels and variou accessories such as palettes and preparatory sketche

BELOW: the tower of St Mary's church tower from where the *hejnał* is played.

Nearby, at Number 45 (tel: 012-422 15 67), is **Jam Michalikowa G**, a famous café which was tradition ally the haunt of the city's Bohemian set, including th *fin-de-siècle* "*Młoda Polska*" (Young Poland) grou which pioneered Secessionism (Art Nouveau). The caf is also the home of the Zielony Balonik (literall "Green Balloon") cabaret troupe, with cabaret still per formed here. The interiors are a pot pourri of Seces sionist decor, including a stained-glass dome, eccentri chandeliers, elaborate mirrors, drawings, and one c the Christ Child's cribs for which the city is renowned

The street culminates at **Florian's Gate** (Brama Flo riańska) **H**. This is the Old Town's only remainin gateway, and features a section of the city wall togethe with four fortified turrets dating from the 14th century The city wall is hung with pictures by local artist (spanning the usual range from kitsch to artistic Beyond Florian's Gate is the **Barbican** (Barbakan) **(**(open May–Oct daily 10am–6pm; entrance fee), a cir cular Gothic bastion built in 1499, and the larges example of its kind in Europe. The rest of the city wall were pulled down in the 19th century, and this area wa laid out as the **Planty**, a wooded park with fountain and numerous benches that extends for almost 3.5 kr (2 miles), encircling the historic centre.

Various monuments erected in the Planty include statue of astronomer Nicholas Copernicus who stud in the city. **Pomnik Grunwaldzki** ❶ on Plac J. Matejki is the monument to Battle of Grunwald in 1410, when Poland defeated the Teutonic knights *page 263*). The monument was commissioned by the pianist and statesman acy Paderewski in 1910, on the 500th anniversary of the battle.

Map on page 200

Modelled on the Paris Opera House, the flamboyant neo-Renaissance late h-century **Juliusz Słowacki Theatre** ❷ (Teatr im J. Słowackiego; Plac iętego Ducha; tel: 423 17 00) is one of the city's leading theatrical venues, le one of the city's most important museums is the **Czartoryski Museum** (Muzeum Czartoryskich; Św. Jana 2; tel: 422 55 66; open Tues–Sat m–6pm, Sun 10am–4pm; entrance fee except on Sun). This palace, former nastery and armoury provides a suitably historic setting for an art collec- which includes German, Italian and Dutch masters, including *Landscape h the Good Samaritan* by Rembrandt. The renowned *Lady with an Ermine*, ted by Leonardo da Vinci around 1490, hangs in an individual room with ench in front of it so that you can savour this enigmatic portrait. The Tent om houses a collection of Turkish effects taken from the Battle of Vienna in 3, including a pavilion and suits of armour. The former armoury houses ient Roman and Greek artifacts.

The walls of the Barbican are three metres (10 feet) thick and it has 130 windows.

prime example of Gothic architecture, **St Mark's Church** ❸ (Kościół Św. rka; open daily) on Św. Marka has impressive interiors including a Passion ne in the apse. The nearby **Stanisław Wyspiański Museum** ❹ (pl zepański 11; tel: 422 70 21; open Tues–Sat 10am–6pm, Sun 10am–4pm, sed Mon; entrance fee) has a collection of paintings by Poland's leading h-century painter, Stanisław Wyspiański. The 14th-century *Madonna of Kru-va* is the best known exhibit. The Baroque **St Anna's Church** ❺ (Kościół

BELOW: the passageway within Florian's Gate.

The arcaded courtyard of Maius College restored almost to its original form.

Św. Anny; open daily) on Św. Anny was designed by Tylman van Game between 1689–1703 as the university church. The stucco works and polychro of the magnificent ceiling, let alone the side chapels, make this a worthw visit. Opposite the church is **Maius College Ⓟ** (Collegium Maius; Jagiellon 15; tel: 422 05 49; Mon–Fri 11am–3pm, Sun 11am–2pm; entrance fee exc Sat). This is the oldest college of Kraków University, established by the Jag lonian dynasty in 1364. It was also Poland's first university college, and second in Central and Eastern Europe after Prague. The Gothic arcaded co yard is magnificent, and you can stroll through it whenever the college is op Admission to the museum is only as part of a guided tour. This takes in original library with its blue skyscape ceiling, senate room, professors' din room and chambers, including numerous *objets d'art*, and scientific inst ments used by Mikołaj Kopernik (Nicholas Copernicus) who studied here fr 1491–95. The Golden Globe of 1510 is one of the first to show the New Wo (America), with the inscription "*America, terra noviter reperta*" ("Americ newly discovered land").

A detour to the **National Museum Ⓠ** (Muzeum Narodowe)(3 Maja 1; op Tues–Sat 10am–6pm, Sun 10am–4pm, closed Mon; entrance fee; tel: 012-2 55 00; www.muzeum.krakow.pl) offers one the city's most important and ext sive galleries. It covers 20th-century art, from Secessionism to contemporary and details Kraków's history as Poland's most important centre of fine Other galleries in the museum include a collection of military uniforms a weapons, and a collection of decorative arts including furniture. Despite vast number of exhibits, you can get around the entire building in a mornin afternoon session without experiencing gallery fatigue. Grodzka leads to

yal Castle and Cathedral, but before this it is worth exploring the numerous lleries and restaurants on this street, such as the traditionally Polish "Pod iołami" ("Under the Angels") at Number 35.

Among the historic buildings is the city's earliest Baroque church, **St Peter d St Paul's Church ⓡ** (Kościół Św. Piotra i Pawła; open daily). In front of : church is an impressive walled courtyard with 12 late-Baroque sculptures of : apostles. The architect modelled his designs on Il Gesù, Rome's renowned uit church. The austere and strikingly simple Romanesque **St Andrew's urch ⓢ** (Kościół Św. Andrzeja; open daily) is one of the city's oldest, with gant stucco work by Balthasar Fontana and a pulpit in the shape of a horse- wn carriage. Parallel to Grodzka is one of the city's most beautiful streets, nonicza (literally the "street of the canons", as it once housed clergymen) with ate Renaissance and Gothic houses. At number 19 is the former **home of pe John Paul II** (Muzeum Kardynala Wojtyly; tel: 012-421 89 63, open ly 10am–4pm, closed Mon; entrance fee) who lived here while serving as shop of Kraków. Besides the exhibition of his personal effects there is also a e collection of sacred art.

e Royal Castle and Cathedral

the end of Grodzka, which is an easy stroll from the main market square, you ve an inspiring view of the **Royal Castle ⓣ** (Wawel; open Mon, Wed, Thur m–3pm, Tues, Fri–Sun 9am-4pm; entrance fee; tel: 012-422 51 55; w.wawel.krakow.pl), built on a limestone hill rising above the Wisła (Vistula) ver. Serving as the royal residence between 1038 and 1596, this complex of ildings includes medieval defensive walls and towers, the royal castle, royal

Map on page 200

The Hen's Foot Watchtower at Wawel Castle, part of the old Gothic castle.

BELOW:
Wawel Castle.

Part of King Sigismund's Flanders Tapestries (which number 136 pieces in all) and throne chair.

BELOW: the Sigismund Bell.
RIGHT: the dome of the Sigismund Chapel.

cathedral, treasury and armoury. The earliest surviving architectural fragmen date from the 10th century, and each architectural genre, from Romanesqu and Gothic to Renaissance and Baroque can be seen here. The immense impor tance of the Wawel to Poland's heritage is summed up by the eminent arti. Stanisław Wyspiański, who wrote: "Here everything is Poland, every stone a fragment, and the person who enters here becomes a part of Poland."

The castle's perfectly proportioned, three-storey arcaded courtyard, from whi the castle extends along four wings, is one of Europe's finest examples of Renai sance architecture. Built from 1502–36, it was designed by the Italian architec Francisco the Florentine and Bartolomeo Berrecci. The royal apartments (op Mon 9.30am–noon, Tues, Fri 9.30am–4pm, Wed, Thurs, Sat 9.30am–3pm, S 10am–3pm) include a magnificent collection of arrases depicting Biblical scen commissioned in the mid-16th century by King Zygmunt August. While ma treasures were saved from the Nazis, having been shipped to Canada prior to t outbreak of World War II, only 142 of the original 360 arrases survived the war. T tour passes through Renaissance and Baroque apartments, and there are usually couple of musicians in period costume performing medieval songs. The **Treasu and Armoury Museum** (open Tues–Sun 9.30am–5pm, entrance fee) includ coronation regalia and royal jewels, including the 13th-century *szczerbiec* ("jagg sword") used at Polish coronations from 1320.

At the entrance to the Gothic **cathedral** (open Mon–Sat 9am–5pm, S 12.30–5pm) is a prehistoric tusk, which has hung here for centuries; superstiti states that so long as the tusk hangs by the entrance the cathedral will be sa Built on the site of an earlier Romanesque church, the triple-naved design includ side chapels that were added later. The most spectacular are the Renaissan

Map on page 200

aplica Zygmunta (Sigismund's Chapel) built from 1519–33, crowned with a agnificent gilded dome, and **Holy Cross Chapel** (Kaplica Świetego krzyża) ith frescos incorporating Ruthenian and Byzantian elements. From the 14th cen- ry the cathedral was used for royal coronations and funerals. Royal tombs vary design from the highly ornate, such as the marble sarcophagus of the Jagiel- nian King Kazimierz IV, completed by Veit Stoss, to the entirely modest, such the tomb of St Stanisław Szczepanowski in the central nave.

The labyrinthine **crypt** is usually much quieter than the cathedral which can full of tour groups, and is the final resting place for members of the royal mily and national figures such as Adam Mickiewicz, Tadeusz Kościuszko ho led uprisings during the partition of Poland), and the 20th-century atesman Marshal Józef Piłsudksi.

One of the cathedral's three towers contains the Zygmunt's Bell (Dzwon ygmunta) which was cast in 1520, and weighs 8 tons. Climbing the steep and amped staircase is a bit of a struggle, but it's worth it, particularly as a Polish perstition states that anyone touching the bell will enjoy good fortune. More- er, an observation terrace provides great views of the Old Town.

Opposite the main entrance to the cathedral is a separate building housing the athedral Museum established on the initiative of Pope John Paul II when he as Cardinal Karol Wojtyła, Archbishop of Kraków.

Beneath the Wawel is the **Dragon's Cave** (Smoczna Jama; open May–Oct ily 10am–5pm), home of the mythical Wawel dragon. The entrance to the ve is marked by an incongruously modern metalwork sculpture of a slimline,)60s-style dragon periodically breathing gas flames. Apparently the dragon as woken from a deep thousand years' sleep by the constant noise as the cas- was constructed, and ventured out in search of mething to eat. As the dragon preferred virgins, he on depleted Kraków of this valuable commodity. ing Krak, by then too elderly to take up the challenge slaying the dragon himself, said that whoever feated the dragon would receive half the kingdom d his daughter's hand in marriage. An apprentice oemaker used ingenuity rather than brawn. Filling a eepskin with sulphur and salt, he sewed it up, uipped it with four wooden legs to make it appear e-like and left it outside the cave. The dragon had it r breakfast. At this point there are two versions of hat happened next. Either the contents made the agon so thirsty that he went to the river and drank so uch that he burst, or the sheep blew up inside him, nited by the fire that the dragon breathed. The shoe- aker consequently married the princess and, true to iry-tale tradition, they lived happily ever after. By the awel, on Bulwar Czerwińskiego (tel: 012-422 08 55) u can join boat trips along the River Vistula.

The crypt of the Royal Cathedral is where the newly ordained Fr Karol Wojtyła (subsequently Pope John Paul II) celebrated his first mass.

BELOW: the fire-breathing dragon of sculptor Bronisław Chromy.

azimierz, Kraków's Jewish Quarter

raków's Jewish quarter, Kazimierz, was originally a parate walled town established in the 14th century King Casimir the Great (Kazimierz Wielki), with own gateways, town hall and market place, centred ound what is now **Szeroka** ⊕ (literally "Wide reet"). Kazimierz became a part of Kraków in the

18th century. In 1941 the Nazis confined Jews to the Kazimierz ghetto befc sending them to the death camps. Of the 68,000 Jews who lived in Kazimie in 1938, only a few hundred survived the war. Kazimierz itself escaped destru tion by the Nazis – but only because they planned to establish a macal museum here of what they termed "vanished races".

Szeroka has retained its Jewish character, though parts of this and sor surrounding streets are still so run-down you would think the war had only ji ended. Restoration work is on-going, and in the meantime the area receiv plenty of tourists, particularly American Jews tracing their roots, or other visitc taking "Oskar Schindler tours". Making the most of this, wandering musicia play nostalgic tunes in Szeroka's Jewish cafés and restaurants. Szeroka al has two synagogues. The **Jewish Museum** (open Tues–Sun 9am–5pm, M 10am–2pm; entrance fee) is housed in the **Old Synagogue** (Stara Synagoga; I Szeroka 24, tel: 012 422 09 62). Dating from the 15th and 16th centuries, I façade has Gothic and Renaissance elements, while period interiors house exhibition of Jewish history and culture. A monument in front of the synagog marks the site where 30 Jews were shot by the Nazis in 1943.

The **Remu'h Synagogue** (open daily 9am–6pm, closed Sat; entrance fee), t smallest in the city, is not only a historic monument but still has a small co gregation. A courtyard opens onto one of Europe's only Renaissance Jewi cemeteries, laid out in 1533 (the other is in Prague). The renowned writer a philosopher Rabbi Moses Isserle, known as Remu'h, was laid to rest here. Tl cemetery has a very poignant atmosphere, with some highly ornate tombstone

One of the most recently restored buildings is the **Isaac Synagogue** (Kupa I open Mon–Thur 10am–7pm, Fri 10am–1pm, closed Sat; entrance fee). Dati

Jewish shop sign in Kazimierz, now a thriving Jewish quarter.

BELOW: remembrance of the struggle for life.

OSKAR SCHINDLER AND PŁASZÓW

Oskar Schindler was a German industrialist living a working in Kraków during World War II, who credited with saving hundreds of Jews by employing th in his factory. Although his motives remain controvers and were not altogether altruistic – he was a businessm at heart and the Jews were effectively slave labour – number of lives saved cannot be disputed. Schindler h now reached hero status to many, immortalised first the award-winning book *Schindler's Ark* by Thom Keneally and later in the Academy Award-winning fi *Schindler's List*, directed by Steven Spielberg, much which was filmed in and around Kraków. Schindle Emalia factory is still standing on Lipowa street a features a small Schindler exhibition near the entranc

Also immortalised in Spielberg's film is the Płasz concentration camp, just south of Kazimierz, which w overseen by the cold-blooded Nazi commander Am Goeth. Many of Kraków's Jews were imprisoned a murdered here. Although the Nazis blew up much of camp as they retreated in 1945, leaving behind little mc than a deserted wilderness, parts of the gate remain a on the hill is a 1960s monument to the victims of t camp. Goeth's villa is now a private residence.

Map on page 200

...m the 17th century, this was the city's largest and originally the most lavishly ...nished synagogue. Retaining a Renaissance façade, the Baroque hall has ...gments of recently uncovered 17th- century wall murals, while the women's ...lery is separated from the main hall by an arcade of Tuscan columns. Hav-...been left unfurnished as a "shell", the slightly austere appearance makes vis-...g this synagogue all the more moving.

...he Jewish Cultural Centre, which includes an art gallery, bookshop and ...é, is nearby at Meiselsa 17, while the former Town Hall (Ratusz) now houses ... **Museum of Mankind** (Muzeum Etnograficzne; pl Wolnica 1; tel: (012) ...) 55 63; open Tues, Wed, Fri, Sat 11am–8pm, Thur 11am–9pm, Sun ...m–3pm; entrance fee). An extensive collection of folk art and culture from ...lages in the Kraków, Podhale and Silesian regions, it includes paintings, ...lpture and folk costumes, as well as exhibits relating to traditional folk-rites ...ch as Christ Child's cribs and Easter eggs. Recreated rooms comprising ...hentic furniture and decor mean you can walk around in what still manages ...feel like someone's home.

...odern Kraków

...e most recent part of the city is **Nowa Huta**, a large post-war housing and ...ustrial area featuring the uncompromising style of "concrete blocks" typical ...the Communist era. This area is hardly on the tourist trail – but that only ...kes it more interesting.

...A statue of Lenin stood in the central square until the beginning of 1990, ...en it was pulled down. At the heart of Nowa Huta is a vast steelworks which ...ounts for around 50 percent of Poland's total steel production and was a

TIP

The International Biennial of Regional Dolls and the Annual Folk Art Fair in September are also held in Kraków, as part of the Museum of Mankind.

BELOW: café-bar on Plac Nowy.

centre of the Solidarity movement in the 1980s (*see page 63*). But it is not
gloomy industrialisation: Nowa Huta also has some historic buildings, includi
the 11th-century Cistercian Abbey in Mogiła, which is opposite the wood
elaborate 15th-century Church of St Bartholomew. The neighbourhood
Bieńczyce features the vast Church of the Holy Mother Queen of Poland, b
in the shape of a ship, which was used as a rendezvous and shelter for oppo
tion groups during the period of martial law declared by President Jaruzelski
December 1981.

Greater Kraków

Various national parks, historic towns, palaces and attractions are within ea
reach of Kraków. The region has also preserved its *Folklor Krakowski*, the t
ditional folklore, which includes a dance known as the Krakowiak (similar to
polka). Many surrounding villages have also retained the architectural st
typical of this region. A visit to the Benedictine Abbey in **Tyniec**, 10 km
miles) from Kraków, is highly recommended. Formerly a Romanesque abb
fortress, it is romantically situated on the summit of a limestone cliff ov
looking the River Vistula. While the church and cloisters are a prime exam
of Baroque, much of the abbey is in ruins. However, during the summer
abbey hosts a series of organ recitals as part of two festivals, "Days of Org
Music" and "Tyniec Organ Recitals". A stroll along the banks of the River V
tula beneath the abbey is also very picturesque.

Around 13 km (8 miles) outside Kraków is the **Wieliczka Salt Mines** (Kop
nia Soli Wieliczka). Listed by UNESCO on the World Cultural Heritage List, t
is Poland's (and possibly the world's) oldest working salt mine, dating fro

BELOW:
the Benedictine
Abbey in Tyniec.

Map on page 200

12th or even the 10th century (Daniłowicza 10; tel: 012-278 73 02; open ily Apr–Oct 7.30am–7.30pm, Nov–Mar 8am–4pm, guided tour only; entrance). Currently the deposits are mined at eight levels, down to a depth of 315 tres (1,030 ft), with the total length of the galleries, chambers and tunnels er 150 km (93 miles). Almost one million visitors a year now come to see the azing features of this salt mine, including a vast underground cathedral rved from salt, including an altar, gallery and chandeliers, three further chapels o carved from salt, a gallery of salt gnomes carved by miners in the 1960s, d caverns with lakes, while the extraordinary effect of refracted light creates magical "underworld". The mining museum exhibits local geology, tools, thing and documents dating back 600 years. There is also a subterranean natorium treating patients suffering from asthma and various allergies.

To the east of Kraków, at the confluence of the Wisła and Raba rivers, lies szcza Niepołomicka, a primeval forest which was formerly hunting grounds the royal court, and which now includes a reserve for aurochs. At the edge the forest in the town of Niepołomice is a castle with a delightful arcaded urtyard, modelled on the Wawel Royal Castle (see page 209) and now serving a regional museum (tel: 012 281 32 32; open Mon–Sat 8am–4pm, Sun 10am– m; entrance fee). Trails from the town lead into the forest. On the other side the Wisła, located about an hour's drive from Kraków, is the village of iślica. This was the main fortress for the Wiślanie tribe between the 9th and th centuries. The crypt of the town's Gothic church has Romanesque foundations and a handsome floor relief, as well as fragments of an earlier church, mplete with a font – evidence that Christianity was already established in s region long before Poland's official conversion to Christianity in AD 966.

The superb acoustics in the underground cathedral in the salt mines have turned it into a spectacular concert venue and state banqueting hall.

BELOW: St Kinga's Chapel in the Salt Mines, Wieliczka.

Map
on page
200

The village of **Igołomia** is the home town of Brother Albert (Ada
Chmielowski). This painter and monk founded the order of St Adalbert
devoted to caring for the poor. Numerous archaeological digs have also tak
place in the Igołomia region.

The beauty of the surrounding countryside is spectacularly displayed throug
out the **Jura Krakowsko-Częstochowska**. This mountain range to the nor
west of Kraków includes limestone hills and cliff-faces, caves, deep valle
and extraordinary rocks in the shape of clubs and needles. The region is a
home to wild boar and roe deer, not to mention 12 different species of bat. P
of the Jura now comes under the auspices of the Ojców National Park (Ojcow
Park Narodowy) which covers an area of 1,890 hectares (4,650 acres). T
most interesting part of this park is the 14-km (9-mile) long valley that follo
the River Prądnik near Ojców, surrounded by thick forests which provide
dramatic backdrop to limestone cliff-faces. The valley's unique flora inclu
the so-called *ojcowska* (shrubby birch). Two caves, Ciemna (literally "dark") a
the larger Łokiełek, are open to the public (tel: 012 389 20 27). It is said t
King Władysław Łokiełek hid here after an attack by King Wenceslas
Bohemia. Some traces of human settlement, found in the Ciemna Caves a
thought to be about 120,000 years old, and are on display in the Władysł
Szafer Museum in Ojców (tel: 012 389 2040, open daily; entrance fee exc
Mon). The town also has ruins of a 14th-century castle.

A few kilometres from Ojców on a dramatic elevation overlooking the Prądn
Valley is the Renaissance castle of **Pieskowa Skała** ("Dog's Rock"). Once the r
idence of aristocratic families, it is now a branch of the Wawel's National A
Collection (tel: 012 389 6004; open Tues–Fri 10am–3.30pm, Sat–Sun 10a
5.20pm; entrance fee), with an exhibition of househo
and castle furnishings dating from the Middle Ages
the 19th century. On the ground floor of the palace
the historic Zamkowa restaurant, while a short wa
from the castle leads to an unusual 25-metre (82-
rock called the Club of Hercules. Pieskowa Skała w
one of several hilltop castles built on the so-call
"Trail of the Eagle's Lair", in order to secure the ro
from Kraków to Silesia during the Middle Ages. M
of those castles are now in ruins, with one of the mo
impressive being Ogrodzieniec, which lies further we

At the plateau's western edge is **Olkusz**, once know
as "silver city". This is Poland's oldest mining regio
Lead and zinc ore, both with a high silver content, we
found in this area. The Błędow Desert (Pustynia B
dowska) covers 30 sq km (11 sq miles) and is the on
large expanse of sand in Poland. It was once mu
larger, but it is progressively giving way to vegetatio

En route to Bielsko-Biała *(see page 260)* is **Wa**
owice, 50 km (35 miles) from Kraków. Set in the va
ley of the River Skawa at the foot of the Little Besk
Mountains, this is the town where Pope John Paul
was born and spent his youth. His childhood home
now a museum (Kościelna 7; open May–Sept da
9am–1pm, 2–6pm; Oct–Apr Tues–Sun 9am–noo
2–5pm; entrance fee) documenting his life and wo
while the Market Place features a 15th-century chur
where the Pope was baptised.

THROUGH LITTLE POLAND

On this route through Małopolska, places of outstanding natural beauty alternate with the Renaissance and Gothic architecture of cities such as Zamość and Łańcut

Map on page 220

Warsaw

n the south and east of Little Poland (Małopolska) large tracts of land have retained the character of primeval forest – the Puszcza Niepołomicka, Puszcza Sandomierska, Puszcza Solska. Amid broadleaf and coniferous oodland live indigenous wolves, lynx, bison and brown bears. Seven national rks in total, about a dozen protected areas and several hundred nature reserves ve been established in the area.

ast of Kraków

you travel from **Kraków ❶** *(see page 201)* eastwards along the E40, which ads through Tarnów, Rzeszów and Przemyśl all the way to Medyka on the kraine border, you will come to yet another region of Małopolska. In Bochnia, t far from Wieliczka, is a second salt mine, almost as old as that in Wieliczka ee page 214). It is also open to visitors.

To the south of Bochnia, in the neglected village of **Nowy Wiśnicz ❷**, stands palace owned by the Lubomirski family. After the war, the property was con-scated by the state as part of the land reform policy, but the land registry doc-ments were never altered, so when democracy was restored to Poland and anges were made to the constitution, the property was legally returned to its rmer owners. It is an impressive structure with five wers, massive walls and a pentagonal courtyard. rmerly a Gothic fortification, the castle was reno-ted in the 17th century by Mattia Trapole. The walls d inside of the palace are decorated with wall paint-gs and stucco work. The next town along the route **Brzesko**, justly famous for its excellent beer, kocim, brewed in the nearby village of the same me. The brewery was founded in 1845 by the ohemian industrialist Baron Goetz. Not far from rzesko, in the town of **Dębno** is a small but inter-ting Gothic castle where a museum keeps an inter-ting collection of weapons, paintings and furniture. The next important settlement along the route rough Małopolska is **Tarnów ❸**, the administra-ve centre for the *powiat* (county) with a charter dat-g back to 1330, was once the seat of the powerful ble Tarnowski family, ancestors of the Polish gen-al Hetman Jan Tarnowski. Some 350 buildings in rnów are listed under the Polish national monument otection scheme. Tarnów is now an important indus-al centre surrounded by large chemical plants, ini-ted by Ignacy Mościcki, president of Poland before orld War II.

Medieval Tarnów is built on two levels with the oper and lower towns connected by steps. The for-er defensive walls were removed and replaced in e late-19th century by a road around the old town

LEFT: a window-view in Lublin.
BELOW: a typical roadside shrine.

centre, thereby preserving the character of what was formerly a provinci
capital during the era of the Austro-Hungarian empire. Sights of particul
interest in the Old Town are the Town Hall with Renaissance attics topping t
roof, its arcades, patrician houses and a vast 15th-century cathedral containi
the tombs of the Tarnowski and Ostrogski families.

Not far from the Old Town is the **Square of the Ghetto Heroes** (Pl
Bohaterów Getta) and, beside the square, the baths where the Jewish comm
nity performed their ritual washing ceremonies. It was from here on 14 Ju
1940 that the first transport left for the concentration camp at Auschwitz wi
738 people on board *(see page 54)*. In the **Church of St Joseph and the H**
Virgin of Fatima, which dates from the 1950s, a chapel is dedicated to t
suffering of the Polish people during the war. Equally impressive is the scul
ture of St Maximilian Kolbe who sacrificed his life in Auschwitz to save a fo
low prisoner. In 1982 Kolbe was canonised by the Pope.

The nearby village of **Wierzchosławice** is the birthplace of Wincenty Wit
(1874–1945), leader of the radical peasant movement which gained momentu
between the two world wars.

Lovers of folk art should take a detour to the village of **Zalipie** ❹, abo
32 km (20 miles) to the northwest of Tarnów. In this unusual village, situat
in a low-lying region beside the Vistula, folk artists have covered the t
interiors and exteriors of their houses, their tables, barns, fences, furniture a
even their dog kennels with colourful and original paintings of plant moti
The town is also renowned for its embroidery, hand-cut silhouettes and stra
dolls. In the house where the painter Felicja Curyłowa (1904–74) lived,
museum keeps alive these unusual rural crafts. The village of **Ciężkowic**

ith a history dating back to the 10th century, lies in the Biała valley. Wooden ᴐuses with open galleries looking out on to the town make a picturesque ght. The **Petrified City** (Skamieniałe Miasto) nature reserve is situated near ięžkowice. An amazing rock formation here has given rise to numerous ᴖyths and legends.

ᴖe Sandomierz Basin

he central region of Małopolska is dominated by a wide depression known as ᴖe Sandomierz Basin (Kotlina Sandomierska). Fields interspersed with large ᴖooded areas are typical of this flat, rural landscape. Most of the farms are ᴖall, about 2 hectares (5 acres) in area, and the narrow strips of cultivated ᴖnd form a regular pattern. The population here has a reputation for militancy, ᴖ tradition which last manifested itself in the winter of 1981 when a strike led ᴖ the foundation of the Solidarity movement *(see page 63)*.

The most important town in this region is **Rzeszów ❺**. Founded in the 14th ᴖntury, the town has always been provincial in character. Up until 1939, half ᴖ its population were Jews, but during World War II almost all of them were ᴖurdered. Two synagogues, rebuilt from the rubble of the war, and a Jewish ᴖemetery serve as memorials to the town's former Jewish community.

The townscape today is dominated by the magnificent 18th-century ᴖubomirski Palace, which is surrounded by bastions and moats; it is now used ᴖ a prison. The Baroque church and the Bernardine Monastery have also been ᴖreserved. A regional museum is housed in the former Piarist Monastery. It ᴖntains a collection of Polish paintings and documents the history of the region ᴖd its people (3 Maja; tel: 017 853 52 78; open Tues–Sun; entrance fee).

Map on page 220

TIP

Every other July since 1969, Rzeszów has been the venue for the World Festival of Polish Folklore Groups Living Abroad.

BELOW: folk art in the village of Zalipie.

Twice weekly, on Tuesdays and Fridays, a bustling market takes place Rzeszów, but sadly this event has lost some of its traditional character a today, with many cheap products on sale, it is reminiscent of a car-boot sal

Situated on the international E40 motorway, 17 km (10 miles) east Rzeszów, is the medieval town of **Łańcut ❻** with its magnificent palace. Th former residence of the aristocratic Lubomirski and Potocki families was bu on old foundations between 1629–41 by Stanisław Lubomirski. At the beginni of the 19th century the structure was expanded into a modern residential pala with the encouragement of Princess Elżbieta Lubomirska (1736–1826). Th renovation was carried out according to plans drawn up by the famous archite Piotr Aigner. Later, at the turn of the 20th century, a façade in the French ne Baroque style was added.

Today the palace is a museum (tel: 017 225 20 08; open Feb–Nov Tues–S 9am–4pm; entrance fee, guided tours only). The centrepiece of the palace is almost square structure with corner towers and a central inner courtyard. A bu wark in the form of a five-pointed star surrounds the complex. The main buil ing houses a Museum of Interior Design where some well-preserved furnishin from the 18th and 19th centuries are kept. The unusual library contains ov 20,000 precious tomes. The upstairs living quarters, the ballroom, large dini hall and theatre, as well as the Turkish room on the ground floor, are all remar able. Visitors to the former stables will find a collection of old Russian icor An international music festival has been held in the palace every May sin 1961. Several outbuildings were added at a later date: the library, a greenhou and a court building which is now a restaurant and hotel. The palace is encor passed by a park laid out on a grand scale. A smaller palace and a riding scho are located within the grounds. To the south of t castle, the old coach house is now used as a museu of about 50 horse-drawn carriages.

BELOW:
Łańcut Palace.

Traditional country fairs are still held in the sm towns around Rzeszów, such as Sokołów, Kolb szowa and Strzyżów. Visitors to these fairs will fi authentic arts and crafts on sale made by local craf people. A few of the villages in this region, in parti ular Medynia Głogowska, Pogwizdów, Medyn Łańcucka and Zalesie, are also centres for the trac tional craft of pottery. Here almost 120 potters pr duce decorative ceramic dishes and sculptures, as w as traditional crockery for everyday use.

A range of hills known as the **Pogórze** lie to t south of Rzeszów. The River Wisłoka meande peacefully through this picturesque landscape. In t many little towns and hamlets, wind-battered farr houses recall a bygone age, but following the expu sion of the native, mainly Jewish, population, the primitive settlements have lost much of their chan

The village buildings of Małopolska we originally built almost entirely out of wood. Althou many examples of this type of construction still exi an exceptionally good one is the small church **Blizne**, which is situated between Rzeszów a Sanok. Built in Gothic style at the end of the 15 century from thick larchwood beams, it has remaine remarkably, unchanged to this day.

orth of Rzeszów

ie section of the Kotlina Sandomierska to the north of Rzeszów is covered
ith the rich forests of the vast **Puszcza Sandomierska**. Mushrooms, berries
d wild game all flourish in this environment. The region is inhabited by the
ssowiaki, a people who pride themselves on their self-sufficiency. Old farm-
uses remain unspoilt, quaint traditions and intriguing rituals survive. Some
pects of the local folk customs have been preserved in the open-air museum
Kolbuszowa ❼. This museum also serves as a venue for cultural events.
During World War II, the German army established two large military train-
g grounds in Puszcza Sandomierska. Several prison and work camps also
rmed part of this complex. The most notorious work camp was in **Pustków**.
me 15,000 people, mainly Poles, Jews and Russians, lost their lives here.
Experiments with V-1 and V-2 rockets were carried out on a strictly guarded
e close to the village of **Blizna** ❽. The underground intelligence wing of the
lish Home Army (*Armia Krajowa*) recorded a major success in its struggle
ainst the occupying forces when locals managed to retrieve a rocket which had
en fired by the Germans and, after dismantling it, smuggled it to London.
The ancient town of **Leżajsk** ❾ lies about 50 km (31 miles) to the northeast
Rzeszów, not far from the River San. Numerous historic buildings and other
minders of a distant past can be found here. Produce markets take place
eekly. In the northern part of the town is a 17th-century Bernardine monastery,
iich was later converted into a fortress. The beautiful and richly decorated
terior of the monastery is dominated by the organ, one of the largest in Poland.
iilt at the end of the 17th century, this instrument, with its 74 organ stops and
394 pipes, spans all three naves of the church. In recent years, organ concerts

**Map
on page
220**

BELOW: the
Coach Museum,
Łańcut Palace.

have been held here every May and their reputation has been spreading. other months the in-house organist will perform on special request. *The Mir* *ulous Image of the Virgin Mary with Child* has been famous since 1634 a painting that performs miracles. On Assumption Day in August, both believe and unbelievers alike are drawn here by the festivities.

Economically, the northern portion of this region, at the confluence of t Vistula and San rivers, is the most interesting. The centre of this area is the v lage of **Tarnobrzeg**. Once poverty-stricken and neglected, its sulphur depos have brought employment and prosperity. The seams of sulphur are exploit in open-cast mines at Machów, and the foul-smelling mineral is then export in granular form via the harbour in Gdańsk.

Baranów Sandomierski ❿ is located at the edge of this sulphur basin, on t right-hand bank of the Vistula. The town is especially renowned for its pala a building regarded by many as one of the brightest jewels of Polish Renaissan architecture. All that remains from the original 16th-century fortress, howev is a rectangular structure with corner towers and a gate. The courtyard w arcaded passageways, an unusual stairway and rooftop attics, which are c tainly the most distinctive features of the palace, were added between 1591 a 1606. Inside, the palace is richly decorated with murals and stucco works a is today the site of a museum as well as a luxury hotel. The museum, housed the cellar, has exhibits relating to the sulphur industry (open Tues–Sun; entran fee). Happily, the excellent wines and food of the adjoining hotel restaurant a not affected by the proximity of this unsavoury chemical.

A short distance to the east of Tarnobrzeg is **Stalowa Wola**, one of Polan newer towns and an important centre for the metal industry. Stalowa Wola w

BELOW: driving through typical Małopolskan landscape.

uilt in 1937, in conjunction with a weapons manufacturing plant. Today, the works manufacture steel and construction machinery. Nearby, on the opposite side of the San, lies the old village of **Radomyśl nad Sanem** ⓫. This is the venue for an unusual patriotic and religious play which is performed every year at Easter. A group of residents, dressed in the colourful robes of Turkish soldiers, lead a military parade through the village. Afterwards they go from house to house wishing the inhabitants luck and asking for a donation to pay for their costumes. They are accompanied by a marching band and countless spectators, many of whom travel great distances to watch the spectacle.

This area is also very well known for its crafts. A little further to the east of Stalowa Wola, along the road leading from Nisko to Janów Lubelski, lie the villages of Łążek Ordynacki and Łążek Garncarski. These two woodland settlements, with craftsmen working in traditional family potteries, are renowned for the production of imaginative and beautiful ceramic designs. The small town of **Rudnik** lies half-an-hour's drive away from Stalowa Wola in the direction of Jarosław. Rudnik is famous for its basket-making. Two manufacturing workshops and several thousand helpers working in their homes produce baskets which are then exported to many different countries all over the world.

Sandomierz ⓬, one of Poland's finest towns, is situated to the north of the Basin on a terrace above the banks of the Vistula. Once the capital of an independent duchy, the town was an important trading port. Founded on the site of an ancient settlement, it is one of the oldest and most picturesque towns in Poland. Thanks to its strategically important fortress, as early as the 12th century it was one of Poland's three largest commercial centres and enjoyed great prosperity during the Renaissance. The Old Town is perched on an oval-shaped hill

Map on page 220

The sundial on the Town Hall.

LEFT: the rooftops of Sandomierz.
BELOW: the clock tower of the Town Hall, Sandomierz.

30 metres (100 ft) above the river valley and has managed to preserve much o its medieval character, including several narrow streets with nooks and crannie although the perfect restoration still cannot conceal a certain urban shabbines Like so many Polish towns, these old quarters successfully convey the impres sion of working communities where ordinary people still lead normal lives.

The remains of a royal palace can be seen at the southern edge of the tow Adjacent to these is a triple-naved Gothic cathedral dating from the 14th cen tury. The Russo-Byzantine frescos in the chancel merit special attention. Adja cent to the cathedral is the Gothic house of **Długosz**, a medieval historian an chronicler of Poland (1415–80). Today, the Diocesan Museum, with its collec tion of art and *objets d'art*, is housed here (open Tues–Sun; entrance fee).

Nearby is the **Church of St James**, which formerly belonged to the Domin cans. This is Poland's best remaining example of a Romanesque brick churc and serves as a memorial to the bloody Tartar invasion of 1259. The plai Romanesque north portal is particularly impressive, while the interior is taste fully finished with glazed bricks. Glass cases contain the bones of the monk who were murdered during the 13th-century Tartar attack.

The marketplace in the centre of the town is surrounded by a number o stylish houses. One, belonging to the Olesnicki family stands out, mainl because of its ornate gallery. The Town Hall dominates the middle of the mar ketplace and the remains of the old fortifications, with the tall Brama Opa towska (Abbot Gate), mark the northern boundary of the Old Town.

BELOW: Church of St James, Sandomierz.

Visitors to Sandomierz should spend some time exploring the surroundin area as there are a number of places of interest. The arable land here is we suited to the production of fruits and vegetables. An old Cistercian abbey an

late-Romanesque church dating from the early 13th century are found in **Koprzywnica** 17 km (10 miles) to the southwest of Sandomierz. In the small village of **Ujazd** ⓭, the impressive ruins of the Krzyżtopór palace can still be seen. This enormous edifice was built in the 17th century by the Ossoliński family, but was partially destroyed soon afterwards by the Swedes. Before the construction of the Palais de Versailles near Paris, this was the largest official residence in Europe. It has some very unusual design features: four towers for the four seasons, 12 large halls for each of the months, 52 rooms for each week and 365 windows. There was even an additional window for leap years which was covered up for the rest of the time.

Some 16 km (10 miles) to the northeast of Ujazd lies **Opatów** with its Romanesque theological college. A far-reaching system of passageways, cellars and vaulted chambers winds its way under the streets and houses. Five centuries ago, this served as a refuge from the marauding Tartars; today part of it is open to the public.

Eastern Małopolska

The economy of the eastern section of Małopolska, which nestles in the valley of the River San, is dominated by agriculture. Those journeying eastwards from Rzeszów should make plans to stop off in **Jarosław** ⓮ close to the Ukrainian border. Sited on the banks of the river, Jarosław is one of the oldest towns in this area. During the Middle Ages its markets and fairs attracted merchants from all over Europe. The Old Town, with its abundance of interesting architecture, is still a veritable paradise for photographers.

The old houses around the marketplace, with their distinctive passageways, covered courtyards, decorated stairways and galleries, are particularly picturesque. The house that formerly belonged to the patrician Italian Orsetti family, built in Renaissance style with an open gallery and attic, is definitely worth seeking out. It now houses the Regional Museum (open Wed–Sat 10am–2pm; entrance fee). Other interesting sights in Jarosław are the attractive Town Hall, a number of older churches, one of which is Russian-Orthodox, and several synagogues. Entering the town from Rzeszów, you will be able to see the late-Baroque **Dominican Monastery** hidden behind its surrounding walls. Outside these walls is a small well. The water in the well not only tastes good, but is also reputed to work magical powers on those who drink it. According to legend, a sculpture of the Madonna was found here in ancient times. Soon afterwards, the sculpture was found to have miracle-working powers. An exceptionally valuable work of art is the Gothic wooden sculpture of Mater Dolorosa from Zbawiec which is now located in the main altar.

Near Jarosław is **Sieniawa**, further downstream, where the recently restored palace of the Czartoryski family is well worth a visit. Equally interesting are Jarzecze with the Dzieduszycki Castle and **Węgierka** with its ruins of a medieval manor house. In the small town of **Pruchnik** ⓯, a few miles to the south of Jarosław, time seems to have stood still for several

Map on page 220

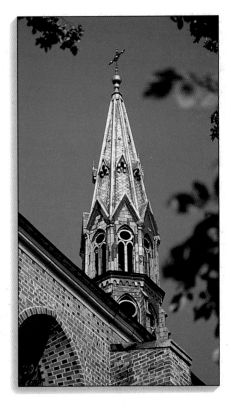

BELOW: cathedral spire, Sandomierz.

centuries. The wooden houses by the marketplace and nearby streets have op
galleries and precise, extremely complex decorative woodwork. Many are ve
old and, as they represent rare examples of Polish architecture, are now officia
listed as ancient national monuments. Long-standing traditions have also be
preserved: for many years now it has been the custom to hang an effigy
Judas publicly on the Saturday before Easter.

The eastern area abounds with sacred myths. Near Jarosław is the Sanctuary of the Holy Virgin in Jodłówka, with a chapel and well. Legend has it that here, too, the Virgin Mary appeared and performed miracles.

East meets west

The border between the Catholic world and the Orthodox, effectively the bo
der between the two main elements of European culture, runs to the east of t
River San. For centuries this stretch of land has been the scene of confrontatio
between the east and west, and the various nationalities in the regions ha
lived and fought both together and against each other. At the end of World W
II, for example, the Ukrainian nationalists fought a bitter and cruel two-year ba
tle for their right to independence. In the end, having suffered enormous destru
tion and the loss of many lives, they gave up their fight. In April 1947, regardle
of whether they had supported the resistance movement, the Ukrainians we
forcibly resettled, either in what was then the USSR or in the former Germ
regions of Poland. Only evacuated and burnt-out villages remained. Even tod
many regions are only thinly populated and settlements can be found that a
almost totally overgrown by woodland and shrubs.

BELOW: a pilgrim in penitential robe.
RIGHT: celebrating first communion.

Characteristic of this part of Poland is the wooden architecture of t
Orthodox churches, which frequently occurs in the old villages. These are re
gems of folk architecture. Some of the more beautiful Orthodox churches a
found in Rudka near Sieniawa and in Chołyniec (both 17th-century),

Pożdziacz and Piątkowa near Przemyśl (18th-century) and in Radruż near Lubaczów (16th-century). Some of the old churches in the Ukrainian villages, also excellent examples of folk art, are now used by the Roman Catholic church. The iconostases have been preserved in many of the churches. These traditional altar screens often show icons dating from the 17th–19th centuries and many are of great artistic value.

The National and Diocesan Museum in the town of **Przemyśl** ⑯ houses an interesting collection of painted icons (Pl Czackiego 2; open Tues–Sun 10am–4pm; entrance fee). The countryside surrounding the border town of Przemyśl, a melting pot of various cultures and traditions since the 7th century, is enchanting. The densely wooded and hilly Przemyśl foothills (Pogórze Przemyskie) stretches out to the south of a town that receives few tourists. In recent years, the Ukrainian minority here has started celebrating its national holiday, the **Feast of St Jordan** again. On a winter morning, the faithful, bearing flags and crosses, congregate on the banks of the San and the deeply religious, almost mystical festival then begins. After the ceremony, the people wash their faces and eyes with river water. Freshly cleansed, they then consider themselves able to face up to their daily lives with renewed vigour.

A charming Renaissance palace belonging to the Krasicki family is located in **Krasiczyn**, 10 km (6 miles) west of Przemyśl. Once the seat of one of Poland's most powerful families, it is a large building with fortifications comprising four bastions and a tower over the entrance. Stylish stucco work and paintings decorate the meticulously restored palace. Not far from Krasiczyn, 16 km (10 miles) south of Przemyśl is **Kalwaria Pacławska** ⑰, where a Franciscan monastery with a painting of the Virgin Mary has been revered for centuries because of its

Map on page 220

LEFT: the round tower of the Renaissance palace in Krasiczyn.
BELOW: old wooden church Nałęczów.

miracle-working powers. In the area around the monastery, the Stations of the Cross are illustrated in 42 picturesquely situated chapels. The wooden houses in the village which grew up around the monastery are also worth taking the time to see. This is an extremely quiet and almost deserted area. Only in August when the annual fair takes place, does it show any real signs of life.

A little further to the south, in the woods around the former village of **Arłamów**, is a holiday hostel that used to belong to the Communist Party and where Lech Wałęsa was kept prisoner for a time *(see page 64)*. Today it is open to the public and, among other activities, hunts are organised in which visiting foreigners can participate. Anyone who enjoys horses and riding will want to visit **Stubno** to the northeast of Przemyśl where the Polish state maintains a stud farm with English thoroughbreds and a riding club.

The Roztocze, which begins a bit further to the north, is also an extremely picturesque region. A unique mixture of flora and fauna can be found in the rolling forest-covered hills. In the most beautiful part of the Roztocze around the towns of Zwierzyniec and Krasnobrod, the **Roztocze National Park** ⑱ (Roztoczański Park Narodowy) has been established. About 10 percent of this 7,900 hectare (19,500-acre) park is under very strict protection. Geologically, the landscape is mixed and the climate changes dramatically with altitude. Consequently the vegetation is very varied: tough steppe plants, an abundance of mountain flora and other flora which require warmth. The wooded regions are also very varied: pine, oak and beech forests proliferate. Running through the centre of the park is the spectacular River Wieprz. Varieties of game, wolf, tarpan, beaver, eagle, osprey and capercaillie are all native species to this park and thrive in great numbers. On the southern faces of the Roztocze hills the

BELOW: Town Hall on Market Square, Zamość.

remains of the Molotov Line fortifications from World War II can still be iden-tified. Maps of hiking routes are available but small areas of the park are restricted and require the accompaniment of a guide.

Zamość

At the northeastern end of the national park in the Zamość Basin (Kotlina Zamo-iska) lies the attractive settlement of **Zamość ⑲**. This fascinating town, founded in the heart of the wilderness during the Renaissance (1579–1616) by the chan-cellor and Grand Hetman of the Crown, Jan Zamoyski, was designed by the Venetian Bernardo Morando.

 Map on page 220

The Old Town of Zamość consists of a palace and residential area surrounded by fortified walls with bastions and gates. This mighty fortress was built so solidly that it was able to resist the attacks of both the Cossacks and the Swedes. The palace, renovated between 1821–31, gives a gloomy barrack-like atmos-phere to the town, despite the fact that a large portion of the complex was turned into a pleasant park after a part of the fortifications were destroyed in 1866. Zamość Old Town is so greatly prized as an example of Renaissance architec-ture that it has been awarded UNESCO World Cultural Heritage status.

Playing with the water pump. Zamość.

The **Market Square** (Rynek Główny) lies at the heart of the Old Town. Its famous Town Hall (designed by Morando between 1591–1600) includes later additions of a grand double staircase (1768) and the octagonal 50-metre (165-ft) high tower (1770) with a Baroque roof. Today it houses local government offices. The square is surrounded by town houses in Renaissance style, linked together with arcades. The German revolutionary and socialist-feminist theorist Rosa Luxembourg was born at Number 37. The Collegiate Church (1587–98), another of Morando's works, is located to the south-west of the market square. The high altar paintings here are usually ascribed to Domenico Tintoretto. The bell tower features an observation terrace (open May–Oct 10am–4pm). Adjoining this central marketplace are two other squares: the Salt Marketplace (Rynek Solny) and the Water Marketplace (Rynek Wodny). The west-ern part of the Old Town is dominated by the palace formerly owned by the Zamoyski family (1585). It was converted into a military hospital in 1831.

BELOW: town house facades, Zamość.

Zamość was once a town with a multicultural pop-ulation, including Poles, Russians, Jews and Armeni-ans. During the Nazi occupation, it was renamed Himmlerstadt. The Polish population was expelled and Germans were brought in to create what Hitler hoped would become the eastern bulwark of the Third Reich. Consequently, the historic buildings, includ-ing the old Orthodox church, the synagogue and an Armenian meeting house survived the war. The Germans were unable to complete their inhumane resettlement plan, but thousands of Poles still lost their lives in the prisoner-of-war camps and mass shoot-ings in the Rotunda, now a Museum of Martyrology (open May–Oct Tues–Sun 9am–8pm), a ring-shaped fort 10 minutes from the Old Town. Many of the town's inhabitants were transported to the extermina-tion camp at Bełżec 42 km (26 miles) away and the Jewish population was completely wiped out.

Lublin

The region of Lublin in the northeastern part of Małopolska is an agricultural area, but with industry concentrated in the larger towns. The largest town in eastern Poland, **Lublin** ⑳, is an important centre for industry, culture and science. It has been a busy trading centre since medieval times and during several periods in its history has been a target for invaders. Its finest moment occurred in 1569 when the Polish and Lithuanian rulers met here to agree the Lublin Union. A period of prosperity followed, but this ended with the First Partition *(see page 30)*. When Poland regained its full independence in 1918, the **Catholic Lublin University** (Katolicki Uniwersytet Lubelski), known as the KUL and the only Catholic university in the whole of eastern Europe, became the centre for Poland's Catholic intelligentsia. In July 1944, after liberation, Lublin was also the provisional capital of Poland and the seat of the transitional government that Stalin installed.

Lublin's Old Town survived World War II relatively intact and many of the old buildings have been restored.

The small **Old Town** (Stare Miasto) is full of interesting sights: the market place with its old town houses (16th–18th century); the cathedral (16th–17th century) and the Dominican monastery (14th–17th century) are noteworthy. The Gothic church has 11 chapels and two are worth seeking out: the Firlej family chapel has a two-tier grave and the dome above the Tyszkiewicz family chapel has a large fresco depicting *The Last Judgement*. The first building on the hill to the east of the town was erected during the 9th century, but the tower that stands there now is 13th century. The Holy Trinity Chapel with its Russo-Byzantine paintings has survived the ravages of time. Recently restored this 15th-century art treasure can now be admired in all its splendour. Western European Gothic architecture and Orthodox frescos make strange bedfellows.

The primarily neo-Gothic castle complex houses a museum of Polish paint

BELOW:
Lublin Castle.

g, folk art and archaeology (open Wed–Sat 9am–4pm, Sun 9am–5pm).
During the years of the German occupation, thousands of Poles were tortured
ıd killed in the neo-Gothic prison (1823) and, following the war, Polish free-
ɔm fighters and anti-Communists were imprisoned here. Lublin used to have a
ɪge Jewish population and they mainly occupied the part of the Old Town
ound Grodzka street, where a few memorial plaques can be seen. During the
)th century, Lublin was also one of the centres of Hassidic Jewry and its Tal-
ud school, the Jeschiwa, was among the most distinguished of its kind any-
here in the world. The school was closed by the Germans and its fine library
undered, but the building remains, now housing Lublin's medical faculty. All
e synagogues and Jewish quarters were destroyed by the Nazis in 1943, but
ɔme graves from both the old and new Jewish cemeteries escaped destruction.
ı 1941 German forces established a ghetto in the north of the Old Town by the
ɪbartowska. In the same year they built one of their most terrible extermination
ɪmps in **Majdanek**, a suburb of Lublin. During the following year most of the
),000 inhabitants of the ghetto were systematically murdered, if not in Maj-
ɪnek, then in Treblinka or Bełżec. A monument on Plac Bohaterów recalls the
ctims of this atrocity. Lublin now has only a small Jewish community.
Between Lublin and the Vistula lies the region known as Płaskowyż Nałęc-
ɔwski. The town of **Nałęczów** which gives this high plateau its name owes its
ɪistence to the mineral springs discovered here in the 18th century. It is still a
ɔpular health resort for patients suffering from circulatory disorders and heart
ɪsease. Many famous Polish writers and artists, including Bolesław Prus and
tefan Żeromski, often came to this spa during its heyday to relax and take the
aters. Biographical museums have been erected in their honour.

Map
on page
220

*The Majdanek
Museum (open daily
Oct–Apr 8am–5pm;
May–Sept 8am–6pm)
details the history of
the death camp.*

BELOW: alleyway
off the Market
Place in Lublin.

Map on page 220

Kazimierz Dolny Castle ruins on the River Vistula.

BELOW: the Market Place in Kazimierz Dolny. **RIGHT:** the Vistula and Kazimierz Dolny.

Kazimierz Dolny to Chelm

On the right bank of the Vistula lies the delightful town of **Kazimierz Dolny**. Founded by King Kazimierz III Wielki (The Great), who died in 1370, Kazimierz Dolny originally earned its living from the grain trade and the town enjoyed great prosperity for many centuries. During the 16th century, the grain merchants built themselves some fine town houses – their naïve interpretation of Renaissance motifs seems quite touching nowadays. Stucco work covers the whole of the façades. Also worth looking out for are Kazimierz Dolny's three regional style 16th-century churches and the unusual grain stores.

A network of footpaths crisscross the landscape in the immediate vicinity of the town. Many visitors enjoy a relaxed walk up to the ruined castle and the watchtower. Kazimierz Dolny has also become a popular haunt with actors, writers and painters, particularly during the summer holiday period and at weekends. In the spring, orchards explode into flower all around this town on the Vistula. In June of each year a fair which includes a folk music competition is held in the town.

A short way downstream from Kazimierz Dolny is **Puławy**. This town can also look back on a rich cultural tradition. Towards the end of the 18th century a centre for Polish culture and a focal point for political activity grew up here on the Czartoryski family estate. It was because of these seditious activities that the family's property around Puławy was confiscated by the Czarist authorities, the members of the family forced into exile and the name changed to New Alexandria.

During the time of Izabella Czartoryska (1789–1810), a fabulous palace with English gardens was built alongside the Gothic, Chinese and Alexander pavilions, the Temple of Sibylle and the small Palace of Marynka. The whole complex is well preserved and open to the public (open May–Nov: Tues–Sun, entrance fee).

The medieval town of **Chełm** ㉒, which was famous for many centuries for its chalk industry, lies at the eastern edge of the Lubelszczyzna. The town itself is perched on a 221-metre (722-ft) high chalk hill known as the Chełmska Góra, an easily defensible spot in the Middle Ages. At the highest point stands an impressive group of buildings including a cathedral, bishop's palace, monastery and gate. In order to mine the chalk on a commercial basis during the Middle Ages, a network of lengthy passageways and deep shafts was carved out of the soft stone. This multilevel labyrinth of chalk cellars some 40 km (25 miles) long and 27 metres (89 ft) deep open to the public (Przechodnia; tel: 082 565 25 30, open Mon–Fri 9am–5pm, Sat, Sun 10am–4pm, entrance fee; guided tours available in English or German via advance booking), warm clothing is advised.

To the south of the line connecting Lublin and Chełm is the **Polesie Lubelskie** region. This beautiful tranquil area is covered with woods, meadows and marshland. The variety of flora and fauna is protected by nature reserves and parks, with the most interesting being Jezioro Białe, Krowie Bagno and the Polesie National Park.

KARPATY

Map on page 238

The mountainous Karpaty region is characterised by beautiful scenery, quaint timber houses and rustic churches. Culturally it is one of the best preserved regions in Poland

The outstanding natural beauty of the **Carpathian Mountains** (Karpaty), Europe's largest chain of mountains after the Alps, extends through the whole of southern Poland. The highest range in the Carpathians are the High **Tatras**, reminiscent of the Alps, which adjoin the **Bieszczady** and the Beskidy, characterised by woodlands, lakes and forests. Hiking trails and established tourist facilities make many areas within these mountain chains readily accessible. Meanwhile, fascinating historic towns, including some of Poland's most renowned spas, provide an ideal base from which to explore the surrounding area, and enable you to combine the urban with the rural.

This unique mountain terrain became a series of national parks in the 1920s–30s, to preserve the countryside from any prospect of industrial development. This foresight means that the natural landscape remains virtually unaffected, with rare animal and plant species thriving among its dense woodlands. The clean air, microclimates and mineral-rich spring waters, also provide a natural habitat for health spas (which date from the 18th and 19th centuries). The western region of the Carpathian mountains is readily accessible to tourists, with convenient road and rail connections, and an established tourist infrastructure, including a wide range of hotels, resorts and guesthouses. The eastern region is far less populated, and consequently less developed. This appeals more to hikers who prefer heading off with a rucksack, tent and their own supplies, and who enjoy exploring rugged and beautiful countryside independently.

LEFT: wintertime in the Tatra mountains.
BELOW: typical country house.

Bieszczady National Park

The **Bieszczady**, a region of primeval forest at the southeastern tip of Poland, is one of those rare places in Europe that has scarcely been touched by tourism. The long, gentle slopes, covering a large part of the *powiat* (county) of Krosno, run along the border with Slovakia and the Ukraine. The highest peak here is the **Tarnica** (1,350 metres/4,500 ft). The steppe-like pastures (*połoniny*) are definitely worth exploring, using the extensive network of hiking trails, which do not present any great difficulties, but are quite long and often require considerable stamina.

More than half of this region is thickly wooded. Right in the middle of the mountain area is the Bieszczadzki **Park Narodowy** – a national park that is a haven for brown bears, herds of bison, lynx, wildcat, sparrow hawk, black stork and kingfisher. Even covering the area by car provides panoramic views from the roadside, with the Bieszczady Loop (Pętla Bieszczadzka) winding through the most interesting sections of the foothills, which is one of the most unusual landscapes in Europe.

With an area less than 3,000 hectares (7,413 acres) the Pieniny National Park is one of the smallest in Poland, but it makes up for its lack of size in scenic beauty and its enormous variety of plant species.

Another major attraction in Bieszczady is the **Solina reservoir** (Jezio Soliński). Also known as the Sea of Bieszczady, this lake covers an area of sq km (8 sq miles) and was created in 1968 when a dam was built. Pleas boats cruise the lake, which also has numerous tourist and holiday centres p viding accommodation and leisure activities.

Some of the original inhabitants of these mountains belong to two sm ethnic groups, the Lemkos (*Łemkowie*) and the Boykos (*Bojkowie*), Gre Catholic and Russian-Orthodox respectively. These groups are now a minori as many of the region's current inhabitants were resettled here by the gove ment from other parts of Poland after World War II. Many of the origina Orthodox wooden churches which are typical of the area have now been co verted into Catholic churches. The best known of these is in **Komańcza**.

Beskid Sądecki

Two main rivers, the Poprad and Dunajec, cross the next mountain region wh is known as the **Beskid Sądecki**. Numerous hiking trails – all of them classifi as "easy" and therefore suitable for less experienced hikers – cross the beau ful wooded slopes of the two main mountain ridges: the Radziejowa, whi reaches a height of 1,261 metres (4,186 ft) and the Jaworzyna rising to 1,1 metres (3,677 ft).

Beskid Sądecki is best known for its numerous mineral-rich springs. T water from these streams, considered highly effective in treating stoma kidney and rheumatic complaints, flows down the hillsides into the Riv Poprad, which rises on the southern Slovakian slopes of the Tatra Mountai and then flows through rocks and woods into Poland.

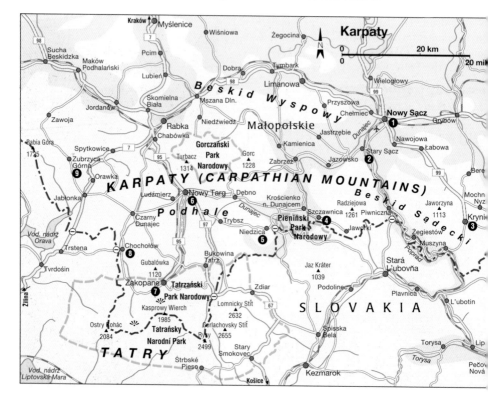

The Beskid Sądecki region is also known for its lively folk traditions. However, the number of mountain villages in which the *Łemkowie* maintain their folk customs in their original form is rapidly diminishing. The foothills of this region are also home to the tiny ethnic group known as the *Lachowie Sądeccy*. The administrative centre for this region is **Nowy Sącz ❶**. Founded in 1292 by the Czech king, Wenceslas II, it developed into a regional centre during the reign of King Kazimierz Wielki (1333–70). The original layout of the town is intact, with some buildings dating from the 15th and 16th centuries. The **Sądeckie Museum** (Lwowska; tel: 018 443 77 08; open Tues–Thurs 9am–3pm, Fri 10am–5.30pm, weekend 9am–2.30pm; entrance fee) contains a collection of folk arts and crafts, as well as Orthodox sacred art. The town has a comfortable hotel, the Beskid (Limanowskiego 1; tel: 081 443 57 70), and a few other guesthouses to choose from.

To the south of Nowy Sącz ("New Sącz") is the small town of **Stary Sącz**, ("Old Sącz") ❷ which dates from the 13th century. The town is linked historically with Kinga, a duchess beatified by the church, who founded a nunnery for the order of St Clare. The fortified convent complex and the town's historic fortifications, as well as several interesting churches, and medieval arcaded townhouses, have survived. With its peaceful setting, mild climate and wealth of cultural events, such as classical concerts in historic churches, and the Annual Festival of Ancient Music, Stary Sącz is thoroughly recommended for a longer stay in the region. Another great attraction is the excursions on the Radziejowa railway into the Poprad valley.

The most historic spa in the Beskidy is the small town of **Krynica ❸**, 45 km (28 miles) to the southeast of Nowy Sącz. This is also one of the most beauti-

Map on page 238

BELOW: farmland in Bieszczady.

ful spas, being surrounded by wooded hills, with various sanatorium facilitie located on the mountain slopes. A cable car (daily in summer) provides acces to the peak of the Góra Parkowa at a height of 741 metres (2,400 ft), from which there are magnificent panoramas and marked trails leading in variou directions. It was during the 18th century that the springs, and the medicina benefits of the waters, were discovered here. The waters continue to be used for drinking and bathing, as well as to treat stomach, intestinal, heart, kidney an respiratory disorders. From the end of the 19th century, Krynica became increas ingly popular as a retreat for famous Polish artists, writers and musicians. On such patient was the world-famous Polish opera singer Jan Kiepura, whose reg ular visits during the 1920s and 1930s helped to boost Krynica's internationa reputation. The renowned naïve artist Nikifor (1895–1968) was born here an continued to work here after World War II.

Touring by car, the region is best explored via the Poprad Loop (Pętl Popradzka), which extends through wonderful scenery from Krynica via th spas of Muszyna, Żegiestów and Piwniczna, all the way back to Stary Sącz. Als worth visiting is the Obrożyska linden tree reserve near Muszyna.

The town of **Szczawnica** ❹, situated on the River Dunajec, between th Pieniny and the Beskid Sądecki mountains, also has a sanatorium. This date from the second half of the 19th century, and specialises in treating respirator complaints, which includes inhalation therapy. The town was regularly visite by the novelist Henryk Sienkiewicz. Fascinating wooden buildings and long standing folk traditions are among the town's other attractions. It is also rec ommended as a base for excursions into the Pieniny, an individual mountai range with a complex geological structure and varied climatic conditions.

BELOW: Topiary Jug in Krynica Park.

Almost the entire mountain range is within the **Pieniny National Park**
ieniński Park Narodowy). The highest peak, **Wysoka**, at 1,000 metres (3,350
, is located in the southern part of the range, and can easily be reached from
czawnica. The route to the peak passes the spectacular gorge known as
ąwóz Homole, which is cut deep into the rock. The mountain peak in the area
at attracts most hikers, however, is **Trzy Korony** or the "Three Crowns",
nich rises to 980 metres (3,200 ft). If you want to reach the summit of Trzy
ɔrony, the best starting point is undoubtedly Krościenko, a picturesque village
ʾ the River Dunajec.

ailing the River Dunajec

raft ride on the River Dunajec, which winds through the dramatically beau-
ul Pieniny gorges, is one of the most popular tourist attractions in Poland. As
ɘ river flows rapidly between steep gorges up to 300 metres (980 ft) high,
.s many sharp turns and a couple of loops, rafting is not for the faint-hearted.
is more dangerous when water levels are higher, but the trips are led by
perienced Góral guides. The two-hour excursion which covers about 15 km
 miles), beginning in **Sromowce Wyżne** and ending in Szczawnica, is an
forgettable experience.
The Pieniny region is divided between Poland and Slovakia, with the border
nning across the top of the mountains and along the Dunajec. Despite the
ggedness of this terrain, it has been a vital route for traders and armies for
nturies. That's why castles and fortresses were built on various hilltops to
ɔtect the route, and to observe any enemy movements. Many ruined castles
d strongholds now provide a poignant reminder of this era.

Map on page 238

BELOW: raft-riding
on the River
Dunajec.

It is a mystery why the Niedzicka museum includes the will of the last Inca ruler, Túpac Amaru. Amaru's daughter Umina married the last owner of the castle, and his will is said to have been discovered within the castle by a descendant, who vanished in mysterious circumstances.

The remains of an ancient fortress known as **Zamek Pieniński** near th summit of Trzy Korony is open to the public. Further west are two 14th-centu castles, **Czorsztyn** and **Niedzica** ❺ (first mentioned in records in 1325 Dunajec Castle), which face one another on opposite sides of the Dunajec. Bo were built on the ruins of pre-Christian fortresses, and were important territo ial markers, frequently occupied by opposing warlords. Czorsztyn is now ruin, while part of Niedzica castle serves as a folk art museum (open Tues–Sun

The **Gorce** and **Beskid Wyspowy** mountain ranges form the region's north ern boundary. Most visitors to this region are experienced mountain-hiker who are undeterred by its remoteness, basic accommodation or the limited roa and rail links.

Podhale

Between Gorce and the Tatra mountains lie the **Podhale** – an area which is great ethnographic and historic interest. The largest town in Podhale is **Now Targ** ❻, a settlement dating from the 13th century. It was traditionally th centre of the entire region, serving as the seat of the royal administration ar judiciary. The town also became famous for its annual country fairs, a traditio that continues today. Additionally, the town market, selling livestock, loc produce and domestic utensils every Thursday, is a principal attraction for loca and visitors. Among the historic buildings, of what is otherwise an unremar able industrial town, are the Church of St Katharina in the town centre, and th small Church of **St Anna** by the town's cemetery, which dates from the 14 century and is thought to have been founded by brigands from the Podha region (presumably trying to salve their conscience).

BELOW: sheep grazing in the Podhale region.

GÓRALS

The Górals (*górale*) are a small ethnic group highlanders, living in the Podhale and Pieniny region Traditionally farmers and shepherds, they speak their ov dialect, and maintain their traditional customs and region costumes – regardless of living among Poles, or, for th matter, the dominant influence of tourism. In fact, as th Górals are a major attraction of the region, tourism actually helping to ensure the continuation of their cultu

A distinctive feature of Góral folk culture is the loc architecture: ornately carved wooden houses ar churches, many of which can be admired in the Tat villages. These traditional houses are often we maintained – one of the greatest ironies of recent Gó culture is that poverty forced generations of them emigrate to the United States, but the money they se back to their relatives was used to preserve the traditior farmhouses they left behind.

In addition to architecture, music and folk dancing a other easily accessible elements of Góral culture, ar there are plenty of opportunities for visitors to enjo performances by Góral choirs, string bands and dan troupes. Some restaurants in Zakopane have regula performances in the evenings.

The sculpture of the Madonna and Child in nearby **Ludźmierz** is revered
throughout Podhale. Every year countless devout Catholics from the Polish and
Slovakian foothills come to Ludźmierz for the festival on 15 August, celebrating the Feast of the Assumption of the Blessed Virgin Mary.
The village of **Dębno**, also near Nowy Targ, is renowned for its beautifully
preserved larchwood church, dedicated to the Archangel Michael. Constructed
during the 15th century using dowels in place of metal nails, the church was decorated with splendid paintings in the early Renaissance style by unknown artists.
Similar paintings can be seen in the churches of **Harklowa** and **Grywald**, but
these are not as well preserved.

Map
on page
238

Zakopane

The small town of **Zakopane** ❼ at the foot of the Tatra mountains was originally a Góral village until it was "discovered" by a Warsaw doctor, Tytus Chałubiński. It became increasingly important in Poland from the 1870s. A growing
number of Polish intellectuals and artists soon began to settle in what was then
a village, drawn by the area's natural and rustic beauty. Moreover, the Górals'
love of freedom and indomitable sense of independence became a source of
inspiration for the entire country, and a symbol for the national struggle against
Prussia, Russia and Austria. Consequently, Zakopane was elevated into a cultural and political centre.
After World War I this small town in the Tatra Mountains continued to be a
meeting point for prominent politicians and artists, many of whom made
Zakopane their permanent home. Elements of Góral culture and folk music also
inspired various artists, such as the composers Karol Szymanowski, Mieczysław

*Typical country
house in the beautiful
Podhale region.*

BELOW:
cow bells for sale in
Zakopane.

Zakopane wooden chapel in Jaszczurówka, designed by the architect Stanisław Witkiewicz.

Karłowicz and Artur Masławski; the writers Jan Kasprowicz, Kornel Makuszyński and Kazimierz Przerwa-Tetmajer, the Dutch pianist Egon Petri and the painter, architect and theoretician Stanisław Witkiewicz (*see page 247*).

Individual museums dedicated to the lives and work of Karol Szymanowski (*see page 111*) Jan Kasprowicz and Kornel Makuszyński have been established in the town. A memorial also stands in the Old Cemetery, honouring many renowned figures who have contributed to public life in Zakopane.

Several artists, such as Stanisław Witkiewicz, built houses in the Zakopane style at the end of the 19th century. This is a synthesis of various types of folk art and was an attempt to integrate elements of local art and architecture with their Polish counterparts. The most beautiful example is the Dom pod Jedlami, built in **Koziniec** in 1897 for the Pawlikowski family. Equally worth seeing the chapel in **Jaszczurówka**, built in 1908.

In Zakopane's **Tatra Museum** (Muzeum Tatrzańskie) there is an important collection of local folk art (Krupówki 10; tel: 018 201 52 05; open Wed–Fri 9am–4.30pm, Sat 9am–5pm, Sun 9am–3pm; entrance fee), while the traditional Góral houses which have survived on Kościeliska street create the unintentional effect of an open-air museum of regional architecture.

Zakopane's reputation as a Bohemian town continues to attract artists, writers and composers, while various cultural events – such as the concerts held in the villa housing the Atma museum – underline the continued importance of art and culture to the locals, as well as visitors. Galleries, such as that run by the famous Polish artist Władysław Hasior, organise regular exhibitions of work by professional artists as well as devoted amateurs. The **Witkacy Theatre** at Chramcówka 15, tel: (018) 200 06 61; www.witkacy.zakopane.pl, has received critical acclaim

d is very popular with visitors – check with the Tourist Offices for details of performances. Zakopane also hosts the annual international **Festival of Highland Folklore** in mid-August, which attracts large crowds.

Map on page 238

The Tatra Mountains

Zakopane is the gateway to one of Poland's greatest natural treasures, the beautiful High Tatry (Tatras) mountain chain, which have established the town as Poland's premier skiing resort. The highest mountains between the Alps and the Caucasus, the High Tatras extend to almost 800 sq km (300 sq miles), part of which is in Poland, while two-thirds are in Slovakia. The highest peak within Poland is the Rysy at 2,499 metres (8,200 ft). The Tatra area is totally enchanting, with alpine scenery and an abundance of attractive water features: streams, waterfalls and lakes, of which the **Morskie Oko** ("Eye of the Sea") is the largest. It can easily be reached by bus from Zakopane, followed by a short walk.

About three million annual visitors, many from western Europe, use the peaks for mountaineering and skiing. The most beautiful spots are connected by an extensive network of hiking trails, which range in difficulty from simple walks to skilful rock climbs. It must not be forgotten that this entire mountain area is part of the Tatra National Park, with its own strict regulations protecting the fauna and flora. If you want to trek in the mountains, it is strongly recommended that you seek the assistance of professional local mountain guides; there is also a volunteer rescue service looking after hikers in case of accidents. You can go skiing in the Tatras in both the summer and the winter, but make sure you take all the necessary precautions and equipment before venturing off, whatever the season, and inform rangers of where you are going.

BELOW: exhibits at the Tatra Museum.

Map on page 238

While you can ski at Zakopane it should be noted that the visitor who com primarily with winter sports in mind will be bitterly disappointed. Lift queue especially for the cable car and funicular up to the main ski areas at **Kasprov Wierch** and **Gubałowka** are horrendous, while the resort's other slopes a spread out around the town and require much walking or bussing around. F more satisfactory are the facilities for ski jumping: five jumps of varyi height are regularly used in international competition, and crowds as the events can be huge.

Besides skiing, ski jumping and hiking Zakopane is an increasingly popul base for other mountain pursuits, such as mountain biking and paraglidin There are now a number of designated biking trails in the resort.

Orawa and Babia Góra

To the north of Zakopane (which can be reached by car or by a four-hour walk) li the extraordinary village of **Chochołów** ❽. The traditional wooden houses a church lining the main street provide some of the finest examples of the Podha region's typical architectural style. A characteristic feature of these houses is t absence of any nails, with pieces of timber skillfully slotted together through joir

From here the road leads on to **Orawa**, the least known of all areas in t foothills. From the gentle hills of this delightful countryside there are wonder views of the nearby Tatra and Beskid Wysoki mountains. As the public transpo system is limited, it is advisable to travel here by car, either from Krakó Katowice or Zakopane. Although this area has only a few places of intere these are certainly special enough (and refreshingly uncrowded) to make t effort worthwhile. Foremost among these is the small holiday village

BELOW: chairlift from Zakopane to Gubalowka.

Orawka, which dates from the 16th century. T exceptional wooden church of St John the Bapti decorated with interesting paintings (including a *b lia pauperum*, an illustration of the Ten Comman ments, on the chancel wall), was built in the 17 century. A little farther on from Orawka is the larg village of **Zubrzyca Górna** ❾, where many wood buildings typical of this region have been preserve

Definitely not to be missed is the **Orawski Pa Etnograficzny** (Orawa Ethnographic Park; op Tues–Sun 9am–3pm during the summer month This is a *skansen* (open-air museum) with rural bui ings from the region, some of which date from t 17th century. This includes an entire farmstead th once belonged to a local mayor, as well as other fa buildings and stalls, each containing original tra tional tools and household objects.

To the northwest of Orawa the mountain of **Ba Góra** rises to a height of 1,725 metres (5,690 ft) number of hiking trails offering varying degrees difficulty lead to the summit, and in clear weather i well worth the climb for the unforgettable and a embracing panorama it offers: of the Tatras, t Beskids, large areas of the foothills and, in t distance, Silesia. If you're tired after the climb w not recover by checking into the mid-market ho Markowe Szczawiny, which is conveniently situat close to the summit.

Witkacy

One personality who is closely linked with Zakopane is Stanisław Ignacy Witkiewicz (1885–1939). Generally known as Witkacy, he was one of the most original exponents of Polish culture, combining the roles of painter, art theoretician, philosopher, writer and dramatist. Although born in Warsaw, Zakopane became the centre of Witkacy's life: his father, Stanisław Witkiewicz, a painter, art critic and creator of the "Zakopane Style", which he applied to architecture and the design of everyday objects, had established himself here.

In 1890, at the age of five, Witkacy made his debut as an artist in the magazine *Przegląd Zakopianski*, and only a few years later his pictures were exhibited in Zakopane for the first time. Brought up to be an artist by his father, he enjoyed the companionship of many of the cultural élite who came to spend their holidays in Zakopane. After the suicide of his fiancée Witkacy fled Zakopane, travelling first to Australia, then to Sri Lanka and on to Russia, where he served as a soldier, surviving World War I. From 1918 he lived permanently in Zakopane, usually staying in one of the guesthouses run by his mother. In 1933, he moved to Witkiewiczówka on Antałówka Hill, and lived in a house built in the Zakopane Style; there are now plans to found a Witkacy Museum here.

Witkacy was a prolific artist. He produced several hundred portraits in his studio, often under the influence of alcohol or hallucinogenic drugs. Even as a young man his paintings were surreal, with visionary and Utopian elements. His early self-portraits reveal carefully chosen colour and psychological depth, but the sharp lines already show signs of the caricature of his later portraits, in which faces were distorted and grotesque.

His *Composition with Three Female Forms* (oil on canvas, 1917–20) is indicative of this development. It is also an example of the way in which he incorporated his impressions of the exotic Tropics and the horrors of the war. Most of his works are exhibited in the museums of Słupsk, Stolp and Warsaw, and in the Tatra Museum in Zakopane. He wrote the majority of his plays in the dramatic surroundings of the Tatra mountains. His major works, including *Mother (Matka)*, *Cobblers (Szewcy)* and *New Deliverance (Nowe Wyzwolenie)*, became popular in the 1960s. In 1925 he founded the Formistic Theatre and put on several productions in Morskie Oko's Eye of the Sea Room, such as *The Madman and the Nuns (Wariat i Zakonnice)* and *New Deliverance (Nowe Wyzwolenie)*. Witkacy was also involved in philosophy and art theory: before World War II he was one of the organisers of the General Vacation University in Zakopane. In conjunction with his belief in "catastrophism", the disintegration of civilisation, the Soviet army's invasion of Poland shocked him into committing suicide.

Witkacy is commemorated in Zakopane cemetery with a symbolic gravestone. The S I. Witkiewicz Theatre on Chramcówki was founded with the aim of producing his plays, so that people can continue to profit from the life and work of this brilliant outsider. ❑

RIGHT: *Composition with Three Female Forms* (1917–20) by Stanisław Witkiewicz.

SILESIA

Silesia offers the beauty of the Sudety Mountains, health resorts, sightseeing and the cosmopolitan city of Wrocław

Long established as the industrial heartland of Poland, Silesia's turbulent history has been dominated by Germany and the Austro-Hungarian Habsburg Empire – a legacy that can be traced throughout the region.

Silesia is thought to have been named after an early Slavic tribe of settlers, the Silings, and was ruled by the Polish Piast dynasty from the 11th century. In the 12th century the region was divided into two duchies: Lower Silesia, governed by Duke Bolesław, while Duke Mieszko controlled Upper Silesia. This historic division has remained, with Lower Silesia was surrounding the city of Wrocław in the northwest, and Upper Silesia, which includes Katowice, in the southeast.

As Silesia prospered during the 13th century, the population also began to diversify, with many new towns and villages principally settled by Germans. Moreover, the death of Bolesław III in 1348 brought the Piast's rule to an end, and Silesia became part of Bohemia. From 1526 Silesia was ruled by Ferdinand I, and remained a part of the Habsburg empire for 200 years. The Silesian wars of 1740–63 resulted in Frederick the Great annexing Lower Silesia and much of Upper Silesia, leaving only part of Upper Silesia under Habsburg rule.

Following World War I, the Treaty of Versailles incorporated a small area of Silesia within Czechoslovakia, and the rest was divided between Poland and Germany in 1921. After World War II Silesia was returned to Poland, after an absence of 600 years. The German population was replaced by those Poles who had been forced to leave the eastern areas of Poland, which had become part of the Ukraine.

Silesia's industrial prowess is, inevitably, an aspect of the region's heritage and character, with various museums depicting the evolution of key industries such as mining and steelworks. However, the region also has numerous attractions which can be visited without going anywhere near an industrial unit.

Wrocław is a fascinating and dynamic city, the Jasna Góra monastery in Częstochowa is Poland's holiest shrine, while the Beskid mountains, part of the Carpathian mountain range, provide endless vistas of outstanding natural beauty.　　❏

PRECEDING PAGES: the Cistercian monastery in Krzeszów.
LEFT: only a few masters of the art of instrument making remain in Poland.

UPPER SILESIA AND KATOWICE

Map on page 254

*In the country's industrial centre, coal and steel
production have shaped the landscape
and its people for centuries*

Warsaw

Katowice

Upper Silesia is the industrial heartland of Poland, offering "attractions"
such as museums of mining or weaving – even industrial towns yield
architectural and cultural gems. The surrounding countryside offers enor-
ous natural beauty, as well as historic towns and villages. During the Middle
ges, Silesia was a gold mining centre. However, the economic policies of
ederick the Great encouraged the mining of coal and iron ore, which led to the
onstruction of iron and steel works. Industrialisation in Silesia made rapid
rides. By the turn of the 19th century, it was a major competitor to the great
dustrial areas beside the Rhine and the Ruhr.

Upper Silesia's main natural resource is hard coal extracted in more than 50
ines. The Katowice steel works are the largest in Poland, while the iron, chem-
al and automobile industries are also major factors. In fact, it's a way of life.
f the region's 2½ million inhabitants almost one million are employed in indus-
al concerns. With such a large population concentrated into a relatively small
ea, many cities have merged to form conurbations. The heavy industry located
tween Gliwice and Dąbrowa Górnicza created a serious pollution problem
hich culminated in it being declared a disaster area in the 1980s. The main rea-
n for this was the Communist regime's planning policies, or rather lack of
anning. Heavy industry was seen as the key to eco-
mic prosperity, which entailed misusing natural
sources and ignoring environmental consequences.
nce the Communist government was out of office, a
ajor clean-up began, with environmentally harmful
d unprofitable factories closed down, while modern
chnology was also introduced to prevent damaging
nissions. An added impetus was the Polish govern-
ent's determination to meet the environmental criteria
tablished as a pre-condition for joining the EU.

LEFT: evening in the Jura mountains.
BELOW: willow trees.

atowice

e capital of Upper Silesia (Górny Śląsk) and centre
the Upper Silesian industrial belt, **Katowice ❶**,
e administrative seat of Śląskie voivodship, is also
scientific and cultural centre. With a population of
0,000, Katowice was once a typical 19th-century
dustrial town, but now embraces some 70 small
wns scattered across the southern highlands. The
dest of them, Bogucice and Dąb, were founded in
e 13th and 14th centuries.

Urbanisation began in the 1860s and for this reason
ere are numerous examples of Revivalism, Art
ouveau and Modernism in the town's architecture;
e theatre and the railway station in particular. Most
the churches date from around the turn of the cenry and were designed in the neo-Romanesque or
o-Gothic styles that were popular at the time.

One particularly striking example of the ecclesiastical style that prevail between the two world wars is the basilica of the Cathedral of Christ the Ki by Xavery Dunikowski. The sandstone structure is the largest 20th-centu church in Poland. The Council Offices, representative of the secular architectu of this period, were a showpiece for Upper Silesia in the inter-war years.

Close by is a Monument to the Silesian Insurgents, commemorating the inha itants who fought against the Germans in the uprisings of 1919–21 for Sile: to join the newly independent Poland. After World War I it required thr uprisings and a plebiscite before Katowice finally joined Poland. Nearby i giant sports and entertainment complex, the Wojewodzka Hala Widowiskow Sportowa, known locally as "the saucer" because of its shape. By the Marl Square is the **Museum of Silesia** (Muzeum Śląskie; al. Korfantego 3; op Tues–Fri 10am–5pm, weekend 11am–5pm; entrance fee; tel: 032 258 56 6 www.muzeumslaskie.pl). The collection of art and sculpture includes a secti devoted to the works of Jan Matejko, Mojżesz Kisling, Jerzy Nowosielski a other 19th- and 20th-century artists. Among the exhibits at the **Archdioces: Museum** (Wita Stwosza 16; tel: 032 251 67 03; open Tues–Thurs 2–6pm, S 2–5pm; entrance fee) is an impressive collection of carved Madonnas. Al worth visiting is the Katowice History Museum (Muzeum Historii Katow ul. Szafranka 9; open Tues–Fri 10am–5.30pm, Sat, Sun 11am–2pm; entran fee; tel: 032 256 1870) it includes a full and thorough exhibition of the city's h tory. On the edge of the city is the Culture and Leisure Park, including a spo stadium, planetarium and observatory, and the Upper Silesian Ethnograpł Park (open Tues–Sun; closed Mon and Sat; entrance fee), showing examples local wooden buildings.

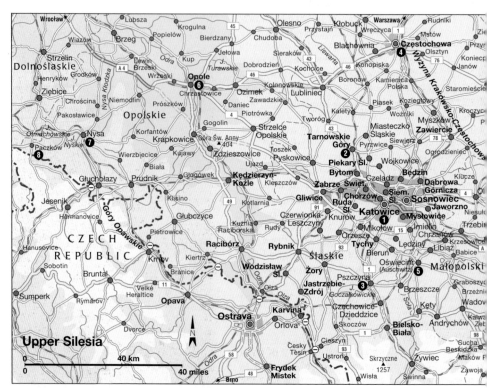

istory and industry

Bytom, 12 km (7 miles) north of Katowice, the Muzeum Górnośląskie
1useum of Upper Silesia; Pl Jana III Sobieskiego 2; open Wed 10am–6pm,
urs–Fri 10am–3pm, Sat–Sun 11am–3pm, entrance fee; tel: 032 281 82 94) has
interesting collection of Polish and European painting, as well as folk arts and
fts, and discoveries from archaeological digs in the region. The town is also
me to the Silesian Opera. A little further north is the mining town of
rnowskie Góry ❷ which developed after rich deposits of silver and lead
re discovered in the area during the 13th century. While this form of mining
ded in the 1920s, the ancient mine in the Bobrowiki district is a great tourist
raction, where you can follow a 1,500-metre (5,000-ft) long trail through
ambers and galleries, at a depth of 40 metres (130 ft). Trolleys and tools have
en deliberately left in place show to help conjure up the working atmosphere,
th guides explaining the history of mining during escorted tours. The huge sil-
r chamber is of particular interest. Another extraordinary attraction in this
ning complex is the so-called Black Trout Gallery, a canal around 30 metres
)0 ft) below ground level, bored out of dolomite rock. A boat takes you across
: 600-metre (1,960-ft) wide canal, which separates two mine shafts.

Map
on page
254

TIP

A more colourful
aspect of the mining
tradition in Tarnowskie
Góry is the annual
Miner's Day Festival in
September.

The regional museum also details the history of mining in the area. The first
am-driven engine in Europe went into operation in the town in 1788, which
o explains why there is a *skansen* (open-air museum) of steam engines.

Gliwice, one of Upper Silesia's oldest towns, has a significant place in the out-
ak of World War II. In 1939 Hitler accused the Poles of attacking a
rman radio station in the town and used this as a pretext for invading Poland. The
ack had, in fact, been carried out by SS troops. The main points of interest in the
ll-preserved medieval town are the Gothic All Saints
ish Church, the neoclassical Town Hall surrounded
restored townhouses, and the Piast Palace Museum.

Będzin is situated on the border between Silesia and
tle Poland (Małopolska). In the 14th century it occu-
d a key position in the new Polish state's defensive
tem. The neo-Gothic Piast Palace, originally 13th-
atury, is now a museum with archaeological and folk
s and crafts, as well as military exhibits. The indus-
l town of Dąbrowa Górnicza, east of Będzin, has
largest iron and steel works in Poland, known as
"Katowice", which began operating in 1976. This
laced the traditional local industry, the mining of
cious metal ores, which ceased at the beginning of
19th century. These tunnels and the Ore Mining
seum at Czarny Pstrąg are now a tourist attraction.
ince the 15th century **Piekary Śląskie** has been a
ine for Catholic pilgrims, and since the 17th century
has been focused on a painting of the Virgin Mary
iekary. The painting's miraculous powers were said
eal people from the Black Death. The last Sunday in
y sees the largest influx of pilgrims, worshipping in
19th-century basilica situated on Cerekwica Hill.

BELOW: a carpenter
works on a house
in a *skansen* (open
air museum).

ning and spa towns

rth of the Silesian highlands is the region of Ryb-
ki Okręg Węglowy, where **Jastrzębie-Zdrój** has
n a spa town since 1861. However, it is also the

site of a large modern coal mining centre, and the mass strikes held here in 19
– together with strikes in Gdańsk and Szczecin – led to the founding of the S
idarity trade union movement *(see page 63)*. Between Katowice and Bielsk
Biała, adjacent to a woodland region, lies the medieval town of **Pszczyna**
Until 1945 Pszczyna Palace was the seat of the Hochberg-Fürstenstein fami
although it was originally constructed for the Piast dynasty, who made the to
the capital of their Duchy. It was refashioned from the original Gothic into
exquisite, highly decorative neoclassical style during the late 19th century by
renowned French architect Hippolyte Destailleur. It is now a Museum of Inte
ors (open Mon 11am–3pm, Tues 10am–3pm, Wed–Fri 9am–5pm, Sat, S
10am–5pm, closed Mon Oct–Apr; entrance fee; tel: 032 210 30 37; www.zame
pszczyna.pl) with a superb collection of decorative arts and furniture from
Renaissance to the 20th century. Concerts of chamber music composed by the f
mer court bandmaster Philipp Telemann, a resident of the town from 1704–8,
held in the Hall of Mirrors. The palace is surrounded by one of Silesia's m
attractive and largest parks, totalling 44 hectares (109 acres). Laid out in an En
lish style, the park is traversed by the River Pszczynka. Interiors at the other e
of the scale, though nonetheless beautiful, can be seen at the Pszczyna Village a
Farm *Skansen (*Zagroda Wsi Pszczyńskiej ul Parkowa; open Tues–Sun 10a
3pm; entrance fee; tel: 032 212 99 99).

To the Black Madonna

Częstochowa ❹, in the Wyżyna (Jura) Krakowsko-Częstochowska region, p
of the Małopolska upland, is a major industrial centre concentrating on metallur
textiles and chemicals, although the city is much better known for the **Jas**

óra Monastery (open daily 9am–5pm, until 4pm Nov–Feb; entrance fee). This is the most important Catholic shrine in Poland for the cult of the Virgin Mary. Pilgrims arrive here throughout the year from around the world, including those who walk from Warsaw, particularly on 15 August, the Feast of the Assumption of the Virgin Mary, and 26 August, the feast day of the Blessed Virgin Mary of Częstochowa. The object of veneration is a painting of the so-called Black Madonna, a miraculous icon of the Blessed Virgin Mary holding the infant Jesus.

This medieval Byzantine icon is believed to be a copy of a painting by St Luke, made on a piece of wood which came from the table on which the Holy family ate. Originating in the Ukraine, the icon was brought to Silesia by Pauline monks led by Prince Władysław of Opole in 1382, and in whose care the icon remained. The prince ordered that the icon be kept in a church and monastery constructed on a limestone hill above the town.

This resulted in a fortified 14th-century monastic complex, extended in the 15th and 17th centuries, which is now one of Poland's most important sacred buildings. The monastery even withstood a heavy siege during the Swedish invasions in the 17th century. When the Swedes inexplicably retreated from the monastery and were subsequently driven from the country, the cult of the Virgin Mary was intensified even further. King Jan Kazimierz laid his crown before the icon and officially declared the Virgin Mary as Queen of Poland. The icon is hung above an early Baroque altar made of ebony and silver in the beautiful Chapel of the Virgin Mary of Częstochowa, which is high Baroque. It is uncovered every day before the first mass and covered again at midday. A poignant showcase in the chapel features walking sticks, crutches and other medical items left behind by people who have been miraculously cured here.

Map on page 254

BELOW: holding mass in Częstochowa with the Black Madonna above the altar.

The basilica is equally magnificent, with priceless votive offerings from several Polish kings exhibited in the treasury. The armoury includes rare weapons and suits of armour including Middle Eastern examples, which Jan III Sobieski brought back with him after his victory over the Turks at Vienna. The library contains numerous rare tomes, illuminated manuscripts and liturgical works. Other rooms which can be visited include the refectory, with its extraordinarily beautiful vaulted ceiling painted with religious scenes.

The **Muzeum Okręgowe** (al. NMP 45; open Tues–Sun 10am–5.30pm; entrance fee; tel: 034 361 50 08) is housed in the Town Hall. Detailing the history of the Częstochowa region, the collection also includes local folk arts and crafts.

The **Jura Krakowsko-Częstochowska** , a rocky area running from Częstochowa to Kraków close to the border between Upper Silesia and Little Poland (Małopolska), is now a popular holiday region. The natural beauty, characterised by caves, wild gorges, gentle valleys and variegated woodland, is the attraction. The highest point is the Podzamcze Ogrodzienieckie at 500 metres (1,650 ft). In the Middle Ages this border area was defended by a series of imposing castles and fortresses, known as eagle's lairs because of their inaccessibility. Ruins of these old castles can still be seen today along the Eagle Lair Route which starts with the Wawel in Kraków *(see page 216)* and finishes with Jasnógorski Castle in Częstochowa. Near Olsztyn beside the Eagle's Lair Route are the ruins of a castle built by Kazimierz the Great, which was badly damaged by the Swedes in 1655. Not far away, in **Potok Złoty**, is a palace formerly owned by the Raczyński family, and a manor house where the romantic poet Zygmunt Krasiński (1812–59) worked. In Mirów and Bobolice further castle ruins testify to the eventful history of this region.

BELOW: Auschwitz.

Certainly worth a short detour are the ruins of Ogrodzieniec Palace, just to the south of **Zawiercie**. The palace was so sumptuously furnished by its owner, a wealthy merchant by the name of Boner, that it even rivalled the opulence of Kraków's Wawel. The oldest building in the Jura Krakowsko-Częstochowska is the small Romanesque Church of St John the Baptist, near Siewierz.

Auschwitz (Oświęcim)

Located on the border between Silesia and Małopolska, where the River Sola flows into the Vistula, Oświęcim ❺ was the site of a 12th-century castle. In 1317 it became the capital of an independent principality, incorporated into Poland in 1457. In 1772, under the First Polish Partition, the town was ceded to the Habsburg Empire. It is now an industrial centre but will always be synonymous with the Holocaust.

Begun in 1940, Auschwitz-Birkenau was the largest Nazi camp complex, with two camps covering an area of 40 sq km (15 sq miles). Auschwitz was a slave-labour camp, largely reserved for political prisoners, members of the resistance and other "opponents" to the Nazi regime, while a second camp, Birkenau, was an extermination camp. A total of 1.5 million prisoners of 23 nationalities lost their lives here, brought by train from all over Europe. At the end of the unloading ramp new arrivals were divided into those capable of work, and hose to be taken straight to the gas chambers. The great majority of the victims were European Jews, together with Poles, Russians and gypsies, who were forced o endure inhuman conditions. Many died as a result of slave labour, hunger, illness and torture, while the genocide reached a peak in 1942 with up to 24,000 people being murdered every day in the gas chambers. The corpses were burned in crematoria and then buried in mass graves. In 1944 the Nazis began destroying the crematoria and some of the camp buildings before retreating, but they did not have enough time to destroy the gas chambers. The camp was liberated by the Red Army in 1945. In 1947 Auschwitz-Birkenau was established as a **National Museum of Martyrology** (ul. Więźniów Oświęcimia 20; open daily Oct–May 8am–5pm; June–Sept 8am–6pm; entrance fee; tel: 033 844 80 00; www.auschwitz.org.pl). Visitors are taken on a guided tour of the camp – children under the age of 13 are not admitted. One of the films shown was taken by troops who liberated the camp in 1945. Other film footage and photos from the camp's archives can also be seen, while the museum depicts the struggle and martyrdom of daily life, with heart-breaking exhibits such as piles of spectacles and shoes belonging to the victims. A monument to the Victims of Auschwitz was unveiled in the grounds of the camp in Birkenau.

Auschwitz concentration camp flag.

Around Bielsko-Biała

Situated by the River Skawa on the way to Wadowice *(see page 216)* is the town of **Zator**, which until 1494 was ruled by Silesian princes and subsequently became part of the Polish Republic. Places of interest are the Old Town walls, the Gothic Church of St George and a palace in an eclectic style but with numerous neo-Gothic features. An important place of pilgrimage in southern Poland is the small

BELOW: Auschwitz camp gate with the inscription *"Arbeit Macht Frei"* ("Work Makes You Free").

TIP

Within easy reach of Wisła are two centres of Beskid folk arts and crafts. Koniaków and Istebna are both renowned for lace-making, and Istebna also has a museum of sacred art, housed in an 18th-century church.

BELOW: hiking in the Karkonosze mountains.

town of Kalwaria Zebrzydowska. Up in the Wadowice Hills is the historic and renowned "Way of the Cross" (Road to Calvary). The route culminates at the Bernardine Monastery's Baroque Church of Our Lady of the Angels. This hill is a setting for performances of a Passion play in Holy Week, leading up to Easter.

The West Beskid Mountains, in the Polish Carpathians, form the southern boundary of Upper Silesia, which includes the towns of Beskid Śląski, Beskid Mały, Beskid Żywiecki and Beskid Makowski. The capital of the region is **Bielsko-Biała**, where the most impressive buildings are the 14th-century Gothic St Stanislaus' Church (Kościół Św. Stanisława), and the 17th-century wooden church St Barbara's Church (Kościół Św. Barbary). Dom Tkacza (Sobieskiego 51; tel: 033 811 71 76; open Tues–Wed 9am–5pm, Thurs 10am–6pm, Fri–Sat 10am– 3pm, Sun 10am–4pm; entrance fee) is a reconstructed weaver's house furnished in a 17th-century manner; the Museum of Textile Technology (Muzeum Techniki Włokienniczej) reflects the town's traditional status within the Polish textile industry (Sukiennicza 7; tel: 033 812 23 67; open Tues–Wed 9am–3pm, Thur 10am–5pm, Fri 10am–6pm, Sat 10am–3pm, Sun 10am–4pm; entrance fee).

South of Bielsko-Biała is **Szczyrk**, Poland's second most popular ski resort after Zakopane *(see page 243)*. Located at the foot of the Skrzyczne (1,257 metres/4,122 ft), this is the destination for some 30,000 winter sports enthusiasts every year. A chairlift takes skiers to the Czantoria mountain station at 854 metres (2,800 ft). The sources of the Czarna and the Biała Wisełka meet in Czarne and continue as the longest river in Poland, the Vistula. Wisła and Ustroń, two other popular holiday resorts, can be reached via the Salmopolska Pass (934 metres/3,063 ft). An abundance of minerals in the spring water has led to the establishment of several spas in this district.

Near the border with the Czech Republic, on the banks of the Olza, is the historic town of **Cieszyn**. From 1282 to 1653 it was the capital of a duchy owned by the Silesian Piasts, which has left a rich architectural legacy, including the Piasts late 13th-century tower. The Chapel of St Nicholas is one of Poland's few remaining Romanesque rotundas, and there are several other medieval and Baroque churches to see. The Market Square features a Renaissance Town Hall and fine burghers' houses of the same period, while early 16th-century fragments of the town walls can be seen on Przykopa.

Map on page 254

The Silesian Lowlands

Further to the west, beside the gently flowing Odra, are the fertile Silesian Lowlands, which become hillier further south. The climate is perfect for agriculture and the area continues to attract holiday-makers keen on outdoor pursuits.

Bordering the Upper Silesian industrial area to the west are the **St Anna mountains** (Góra Św Anny), which reach a height of 404 metres (1,325 ft). Mount St Anna was the site of a fierce battle between Polish insurgents and the German army in 1921. This mountain lies at the heart of the German-speaking region and mass is usually conducted in two languages. The village of Góra Św. Anny, situated on the Chelmer Ridge, has been the centre of the cult of St Anna since the beginning of the 17th century. A Franciscan monastic complex built here in the mid-18th century includes no less than 37 chapels, two devotional churches and the Basilica of St Anna. A Renaissance figure of St Anna with the Madonna and Child, can be seen in the parish church.

Opole ⑥ was initially a fortified settlement inhabited by the Opolanie tribe, and the town was established on the River Oder in the 13th century; it soon

BELOW: the marketplace in Opole.

Map
on page
254

TIP

Every year in the third week of June Opole is flooded with visitors who come here to enjoy the Festival of Polish Songs.

BELOW: glass worker in the Karkonosze mountains.

became the capital of the Opole principality. Reminders of the past include the massive Piast Tower, part of the former castle of the Opole princes. Other elements of the town's fortifications include fragments of the town wall, and a bastion. The town centre, on the banks of the Młynówka Canal, has retained a delightful Renaissance atmosphere. The Town Hall in the Market Square has a distinguished Italianate character, which isn't surprising as it was intended to be a copy of the Palazzo Vecchio in Florence. The surrounding buildings combine Gothic, Renaissance and Baroque elements. However, it is the town's sacral buildings which are the most impressive. The Gothic Church of the Holy Cross (now the cathedral) dates from the 15th century, while the 14th-century Franciscan Monastery complex includes a church with the St Anna Chapel, also known as the Piast Chapel, where the Piast princes of Opole were buried.

The road to Wrocław *(see page 267)* leads past the Opole Village Museum, a *skansen* displaying farm buildings from the Opole region, including cottages, windmills, a forge and granaries from the 17th century.

Towards the Góry Opawskie

Nysa ❼, to the southwest of Opole on the Nysa Kłodzka River, was the capital of Wrocław's bishops for several hundred years until 1820, with its most prosperous period during the 16th and 17th centuries when it was a centre of handicrafts. When the Red Army "liberated" the town in March 1945, around 80 percent of it was destroyed in the process. The town's original fortifications, comprising 28 bastions and four towers, were reduced to a couple of 14th- and 15th-century town gates and a fragment of the town wall. The postwar expansion followed the opening of a factory producing pick-up trucks. The town's sacred buildings are well worth seeing, with the **Church of St Jacob** in the town centre a wonderful example of Gothic architecture, with numerous Gothic, Renaissance and Baroque sculptures. Comprising three naves, 19 chapels, three porches and a belfry (added in the 16th century), the monumental proportions are impressive considering it was built in the 13th century. The Church of SS Peter and Paul, built in the 1720s, contains one of finest Baroque interiors in Silesia. The man-made Nysa Lake to the west of town provides various watersports.

A few miles further west, at the foot of the Gold Mountains, is **Paczków ❽**, a town popularly known as "Poland's Carcassonne" because of its perfectly preserved medieval fortifications, comprising stone defensive walls, 18 turrets and four city gates. In the market square is the fortified Church of St John, a massive triple-naved Gothic church with a carved portal adorning the west wall and an ornamental Renaissance attic. The Renaissance altar is a work of art, with the interiors also featuring Gothic sculptures. The surrounding burghers' houses provide fine examples of various architectural genres. Up in the Góry Opawskie hills beside the border lie some picturesque little towns such as the historic spa **Głuchołazy**. In the market square stands a linden tree surrounded by burghers' houses. The town's other impressive features are the Baroque twin-towered Church of St Lawrence and the Lower Gate Tower, part of the original defensive system. q

Teutonic Knights

The Order of St Mary of the Germans in Jerusalem was the last of the religious-military orders. It was founded in 1198 as part of the Hohenstaufen emperors' crusades and employed as an auxiliary force against infidel armies. It won territory in Palestine, Greece, Italy and Germany.

The order greatly expanded its power base under the fourth Grand Master, Hermann von Salza, when the Teutonic Knights began expanding in central Europe with the backing of German overlords. In 1211, the knights defeated the Cumans in Transylvania but when they became too powerful for the Hungarian king they were expelled. In 1226 Duke Konrad of Mazovia employed the knights in his struggles with the Prussians, a pagan tribe that repeatedly invaded and laid waste to the north of the dukedom. Konrad gave the knights land north of Toruń in exchange for their protection and the conversion to Christianity of the Prussians.

The duke wanted to retain sovereignty over the land he entrusted to the knights, but the agreement turned sour. The conflict between Germans and Poles would continue for 250 years. Instead of being converted, the native Prussians were simply wiped out and their names passed to their exterminators. Bismarck's Prussians were in fact descendants of the people who had eliminated the original tribe and whose ethnic origin was quite different.

One important element was the signing of the "Golden Bull of Rimini", ratified in 1226, which allowed Emperor Friedrich II to call upon the knights in any lands that he had conquered. This papal edict encouraged him to extend his empire further, and the knights captured regions around the Baltic. In 1308, the order won control of the region around Gdańsk and moved its headquarters to the castle at Marienburg, now Malbork.

At the head of the knights' hierarchy was a Grand Master, elected for life, who had five regional commanders-in-chief. The dioceses were led by knight-priests. Knights and priests had equal status, but they were all sworn to obedience, poverty and chastity. The white cloak with the black cross became the knights' uniform. The achievements of the Teutonic Order can be attributed to their expansionist policies, cultivation of farmland and the resettlement of Germans. This was underpinned by an efficient bureaucracy and the cities it controlled in the Hanseatic League such as Gdańsk, Toruń and Königsberg, which traded cereals, timber and amber. This wealth encouraged architects and craftsmen – Pomerania and Mazuria have magnificent castles and churches from this period.

After the unification of Poland and Lithuania the order started to decline and the rivalry came to a head in the Battle of Grunwald in 1410. The order's Grand Master, Ulrich von Jungingen, died in the battle. Under the Second Peace of Toruń of 1466 the knights ceded Gdańsk and Malbork to the Poles. Marienburg Castle was captured in 1457 and their headquarters moved to Königsberg.

The order was finally dissolved in Germany by Napoleon. The surviving branch of the order has headquarters in Vienna. ❑

RIGHT: the gates of Malbork Castle.

POLAND'S LIQUID ASSETS

Spa towns throughout Poland specialise in treating specific illnesses and provide a wide range of reviving and relaxing treatments

The earliest Polish health spas were established in the 12th century and entered a golden age during the 18th and 19th centuries when it was fashionable for high society from France, Germany, Austria and the United States, to "take the waters" and mingle.

Today there are more than 40 spas in Poland, offering a range of treatments including mud baths, inhalations, hydrotherapy, kinetic therapy, and of course drinking mineral water, with each spa's water having its own mineral profile. Individual spas specialising in treating specific illnesses include Połczyn Zdrój, renowned for treating rheumatism, and Ciechocinek, the first choice for curative baths in the treatment of respiratory illnesses. The range of resort locations also means that spas can be chosen on the basis of their setting and surrounding attractions, as well as their range of facilities. On the Baltic Coast for example, there is a clinic in Sopot, while the largest spa on the coast is in Kołobrzeg.

There are a few spas in central Poland such as Inowrocław and Nałęczów, while the greatest concentration of spas is in the south, along the Carpathian mountain range.

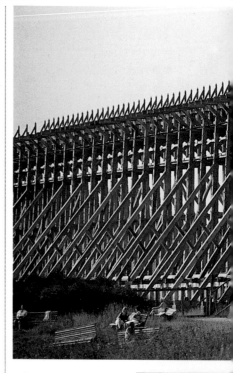

△ **SALT WONDER WORKS**
Ciechocinek's amazing salt-filtering graduation towers extend to a total of 1,750 metres (5,741 ft) with the earliest tower dating from 1824.

▷ **TAKING THE WATERS**
Mineral waters smell worse than they taste. The traditional way to "take the waters" is to drink from a porcelain tankard while walking slowly.

HEALTH FROM A BOTTLE

Each spa resort has a water source with a different mineral profile. Some spas such as Kudowa Zdrój in the south of Poland have three separate water sources, each offering variations on the theme, including hydrocarbon-calcium-soda, chalybeate and boron, which is quite a mouthful in more ways than one. Numerous spas also bottle and distribute their waters throughout Poland. Ciechocinek for example has been bottling the Krystynka brand since 1903, and the Kujawianka brand since 1962. Similarly, the Kołobrzeg spa markets the Perła Bałtyku (Pearl of the Baltic) mineral water, while Polanica Zdrój is the source of Staropolanka (Old Polish). Other spas market mineral water under their own name, such as Kryniczanka, bottled since 1808 in the spa town of Krynica.

CURATIVE EFFECTS
In the past, the saline mist produced during the filtration process was inhaled by respiratory patients walking through the tower for its high level of iodine.

△ **SWIMMING POOL**
In between Ciechocinek's towers is a natural salt water swimming pool, also used as part of a range of treatments.

◁ **SEASIDE SPA**
The clinic at the delightful 19th-century seaside town of Sopot is perfectly located right by the sandy beach and the pier.

▷ **HAND PUMP**
The traditional way of filling your glass, the old fashioned hand-pump, is a feature of some Polish spa towns – many are still in working order although some are purely decorative.

WROCŁAW AND LOWER SILESIA

Maps
City: 268
Area: 274

Wrocław's long and turbulent history provides a packed sightseeing itinerary which contrasts with the relaxed scenic beauty of the surrounding Lower Silesian countryside

he most important city in Silesia and capital of Dolnośląskie voivodship, Wrocław is characterised by broad thoroughfares and imposing buildings, which are handsome and robust rather than beautiful. And despite the city's varied architecture, with definitive examples of every genre, there is a distinct sense of harmony. This is not due to some master plan, but to their character: big, old and beckoning. The buildings merit closer examination. Arriving in Wrocław by train means you get the picture straight away. The railway station's late 19th-century neo-Gothic white stucco building, with various gables, turrets and castellations, houses a main hall that is 200 metres (650 ft) long. But then it was built as one of the largest stations in Central and Eastern Europe. And yet, even within the city it is easy to escape, with quiet walks through parks or riverside greenery, and around the city's islets, linked by small bridges.

Changing rulers and artistic heyday

Wrocław's location, close to the borders with both Germany and the Czech Republic, is one reason why the city frequently changed hands, and nationalities, during its long history. Wrocław dates from the 9th century, with the earliest settlement established on small islands within the River Odra by a Slavonic tribe called the Ślężanie. This settlement was already recorded in the 9th century by the so-called "Bavarian Geographer". During the 10th century this developed into a Slavic trading post, benefiting from its advantageous position on the routes between western Europe and Russia and between the Baltic and Mediterranean. Briefly taken over by a 10th-century Bohemian prince called Wrotisłav, after whom the city takes its name, the Piast prince who became the Polish Duke Mieszko I incorporated Silesia into Poland in AD 990. In the year 1000 the first Silesian episcopal seat was founded in Wrocław. The town recovered quickly from the Tartar invasion in 1241, and in 1259 became the capital of Piast dukedom. After joining the Hanseatic League, Wrocław prospered during the 14th and 15th centuries under Bohemian and then Austrian rule, developing into one of Central and Eastern Europe's largest cities.

The city's architecture reflects its varied rulers. Romanesque dominated during the Piast era, with Gothic established by the Bohemians, which includes the late-Gothic town hall. The Austrian Habsburg dynasty ruled during the Baroque, with Silesia coming under 200 years of Prussian rule during the partitions of Poland, and becoming part of Germany between the two world wars. During this period the artist Adolph von Menzel (1815–1905) and Ferdinand Lassalle (1825–64), the founder of social democracy, lived in Breslau, the German name for Wrocław.

LEFT: ornately decorated house in Wrocław's market square.
BELOW: statue of Alexander Fredro.

An industrial centre

In 1939, with a population of 700,000, **Wrocław ❶** was one of the Third Reich's largest cities. However, 75 percent of the town, including many historic buildings and monuments, were destroyed during World War II, with a massive rebuilding programme beginning in May 1945 within days of the Polish authorities regaining control of the city. Having expelled the German population, the city was resettled by Poles from Polish territories which had, in turn, been lost to the Ukraine. With a current population of 640,000, Wrocław is now Poland's fourth largest city, with the university one of Poland's most historic and prestigious. Together with ten further education colleges this also ensures a high youth quota, and the inevitable accompaniment of student and alternative cultures. Meanwhile the city's cultural events include the annual Festival of Polish Contemporary Music (February), Jazz on the Odra festival (May), and the Festival of Modern Polish Plays (June).

Ostrów Tumski

During the 9th century, the earliest settlement was established on what is now **Cathedral Island** (Ostrów Tumski). Around 1000 the episcopal church was built here and, until the Tartar attack of 1241, this was also the site of the Piast dukes' original residence. Ostrów Tumski continues to be the city's spiritual centre, with several churches, and although it ceased technically to be an island after a tributary of the River Oder was filled in during the 19th century, Ostrów Tumski continues to feel isolated from the bustle of the city. An evening stroll is particularly delightful, with gas lamps still lit to illuminate the views.

The **Cathedral of St John the Baptist ❹** (Katedra Św. Jana Chrzciciela

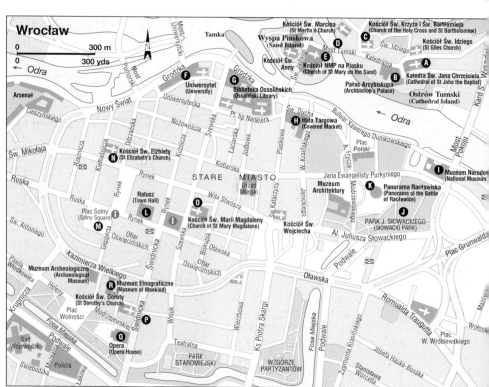

pen daily10am–3pm), dating from the 13th century, is the largest and most important church on Ostrów Tumski. The three chapels in the ambulatory provide contrasting styles: the Italianate Baroque of St Elizabeth's; the Gothic chapel of Our Lady Mary; and the Duke's Chapel, designed by the Viennese master architect Fischer von Erlach. Other outstanding features include an impressive Renaissance stone portal, a triple-winged altarpiece dating from 1522, and an alabaster pulpit.

To the right of the cathedral's main portal stands the neoclassical **Archbishop's Palace** ❸ (Pałac Arcybiskupa), now the home of the Papal Institute of Theology. It is the first in a series of historic buildings along Katedralna ("Cathedral street"). The archbishop now resides at Number 11 Katedralna. The second largest church on Ostrów Tumski is the Gothic **Church of the Holy Cross and St Bartholomew** ❹ (Kościół Św. Krzyża i Św. Bartłomieja; open daily), also an architectural rarity. The building actually comprises two churches. The elegantly appointed Gothic Church of the Holy Cross (Kościół Św. Krzyża) on the ground floor. Meanwhile, the crypt houses the Greek-Catholic (Uniate) Church of St Bartholomew, which is the final resting place for two of Wrocław's most renowned bishops, Nanker and Lubusz.

The impressive **Cathedral Bridge** ❹ (Most Tumski) was constructed from iron in 1889. The bridge displays figures of St Hedwig and John the Baptist and links Ostrów Tumski with the **Sand Island** (Wyspa Piaskowa).

Wypsa Piaskowa is dominated by the Gothic **Church of St Mary on the Sand** ❺ (Kościół nmp na Piasku; open daily). Built over a 12th-century Romanesque chapel, this lofty edifice has an interesting 16th-century icon of the Blessed Virgin Mary in the north aisle, originating from east Poland.

Maps
City: 268
Area: 274

Cathedral Bridge was constructed at the end of the 19th century. It joins Cathedral Island to the Old Town.

LEFT: nuns visiting Wrocław.
BELOW: the marketplace at Wrocław.

Church of St Mary on the Sand has a Piast vault (the aisles have an asymmetrical tripartite rib) which is only seen in this region.

BELOW: the Aula Leopoldina of Wrocław University.

Around the Old Town

A monumental white Baroque façade, dating from 1811, Collegium Maximus forms the main building of the **University** (Uniwersytet; open daily 10am–3.30pm, closed Wed; entrance fee). Situated on the leafy banks overlooking the River Oder, it was established on the site of a medieval castle which guarded the ford across the river. The façade's elegant Astronomical Tower is crowned by a globe, encircled by statues personifying the four academic sciences: law, theology, astronomy and medicine. The interiors are all eclipsed by the magnificent Aula Leopoldina Assembly Hall (Pl. Uniwersytecki 1; tel 071 340 26 18; open Mon, Tues, Thurs 10.30am–3.30pm, Fri–Sun 11am–5pm; entrance fee). This is one of Poland's most beautiful Baroque halls, where the flamboyant architectural details, *trompe l'oeil* paintings, frescos and sculpture all harmonise perfectly. Nearby is the Baroque **Ossoliński Library** (Biblioteka Ossolińskich; tel: 344 44 71; entrance fee) erected on the site of a former Augustinian monastery. Its collection of illuminated manuscripts includes the Florentine publication of Dante's *Divine Comedy* of 1481 and original manuscripts of Polish writers such as Adam Mickiewicz and Henryk Sienkiewicz.

Passing the 19th-century red brick **Covered Market** (Hala Targowa; open daily), formerly a tram depot, you can head to the **National Museum** (Muzeum Narodowe; pl Powstanców Warszawy 5; tel: 071 343 88 39; open Tues, Wed, Fri, Sun 10am–4pm, Thurs 9am–4pm, Sat 10am–6pm; entrance fee except Thurs). Overlooking the River Oder on one side and a wooded park on the other, this neo-Renaissance building dates from the 1880s. An extensive collection of Silesian art includes ultimate examples of Gothic including a sarcophagus from the Church of the Holy Cross, bearing a Latin

scription: "Prince Henryk IV passed away in the year 1290 after years of perb leadership in Silesia, Kraków and Sandomierz." Reliefs on the side of e sarcophagus depict two eagles, representing the Polish crown and the incipality of Silesia. There is also an extensive collection of Polish paintings om the 17th to 20th centuries, including plenty of modern, conceptual and ant garde Polish art.

A stroll across the **Słowacki Park** (Park J. Słowackiego; open daily) leads an ugly modern building resembling a giant circus tent. Nevertheless, this pur-se-built rotunda houses the city's most popular tourist attraction, the **norama of the Battle of Racławice**  (Panorama Racławicka, Purkiniego ; open daily 9am–5pm; entrance fee; tel: (071) 344 23 44). The exteriors are ally forgotten once you climb a circular staircase to the dome, which dis-ays this painting in the round. Depicting the victorious battle won by Koś-uszko's Polish army against Russian forces in 1793, it is 114 metres (370 ft) ng and 15 metres (50 ft) high, and took nine months to complete. It is a truly ectacular painting: incredibly life-like and, despite the fact that you view it om a special platform, it is easy to become totally lost in the view and the his-ric struggle between opposing forces.

This genre of painting, hung in the round to heighten the three-dimensional alities, was very popular during the 19th century, until overtaken by cinema. inted in Lwów in 1893 by the artists Wojciech Kossak and Jan Styka to mark e 100th anniversary of the battle, it was first exhibited in Lwów (part of)land between the two world wars). In 1939 it was put into storage, which is here it remained after the war – the symbolic significance of the painting ing the struggle for independence. Only in 1980 when the Solidarity move-ent began to gain ground and could exert some pres-re on the Communists, was it decided to restore the inting, which took five years to complete.

The entry to the Piwnica Świdnicka (the 13th century beer cellar) in Wrocław Town Hall.

BELOW: the Town Hall, Wrocław.

round the Market Square

fter the Tartar invasion of 1241, a new town on the ft bank of the Odra began to emerge. The **Old Town** tare Miasto) was laid out in a chequerboard style ound the **Town Hall** (Ratusz), with the circular azimerza Wielkiego following the course of the wn's original fortifications.

The Town Hall is one of the finest examples of othic in Central and Eastern Europe, while definitive Silesian Gothic style. The flamboyant façade is corated with tracery as well as fine carvings, with arched roof crowned by a spire and featuring a tur-t on each corner. The central gable features an orna-ental 16th-century astronomical clock, with clocks each façade of the spire too. Next-door cafés allow u to marvel at the façade at leisure.

Equally impressive interiors feature inlaid panelling, intings and Renaissance portals, as well as The Grand all and the Prince's Room. The **Historical Museum** Muzeum Historyczne, Ul. Sukiennice 14/15; open ed–Sat 11am–5pm, Sun 10am–6pm; tel: 071 347 16) is housed in the Town Hall's upper floors, while the th-century cellar, **Piwnica Świdnicka** serves local ers including the eponymous Świdnicki beer. The

TIP

Some rooms in the Town Hall are used for temporary exhibitions, such as the highly successful Lego exhibition of famous buildings from around the world, popular with children.

Market Square (Rynek) is truly extraordinary, for the range of architectural style and the sheer scope, number and layout of the buildings. Unusually, the Tow Hall is not situated in the centre but on one edge of the Market Square. The prim location would be too much for one building, and indeed it is shared by a group of buildings arranged as an "inner square". One side of this inner square is taken u by the New Town Hall (Nowy Ratusz), which continues the Gothic theme but an example of more subtle 19th-century neo-Gothic. Moreover, there are mor buildings within the inner square, with a few alleyways providing access to wh were originally artisans' workshops.

The perimeter of the Market Square includes numerous burghers' house with Numbers 2–11 dating from the 13th century. "Under the Griffins" (Po Gryfami) at Number 2 has an amazing portal with a crest bearing griffins, whi a series of griffins also ascend the top five storeys of this building in a *tour-de force* of Mannerism.

The southwest corner of the Market Square opens onto another market squar **Plac Solny** Ⓜ which is lined with Renaissance buildings and the early 19th century neo-Gothic New Stock Exchange (Nowa Giełda). In addition to th Market Square's civic buildings, the Gothic **St Elizabeth's Church** Ⓝ (Kości Św. Elżbiety), in the northwest corner, dates from the 14th century. The 8 metre (282-ft) tower makes this the city's tallest church.

The most outstanding feature of **Church of St Mary Magdalene** Ⓞ (Kości Św. Marii Magdaleny) is something older rather than taller, in nearby Szewsk This triple-naved Gothic basilica has a 12th-century Romanesque portal, fro a Benedictine abbey formerly in the vicinity, which was built into the sou wall during the 16th century. For a change of ambience, from ecclesiastical

BELOW: the River Oder at night.

ular, and from Gothic to multi-period, continue to **Świdnicka ⓟ**. This is
city's principal thoroughfare, just as it has been since the mid-13th century.
offers prime shopping opportunities, with department stores and boutiques,
ile wide pavements and the mostly pedestrianised street provides plenty of
ce for street traders, and performers. It is also one of the city's most archi-
turally varied streets, the oldest building being the 14th-century **Church of
Dorothy**. The elegant neo-classical **Opera House ⓠ** was completed in 1840,
ile the Centrum Department Store dates from the 1920s. Its many other
partment store rivals date only from the 1990s.

he former palace of the Spaetgen family houses the **Ethnographic
useum ⓡ** (Muzeum Etnograficzne)(Kazimierza Wielkiego 34; open Tues,
d, Fri–Sun 10am–4pm, Thurs 9am–4pm; entrance fee; tel: 071 344 33 13)
h a large collection of dolls dressed in various national costumes. Next door
he **Archaeological Museum** (Muzeum Archaeologiczne; ul. Kazimierza
elkiego 35; tel: 071 347 16 96). Housed in the city's former arsenal, dating
m the 15th century, it is encircled by medieval fortifications, and is now pre-
minantly an arms and weapons museum (open Tues–Sat 11am–5pm, Sun
am–6pm; entrance fee).

rth of Wrocław

e of the oldest Silesian towns, **Oleśnica ❷** stands on a hill 30 km (19 miles)
theast of Wrocław. It was the seat of the Oleśnica dukes between the 14th and
h centuries, with the 14th-century castle one of Poland's most beautiful and
t preserved Renaissance examples. In addition to an entrance gate decorated
h heraldic motifs, the inner courtyard features arcaded galleries.

*Ul. Modrzejewska is
home to one of
Poland's most
renowned hotels, the
Monopol. Built in
1892 in the
Seccesionist style, it
is full of exquisite
original features,
though in need of
renovation to restore
its former splendour,
when guests such as
Marlene Dietrich
stayed there.*

BELOW: the
wooden Church of
Peace in Świdnicka.

*Map
city: 268
area: 274*

Trzebnica ❸ is situated in a shallow valley of the Trzebnickie Hills (Wzgór Trzebnickie) north of Wrocław. The mild climate means that grapevines we cultivated here during the Middle Ages. The town is also renowned for its mineral springs, though the principal reason for visiting is the monastic complex the former **Cistercian Abbey**. Founded in 1202 by Duke Henryk Broda (Henry the Bearded), the church was built around a Romanesque basilica a is now one of Poland's most precious monuments. The showpiece in the basilica is the early-Gothic Chapel of St Jadwiga to the right of the chancel. It w built in 1680 in memory of Princess Jadwiga, wife of the founder. Canonised 1267 for contributing to the advent of Christianity and numerous charitab works, she is the patron saint of Silesia. On 15 October every year pilgrim arrive to celebrate St Jadwiga's feast day, just as they have done for centurie

West of Wrocław

Środa Śląska ❹ is one of the most historic settlements on the trade rou between Germany and Russia. Its medieval town centre has been preserve with particular points of interest being the unusual, oval-shaped marketplac fragments of the town walls and the Parish Church of St Andrew, which h retained its late-Gothic interiors, despite repeated alterations.

About 50 km (31 miles) north-west of Wrocław is the village of **Lubia** where the large Baroque monastery complex was the first Cistercan settleme in Silesia. The oldest of the monastery churches, which dates from the 13 century, was the first of its kind to be built in brick, and the largest of its ki in Europe. The main building measures 223 metres (724 ft) in length, and is or of the finest examples of Baroque. Michael Willmann, a famous painter and

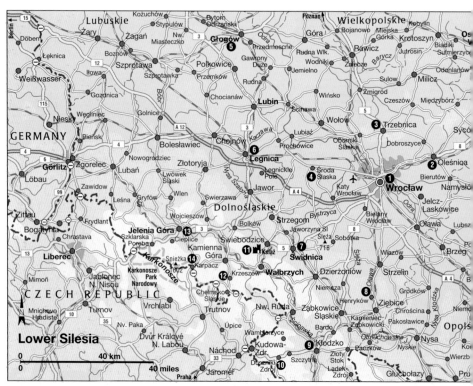

m of artists were commissioned to work on the project. Another fine exam-
: of Baroque is the three-aisle St Walenty church, dating from the 1740s.
Further along the Odra, near the confluence with the River Kaczawa lies **Pro-**
owice, where the walls of a ruined 13th-century castle have survived more or less
act. As early as the 10th century, **Głogów** ❺, about 40 km (25 miles) upstream,
s the seat of the Piast princes and one of Poland's strongest fortress towns. After
45, the town played a key role in Prussia's military strategy. Destroyed during
orld War II, the late Baroque church and the Corpus Christi College, the work of
Italian architect Simonetti, were subsequently rebuilt. So, too, was the town's
st important monument, the **Piasts' Castle**, detailed in the town's Archaeolog-
and Historical Museum (ul. Brama Brzostowska 1; tel: 076 834 10 81; open
d–Sun 10am–5pm; entrance fee). Dukes of the Piast dynasty resided here from
13th century, but the current style of the castle reverts to its Baroque 17th-cen-
y incarnation, except for the cylindrical Gothic tower.

ince 1957 the area between Legnica and Głogów has been the centre of the
ion's copper industry, but the cost to the environment has been disastrous.
mospheric pollution is high and this is now regarded as one of the most
ghted areas in Poland. At the heart of this region lies the former trading
lement of **Lubin**, a charming town with several examples of Gothic archi-
ture, fragments of town wall, a fortified tower, a church and castle ruins.
The copper industry brought rapid economic expansion to **Legnica** ❻, (which
be followed in the town's Copper Museum), but the town is also renowned
producing some of the country's finest pianos, and for once having the
gest garrison of the Red Army in Poland. Legnica was originally the capital
the Trzebovites, a Slavic tribe, before becoming a Polish episcopal seat and,

Map
on page
274

BELOW: examples
of typical Silesian
woodcarving.

due to its favourable location on the River Kaczawa, an important trading ce tre. As the capital of the Piast duchy until the 17th century, the town has so suitably grand architecture. The duke's early Gothic Castle also has Romanesc elements and a Renaissance portal by Johannes von Amberg. After a serious f in 1835, it was refurbished according to a design by Karl-Friedrich Schinkel, t architect responsible for many of Berlin's neo-classical buildings.

The delightful Old Town includes the Academy for the Nobility and the "h ring" tenement houses, so-called because of their narrow stature. Other imp tant buildings are the Church of SS Peter and Paul, principally Gothic witl Romanesque font, and the former presbytery of the Baroque **Church of John**, which contains the Mausoleum of the Legnica and Brzeg Piasts.

Not far from Legnica is **Legnickie Pole**. This was the scene of a fierce bat in 1241, when an army composed of Silesian knights fought bitterly agair the Tartars. The mother of Henryk II the God-fearing, who led the Europe army and was killed in battle, founded a church in honour of her son. Sub quently, it was in her memory that the Benedictine Abbey, comprising t Church of St Jadwiga was founded in the 18th century. The vaults of t Baroque church, the work of Kilian Ignaz Dientzenshofer, are decorated w frescos by the Bavarian master Cosmas Damian Asam.

In the town of **Chojnów** stands a Renaissance palace, built during the re of the Prussian King Friedrich III. Subsequently extended, it now house: museum. You can also see a Gothic church and the impressive remains medieval fortifications. From the 12th century onwards the town

BELOW:
craftsman at work.

Złotoryja prospered from the mining of local gold deposits. Once these h been exhausted, the inhabitants began producing textiles instead. A number

medieval buildings have survived: fragments of original town walls, including a bastion, Romanesque Gothic Parish Church of the Virg Mary, the Church of St Hedwig and the Gotl Baroque Franciscan monastery.

Świdnica-Jawor region

Jawor was the capital of the Świdnica-Jawor duc ruled by the Piasts for a short period during the 1 century, and the Market Square is still overlooked imposing town residences. A Regional Museum housed in the Franciscan Monastery. The **Protest**: **Church of Peace** is also worth seeing for its ha timbered exteriors, and wooden interiors hung w unusual paintings dating from 1710.

Perched on top of a basalt hill is the town **Strzegom**, one of Silesia's oldest settlements. Ev before the birth of Christ there was a castle he which was subsequently used by the Poles a: fortress. The medieval **Church of SS Peter and P**: features elaborately carved portals with gable w dows, and Mannerist interiors. Until 1456, the Chui of St Barbara was a Jewish synagogue. Beyond original town walls, with their ancient Beak Basti lie numerous historic quarries and mines which w once an important source of basalt and granite.

In the centre of the medieval town of **Bolków** the Nysa Szalona stands Poland's oldest stone cas

th-century), with a tower that provides a fine view over the surrounding
ion. The marketplace also occupies the highest point of a hill, where you can
oll beneath historic arcades, past the Town Hall and the Parish Church of St
wiga. Situated on the Bystrzyca river, **Świdnica ❼** was originally a fishing
lement that developed into a trading centre from the 12th century, being on
key route between Kiev and Germany. Between the 13th and 14th centuries
as the capital of the Piast's Świdnica-Jawor duchy (which extended to the
ourbs of present-day Berlin) and developed into a fortified town. During the
h and 16th centuries, under the Piast dynasty, the town was renowned for
en and brewing beer (with grapevines also cultivated around the town).
Świdnica's **Market Square** is surrounded by 16th- to 18th-century burghers'
ases, while the town walls are as decorative as they are defensive, bearing
utiful stone sculptures. The Church of SS Stanisław and Wacław, a blend of
thic and Baroque, has the highest church tower in Silesia (100 metres/340 ft),
 one of the most splendid interiors, with an ornate organ and various sculp-
es and paintings.

n the former cemetery stands the beautiful half-timbered **Evangelical
urch of Peace**. This dates from the end of the Thirty Years War in 1648,
en Silesian Protestants were allowed to build three "churches of peace" in
idnica, Jawor and Głogów (this last church has not survived). However, this
luded significant restrictions: the churches had to be located outside the
vn, they could not be constructed from stone or have a tower, and had to be
mpleted within a year. Even these "concessions" were grudgingly made by the
bsburg authorities (Silesia was then part of the Austro-Hungarian Empire).
vertheless, this didn't mean modest churches – far from it. Gilded interiors,

Map
on page
274

*Near the town of
Bolków is the former
concentration camp
of Rogoxnica. It is
now a mausoleum
and an exhibition on
the site remembers
the victims of crimes
committed here by
the Nazis.*

BELOW: flowers and
shutters of a house
neighbouring the
Wang Church.

Details of hunting frieze on a door in Brzeg.

BELOW: the courtyard of the Museum of Silesian Piasts, Brzeg.

wooden balconies, frescos and an imposing altar create a splendid effect, with a fascinating half-timbered façade. The **Scenic Park of Ślęża,** criss-crossed mountain streams flowing into the Ślęża, which then joins the Odra northw of Wrocław, contains the **Góra Ślęża**, the highest peak (720 metres/2,360 ft) Poland north of the Sudety mountains. Two thousand years ago this isola mountain rising from an immense plateau became a sacred site for the Ślęża (an early Slav tribe), who performed pagan rites on the peak. Remains of scul tures can still be seen here, while clearly marked tourist trails lead to archa logical digs in the area, yielding stone dykes and cult statues.

Sacred objects and sculptures dating from the 3rd to 1st centuries BC can a be seen in the museum in **Sobótka**, a small town situated at the foot of Góra Ślęża. The town's other attractions, such as the 14th-century churches St Anna and St Jacob, ensure that it's a popular destination all year, particula as a weekend break from Wrocław.

South from Wrocław

Between the rivers Odra and Oława, to the southeast of Wrocław, lies the f mer episcopal town of **Oława**. By the marketplace is a 14th-century Town H later converted into neoclassical by the renowned Berlin architect, Karl-Friedr Schinkel. **Brzeg**, further south, has a superb Renaissance castle housing Museum of the Silesian Piasts (pl Zamkowy 1 tel: 077 416 32 57; op Tues–Sat; entrance fee). This dynasty was instrumental in the history of low Silesia. Resembling the Wawel in Kraków *(see page 209)*, the castle features arcaded courtyard. There is more Renaissance architecture to be seen in Market Square, with a fine Town Hall, while a delightful park incorporates

:dieval town walls. The foothills of the Sudeten mountains begin around rzelin, about 45 km (28 miles) south of Wrocław, and these hills provide st of Poland's granite. Within the town, the **Church of St Gotthard**, a manesque rotunda dating from the 12th century, certainly merits a visit.

Map on page 274

Heading southwest, **Henryków** ❽ is one of Silesia's oldest Cistercian monasies, founded by Henryk Brodaty in the 13th century. This complex includes : Monastery Church of St Mary, with Gothic and Baroque features that include borately carved monks' stalls, valuable sculptures and paintings. The *Księga nrykowska* (Henrykowska Book) manuscript containing the earliest example written Polish, was completed in the abbey during the 13th century. In the bey garden is the largest yew tree in Poland – the trunk measures 12 metres) ft) in diameter.

Ziębice, at the source of the River Oława, has retained its medieval town ntre and fortifications. The Church of St George has fascinating interiors lecting various architectural styles. Next to the former monastery hospital nds the Church of SS Peter and Paul, laid out in the shape of a Greek cross.

On the edge of the **Kłodzko Basin** (Kotlina Kłodzka) is the town of bkowice Śląskie, renowned for its glassworks. The town's bastions and fored towers, the Gothic Church of St Anna and the Dominican Monastery are ong the historic attractions. Of Poland's first Renaissance palace only ruins w remain, with a romantic cloistered courtyard.

The former Cistercian monastery is worth visiting in **Kamieniec Ząbkowicki**, ether with the ruined neo-Gothic **Hohenzollern Palace**, poignantly set on a l within an English-style park. Built between 1838–63 by Karl Friedrich ninkel, this palace was one of the final but also most remarkable works by this

BELOW:
landscape at
Ogorzelecon near
Jelenia Góra.

renowned Berlin architect. The palace was destroyed by fire during World War II, but a British-based Polish émigré has now pledged to restore the palace.

On the border between Silesia and Bohemia at the foot of the mid-range Sudetens in the Nysa Kłodzka valley lies the beautiful episcopal town of **Bard** In the early Middle Ages, pilgrims came to the town in large numbers to pa homage to the Virgin Mary, and the single-nave Baroque church contains wood-carving as well as a Gothic sculpture of *Our Lady of Sorrows*.

Around Kłodzko

Adjoining the foothills of the Sudeten is the large basin through which the Ny Kłodzka, Bystrzyca, Ścinawka and Biała Lądecka rivers flow. At the centre this basin is **Kłodzko **, founded in 1223. Its oldest feature is the Gothic sto bridge, built around 1390 and decorated with Baroque reliefs. There is also citadel, as well as three large monasteries belonging to the Franciscans, t Order of St John and the Jesuits. The Franciscan St Mary's Church is dec rated with paintings and frescos by the the Prague maestro Scheffler. A featu of the twin-towered parish church is the Baroque altar designed by Tausch.

The Kłodzko region is a beautiful part of Silesia surrounded by forest-cover mountains. Other aspects of the region's natural beauty are the **Jaskin Niedźwiedzia** (the "Bear Cave") with almost 2 km (1 mile) of tunnels, as we as the labyrinths and fascinating rock formations known as **Błędne Ska** ("Erratic Rocks"). However, this region is best known for its mineral wat springs. The earliest recorded mention of these waters' medicinal benefits da from 1272, with the earliest spas established during the 17th century in t towns of Polanica, Duszniki, Kudowa and Lądek.

The oldest of the Sudeten spas, **Lądek-Zdrój**, w known for its curative mineral springs even before was granted a town charter in 1282. The spa Kudowa-Zdrój is on the Czech border, with near Czerna having a macabre Baroque chapel, the flo and walls of which are covered with some 3,00 human skulls.

Chopin stayed in **Duszniki-Zdrój ⑩**, one of t most beautiful spas on his journey through Pola that eventually led to his permanent exile in Paris. commemorate the visit the town holds an annu Chopin Festival. The 17th-century paper mill, whe some fine frescos were recently discovered, is now museum devoted to the history of paper productic for which the town was once known.

Another attraction in this area is **Wambierzyce**, the foot of Góry Stołowe. On a hill in the centre of t town, a staircase leads up to a monumental Baroq basilica and a group of calvary chapels which h been the site of pilgrimages since 1218. Near t church is a delightful exhibition of mechanical Chri mas cribs.

Westwards along the Sudetens

Wałbrzych, the largest town in the region, has little offer tourists, being an important industrial and mi ing centre. However, the town does have a neoclas cal Evangelical Church with an oval galleried interi

The Kłodzko region provides a natural habitat for the protected yellow European globe plant, known as the "Kłodzko rose", which flowers in June on mountain meadows.

BELOW: Kłodzko on the River Neisse.

esigned by K.G. Langhans, whose work includes the Brandenburg Gate in
Berlin. The Museum of Industry and Technology covers mining installations,
minerals, fossils and porcelain. Soon after the Communist government was
ousted, several large industrial plants were closed in the area, and in parts the
landscape makes a pitiful sight, though the scenery beneath the Sudetens in the
west makes a marked contrast.

Moreover, not far from the outskirts of Wałbrzych is Silesia's largest castle,
Książ ⑪ (open daily; entrance fee). Constructed by Bolko I, the prince of
Świdnica in the 13th century, the castle is set in a park surrounded by
multicoloured rhododendron bushes, while a ravine with a small river isolates
the castle on three sides. Up until the 15th century the palace belonged to the
Piasts of Świdnica, and later to the German Hochberg family, who converted the
castle into a Baroque citadel. The Nazis began to convert the building into a
headquarters for Adolf Hitler, and by excavating a giant bunker destroyed parts
of the original building. However, remains of the medieval stone tower and the
Renaissance wing have survived, while the museum's collection includes
ceramic tiles and decorative glassware. An English-style garden laid out on the
slopes around the palace, planted with exotic trees, is a very pleasant place for
a stroll. Among various terraces in this garden is the Water Terrace, with a grand
total of 27 fountains.

Of special interest in **Kamienna Góra** are the ruins of a large Renaissance
palace, a row of Baroque houses with arcades on the Market Square, and an
interesting exhibition detailing the history of weaving in the town's small
Museum of the Silesian Textile Industry.

The Cistercian abbey of **Krzeszów** ⑫ is one of the most outstanding examples of late Baroque architecture in Silesia. Behind
the ornamental and monumental façade, with its twin
towers, the white and gold interiors are laid out in a
circular manner, decorated with wall-paintings,
canvases and sculptures. It is thought that the
renowned architect, Kilian Ignaz Dientzenhofer, was
involved in the initial work. The neighbouring Church
of St Joseph is famed for its frescos, attributed to
Michael Willmann, a painter often referred to as the
Silesian Rembrandt.

In nearby **Chełmsko Śląskie**, a street of centuries-
old weavers' cottages has been preserved, among
them the House of the Twelve Apostles. The River
Bóbr and its tributaries, the Kamienna and the Łom-
ica, flow through the densely populated and heavily
industrialised area of **Kotlina Jeleniogórska**. The former episcopal town of **Jelenia Góra** ⑬, situated in a
low valley surrounded by mountains, is now the
region's administrative and cultural centre. From the
Middle Ages it was an important regional trading centre, and developed rapidly as it became industrialised.
But the town has also long been a major tourist attraction, with numerous historic sights.

At the centre of Jelenia Góra is the Market Square
with its imposing **Town Hall** dating from the 17th
century, surrounded by colourful arcaded burghers'
houses of the same period. An unusual feature of the
Grace Church is not so much the huge 18th-century

Map
on page
274

*The Town Hall in
Jelenia Góra stands
out among the pas-
tel-toned façades of
the burghers' houses.*

BELOW: preparations
for Corpus Christi
in Krzeszów.

organ, but the theatrical three-storeyed gallery. The Parish Church of St Erasmu and St Pancras has a Renaissance tower, subsequently refashioned in a Baroqu style, while the impressive main altar is the work of two Norwegian sculptor Weisfeld and Kretschmer.

Beyond the fragments of the medieval town walls stands the Protestar **Church of the Holy Cross**, dating from 1718, which was, designed by th Swedish architect Franz. The interior is decorated with frescos painted by th Prague master A. F. Schaffler, assisted by local artist J. F. Hoffmann. There i also a museum exhibiting 17th- and 18th-century glass, ranging from every day functional glassware to works of art.

The spa town of **Cieplice**, one of Poland's most historic, now falls withi Jelenia Góra's town boundaries. It once belonged to the Order of St John, an records from 1281 show that the monks used waters from hot sulphur spring to treat various illnesses such as skin complaints. During the 18th- and 19th century Cieplice was established as an essential rendezvous for the fashior able and wealthy, who easily outnumbered the minority of genuine patien looking for a cure. Of special interest are the monastery, with its Church c St John the Baptist, the former Schaffgotsch Family Palace dating from th late 18th-century, and a park housing the **Museum of Natural History** (u Wolności 268; open daily 9am–4pm; Oct–Apr 9am–6pm, closed Mo May–Sept; entrance fee; tel: 075 755 15 06), with an extensive collection c birds and butterflies.

The town also has a reputation for producing excellent cut glass, as well a being a centre for manufacturing paper. The town of **Lwówek Śląski** on th River Bóbr, dates from 1217. The first town on Polish soil to adopt the Magde burg laws, it was formerly a centre of gold minin Some splendid Gothic monuments give the town i essential character, including well-preserved defer sive walls and turrets, the twin-towered Church of th Assumption with superb portals, and the Town Hal which incorporates Renaissance elements and has vaulted vestibule.

The Karkonosze

The main mountain range, the **Karkonosze**, some times known by its German name, the Riesengebir (meaning Giant Mountains), stretches for 36 km (2 miles) between **Przełęcz Szklarska** (885 metre 2,900 ft) in the west and **Przełęcz Kowarska** (72 metres/2,384 ft) in the east. These mountains ar known for their unusual rock formations and tw lakes **Mały and Duży Staw** ("Large" and "Small lakes) which were formed in the Ice Age, as well a romantic waterfalls, alpine meadows and peat-bog

The highest mountain is the **Śnieżka** (1,602 metre 5,254 ft), followed by the Szyszak and the Szrenic with the peak of Śnieżka also the site of two mar made features: St Laurentius' Chapel dating from th 16th century and, dating from the 1960s, the sauce shaped meteorological observatories. Reaching th top of this mountain doesn't necessarily entail a lon hike, as a chair-lift can do much of the work for you Pines and mountain ash grow up to a level of 1,25

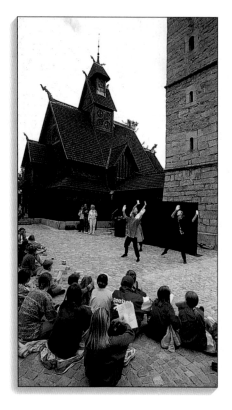

BELOW:
a performance of a religious play outside the Wang wooden church.

etres (4,000 ft). Beneath this the vegetation consists of dwarf pines and arpathian birches. Deer, mouflons and owls are plentiful on the hillsides. The **arkonosze National Park** covers an area of 5,500 hectares (13,590 acres) and well supplied with guesthouses for those wishing to explore it on foot. However, some of the thickly wooded mountain slopes have been affected by atmospheric pollution, largely caused by power plants on the Czech side and in what as the German Democratic Republic.

Szklarska Poręba, at the foot of **Mount Szrenica**, occupies a picturesque ot on the banks of the Kamienna River. Skiers can reach the pistes on the earby **Szrenica** via chair lifts, leading to trails catering for various standards f expertise. Moreover, the microclimate means that the snow often remains here ntil the end of April.

The most popular skiing and holiday resort is **Karpacz ⓮**, at the foot of nieżka mountain. This makes a good starting point for excursions and skiing ong various trails in the Karkonosze, with the town's cultural attractions cluding the Toy Museum exhibiting dolls from all over the world. In the arpacz Górny district is the **Wang**, a 13th-century wooden church, which as sold by the village of Wang in Norway at the beginning of the 19th century, because the congregation had become too big for the church. Dismantled, was brought here in sections and reassembled in 1842. It is a traditional orwegian "*stave*" church, with a vast sloping roof, a design that was typical Norway during the 12th and 13th centuries. Two of the dragon's heads oking down from the gable are claimed to be made from Viking long ships. ome of the beams feature detailed carvings of mythical creatures, while rved figures on the portal narrate a Nordic saga.   ❑

Map
on page
274

An example of Lazarus carving at the Wang Church.

BELOW: Wang Church interior.

WIELKOPOLSKA – GREATER POLAND

*Wielkopolska isn't famous for its scenery, but its fascinating
history makes up for anything it lacks in landscape*

One of Poland's largest provinces, Wielkopolska, literally "Great
Poland", is also the most historic. Situated in the west of the
country, along the central and lower reaches of the River Warta
(the main tributary of the Oder), Wielkopolska provided the foundation for the first sovereign state of Poland.

It was the Piast dynasty who united the scattered territories of the
Polanie tribe into a single dominion, which they ruled from an island
on the Lednica lake, between Poznań and Gniezno.

Gniezno subsequently became the capital of this state, and also
the centre of Catholicism. The archdiocese founded in the town in
1000 resulted in the magnificent cathedral. This is an important sacral
building, exemplifying Romanesque architecture, which is also
intrinsically linked with the evolution of the early state of Poland.
Although Kraków and then Warsaw assumed Gniezno's role as the
capital city of the country, Gniezno is still considered to be the spiritual centre of Poland.

The region's principal city, Poznań, has always been an important
trading centre, and continues this historic role by hosting the largest
trade fairs in Central and Eastern Europe. An attractive city to visit,
and one of Poland's greenest, Poznań also makes a good base from
which to tour the surrounding countryside.

Among the attractions within easy reach of the city are the Ostrów
Lednicki Piast Museum, which includes the remains of the Piast's
ducal castle, the Gothic Kórnik Palace, the French Renaissance
Gołuchów Palace, and the neoclassical Rogalin Palace, which are
all museums set in magnificent parks. And if you want to get away
from it all there are plenty of secluded villages, lakes and forests in
which to enjoy tranquillity and natural beauty. ❑

PRECEDING PAGES: the Cathedral Island in Wrocław.
LEFT: the early Slavic settlement of Biskupin.

POZNAŃ

*The industrial centre and trade-fair city of Poznań is one
of Poland's oldest cities and the capital of the
Wielkopolska (Greater Poland) region*

Poznań divides quite naturally into four equally interesting sections, that can easily be navigated on foot, and which are never far from a park or some other greenery. The most historic part of the city, Ostrów Tumski, is full of Romanesque and Gothic architecture. The Old Town is characterised by Renaissance and Baroque, while the "New Town" district contains 19th-century neoclassical "statement" buildings. Further west is the most modern part of town, with generic contemporary European architecture, spreading out past the main railway station to the international trade halls, which host the largest international trade fairs in Central and Eastern Europe.

This combination ensures that the city has as many business visitors as tourists, with an established infrastructure to handle both, and the town is continually being smartened up – although it is very attractive it is not yet a "showpiece" on the same level as Kraków. There are numerous business and tourist hotels, which tend to be outside the historic centre, but these are in great demand when the numerous trade fairs are on, so dates and accommodation need to be checked well ahead.

The history of Poznań

As the capital of the Wielkopolska (Greater Poland) region, in the centre of western Poland, Poznań is a thriving industrial and commercial hub, with a long history as a major trading centre.

One of Poland's oldest cities, Poznań dates from the 9th century, when a fortified settlement was established on an island in the River Warta. As this expanded it became the capital of the Polish state in the late 10th century, which also included Gniezno and the surrounding region *(see page 301)*. Duke Mieszko I was baptised here in 966, converting the Slavs from pagans to Christians, and Poznań became a bishopric in 968. In 1253 Poznań was granted its own charter under the Magdeburg Laws.

As trade flourished the town prospered, particularly during the 16th century, with Poznań a key "transit point" on numerous European trade routes: from western Europe to Russia and Lithuania, and from the Balkans to Scandinavia. However the Swedish invasion in the 17th century devastated the city, and during the partitions Wielkopolska, together with Silesia, was annexed by Prussia. In towns and villages patriotic organisations were formed to resist the "Germanisation" policies being actively exerted on the region. Poznań played an important part in the battle for Poland's full independence, with the Wielkopolska Uprising, which began in Poznań on 27 December 1918, overthrowing the Prussians *(see page 37)*.

LEFT: Poznań's Old Town.
BELOW: a fountain outside the Renaissance Town Hall.

Wielkopolska subsequently rejoined a newly-independent Poland. During World War II more than half of the city was destroyed, but a rebuilding and restructuring programme got underway immediately, and Poznań's population was soon twice its pre-war total. Since 1925 international trade fairs have been held in Poznań, which developed from the city's medieval tradition of holding a major midsummer fair. The main event, the Industry Fair, takes place in June with ten additional specialist fairs, such as Salmed for medical equipment, Polagra (agricultural) and Multimedia. The reason for the success of these fairs is the "bridging" function they perform between Central and Eastern European markets, as well as their suitability for small and medium-sized companies.

In addition to the university, Poznań has ten institutes of Higher Education, a branch of the Polish Academy of Sciences and numerous scientific institutes, including the Western Institute which provides links between Poland's industry and the European Union, particularly Germany.

The Baroque spires on the two towers of the Cathedral of SS Peter and Paul in Poznań were reconstructed after World War II.

As well as historic churches and civic buildings, palaces and specialised museums, this highly cultured city has several theatres including the National Theatre (Teatr Narodowy), a Philharmonic Orchestra, three well-known boys' and male-voice choirs, not to mention hosting the renowned Henryk Wieniawski Violin Competition which takes place every five years.

Ostrów Tumski – Poznań's heart

The earliest settlement and site of Christian worship was established on Ostrów Tumski (Cathedral Island), the peninsula between the River Warta and the River Cybina, which continues to be the city's religious and spiritual centre. Just beyond the River Cybina is the late Romanesque **St John's Church Ⓐ** (Koś-

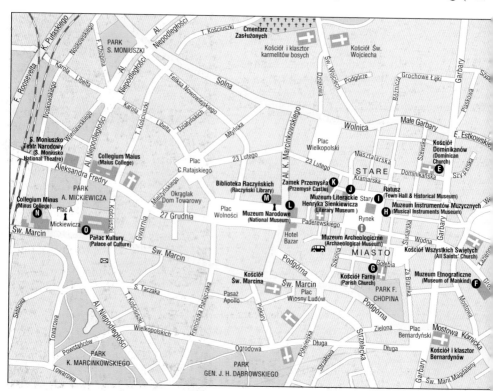

...iół Św. Jana; open daily), one of the first brick-built churches in Poland. The neighbouring **St Margaret's Church**  (Kościół Św. Małgorzaty; open daily) stands in what was until the 18th century the independent municipality of Śródka, a district which has retained a distinct atmosphere.

Crossing the River Cybina to Ostrów Tumski, the most important of several sacred buildings is **Cathedral of SS Peter and Paul** (Katedra Św. Piotra i Pawła; open daily). The foundations of the first Romanesque church built here in 968, and even pre-Romanesque fragments can be seen in the crypt, with the building continually extended and refurbished until the 16th century. Reconstructed after World War II, the cathedral now resembles a Gothic basilica with three naves and radiating towers. Two Baroque towers dominate the entrance, and while it is certainly imposing, this geometric façade is no preparation for the grandeur within. The Gothic main altar with a beautiful triptych dating from 1512, crafted in a Silesian workshop, is often cited as the most outstanding feature. But there are also 12 impressive chapels, including the magnificent neo-Byzantine Golden Chapel, dating from the 19th century, containing the tombs of the nation's founder Mieszko I, as well as his successor and the first king, Bolesław Chrobry. Polish rulers were buried here from the 10th to 13th centuries, which gives the cathedral immense national status.

Nearby are two churches, **Church of the Blessed Virgin Mary** (Kościół Najświętszej Marii Panny; open daily), dating from the 15th century, which has survived entirely in its original form, and the early 14th century **Psałteria**, the house where cathedral choristers once lodged. Also near the cathedral on Mieszka I are the **Bishop's Palace** (Pałac Biskupów) and canons' homes. To the north stands a building that houses the present Lubrański Academy (1518),

Map on page 290–91

BELOW: Cathedral of SS Peter and Paul – the Golden Chapel.

The interior of Poznań's Parish Church has a painting hanging over the altar which details an episode from the life of Saint Stanisław.

BELOW: horse and cart in Poznań.

with an attractive arcaded courtyard, once the site of Poznań's first university. The neighbouring **Archdiocesan Museum** (Muzeum Archidiecezjalne) has an interesting collection of sacred art from the Wielkopolska region (ks Ignaceg Posadzego 2; tel: 061 852 61 95; open Mon–Sat; entrance fee). The moder architecture of the adjoining seminary, where priests are trained to work in Pol ish émigré parishes around the world, is a sharp contrast to the other building in this historic part of the city.

Around the old town

In 1253 two Wielkopolska dukes, Przemysł I and Bolesław Pobożny, founde a new town on the left bank of the River Warta. This revolved around what i now the **Old Market Square** (Stary Rynek), which is one of the finest medieva urban complexes in Poland.

The **Dominican Church**  (Kościół Dominikanów; open daily) in Domin kańska is one of the city's finest churches. It was the Dominicans who intro duced the techniques of Gothic brick architecture to Poland, and fragments o the original monastery and Rosary Chapel can still be seen in the south wing Retaining an impressive Gothic brick portal, dating from the 13th century, th church was subsequently rebuilt in a magnificent Baroque style.

A 19th-century former Masonic Lodge houses the **Ethnographic Museum** (Muzeum Etnograficzne; Grobla 25; tel: 061 852 30 06; open Tues–Wed Fri–Sun 10am–3pm; entrance fee except Sat). It doesn't take long to see a lo here, with an extensive but compact collection of folk arts and crafts from th Wielkopolska region, as well as the paraphernalia involved in traditional cele brations such as Easter. Now acting as the principal church in the city, as wel

as being one of the finest Baroque churches in Eastern Europe, **Parish Church** Ⓖ (Kościół Farny; open daily) on Gołębia, was built by the Jesuits in the second half of the 17th century. Massive ornate columns lining the walls do not support the building, they are purely decorative which is typically Baroque. Being purely aesthetic and inspirational, and together with elaborate stucco work, the effect is as palatial as it is religious. The neighbouring building is the Jesuit College which currently houses the city administration.

While Ostrów Tumski and both banks of the River Warta may seem dominated by churches, the Market Square is entirely a case of civic showmanship, with the Town Hall, ornate palaces and highly individual burghers' houses with polychrome decorations creating an impressive effect, particularly stunning when floodlit at night. By one corner of the Market Square is the **Archaeological Museum** (Muzeum Archeologiczne). The exhibits, ranging from the Stone Age to the Middle Ages, are housed in a beautifully restored former palace, which is also Poland's second oldest museum (Pałac Gorków, Wodna 27; tel: 061 852 61 95; open Tues–Fri 10am–4pm, Sat 10am–6pm, Sun 10am–3pm; entrance fee). One of the city's most unusual museums is the **Musical Instruments Museum** Ⓗ (Muzeum Instrumentów Muzycznych; Stary Rynek 47; tel: 061 852 08 57; open 10am–5pm Tues–Sat, Sun 10am–3pm; entrance fee except Sat). Housed in a beautiful burgher's house which needn't take long to negotiate, there are more than 2,000 historic instruments from Poland and other parts of Europe, including a room dedicated to Chopin with pianos that he played. Even if you're not musical, the instruments are impressive for their craftsmanship alone, and qualify as works of art beyond their musical status. The most outstanding building on the Market Square is the **Town Hall** Ⓘ (Ratusz). Built between 1550–55,

Map on page 290–91

TIP

An annual highlight in Poznań's Market Square is the Swietojański Fair (St John's Fair) in June, which sees colourful market stalls as well as street performers out in force.

BELOW: the Musical Instruments Museum, Poznań.

this is one of Europe's finest Renaissance buildings, with the façade comprising three floors of arcaded loggias surmounted by a high ornamental attic and turrets, above which extends an ornamental tower. The exquisite harmony and unmistakeably Italianate style stem from the architect being Giovanni Quadro of Lugano. Original Renaissance interiors are also exhibits in themselves, particularly the splendid Great Hall's coffered ceiling resting on two impressive pillars (concerts are held in the hall during the summer), and the Courtroom with decorative portraits, while more portraits can be seen in the Royal Chamber. The Town Hall also houses the **Historical Museum of the City of Poznań** (Muzeum Historii Miasta Poznania; ul. Stary Ryneki; tel: 061 852 56 13; open Mon, Tues, Thurs, Fri 9am–4pm, Wed 11am–6pm, Sat 10am–4pm, Sun 10am–3pm; entrance fee except Sat). A daily attraction at noon sees two mechanical kid goats, made from metal, emerge from above the clock on the tower and playfully lock horns to the sound of a bugle call. Locals are just as enchanted by this as tourists. In front of the Town Hall is an ornate rococo fountain of Proserpinae, and a copy of the 16th-century pillory formerly used for floggings.

The Town Hall is one of several buildings in the central area of the Market Square, with fortunately only one "intrusion" in the form of a small 1960s-style "concrete block" tucked among historic neighbours. A terrace of arcaded 16th-century vendors' houses, from which herrings were sold, are smaller and simpler than the ornamental burghers' houses lining the square, but equally interesting, and street traders still vie in front of them for pole positions. Behind the Town Hall is the neoclassical white stucco single-storey Guard House (Odwach) housing the **Historical Museum of the Wielkopolskie region** (Wielkopolskie Muzeum Historyczne), which has various temporary exhibitions (Stary Rynek 9; tel: 852

BELOW: the Town Hall in Poznań.

67 39; open Tues–Sat 9am–4pm, Sun 10am–3pm; entrance fee). While this is a small museum, with modest interiors and exhibits generally comprising documents, pictures, photographs and other ephemera, they provide a very personal insight into regional life and history. An exhibition of the region's officers killed in the Katyń massacre (*see page 50*) is particularly moving.

The life and works of the renowned Polish author, who won the Noble Prize for Literature in 1905 with *Quo Vadis*, are detailed in the eponymous **Literary Museum dedicated to Henryk Sienkiewicz ❶** (Muzeum Literackie Henryka Sienkiewicza; Stary Rynek 84; tel: 852 24 96; open Mon–Fri 10am–5pm; entrance fee except Fri, reservations required for groups) Even if this author is unknown to you, his "museum home" is still worth visiting to see how this type of burgher's house was decorated at the beginning of the 20th century and to gain some idea of what life was like for its resident.

Being the heart of the Old Town, the Market Square is a key rendezvous and place to promenade. Burghers' houses feature smart boutiques and galleries, together with numerous restaurants and cafés ranging from expensive to fast food outlets. Additionally, **Park F. Chopina** is only 250 metres (270 yards) from the Market Square, and is an ideal spot for a picnic among greenery.

Przemysł Castle to Freedom Square

While most of the city walls were pulled down at the beginning of the 19th century, medieval fragments, including a tower, have survived on Przemysław Hill to the northwest of the Market Square, in the vicinity of **Przemysł Castle ❸** (Zamek Przemysła; tel: 061 646 52 76; open daily 11am–7pm). This impressive castle houses the Museum of Decorative Arts (Muzeum Rzemiosł Artystycznych).

Map on page 290–91

TIP

One of the most atmospheric restaurants in the Market Square is Stara Ratuszowa at Number 55. A *fin-de-siècle* Bohemian townhouse, complete with antique interiors, it serves traditional Polish food (including regional dishes).

BELOW: painted houses line the Old Market Square.

Shimmering copies of classic icons for sale.

BELOW:
relaxing in front of etchings stall.

Arranged over two floors, the extensive collection is concentrated without being time-consuming, providing the finest examples of Gothic and Renaissance sacred art and furniture, Gobelin rugs, Limoges porcelain and decorative enamelwork, together with crystal and glassware, and silver and gold *objets d'art*, many of which were formerly owned by eminent Poles. The 20th-century galleries also provide definitive examples of Secessionism and Art Deco (Góra Przemysława 1; tel: 85 22 035; open Wed–Sun; entrance fee). Beyond the square at the foot of this hill are two churches facing each other, and both merit a visit. The façade of **St Joseph's Church** (Kościół Św. Józefa) is classic early Baroque. The Gothic façade of **St Adalbert's Church** (Kościół Św. Wojciecha) may seem to tell the whole story, but the interiors include wonderful Seccessionist polychrome. Moreover, many renowned Poles have been laid to rest here, including Józef Wybicki (1747–1822), who composed the Polish national anthem. Heading for **Freedom Square** (Plac Wolności) marks a change of character, with this area dominated by 19th-century neoclassical "statement" buildings, not to mention a modern urban buzz (which the pedestrianised Market Square area is blissfully free from). This area is also more ragged and not yet as manicured as the Old Town. Plac Wolności is actually a vast rectangle rather than a square, harbouring skateboarders as well as locals chatting on benches, overlooked by several important buildings.

The **National Museum, Painting and Sculpture Galleries** Ⓛ (Muzeum Narodowe, Galeria Malarstwa i Rzeźby)(Marcinkowskiego 9; tel: 061 852 56 59; open Tues 10am–6pm, Wed 9am–5pm, Thurs 10am–4pm, Fri–Sat 10am–5pm, Sun 10am–3pm; entrance fee except Sat) is housed in a neoclassical building. It contains one of the most comprehensive collections of Polish paintings, including works by Jan Matejko, Poland's greatest historical painter *(see page 112)*.

European masters such as Ribera, Bellini and Bronzino can also be seen, together with a range of folk arts and crafts. At the opposite end of the square is the neoclassical Arkadia building, currently a casino, though its provenance is more cultural, with concerts given here by Paganini in 1829 and Liszt in 1843. **Raczyński Library**  (Biblioteka Raczyńskich; open Mon 1–3pm, Thurs 4–6pm) takes the form of an outstanding neoclassical building, dating from 1829, with the sublime colonnade featuring 24 Corinthian columns. Modelled on the Louvre in Paris, it reflects the initially peaceful Prussian regime, which changed over the following decades as the Prussians attempted to "Germanise" the city.

A centre of the Polish Nationalist Movement against the Prussians was the nearby **Hotel Bazar** at Marcinkowskiego 10. Dating from the 1840s, this is one of Europe's oldest hotels, with the neoclassical atmospheric style being the work of renowned Berlin architect Schinkel.

Poznań art and culture

On **Adam Mickiewicz Square** (Plac Adama Mickiewicza) are two interesting monuments, one to the eponymous romantic poet and the other in memory of the worker's uprising of 1956, known as the "Poznań June". Like the Berlin Uprising of 17 June 1953, this was a spontaneous insurrection against the injustices of Communism, and one in which many people lost their lives.

This square is overlooked by the distinctive neo-Gothic architecture of **Minus College**  (Collegium Minus; open Mon–Fri 8am–8pm), the university concert hall which is renowned for the quality of its acoustics. This is a regular venue for the city's Philharmonic Orchestra and the Poznań Ballet, while also hosting the Henryk Wieniawski International Violin Competition. Opposite

BELOW: the Raczyński Library.

Map on page 290–91

Map on page 290–91

Plac Adama Mickiewicza is the **Palace of Culture** ◯ (Pałac Kultury; tel: 06 853 60 81; open Mon–Fri 10am–8pm, Sat 11am–6pm). This *fin-de-siècle* neo Romanesque building, originally known as the Kaiserhaus, was the Germa Emperor Wilhelm II's former palace, and now houses various institution Although its appearance can seem like a grey bulk, it is worth visiting for its pro gramme of interesting temporary exhibitions covering a wide range of subject Its location on **St Martin's Street** (Święty Marcin) means that, the Palace o Culture is also on the prime shopping street, which has all the atmosphere of modern, lively city. Parallel to this street is Aleksandra Fredry, which is als retail terrain and includes the extraordinary Okrąglak Dom Towarowy ("Round about" Department Store), a 1950s glazed rotunda. Further along Fredry is th S Moniuszko National Theatre (neoclassical S Moniuszko Teatr Narodowy

Poznań's parkland

You are never far from a park in Poznań, with 20 percent of the city bein green. North of the city centre lie the remains of a large citadel which wa almost completely destroyed in 1945. Today, the **Park Cytadela** occupies thi site, together with a cemetery for Red Army soldiers who died during Worl War II, and the Poznań Citadel Museum (open Tues–Sun), which details th struggle against the Prussians during the partitions, as well as other aspects o military history, including the city's wartime fate.

Wilson Park, in the Łazarz district, includes Poland's (and one of Europe's largest palm houses. A number of pavilions totalling 4,000 sq metres (4,700 s yards) contain around 17,000 tropical plants, including 700 species from sub-trop ical and tropical countries. An adjoining aquarium contains plenty of local an exotic fish. The city limits to the southwest of this par see the start of the Wielkopolski National Par (Wielkopolski Park Narodowy), with diverse land scapes, woods, hills and lakes to explore, together wit *skansens* and agricultural museums.

Adjoining the northern outskirts of Poznań is a larg area of park and woodland with a series of four lake Part of **Lake Strzeszyńskie** is an open-air swimmin pool, with a motel and a camp site also on its shore **Lake Kierskie**, which covers an area of 300 hectare (740 acres), is very popular with sailing enthusias who find the wind conditions to be near perfect.

Also within easy reach of the city centre pa Ostrów Tumski is **Lake Maltańskie**, one of the fine rowing and canoeing regatta courses in Europe, cre ated on this lake between 1985–90. The world cano ing championships were held here in August 1990. I sunny weather the lakeside is very popular for a stro with walking and cycling trails encircling the lak while cafés and beer gardens provide refreshment On the eastern edge is an artificial ski slope, for prac tising at any time of year.

East of the lake is Wielkopolska Zoo, Poland largest and most comprehensive. The animals are kep in spacious compounds under conditions that closel resemble their natural habitat. If you don't want t walk that far, a miniature railway runs along the lak side (from Kościół Św. Jana, May to September).

BELOW: exhibit in the Poznań Citadel Museum.
RIGHT: statue of St John Nepomucene.

AROUND POZNAŃ

This chapter features a one day trip that can be made from Poznań to the beautiful lakeland landscape and quiet bucolic villages that surround the city

Map on page 302

Poznań is situated in the centre of a large agricultural region, which includes forests and nature reserves, with good road and rail links making it easy to visit historic towns and villages – and to enjoy the pastoral views on the way. Nor do you have to go far to escape the city, and be in the midst of fascinating countryside. In fact, on the southern outskirts of **Poznań ❶**, only 15 km (10 miles) from the city centre, lies the **Wielkopolski National Park**, which covers an area of about 10,000 hectares (24,750 acres). This has the archetypal characteristics of the Polish lowlands: deciduous woods with many different types of vegetation, moraine hills and lakes. The most beautiful part of the park is Lake Góreckie, where the ruins of a castle remain on one of its islands.

Kórnik to Szamotuly

Two popular destinations around 20 km (12 miles) south of Poznań are Kórnik and Rogalin. The small town of **Kórnik ❷**, with a three-nave Gothic church on the Market Square, is idyllically set on the shores of Lake Kórnickie. An impressive arboretum can be seen in the adjoining park (open daily; entrance fee), laid out in an English style. (It contains 3,000 species of trees and shrubs from around the world, which is the most extensive collection in Poland). The centrepiece of the park is **Kórnik Palace**. Originally built in the 16th century, it was redesigned in an English neo-Gothic style in the mid-19th century by the aristocratic owner Tytus Działyński, incorporating designs by the famous Berlin architect, Karl-Friedrich Schinkel. Gothic features, which include a bridge over the moat, were intended to recall Poland's historic splendour, with the refurbishment also providing a suitable home for the owner's collection of historic books and paintings. Bestowed to the nation in 1924, the castle houses a museum (Zamkowa 5; open Tues–Sun 10am–3.30pm; entrance fee; tel: 061 817 00 81) including furniture, paintings, military weapons and armour. The library has one of the most valuable collections of Polish books in the country, with over 350,000 volumes, including one by Napoleon. A neighbouring building houses historic horse-drawn carriages.

The main attraction in **Rogalin ❸**, a village beside the River Warta, is the beautiful park and palace on the edge of an oak forest. Laid out in the late 18th century in a French Baroque style, with an English-style landscaped park laid out at the beginning of the 19th century, this is home to the greatest number of ancient oak trees (over 1,100) of any forest in Europe, some of which are 800 years old. The most famous are three oaks named after the legendary Slav brothers Lech, Czech and Rus, the founders of Poland, Bohe-

LEFT: boat on Lake Kórnickie in Kórnik.
BELOW: sculpture in Rogalin park, overlooking the Palace.

The Rogalin Chapel, built in pink sandstone, serves as a parish church and a mausoleum for the Razcyńskis family.

mia and Russia. The late Baroque–early neoclassical **Rogalin Palace**, former owned by the Raczyński family is now a museum (tel: 061 813 80 30; clos renovation). The collection includes a range of clocks, furniture, tapestries, porc lain and 18th- and 19th-century Polish paintings. Separate pavilions house i exhibition of 20th-century Polish and European art, and horse-drawn carriage

Superb Gothic architecture can be seen in the small town of **Szamotuły ①** 35 km (22 miles) northwest of Poznań. The Gothic Collegiate Church has mai nificent interiors, with the late 15th-century **Górków Castle** (Zamek Górkó now a museum (Wroniecka 30; open Tues–Sun; entrance fee; tel: 061 292 ① 13). In addition to the castle's interiors, the collection includes Poland's mo comprehensive collection of icons and Russian Orthodox sacred art. The cast is adjoined by fragments of a moat and defensive system, with the superb thre storey late-Gothic Halszka Tower housing an exhibition of the region fro ancient times to World War II. Around the Market Square are numerous la 19th- and early 20th-century burghers' houses, with another interesting 19t century building formerly used by the mounted postal service.

An essential detour, less than 10 km (6 miles) northeast of Szamotuły, brin you to **Słopanowo**, where a stunning wooden church dating from 1699 featur beautiful folk interiors, 16th- and 17th-century sculptures and a late 17th-centu polychrome wall.

The origins of the Polish state

The **Szlak Piastowski**, a road that leaves Poznań in a northeasterly directio passes several places marking the origins of the Polish state. Consequently, th road is named after the first dynasty of Polish kings, the Piasts. The first place (

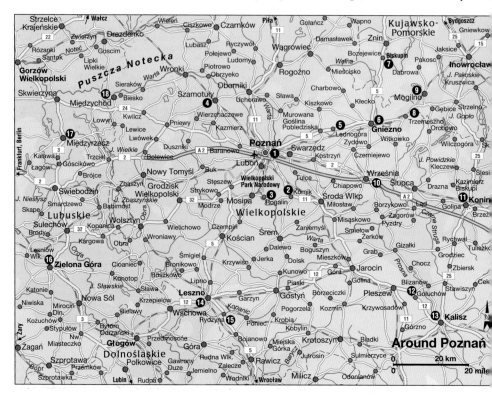

terest along this route is the village of **Lednogóra ⑤**, located on Lake Lednica. On Ostrów Lednicki, the lake's largest island, is a fascinating archaeological site, the **Museum of the First Piasts in Lednica** (Muzeum Pierwszych Piastów na ednicy; Dziekanowice 32; open Tues–Sun 9am–5pm during the summer; ntrance fee; tel: 061 427 50 10; www.lednicamuzeum.pl). This has the oldest rchitectural fragments of brickwork in Poland, and includes the remains of alatium, the Pre-Romanesque late 10th-century residence of Mieszko I, founder f the Polish state. Massive earthworks mark the site of a castle built here in the 1th century. The island was originally connected to the shore by a series of ridges with a total length of about 700 metres (2,300 ft). On the opposite hores of the lake is the **Wielkopolski Ethnographic Park** (Wielkopolski Park tnograficzny; open Tues–Sun 9am–5pm during the summer; entrance fee). his *skansen* (open-air) museum has plenty to see with around 50 primarily vooden buildings, such as an 18th-century Wielkopolska farmstead, a manor ouse, and the oldest Polish windmill dating from the late 16th century.

Further along this route is the hilltop town of **Gniezno ⑥**, Poland's first capital. he earliest inhabitants settled here in the 7th century, with a fortified settlement uilt in the 9th century and the first church founded around 970, after Poland onverted to Christianity in 966. Gniezno's 14th-century **cathedral** (open daily am–5pm, closed to tourists noon–1pm) is the grandest Gothic church in Poland, nd the seat of Polish archbishops since the year 1000. A three-naved basilica vith 14 chapels, featuring ornate portals and grilles, this is also the final resting lace for the first Polish martyr and one of the country's most important saints, St dalbert (Wojciech). His silver sarcophagus is in the centre of the main nave. he cathedral's magnificent pair of Romanesque bronze doors date from 1170, and

Map on page 302

Statue of Bolesław Chrobry (The Brave).

BELOW: Gniezno Cathedral at night.

Details of bronze doors of Gniezno's Cathedral, one of the finest surviving examples of Romanesque decorative art.

BELOW: the Old Fort at Biskupin.

illustrate the life of St Adalbert through a series of panels on each door. The sai is shown leaving the St Alexis Monastery on the Aventine, Italy and arriving Gniezno in 996. The following year he baptised the pagan Prussians, before bei killed by them. King Bolesław Chrobry is shown buying his body from the Pru sians, with the final scenes showing the saint being laid to rest in the cathedr

Collections of ancient books and works of art, some dating from the 10 century, are kept in the church archives and the **Museum of the Archdiocese Gniezno** (Muzeum Archidiecezji Gnieźnieńskiej; Kolegiaty 2; tel: 061 426 78; open Tues–Sat 9am–4pm; entrance fee). It doesn't take long to see tl Gothic and Baroque sacred art here, together with various ecclesiastical item and it's certainly worth it. A delightful stroll past various historic churches al buildings, past a lake surrounded by greenery, leads to the **Museum of the Oi gins of the Polish State** (Muzeum Początków Państwa Polskieg Kostrzewskiego 1; open Tues–Sat 9am–5pm, Sun 9am–3pm; entrance fee; tt 061 426 46 41). This ugly modern building hides a treasure trove of archae logical fragments covering the history of the Piast Dynasty. An audio-visu display may seem a bit dated, but it does the job effectively, detailing the town history up to the Middle Ages. Once Kraków became the capital in the 11 century, Wielkopolska's nobility tried to reverse the town's declining statu but to no avail – the town gradually fell into provincial obscurity.

North of Gniezno is **Biskupin** ❼ (open daily, Apr–Oct; booking tel: 052 3(50 55; entrance fee), an archaeological reserve where in the 1930s an ear Slav settlement on the Biskupin Lake peninsula was discovered, with artifac from the Bronze Age in well-preserved wooden buildings going back 2,5(years. Part of the settlement has been reconstructed, offering an insight in

:historic Slav life. Continuing along the Szlak Piastowski from Gniezno lie
: five towns of Trzemeszno, Mogilno, Strzelno, Kruszwica and Inowrocław.
Trzemeszno ❽ sections of the magnificent church show its 10th-century
.gins, although it is essentially Baroque in character. In the vicinity of
zemeszno are several lakes, most of which have a rather unusual, elongated
.ape. This is because they fill glacial channels created during the Ice Age.
One of the first Benedictine monasteries in Poland was built in **Mogilno ❾**
.ring the 11th century. A Romanesque church was built at the same time, and
.hough repeatedly refashioned, it has retained many original elements includ-
; the crypt. Further points of interest along the Szlak Piastowski are described
the chapter on Gdańsk and the surrounding area *(see page 302)*.

Map
on page
302

st of Poznań

.e eastern part of the Wielkopolska region is a flat, exclusively agricultural
:a with sparse woodland. One of the country's major trunk roads, the E30
.ernational Expressway, leads through it from Poznań to Warsaw. It remains
expressway until Września, and is subsequently a motorway as far as Konin.
About 50 km (30 miles) from Poznań is **Września ❿**, where several monu-
:nts commemorate the local people's heroic struggle against the Prussians'
.empted "Germanisation" during the partition of Poland. The school where
.pils went on strike to demand religious education in the Polish language in
'01, which led to a chain of protests throughout Wielkopolska, is now the
:gional Museum dedicated to the Children of Września (Muzeum Region-
.e im Dzieci Wrzesińskich; Dzieci Wrzesińskich 13; open Mon–Sat
am–5pm, closed Sun; entrance fee; tel: 061 436 01 92), with reconstructions

> 👁 **TIP**
>
> There is an interesting
> narrow-gauge and
> steam engine rail link
> between Biskupin and
> nearby Wenecja. Here
> there is also a
> delightful railway
> museum (open
> Apr–Sept) from where
> you can take a
> "historic" train ride.

BELOW: rural
modes of transport.

of the original classrooms. The small town of **Miłosław**, 16 km (10 miles) sou of Września, is famous for the battles that took place here during the revoluti of 1848. Its 18th-century church and neoclassical palace, both in the attracti setting of a large park, are well worth visiting. In the chapel in the neighbou ing village of **Winna Góra** is the grave of the Polish general Jan Dąbrowski national hero from the time of the Napoleonic Wars, while the palace (op Tues–Sun; entrance fee) has an exhibition detailing his life.

The village of **Ląd** on the Warta River is one of the most important sites the Cistercian order in Europe, with an extensive monastery. Built in the 13 century and remodelled in the mid-17th century, this is now one of the mo beautiful examples of Gothic and Baroque architecture in Poland. The mon mental architectural style, with its splendid interiors and fine collection of 14t century wall paintings, is an impressive sight. The Passion Plays staged at Eas attract people from across the country.

Konin , on the River Warta, has retained a medieval urban layout in the O Town, which includes the **Old Market Square** (Stary Rynek) with numero 19th-century buildings. There is also a late 14th-century Gothic church set in garden that includes a 2.5 metre (8-ft) high sandstone mile post dating fro 1151. The postwar area of Konin contains sports and cultural centres hosti large-scale events such as the annual Children's Song and Dance Festival June. But this is also an industrial centre, with power plants and factori (including an aluminium smelter) taking advantage of the area's deposits brown coal. It is also rapidly expanding, and the town's population has increas sevenfold since 1960. A palace in the **Gosławice** district of Konin houses th **Regional History Museum** (Muzealna 6; open Tues–Sun 10am–4pm; entran

BELOW: sheep herd on the move.

Map
on page
302

e; tel: 063 240 11 11) with a good collection of jewellery, Polish coins and th- and 20th-century Polish paintings. As Konin has a long history of mining, ere is also a gallery of paraffin lamps. Next door is a small *skansen* (open es–Sun 10am–4pm; entrance fee) with 19th-century farm buildings, and a othic church dating from 1444. The countryside around Konin is popular with liday-makers, with the area's towns also providing aesthetic sights. Stary cheń, 13 km (8 miles) northeast of Konin attracts numerous pilgrims, who me to the mid-19th-century neo-Gothic church to see the small painting of St ary of Licheń. **Ślesin**'s triumphal arch, erected in 1811 in honour of Napoleon onaparte, is the only monument of its kind in Poland.

Koło and Uniejów are two interesting small towns on the River Warta. **Koło** home to an architectural rarity: a Gothic church with Art Nouveau interiors, ile **Uniejów**'s main attraction is a Gothic castle. This can also be experi-ced as a resident, having been converted into a comfortable hotel, with the sur-unding park providing various walks among a variety of trees and bushes.

round Poland's oldest towns

cturesquely located between moraines on the edge of the Warta valley, en ute to Kalisz, are Żerków and Śmielów. The main feature of the quiet town of rków is a delightful Baroque church. The renowned Polish poet Adam Mick-wicz stayed in the village of **Śmielów** on a number of occasions, which helped put the place on the map. The village and surrounding area features in Mick-wicz's *Pan Tadeusz*, one of Poland's most significant poetic works. The neo-ssical Śmielów Palace, dating from 1800, is an appropriate location for the lam Mickiewicz Museum (tel: 062 740 3164; open daily 10am–5pm; entrance e except Sat), detailing his life and the Romantic era.

BELOW:
European bison.

By the village of **Gołuchów** ⓬ is the magnificent e 16th-century French Renaissance Gołuchów Palace en Tues–Sun 10am–4pm; entrance fee; tel: 062 761 94). In addition to rooms decorated with interesting rniture, porcelain and Polish and European paint-gs from the 16th and 17th centuries, there is an quisite collection of Ancient Greek vases. The lace is set in Wielkopolska's largest landscaped park, ich includes a Forestry Museum within an out-ilding, while the outlying of the park are a reserve r European bison. An unusual sight worth visiting the Gołuchów woods is the "Erratic", a huge boul-r left over from the Ice Age with a circumference 22 metres (71 ft) and a height of 3.5 metres (12 ft).

As the second largest town in the region is alisz ⓭ is also one of Poland's oldest, retaining its dieval layout of narrow streets. The town was first entioned 1,800 years ago in the writings of the eek traveller Ptolemy. Formerly an important stop the amber trade route from the Baltic, Kalisz is w an equally important Polish textiles centre.

The Old Town's most interesting buildings include e **Cathedral of St Nicholas**, dating from 1253, with splendid late Renaissance stucco work and roque altar; the late-Baroque Collegiate Church of Joseph, as well as the Bishop's Palace and Town ll, both neoclassical. The **Franciscan church and**

monastery dating from the 13th century, was rebuilt during the Baroque e while fragments of the defensive walls can also be seen. The avant garde desi of two modern churches in the **Asnyka** district provide an interesting contra to the town's wealth of traditional architecture.

Idyllically located on the banks of the River Prosna is the Wojcie Bogusławski Theatre, a sublime confection of white stucco neoclassicism. Th adjoins the Town Park, one of the country's oldest public parks founded 1798. Some of Poland's greatest writers, such as Adam Asnyk, Maria Konc nicka and Maria Dąbrowska lived and wrote in Kalisz. The town's cultu calendar also includes several festivals such as the Mieczyław Kosz Intern tional Jazz Pianists Festival. The **Kalisz Regional Museum** (Kościuszki open Mon, Wed 10am–3pm, Tues, Thurs 11am–5.30pm, Fri–S 10.30am–2.30pm; entrance fee except Sun; tel: 062 757 16 08) has a good co lection of archaeological, historical and ethnographic exhibits, while also deta ing the history of the town's textile trade.

Wielkopolska's southern border is formed by the Ostrzeszowskie Hills. T park in **Antonin**, a village on the busy road from Poznań to Silesia, contai many ancient oak trees and an extraordinary neoclassical wooden hunti palace. Odd, perhaps, but why have a mere shooting lodge if you're a disti guished aristocrat who can afford a four-storey hunting palace? Considered o of the most remarkable buildings in Europe at that time, the body of the pala is a large hexagonal tower (containing a circular galleried staircase), from whi four short evenly spaced wings extend. The intention was to create an entire new architectural form, and it certainly succeeded. Built at the beginning the 19th century, it was designed by the renowned Berlin architect Karl-Friedri

BELOW: lush and green pastures.

hinkel. Frédéric Chopin was a guest at the palace, which explains the Chopin ncerts every Sunday. Moreover, every September a festival called "Chopin in Colours of the Autumn" is held here.

outhern and western Wielkopolska

ie intensively cultivated agricultural region of South Wielkopolska has the ghest concentration of farms of any region in Poland. The area is, however, ually rich in architectural monuments and places of historical interest.

Dating from the Middle Ages, the Market Square in **Leszno** ⓮ has numerous posing 17th- to 19th-century burghers' houses. But they are still over- adowed by the elegant Baroque Town Hall, dating from the 1780s, with a iking colour co-ordinated façade of sienna, yellow and white. It was designed the Italian architect Pompeo Ferrari, who also designed the splendid Baroque rish church. The Regional Museum (pl Metziga 17; open Tues–Sun; entrance ; tel: 065 529 61 40) has an impressive collection of coffin portraits, which re very traditional in Poland, as well as folk art. The town is also well known r the Akwawit indoor swimming pool, the largest in Poland, which includes 2-metre (170-ft) chute.

On a hill in **Lubiń** around 30 km (19 miles) to the northeast of Leszno, stands Benedictine monastery built in the early 18th century, with neighbouring ildings housing a Regional Museum covering local history and folk arts.

One of Poland's most beautiful and striking sacred buildings is the Church of Philippians on the **Holy Mount** by the town of Gostyń, a replica of the nta Maria della Salute church in Venice. Beneath a massive dome, the interiors lude a painting of the Madonna dating from 1540. A view of the town forms

Map on page 302

BELOW: haymaking in Jelenia Góra.

In Strzyżewice, a suburb of Leszno, there is an airfield for gliders, where the world gliding championships have twice been held.

the background of the painting – almost certainly the earliest example of i kind in Polish art. Also worth seeing in the nearby village of **Pawłowice** are th Gothic church with Renaissance interiors and the neoclassical Palace set in beautiful park with several lakes. Near Leszno in the direction of Wrocław *(se page 267)* is the small town of **Rydzyna** , which is registered in its entire as a historical monument of outstanding quality. The 18th-century layo includes the Market Square surrounded by burghers' houses, while the rococ monument to the Holy Trinity dates from 1760. The Baroque Rydzyna Castl dating from the 17th century, houses a museum, hotel and restaurant.

Some of the lakes near **Boszkowo**, a village northwest of Leszno, are we worth exploring. The largest of the area's numerous convalescent homes (man of which are open to tourists) is situated by the clear waters of Lake Dominick

The town of **Grodzisk Wielkopolski**, lying midway between Poznań an Zielona Góra, is renowned for brewing a strong wheat beer. This also has superior flavour attributed to the local spring water, whose special qualitie were discovered in the 14th century. Monuments to Grodzisk's glorious pas including a fine Renaissance church, can be seen throughout the town.

Wolsztyn, on the River Obra, is a popular with watersports enthusiasts, pa ticularly canoeists, as the surrounding area contains many lakes. Moreover, th lakes are linked by either the river or small canals. The choice of accommod tion includes an irresistible opportunity to live like a prince for a fraction of th price, with a tourist hostel located in what was once a neoclassical palace (te 068 384 27 46). The town was once a centre of woollen cloth production, an includes an 18th-century Baroque church, while the Regional Museum is house in the former workshop of the outstanding Polish sculptor Marcin Rożek.

BELOW:

country girls pose for the camera.

Around Zielona Góra and Ziemia Lubuska

The western part of Wielkopolska includes a densely wooded region with many rivers and lakes, extending along the border with Germany, which follows the Odra and Nysa-Łużycka rivers. Attractively situated close to the Odra valley at the foot of a chain of hills is the region's administrative centre and the capital of Lubuskie voivodship, **Zielona Góra** ⓰. This was traditionally a wine-growing area, with a vine-covered hill in the centre of town the only symbolic remains of this practice, where a palm house also houses a restaurant. However, this tradition is celebrated in the colourful September Days of Zielona Góra Harvest Festival, also called "a Holiday of Vine Gathering".

The **Lubuskie Regional Museum** (Niepodległości 15; open Wed–Sun; entrance fee) documents the history of wine production in the area, with a collection of tools and pots used by vine growers, as well as archaeological and ethnographic exhibits. The town also has one of Poland's most renowned distilleries, with Polmos Zielona Góra producing a wide range of clear and flavoured vodkas. Much of Zielona Góra's original layout dates from the town's charter, granted in 1323. The most impressive sights include the **Cathedral of St Jadwiga** with its monumental Gothic architecture dating from the 13th century, the neoclassical Town Hall with an elegant clock tower, and 15th-century fragments of the defensive walls. Despite the name, the **Church of the Virgin Mary of Częstochowa** is actually Evangelical, with this half-timbered building dating from the mid-18th century. There are also various early 20th-century buildings, providing a wide range of Secessionist and eclectic styles.

There are a number of interesting towns in the southern part of Ziemia Lubuska, a region which formerly belonged to Lower Silesia. In **Kożuchów**, for

Map on page 302

BELOW: resting tired legs.

example, large sections of the medieval town walls have survived, while the 13th-century church with Baroque interiors is also particularly impressive.

Żagań, situated on the River Bóbr, was the capital of an independent Piast duchy from 1270s, and has preserved its original medieval town structure, including fragments of the 12- to 14th-century town ramparts. The neoclassical Town Hall is surrounded by 17th- and 18th-century burghers' houses, while the Augustinian Monastic Complex, including a 15th-century parish church, monastery and a granary, offers a wide range of architectural styles. The monastery houses an early 18th-century library while another part of this complex is a hotel. The town also has the ruins of a Franciscan monastery, dating from the 13th century and refashioned in the 18th century. However, Żagań's finest architectural monument is the early 18th-century **Wallenstein Palace**, approached by a bridge over a moat, and picturesquely situated on the banks of the Bóbr, in a park with many rare species of trees.

Until the end of the Communist regime the town of **Żary**, originally founded in 1260, had a long history of producing the finest cloth and linen in the country. Recalling the town's medieval heyday are the 14th-century Town Hall with a Renaissance portal, a few 13th- and 14th-century Gothic churches, and sections of the ramparts and watchtowers from the 14th century. The Dewin Biberstein late 18th-century palace and burghers' houses by the Market Square provide prime examples of other architectural styles.

By the banks of the Warta lies **Gorzów Wielkopolski**, a town granted its municipal charter in 1257. As the principal town of this region it has a current population of 120,000 and several large textile factories. Particularly interesting is the 13th-century Gothic cathedral, with a substantial defensive tower dating from the 14th century, a 15th-century presbytery and a Renaissance altar. The imposing half-timbered granary on the banks of the River Warta was built in the 1770s, and is now a museum of historic and modern paintings. The town's main museum is housed in a *fin-de-siècle* Secessionist Palace (Warszawska 35; tel: 095 732 28 4 open Tues–Sun; entrance fee), with a collection of decorative arts and crafts, and Polish portraits. Every August the town sees gypsy groups converge for the annual international meeting for the Romane Dyve festival of gypsy musical groups.

South of Gorzów, surrounded by beautiful woodland and lakes, is the holiday resort of **Lubniewice**, while heading northeast brings you to **Strzelce Krajeńskie**, where the medieval fortifications, built of uneven blocks, have been preserved almost entirely intact.

The moraines and lakes of Łagów

Along the historic border between Wielkopolska and Ziemia Lubuska, to the north of the E-30, the main Berlin to Poznań road, are several places worth visiting. **Łagów** is set in a particularly beautiful location between high moraines and two lakes. Its most outstanding architectural monument is a castle, built in the 15th century for the Order of St John, with a watch

ɔwer providing a wonderful view of the surrounding area. The castle now houses
hotel and restaurant. Łagów is still protected by a medieval wall, interrupted
nly by two gates leading into the town. The nearby lakes offer good leisure facil-
ies, and not surprisingly are popular in the summer months. On the western bor-
er of Wielkopolska lies the small town of **Międzyrzecz ⑰**, a good base from
which to tour the area. Dating from the 10th century, the town is perched on a
mall hill above the River Obra. The carefully preserved ruins of a 14th-century
Gothic castle are worth seeing, with the grounds including the 18th-century House
of the Starostas (town governors), now a museum with historical and ethnographic
xhibits, including some unique 17th-century coffin portraits. The neoclassical
own Hall, built in 1813, has a neo-Gothic clock tower, while the 16th-century
Gothic parish church with a wooden spire and beautiful star vaulting, also has
horoughly modern interiors.

North of Międzyrzecz, in the hilly area close by the lakes, is **Rokitno**, the site
f a Baroque church, which is the destination for countless pilgrims who wor-
hip its image of the Virgin Mary. Surrounded by woodland, the village of
Gościkówo is situated 10 km (6 miles) south of Międzyrzecz. The main attrac-
on is a former Cistercian monastery, dating from the 13th century but with
Baroque additions.

To the west and southwest of Międzyrzecz is an extensive system of **fortifi-
ations**, which the Nazis constructed from 1934–8. One of the world's largest
military fortifications, the complex consists of 55 individual defensive shelters,
with walls of reinforced concrete up to 2.5 metres (8 ft) thick. The fortifications
re connected by a network of underground corridors totalling 30 km (19 miles)
a length, through which electric trains ran. Part of the underground area also

Map
on page
302

BELOW: fishing on
the lake in Łagów.

housed armaments factories. In January 1945, the entire complex was capture
by Soviet tank units and large sections were blown up. The ominous remair
can be visited, though it is a rather hazardous undertaking if unescorted. The be:
place to enter the complex is at **Kaława**, a village 8 km (5 miles) south c
Międzyrzecz. If you do, you won't be alone. Some of the tunnels have becom
a winter shelter for huge colonies of bats, up to about 30,000 in total, whic
includes 10 different species of these flying mammals. Consequently, this ha
been declared the Nietoporek nature reserve.

The Warta lakes

One of Wielkopolska's most scenic areas, the Międzychodzko-Sierakowski
Lakes, extends northwest of Poznań beside the lower reaches of the Wart
With over 100 lakes, moraines, woods, footpaths and recreational facilities,
has become a very popular area with holiday-makers.

There is a large holiday centre on the shores of **Lake Jaroszewskie**, whi
Lake Lutomskie, with its steep banks and impressive beech forest, forms part c
a nature reserve. A route called the "black path" leads to the town of **Sieraków**
located 3 km (2 miles) away. By the altar of the town's Renaissance church i
a painting that originated from Rubens' studio. Another attraction is the stu
farm, which raises a horse breed unique to the region and offers riding holiday.
A large holiday centre by the side of Lake Mierzyńskie also attracts many vis
itors during the summer.

The town of **Międzychód** ⓯, situated between the River Warta and Lak
Kuchenne, has a delightful Old Town with gabled houses. Between the Wart
and the Noteć lies one of the country's largest forest areas, densely covere

BELOW: horseback
riding holidays
are popular with
visitors.

ith pines, which is the **Noteć Primeval Forest**. In the autumn mushroom-ickers from all over the country flock to this hilly area.

orth Wielkopolska

orth Wielkopolska is a hilly, mainly wooded region with many lakes. One of s beauty spots is the **Noteć Valley**. Nestling among the hills and between three ikes, Chodzież occupies a picturesque site. This town has three factories pro-ucing porcelain, making it one of the main centres of this industry in Poland.

On the banks of the River Gwda, a tributary of the Noteç, lies the 15th-century wn of **Piła**, the administrative centre for North Wielkopolska. The centrally ocated Gromada Hotel (tel: 067 351 18 00) is recommended as a base from vhich to make day trips to the many different points of interest in this part of Vielkopolska and Pomerania. Piła was badly damaged during World War II, but ie town has an early 20th-century neo-Gothic church of St Stanisław Kostka and ie modernist 1930s church of St Anthony, with its 7-metre (30-foot) high sculp-ire of Christ, said to be the tallest in Europe. This is also the home town of tanisław Staszic, a priest, scientist, and politician who reformed the Polish conomy at the end of the 18th and early 19th centuries. His family house is ow a museum detailing his life and work. The town's lakes include beaches and ccreational areas, while Lake Rudnicki is part of a nature reserve, harbouring ild boars and various species of birds and trees. Piła is also the home of Polo-ia, one of the best speedway clubs in Poland. North of Piła, and over the bor-er into Pomerania, are the remains of the German-built Pomeranian Wall, a efensive line crossing an area of forests and lakes. This World War II relic is escribed in detail in the chapter on West Pomerania *(see page 321).* ❑

Map on page 302

BELOW: the woods provide natural habitat for many wild animals and their young.

THE NORTH

The well-forested countryside that surrounds the post-glacial lakes of the north is gentle and undulating, while the city of Gdańsk provides an urban centre for the region

The Baltic coastline, with its secluded beaches fringed by pine trees, includes many attractive resorts and spa towns, as well as major ports such as Gdańsk and Szczecin.

As the capital of Western Pomerania (Zachodnio-Pomorskie), which borders Germany, Szczecin's historic importance is demonstrated by monumental buildings such as the Castle of the Pomeranian Duke's and the Pomeranian Parliament Building. The city is also a gateway to other Hanseatic towns such as Stargard Szczeciński, as well as national parks and seaside resorts. The surrounding countryside also features vast expanses of agricultural land, with potatoes the most important crop.

The tri-city of Gdańsk, Sopot and Gdynia is the largest municipal area in northern Poland. The historic centre of Gdańsk, with numerous buildings that were designed to impress, reflects its long history as the most important Polish port. Sopot has remained a delightful seaside resort, characterised by 19th century pavilions and *fin-de-siecle* villas, while Gdynia is a modern marina and port with dockyards, essentially dating from the 1920s.

A lasting legacy of the Teutonic Order of Knights, who dominated this region from the 13th to the 15th century, are a large number of castles. Some are now picturesque ruins on hillsides, while others are museums. The most impressive is the vast castle in the town of Malbork, south of Gdańsk, and there are well-preserved fragments of a Teutonic castle in the delightful town of Toruń, the birthplace of Copernicus. The town also has prime examples of Gothic architecture. To the east the area is bordered by Warmia i Mazury, which includes the Masurian lake district – with over 1,000 lakes it's Poland's most popular holiday destination. ❑

PRECEDING PAGES: Gniezno Cathedral.
LEFT: the wandering dunes at Łeba.

WEST POMERANIA AND SZCZECIN

Maps:
Area 322
City 323

Western Pomerania is the top sea and sun destination in Poland, while the capital of the region, Szczecin, has all the buzz of a busy port town and a fascinating past

West Pomerania's 200-km (124-mile) stretch of coastline means a choice of secluded beaches as well as seaside resorts with various facilities. Similarly, the Pomeranian lake district provides tranquil havens, with its series of inter-connected lakes surrounded by forests, as well as attractive resorts. Among the national parks are the islands of Uznam and Wolin, while the Słowiński National Park is renowned for its "wandering dunes". With numerous historic towns and villages, the region provides a range of attractions.

Slavic tribes, ruled by various dukes, first settled in this part of Pomerania in the 9th and 10th centuries. At the end of the 10th century the area was unified by the Piast dynasty, the first Polish kings, though control of the region fluctuated between the early Polish state and the Brandenburg Margraves (German nobles). In the 12th century the Margraves were forced to cede territorial claims to the Polish king, Bolesław Krzywousty, who once again united the region's leaders. However, in league with the Danes, the Margraves subsequently re-established control, with the Greifen family, originally Slavic but then "Germanised", ruling from the early 13th–16th centuries. In the 17th century, the region was annexed by Sweden and then by Prussia in 1720, after which the region was again "Germanised" and not returned to Poland until after World War II. The region's post-war prosperity rests on a combination of industry, fishery, agriculture and forestry.

LEFT: sheaves of corn after the harvest.
BELOW: Szczecin harbour.

Szczecin

The capital of West Pomerania and Zachodniopomorskie voivodship, **Szczecin ❶**, is near the border with Germany on the River Odra (Oder). This river, and the fact that Szczecin is only 65 km (40 miles) from the Baltic, has ensured its status as the second-largest Polish port and a junction for land traffic.

Szczecin evolved from a 9th century Slav settlement. In 1237 the city was granted its municipal charter, and joined the Hanseatic League in 1251. Establishing the city as the capital of their duchy, the Pomeranian dukes began to build their magnificent castle in 1346. Between the 13th and 18th centuries the harbour developed into an important commercial centre, particularly for fish and grain, trading with the major Baltic ports, including Lubeck, Tallin, Stockholm and Gdańsk. Sixty percent destroyed by Allied bombing during World War II, the city was rebuilt and expanded after the war. As a cultural and educational centre, it has a university, five institutions of higher education and the Higher Maritime Academy, a Philharmonic orchestra and several theatres.

The city's attractions are concentrated in the centre, and can easily be seen on foot, with broad boulevards, river banks, parks and squares providing various settings for historic architecture. While Szczecin is an attractive city sightseeing is a case of robust, handsome "highlights", rather than continual refined aesthetics. A prime example of Pomeranian ecclesiastical architecture located on the banks of the River Oder, is **St John the Evangelist's Church** (Kościół Św. Jana Ewangelisty; open daily). One of the few buildings to survive the war, the 14th-century façade yields simple interiors with fragments of the original wall paintings in the right-hand aisle.

Further along by the banks of the Oder is the **Old Town Hall** **B** (Ratusz Staromiejski; open Tues–Sun; entrance fee). Dating from the 17th century, it was burned down in 1944, and reconstructed in its original Gothic style. This includes an extraordinary gabled roof, while the decorative terracotta façade is typical of Hanseatic towns around the Baltic. The building now houses the **Museum of the History of the City of Szczecin** (Muzeum Historii Miasta Szczecina; ul. Mściwoja 8; open Tues, Wed, Fri 11am–6pm, Thurs, Sat–Sun 10am–4pm; entrance fee; tel: 091 437 52 55) with a collection of engravings that dates from the 17th and 18th century. Nearby are the elegant **Loitz House** **C** (Kamiennica Loitzów), formerly the residence of a wealthy 16th-century merchant family, now a College of Fine Art, and the far more majestic **Castle of the Pomeranian Princes** **D** (Zamek Książąt Pomorskich). Built between the 14th and 17th centuries, it was reconstructed after World War II in a Renaissance style, retaining Gothic elements. Originally housing the dukes' valuable art collection, it comprises five wings and two inner courtyards which are an impressive sight. In addition to a library, there is a concert hall within the former

TIP

During the summer, concerts are held at noon on Sundays in the Szczecin Castle courtyard and the concert hall.

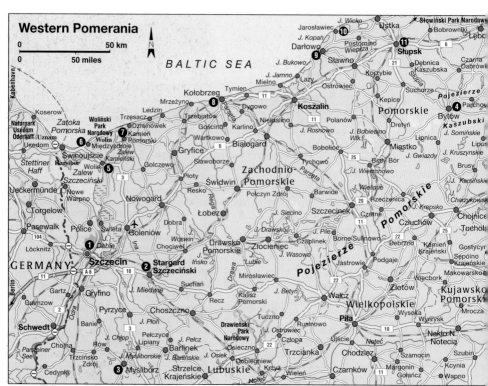

chapel, while the belfry's observation tower provides a magnificent panorama of the city and the harbour. The east wing houses the Castle Museum (ul. Korsarzy 34; open Tues, Wed, Fri 11am–6pm, Thurs, Sat–Sun 10am–4pm; entrance fee; tel: 091 433 88 41) which details the castle's history. Among the most interesting exhibits are six sarcophagi of Pomeranian dukes from the early 17th century. At the foot of the castle are fragments of the town's medieval defences, the **Maiden's Tower** **E** (Baszta Panieńska; summer months open 10am–6pm; entrance fee), also known as the Bastion of Seven Cloaks.

Walking along **Chrobry Embankments** **F** (Wały Chrobrego) takes you past an eclectic group of red-brick buildings. Dating from the early 20th century and built on the site of the former town walls, these buildings house the Maritime Academy and the **Museum of the Sea** (Muzeum Morskie; tel: 091 433 60 18; open Tues, Wed, Fri 10am–6pm, Thurs, Sat–Sun 10am–4pm; entrance fee) including maritime, ethnographic, and archaeological exhibits. Proceeding further north brings the harbour into view, from where boats leave on sightseeing tours of the river, and cruise further north to the port of Świnoujście by the Baltic. Strolling through **Żeromskiego Park** **G** (Park Żeromskiego; open daily) takes you through wooded greenery, including numerous trees and shrubs from around the world, as well as the **Mickiewicz Monument** **H** (Pomnik Adama Mickiewicza) honouring Poland's most romantic poet *(see page 108)*.

The north of the city

The streets and squares of the northern part of the city are laid out in a star-shaped pattern, with the radial roads meeting at **Grunwald Square** (Plac Grunwaldzki). Unlike the city centre, which was badly damaged during World War

Maps:
Area 322
City 323

The reconstructed Castle of the Pomeranian Princes. Climb the bell-tower for a great view of the city.

BELOW: the Church of SS Peter and Paul, Szczecin.

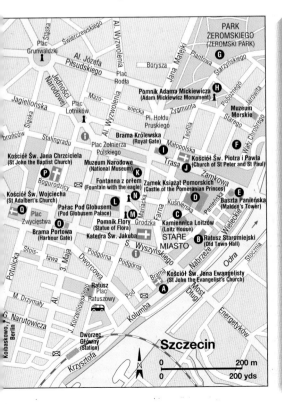

The tune that now traditionally accompanies all brides down the aisle, The Wedding March, was first played by its composer Felix Mendelssohn-Bartholdy in 1827 at Szczesin's St James' Cathedral.

II, the surrounding area was relatively unscathed. If perhaps ready for refurbishment, the area's houses are, nevertheless, attractive. The ornate and ceremonial **Royal Gate ❶** (Brama Królewska), also known as the Gate of Prussian Homage, is one of the city's landmarks. Replacing an earlier Gothic gate, this was built by the Prussians at the beginning of the 18th century as a reminder of the Prussian purchase of the city from the Swedes in 1720. This highly artistic gate now houses an art gallery.

The **Church of SS Peter and Paul ❶** (Kościół Św. Piotra i Pawla; open daily) is a superb example of Pomeranian Gothic sacral architecture, with an ornate façade featuring an impressive rose window. The façade is decorated with glazed terracotta mascarons, while the interiors include an 18th-century wooden ceiling, buttresses and an historic portal from a monastery in Grabów.

The Baroque Parliament Building of Pomeranian States on Square of the Polish Soldier (Plac Żolnierza Polskiego), built in the 1720s, now houses the **National Museum ❶** (Muzeum Narodowe; open Tues, Wed, Fri 10am–6pm, Thurs, Sat–Sun 10am–4pm; entrance fee; tel: 091 431 52 67). A fascinating collection encompasses medieval sculptures from eastern Pomerania, Polish paintings from the 18th to the early 20th centuries, the history of Szczecin and Pomerania, silver, folk arts and crafts. Among the sacred art are some beautiful altarpieces. Modern Polish art is displayed at the museum's annex across the road in the neoclassical Pałac pod Głowami (Palace under the Heads), named after the busts which decorate the windows. This is one of several neoclassical buildings in the immediate area.

BELOW: detail of brick heads on the Church of SS Peter and Paul.

The **Pod Globusem Palace ❶** (Pałac Pod Globusem; open daily) was built in the 1720s for the Governor of the Province of Pomerania, and features a dec-

orative tympanium. Opposite the 18th-century Baroque **Statue of Flora** Ⓜ (Pomnik Flory), is one of Pomerania's largest Gothic churches, St James' Cathedral (Katedra Św. Jakuba). After the war, only the bomb-damaged tower and the choir remained, until reconstruction began in 1971. Few of the original features have survived, though the 14th-century altar triptych and Baroque epitaphs are worth seeing. The Baroque **Fountain with the eagle** Ⓝ (Fontanna z orłem) is indeed crowned with a majestic sandstone eagle. Erected in 1723, it also served as a well, being part of the city's newly established water system. The willows surrounding the fountain really do make this a "green oasis", and the best view of the fountain is with the Pod Globusem Palace as the backdrop.

Harbour Gate Ⓞ (Brama Portowa) was also built by the Prussians at the start of the 18th century, on the site of an earlier Gothic gate. Among the ornate inscriptions and carvings is a panorama of Szczecin. The late 19th century neo-Gothic **St John the Baptist Church** Ⓟ (Kościół Św. Jana Chrzciciela; open daily) is arranged in the form of a cross. It is often known as the "Polish church" as even during the Prussian regime mass was occasionally celebrated in Polish. The early 20th century **St Adalbert's Church** Ⓠ (Kościół Św. Wojciecha; open daily) pays homage to Poland's most famous saint, with stained-glass windows depicting his life. As the garrison church, there are also monuments to Polish troops who lost there lives in various uprisings and wars.

Further north is Jasne Błonia where a monument was erected to commemorate the dramatic events of 1970, when many dockers were killed during an uprising against the Communist regime. Directly adjoining the woodland of the Wkrzańska Forest is **Jan Kasprowicz Park** (open daily). Founded in the late 19th century, it includes an amphitheatre together with

Map on page 323

The Gothic Cathedral of St James was badly damaged in 1945: restoration was completed in 1982.

BELOW: the Old Town, Szczecin.

various rare trees and shrubs. The southern districts of Zdroje and Dąbie, both originally villages, border onto delightful countryside. The Emerald Lake, created on the site of a former chalk quarry, is named after the colour of the water. Around the lake are marked trails through the **Beech Tree Forest** (Puszcza Bukowa), with the highest hills providing a wonderful panorama of the city and surrounding lakes and forest.

A comprehensive tram service operates in Szczecin. A local map (from the tourist office) details tram routes.

BELOW: writing postcards home.

South and east of Szczecin

One of the most popular and interesting towns, situated by the River Ina about 35 km (16 miles) to the east of Szczecin, is **Stargard Szczeciński ❷**. It provides a great day out and a leisurely stroll will take you past all the Gothic and Renaissance attractions, set amid a delightful "country town" atmosphere.

The Market Square includes the ornate late Gothic Town Hall, with a wonderful flourish of mascarons on the façade, neighboured by Gothic and Renaissance burghers' houses and the former police station, which houses the Regional Museum covering local history. The twin-towered **Church of the Blessed Virgin Mary** (Kościół Najświętszej Marii Panny), was designed by Henryk Grunsberg, one of the most renowned Gothic architects. Construction began in 1292, but continued until the end of the 15th century. The 15th-century Gothic **St John's Church** (Kościół Św. Jana) has Pomerania's tallest tower at almost 100 metres (328 ft), not to mention an impressive vaulted nave.

The town's powerful defensive system has survived remarkably well. Dating from the 13th and 14th centuries, the city walls enclose the Old Town, with attractive parks laid out along the walls. Several gates and towers provided aesthetics as well as defence. The oldest tower is the imposing red-brick Brama

Pyrzycka, dating from the 13th century, set among wooded greenery. One of the most unusual is the 15th-century Mill Gate. The tallest is the Morze Czerwone Tower (Red Sea Tower) at 34 metres (111 ft), while the Harbour Gate crosses a tributary of the River Ina, with a tower on each bank. The village of **Chojna**, originally a 10th-century Slav settlement, is also a popular destination. The remains of the 15th-century **Church of the Blessed Virgin Mary** (Kościół Najświętszej Marii Panny), is currently being restored, while the Augustinian Monastic complex dates from the 13th century, and the Town Hall is 15th-century. Fragments of the defensive walls and two splendid gates are 15th century.

There are more defensive walls and impressive 15th-century gates to be seen in **Trzcińsko Zdrój**, set by the picturesque Trzygłowski lake and park. Traditionally a cattle and sheep trading town, a spa was established in 1895. The church dates from the 13th century and has a vast stone tower, while the 15th-century Town Hall includes an ornamental façade and vaulted interiors.

Heading south are a number of towns which played a prominent role during the war, with forts by the Oder erected by Polish and Russian soldiers in April 1945, shortly before the capture of Berlin. A monument on a hill near Cedynia, Poland's most westerly town, recalls the battle between Mieszko I and German Margraves in 972. The town also has a 13th-century church and the remains of a 14th century abbey. The Cedyński Landscape Park, which includes a reserve for rare plants, is within easy reach of the town.

Myślibórz ❸, a small town close to a number of lakes, is encircled by the remains of a medieval wall. The walls of the late 13th-century parish church are also worth seeing, being constructed of loose stones arranged on top of one another, a building method typical of early-Gothic churches in Pomerania. The

Map on page 322

BELOW: the Old Town of Szczecin overlooking the River Odra.

TIP

During summer there is a varied programme of cultural events: in Swinoujscie there is an Arts Festival (June), Days of the Sea (July) and Polish Songs of the Sea (September); In Międzyzdroje the annual International Festival of Choral Music and the Comedy Film Festival.

BELOW:
statue guarding the ruins of the church in Wolin.

grand Town Hall is Baroque. Among various sights in **Pyrzyce** are the well-preserved town walls with three medieval gates, and the early 16th century Church of the Blessed Virgin Mary, with notable stained glass windows. To the east, by the lower reaches of the River Drawa, large wooded areas extend across Drawska Forest. This countryside is perfect for outdoor pursuits, such as hiking and cycling. Meanwhile, the section of the River Drawa between Czaplinek and Krzyż is a kayaker's paradise.

The Pomeranian Lakes

West Pomerania's landscape is dominated by lakes, most of which are ringed by delightful wooded hillsides. The **Drawskie Lakes** (Pojezierze Drawskie), including the towns of Drawsko Pomorskie, Połczyn Zdrój and Szczecinek, is the most attractive region. The largest and most beautiful of the 200 lakes is Lake Drawsko, with the popular tourist town of **Czaplinek** on its southeastern edge. Travelling northwards through the picturesque Valley of the Five Lakes leads to **Połczyn Zdrój**. This popular spa town has been renowned for the medicinal benefits of its waters since the 14th century. Nestling between high moraine hills, the town's attractions include a castle dating from the 13th century and the Gothic Church of the Blessed Virgin Mary. The **Pomeranian Wall** (Wał Pomorski) stretches from Szczecinek through Wałcz and Tuczno to Krzyż. This defensive barrier built of reinforced concrete by the Germans in the 1930s was part of an ambitious system of fortifications. It was only in February 1945 that Polish soldiers managed to break through. Monuments and military museums in Podgaje near Jastrowie, in Wałcz and in Mirosławiec serve as memorials to the fierce battles waged in this part of West Pomerania. The best preserved fragments of the wall can be visited near Wałcz.

This town, on the shores of two lakes, also has a vast military cemetery where victims of World War II are buried. The **Bytów Lakes** (Pojezierze Bytowskie), found among wooded hills, begin east of the Drawa Lakes. **Bytów ❹**, on the edge of the Bytów Lake District, has a Gothic castle built by the Teutonic Knights which is now a Regional Museum of Western Kashubia, with a collection that includes folk arts and crafts. The castle also houses a hotel and restaurant. The town's other attractions include the Gothic tower of St Catherine's church, the 18th-century neoclassical former post office, and a half-timbered 19th-century granary.

Along the Baltic Sea coast

Świnoujście occupies three islands: Uznam, Wolin and Karsibór. While this is a major port for cargo ships and passenger ferries to Hamburg, Copenhagen and Ystad, it is also a tourist centre. The western end of Świnoujście has long sandy beaches, with Poland's tallest lighthouse (68 metres/220 ft), and being a long established spa town there are various Seccessionist spa buildings. The town of **Wolin ❺**, in the south of the island of Wolin, was one of the oldest Slav settlements, flourishing during the 9th and 10th centuries. A Slav burial mound and cemetery both date from the 9th century. However, it was also a Viking stronghold, which accounts for the annual Viking Festival. Part of the island is a national park, established to protect the unusual geological formations, cliffs and offshore rocks. The remote eastern edge of the park has several lakes which link to form a small lake district. This includes Lake Turkusowe at the southern end of the park, with Lake Gardno close to the seashore. Eagles, water fowl and other protected species such as wild boar can be seen in the woods surrounding the lakes, with a small bison reserve at the edge of the park. Having attractive sandy beaches, impressive cliffs, and dense forests on either side, makes **Międzyzdroje ❻** one of the most popular Baltic resorts. In addition to numerous sports facilities, the spa operates from attractive wooden buildings dating from the 19th century. The Natural History Museum (open Tues–Sun 10am– 6pm) will also enable you to get the most out of visiting Wolin.

Kamień Pomorski ❼, a town which joined the Hanseatic League in the 14th century, is situated by the Kamieński Lagoon about 10 km (6 miles) from the sea. This was once an important trading centre, with a mint issuing Pomeranian coins in the late 12th century. Retaining its original medieval lay-out, the town's most important building is the Romanesque-Gothic cathedral. Elegant features animate the red-brick façade, while the interiors include a 12th-century baptismal font, a 17th-century wrought-iron screen and Baroque organ, which can be heard during the town's Summer Festival of Organ Music. The late Gothic Bishop's Palace, the 14th-century Church of St Nicholas, now housing the Regional Museum, and St Mary's Church, built in the 18th century, are also prime examples of sacred architecture. Fragments of the town walls include the 15th-century Wolin Gate, which leads into the Old Town and the late-Gothic Town Hall. To explore the lagoon, boats can be hired by the day at the harbour.

The coast is lined with numerous holiday villages such as Dziwnów, Dziwnówek, Mrzeżyno, and Dźwirzyno, which are renowned for their recreational

Map on page 322

European bison in a reserve at the Wolin National Park.

BELOW: fishing boats at low tide.

facilities. Parts of the coast have suffered from erosion, which is particularly evident in Trzęsacz, where the ruins of a 14th-century Gothic church, originally built 2 km (1 mile) from the coast, have been lapped by the sea since 1901 Founded in the 13th century, **Trzebiatów,** beside the River Rega, has managed to preserve its delightful medieval character. The main sights are the Gothic S Mary's Church, dominated by a stately 90-metre (295-ft) steeple which is typical of West Pomeranian architecture and contains one of Poland's heaviest bells (7.2 tons). Scaled-down Gothic can be seen at the delightful Holy Ghos Chapel. Fragments of the town walls include the late-Gothic Kaszana tower. A great way to see the surrounding countryside is from a narrow-gauge passenger train which operates between Trzebiatów and other coastal towns.

Kołobrzeg ❽, at the mouth of the River Parsęta, is both a port and major holiday spa resort. The town dates from AD 1000, when King Bolesław Chrobry established an episcopal see and prospered as a member of the Hanseatic League. A great asset was salt production, which also fostered production of salted herrings. Almost 90 percent of Kołobrzeg was destroyed in World War II but the Old Town has now been rebuilt, much of it very recently. The Gothic Collegiate Church of St Mary is the town's most impressive building, with leaning columns supporting a vaulted ceiling. These pillars may give the impression that the church is about to collapse, but they have leaned at an angle since the 16th century. Gothic features include a bronze font, a vast chandelier, and beautifully carved stalls. It's an effort to climb to the top of the brick steeple, but the reward is a magnificent panorama of Kołobrzeg and its surroundings. Fragments of the medieval city wall include the **Gun Powder Tower** (Wieża Prochowa), while the Military Museum exhibits weapons and other items salvaged

BELOW: the shifting dunes at Łeba.

Map
on page
322

in 1945 (open Tues–Sun; entrance fee). Lying beyond the dunes east of Koło-brzeg are more holiday villages, with Ustronie Morskie, Sarbinowo and Mielno popular with tourists especially during the summer. Around this area the countryside has an extraordinary beauty, combining lakes and flooded meadows.

The sleepy fishing village of **Darłowo** ➒, by the mouth of the River Wieprza, was granted its municipal charter in 1270. The Pomeranian Duke Eryk I, who also ruled Denmark, Sweden and Norway, established the 14th-century castle as the capital of his dukedom. This magnificent castle is now a museum (tel: 094 314 23 51; open Tues–Sun; entrance fee) with an interesting collection of folk arts and crafts, furniture, armour, sacred art and portraits of Pomeranian dukes. Duke Eryk also founded the Scandinavian Gothic-style St Gertrude's Chapel, which is a rarity, being twelve-sided. He is buried, together with other Pomeranian dukes, in the Gothic St Mary's Church. The Old Town has retained a medieval character, which includes the town walls and one of the Gothic town gates. A Baroque Town Hall overlooks the market square.

The neighbouring village of **Darłówko** is another popular seaside resort, as is the small town of **Sławno**, 20 km (12 miles) from Darłówko, which has several monuments that are well worth a detour, including the medieval town wall, the huge Gothic St Mary's Church, and various burghers' houses.

Jarosławiec ➓ is one of Poland's most attractive seaside resorts, partly due to its proximity to Lake Wicko. The traditional fishermen's cottages and half-timbered houses surrounding the lake, and the 17th century lighthouse, create a delightful atmosphere. At the mouth of the River Słupia is Ustka, a small port and popular resort. The harbour was built to serve **Słupsk** ⓫, a busy town situated some 20 km (12 miles) inland. One of the largest coastal resorts, Słupsk's attractions include the 14th-century Gothic Parish Church and the Renaissance Castle of the Pomeranian Dukes. This houses the **Museum of Central Pomerania** (open Tues–Sun; entrance fee; tel: 059 842 40 81) as well as a gallery devoted to the works of Witkacy *(see page 247)*. The castle's grounds also include the Dominican Church of St Jacek, with its ducal tombs and Baroque organ.

The **Słowiński National Park** encloses four lakes: Łebsko (the third largest in Poland), Gardno, Dołgie Wielkie and Dołgie Małe. Separated from the sea by a small beach, the lakes are a refuge for numerous birds. However, the park is most renowned for its unusual 'moving" sand dunes, along the coastline between Rowy and Leba. In some areas the dunes are moved up to 10 metres (30 ft) per year by the wind. The tallest dune is just over 40 metres (130 ft) high, and the largest extends to around 300 hectares (740 acres). In the western part of the park are the remains of V-2 rocket launch pads, abandoned by the Nazis at the end of World War II, which now attract a lot of visitors.

Kluki, a remote fishing village on the edge of Lake Łebsko, has some fine half-timbered houses and a *skansen* (open-air museum) with a collection of historic regional buildings. Most of the local inhabitants are descended from the Slavic Slovincian tribe. The coastal village of **Łeba** is an attractive seaside destination and a fishing port, and is a good base from which to explore the Słowin National Park. ❏

BELOW: visitors to Słowinski National Park, near Łeba.

GDAŃSK

Gdańsk was reduced to rubble during World War II, but it has been reconstructed and today looks much the same as in the Hanseatic era when it was built by rich shipowners and merchants

The most important city along the Baltic Coast is actually a "Tri-City", comprising Gdańsk, Sopot and Gdynia, which together extend along the Bay of Gdańsk for 20 km (12 miles). Originally separate towns, the suburbs of each have linked to create a conurbation inhabited by almost 800,000 people, which is well connected by road, rail, ferry, bus and tram links.

These three cities have nevertheless retained their own distinct characters. Gdańsk is the historic and cultural centre, with outstanding examples of Gothic, Renaissance and Baroque architecture. Sopot is a traditional seaside resort, which developed in the 19th and early 20th centuries, and is characterised by Art Nouveau villas, while the maritime character of Gdynia dates from the 1920s, when the city was "purpose-built" to provide a modern harbour and docks.

Historic pearl of the Baltic

Gdańsk has long been an important port and trading centre. Originating as a Slavic fishing village, a defensive settlement was established in the Gdańsk area during the 9th century. From the 10th century this was a seat of the Pomeranian dukes, with Poland's most important saint, Adalbert, baptising the local inhabitants in AD 997. The earliest recorded mention was in 999, within *The Life of Saint Adalbert* written by a Benedictine monk. Being a river port on the Vistula also meant that Gdańsk was an important link in the early Middle Ages with the historic capital of Kraków (*see page 201*), with grains, furs, leather and amber among the most important commodities.

The region's evolution was also dictated by Polish-Prussian rivalry. In 1226 the Mazovian Duke Konrad Mazowiecki asked the Teutonic Order of Knights (*see page 22*) to help in his struggle against the heathen Prussians, in order to control the area around Toruń in East Pomerania. The Teutonic Knights agreed, but it soon created another problem, as the Knights used this as an opportunity to strengthen their presence in East Pomerania. Gdańsk and East Pomerania came under the control of the Teutonic Knights in 1308, the same year in which the Main Town district received its town charter. The Knights also founded the New Town (Nowe Miasto) in 1380, which subsequently merged with the Main Town, while also incorporating the neighbouring East Pomeranian town, now known as the Old Town district. The Knights also transferred their capital from Venice to nearby Malbork.

As a member of the Hanseatic League, Gdańsk developed into a prosperous town during the 14th century, and the town's burghers set about constructing major civic buildings, with St Mary's Church intended to be the largest brick-built church in the world.

LEFT:
the Golden House.
BELOW: the Neptune
Fountain, symbol of
the city of Gdańsk.

The princes of East Pomerania and Greater Poland (Wielkopolska) attempted to resist the growing dominance of the Teutonic Knights, and a Polish triumph in 1454 brought Gdańsk and East Pomerania under Polish rule. This was further ratified by the Teutonic Knights agreeing to the Second Peace of Toruń in 1466. Being granted exclusive rights to Poland's maritime trade in the 15th century resulted in Gdańsk enjoying even greater prosperity, with two-thirds of Poland's external trade passing through the town. Gdańsk continued to have the status of an independent town until the partitions of Poland brought it under Prussian control in 1792, regaining its original status as a free town during the Napoleonic era. Between the two World Wars, Gdańsk was under the protection of the League of Nations.

The most famous chronicle of the wartime years is The Tin Drum, by the German writer Günter Grass. Born in Gdańsk (or Danzig as it is known in German) in 1927, he describes this period through the eyes of a child.

It was in the Westerplatte region of Gdańsk that the first shots of World War II were fired, and Gdańsk remained in the active war zone for longer than any other region, with the occupation lasting until the Nazis surrendered on the Hel peninsula in May 1945. By the end of the war Gdańsk was reduced to rubble, though much of this was inflicted by the "liberating" Red Army, who thought of Gdańsk as "Danzig", in other words German.

Following the end of World War II, Gdańsk became a part of Poland and despite the town's devastation and Poland's precarious economic situation there was never any question that the city would be reconstructed. The question was how this should be done. It was suggested that a new, modern city be built on this site, but it was eventually decided to reconstruct the city in its historic style. This presented a huge challenge for architects and planners. Although some fragments of the original buildings, such as church walls, towers and gates, could be retrieved from the rubble, many of the landmarks were totally

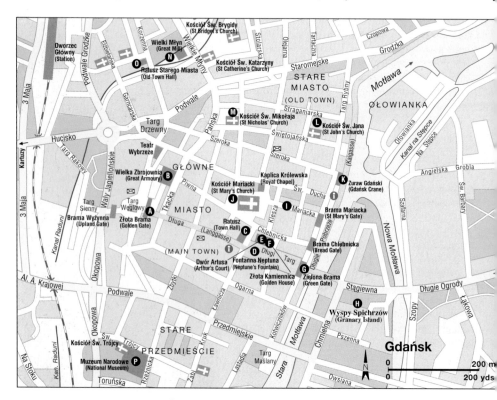

Gdańsk

0   200 m
0   200 yds

estroyed. It was a massive undertaking, and it wasn't until 1975 that the recon-
truction programme was completed. Indeed, St John's Church was only fin-
shed in the 1990's. The historic granaries are still waiting their turn.

In 1997, Gdańsk, now with a population of nearly 500,000, commemorated
s millennium, and the city continues to be Poland's largest port as well as an
mportant industrial, scientific and cultural centre, not to mention a major tourist
ttraction. Among the city's varied cultural repertoire is the Baltic Philharmonic, with annual events including the Festival of Organ Music, the Film Fes-
val and the Dominican Fair in August. First established during the mid-13th
entury and revived in 1972, this market offers numerous folk arts and crafts,
ntiques and bric-a-brac, amber jewellery and various other local specialities,
vith various concerts and events organised to coincide with this fair.

Map on page 334

Gdańsk's historic centre

Much of the historic centre was originally constructed as a showcase of the
city's prosperity. The buildings were designed to impress. From grand and
imposing to flamboyant and ornamental, the city is beautiful but never osten-
tatious. The burghers had that rare combination: wealth and style. As much of
the historic centre is pedestrianised, a walking tour is the best way to explore,
with the numerous cafés, boutiques and galleries providing plenty of refreshing
stops en route. Nine principal thoroughfares each link to a waterside gate that
provides access to the harbour, so you are never far from a sea view.

The principal thoroughfare, Długa (literally "Long street"), is best approached
through the **Golden Gate Ⓐ** (Złota Brama). Designed by Abraham van den
Blocke between 1612-14 in a Renaissance style, it was inspired by a triumphal

*The statues on the
Golden Gate are
copies of the origi-
nals made in 1648.*

BELOW: Solidarność
plaque, Gdańsk.

CRADLE OF SOLIDARITY

Gdańsk is now best known as the birthplace of the
trade union movement Solidarity *(Solidarność)*, which
challenged the Communist regime and shaped Polish
history during the 1980s. Lech Wałęsa, the union's leader
and President of Poland (1990-95), wrote:

"Visitors… have no trouble finding their way to the
monument… outside the Gdańsk shipyard. Striking
workers were murdered here in December 1970, in a hail
of fire from the militia. They sacrificed their lives for more
than Gdańsk – even at a time when nobody had foreseen
what far-reaching effects their struggle would have on
the future of all of Europe. Their resistance and deaths
were experiences from which we learned lessons…

"The resounding slogan of 1980 was 'good bread for
good work'. Of course, the call for freedom was within
everyone's heart all over Poland, but it was also clear to
every one of us that such a cry at that time could have
triggered off a swift Soviet intervention.

"And yet 10 years later, we have attained our goal – in
a revolution without force and without bloodshed, a
revolution which overthrew the Communist regime and
set an example for democratic freedom initiatives
throughout central and eastern Europe."

The Gdańsk Town Hall clock and tower. The statue at the top of the tower is of King Zygmunt August.

BELOW: guard at entrance to Gdańsk Town Hall, now the Historical Museum.

Roman arch, and the view along Długa is equally triumphant. As this was th route along which Polish kings paraded when attending events in the city, it' hardly surprising that Długa features numerous impressive buildings. An imme diate example is the neighbouring Court of the Fraternity of St George (Dwó Bractwa Św. Jerzego). This Gothic mansion was built in the late 15th century as the seat of this fraternity.

Before continuing along Długa, turn left into Tkacka to see the **Grea Armoury B** (Wielka Zbrojownia). A magnificent example of Renaissanc architecture, the intricate symmetry of its four-gabled façade was designed b Dutch architect Anthonis van Opbergen. He was highly regarded in Gdańsk, an also built the Kronborg in Helsingør, Denmark, more popularly referred to a "Hamlet's Castle". The armoury now houses the Państwowa Wyższa Szkoł Sztuk Plastycznych (the Academy of Fine Arts; open Tues–Sun; entrance fee)

The **Town Hall C** (Ratusz) is unusual in not occupying a central position i a square, but forming part of a terrace of buildings at the far end of Długa. Nev ertheless, this red brick 14th-century Gothic building stands out as the larges building in the street, with its elegant Renaissance tower crowned by a gilde statue of King Zygmunt August, dating from 1561. Needless to say, the view from the top of the tower is magnificent. The interiors are equally impressive and the Red Room, originally the setting for the Town Council's debates, i truly a showpiece. Set against a vivid red and gilded background, this room' wealth of sculptures and ornamental carvings, are dominated by numerou paintings – 25 on the ceiling alone, while a series of seven allegorical painting are the work of Hans Vredeman de Vries. Many of the furnishings are original having been shipped from Gdańsk prior to the outbreak of war for safekeeping

Map
on page
334

oused amid these sumptuous interiors is a stylish restaurant and the **Histori-** **al Museum of the City of Gdańsk** (Muzeum Historii Miasta Gdańska, Długa 7; open Tues 10am–3pm, Wed–Sat 10am–6pm, Sun 11am–4pm; entrance fee xcept Tues; tel: 058 767 91 00). At this point Długa broadens out to form ługi Targ ("Long Marketplace"). The architectural magnificence is also height- ned, as this is where the very wealthiest merchants and ship-owners built their sidences. The beginning of this street is marked by the decorative **Neptune's** **ountain** ❿ (Fontanna Neptuna). Enclosed by its original wrought iron railings, is statue of Neptune, symbolising the city's maritime links, dates from 1613.

Another impressive building is **Arthur's Court** ❺ (Dwór Artusa) , the tradi- onal seat of the Gdańsk Merchants' Guild and Poland's first stock exchange. The ghly individual Mannerist architecture includes windows that dominate the main çade (equal to three storeys of the neighbouring houses). The vaulted entrance hall ontains various historic features, including an ornate tiled stove. One of the few uildings not to be totally destroyed during World War II, this is now a museum (tel: 58 301 43 59; open Tues, Thurs, Sat 10am–5pm, Wed 10am–4pm; entrance fee).

Façades of neighbouring buildings are equally definitive of other architectural enres. Baroque *in extremis* is the only way to describe the **Golden House** ❻ Złota Kamiennica). Dating from the early 17th century, this four-storey house as built for the Mayor of Gdańsk and was named after its gilded bas reliefs, omprising mythological figures including Achilles and Cleopatra. Home to e Cunard Line between the world wars, this is now the Maritime Institute.

The marketplace culminates in another gateway, the ornate quadruple arched reen Gate ❼ (Zielona Brama). Designed in a Flemish Renaissance style, is was also an official residence of Polish kings when visiting the city.

In the 14th century Europe became fascinated with the stories of England's King Arthur and Camelot, and many towns such as Gdańsk attempted to emulate the chivalrous spirit in their self-styled courts.

BELOW: relief detail the Golden House.

Gdańsk's waterfront

The Green Gate opens onto the wharf by the Motława estuary, formerly the site of the town's harbour. Boats leave from here for trips along the coast to Sopot, Gdynia and Westerplatte, or across the Bay of Gdańsk to the popular holiday resort of Hel on the Gdańsk peninsula (*see page 345*). Across the estuary on **Granary Island** (Wyspa Spichrzów) are numerous historic granaries, some of which are still awaiting restoration. Part of this area is also being redeveloped as the city's modern commercial and banking centre. Turning left leads to the Bread Gate (Brama Chlebnicka), with the waterfront featuring numerous galleries selling souvenirs, antiques and above all, "Baltic Gold" or amber, alongside cafés and bars. Amber is almost the only thing you can buy, together with antiques, in the boutiques and galleries along the street **Mariacka** , entered through St Mary's Gate (Brama Mariacka). One of the city's most beautiful streets, with its original granite cobblestones, it is also one of the most individual, characterised by "*perrons*". A feature of grander houses in numerous Baltic cities, this comprises a small but ornate flights of steps from the pavement to a terrace by the entrance to each building (rather like a box at the theatre). This was a prime place for the residents to sit and watch passers-by, as well as being seen themselves. Totally rebuilt after World War II, the first task was to determine exactly which fragments could be used where, as masonry was scattered all over the street. Furthermore, there was little documentation to draw upon as the archives were destroyed during the war, which meant the architects frequently resorted to photographs as their source material. There was at least one surviving *perron*, which was an invaluable starting point.

At the end of Mariacka is the transcendent **St Mary's Church** (Kościół Mariacki). This monumental red-brick Gothic building is thought to be th

world's sixth largest church, able to accommodate a congregation of 25,000 or crowds of tourists). Not surprisingly, it took more than 150 years to complete, from 1343–1502. Austere through its simplicity, but undoubtedly beautiful, the initial impact is provided by the scale and height of the three-naved arrangement. It is certainly worth looking up at the Baroque organ, and the magnificent vaulting, much of which was reconstructed following a fire in 1945.

While many original treasures were looted by the Nazis (or ended up in Polish museums), this still leaves plenty to see: 13 Gothic altars, over 30 Renaissance and Baroque epitaphs and a stunning sculpture of the so-called Beautiful Madonna. An astronomical clock, the work of Hans Duringer in 1470, is one of the world's largest medieval clocks, revealing the phases of the moon as well as the positions of the sun and the moon. Another outstanding feature is a triptych by Hans Memling entitled *The Last Judgement*, dating from 1466–73. This painting was actually en route to a church in Tuscany when it was intercepted by the citizens of Gdańsk. A copy now hangs in the church, with the original in the National Museum (Muzeum Narodowe). If you feel like climbing the lofty tower a wonderful view across the historic centre is your reward.

Neighbouring the church is the elegant **Royal Chapel**, built in 1678–81. Founded by King Jan III Sobieski, it is thought to be the work of Tylman of Gameren, the Dutch architect responsible for many of Poland's most beautiful Baroque buildings; sculptures decorating the façade are by Andreas Schluter.

Returning to the riverfront, the 15th-century **Gdańsk Crane ⓚ** (Żuraw Gdański) was meticulously restored after World War II. Housed in the largest double-towered gate on the waterfront, it handled cargos as well as raising ships masts. Capable of lifting up to 2,000 kg (2 tonnes), it is one of the largest industrial constructions to have survived from the Middle Ages, and seeing the crane in action is a major attraction. This building now houses the Central Maritime Museum (Centralne Muzeum Morskie, Szeroka 67–8; open Tues–Sun 10am–3pm; entrance fee; tel: 058 301 86 11). Adjoining the crane is a restaurant of the same name, which provides a panoramic view of the Motława. There are two prime examples of sacred Gothic architecture on Świętojańska. The **St John's Church ⓛ** (Kościół Św. Jana), which has only recently been reconstructed after its wartime devastation, has an impressive altar and various tombs of city dignitaries. The **St Nicholas' Church ⓜ** (Kościół Św. Mikołaja) was one of the few buildings to survive the war intact. The Gothic façade gives way to highly gilded Baroque interiors, with a beautiful altar where a central painting is surrounded by gilded figures.

The Old Town

Although the **Old Town** (Stare Miasto) district was not rebuilt to the same extent as the Główne Miasto, there are numerous historic buildings and architectural styles. It has a different character: less densely built up, and providing greater variety, with broader streets and more open spaces interlaced with greenery. The parish church St Catherine's Church (Kościół Św. Katarzyny) on Wielkie Młyny has a magnificent Gothic tower with unusual ornamentation soaring above the façade, while the interiors feature late Gothic vaulted ceilings and

Map on page 334

It is claimed that the St Mary's Church Astronomical Clock has only lost three minutes in the first hundred years of service.

BELOW: the riverfront with the Gdańsk Crane.

Map on page 334

Baroque details and monuments. This includes the tomb of the renowned Gdań astronomer, Jan Heweliusz, also known as Johannes Hevelius (1611–87), wh published one of the first detailed maps of the moon and a catalogue of star However, earning little money from astronomy, he was also a successful brewe with profits from the brewery providing funds to establish an observatory (th Hevelius beer brand continues to be very popular). Immediately behind th church is St Bridget's Church (Kościół Św. Brygidy), which played a significa role in Poland's recent history, being known as the "Solidarity church". Durin martial law in 1981–3 anti-Communist groups met here to worship, which wa then considered an act of "political opposition". This church is also unusual not having recreated period interiors. Instead a modern layout, in a form «sacred minimalism" creates a poignant setting for contemporary works of ar including a monument to Fr Jerzy Popiełuszko, the outspoken supporter of So idarity who was murdered by the Communists.

Both St Brigitte's and St Catherine's Church are part of a cluster of build ings around the **Radunia Canal** (Kanał Raduni), at the heart of the Old Tow. The combination of a small park and other stretches of greenery, canals ar cascades gives this area a relaxed identity.The **Great Mill**  (The Wiel Młyn) completed in 1595, and the Small Mill (Mały Młyn) are both prin examples of medieval architecture. The former is a terrific structure with sloping tiled roof, now housing an elegant shopping centre (open daily 11am 7pm). The 16th-century **Old Town Hall** (Ratusz Starego Miasta)  (ope Mon–Sun 10am–8pm; tel: 301 10 51) with its Dutch appearance, has sple did interiors; although not on the same scale as the main Town Hall it is wort seeing, with some beautiful paintings and fine examples of the Gdańsk chest

BELOW: Gdańsk Shipyard Monument.

Heading further north in the direction of the shipyard is the Monument to the Shipyard Workers (poignar Pomnik Poległych Stoczniowców). Three huge crosse on which much smaller anchors are attached, soar abov Gate 2 of the entrance to the Gdańsk shipyards, con memorating the 28 people who died when the Decen ber 1970 strike was suppressed. The crosses symboli Faith and the anchors Hope, while metal figures dockyard workers feature at the base of the crosses. Th monument was unveiled in 1980 by the Solidarit movement, the year in which the trade union moveme was legally recognised by the government. The Con munists did not dare touch the monument because its powerful significance. **Roads to Freedom** (Dro; do Wolności; open Tues–Sun 10am–4pm; entrance fe tel: 058 769 29 20) is a museum in the shipyard tracin the history of the Solidarity movement and the defeat the Communist régime.

South of Długi Targ is **The Old Suburb** (Star Przedmieście). Among the area's most importar buildings are the Church of the Holy Trinity (Kościo Św. Trójcy) built at the beginning of the 16th centur with a former Franciscan monastery housing th **National Museum**  (Muzeum Narodowe; Toruńsk 1; tel: 058 301 70 61; Tues–Fri 9am–4pm, Sat–Su 10am–4pm; entrance fee except Sat). The extensiv collection includes Polish paintings, *objets d'art* an furniture, such as the renowned Gdańsk chests.

Amber

Fondly referred to as "Baltic Gold", amber is Poland's national stone and a visible element of daily life, whether it's in the form of rings, earrings, necklaces, bracelets or cuff-links, not to mention various decorative items for the home such as lampshades and jewellery boxes. Amber varies enormously in terms of shape and size, while the colour ranges beyond amber from yellow to white, red and green. Being transparent, amber is usually streaked with various colourways, while the inherent flaws add character.

Artificial amber can be convincing and inexpensive (if sold honestly), prepared from substances such as camphor. The genuine article is actually fossilised resin that seeped from deciduous and coniferous trees and has solidified and "matured" over thousands of years. The resin frequently trapped insects and flora, resulting in numerous pieces of amber containing perfectly preserved specimens of prehistoric life. Polish amber has even included fragments of date trees and tea bushes from the primeval forest which originally occupied the Baltic coastline.

Beyond the technical explanation, various legends define amber as the solidified tears of the passing of time, and more specifically as the tears of the Heliades, the sisters of Phaeton, who couldn't stop weeping after his death. Phaeton's father was Helios, god of the sun, who drove the chariot that dragged the sun across the sky from sunrise to sunset. One day Phaeton drove the chariot, but brought the sun too close to the earth: mountains burned and seas evaporated into deserts. Phaeton's punishment was to be struck by a fatal thunderbolt by Zeus. To stop his sisters from weeping the gods turned them into willows on the banks of the River Edrin, into which their tears continued to flow. En route to the Baltic the teardrops turned into amber. Locals who collected the amber on the beach assumed it was a gift from the gods.

Amber continues to be collected from beaches as the sea washes it up from beneath the surface of the sand. The best time to go amber-hunting is after a storm. The region between Chlapów and the Sambian peninsula yields the largest amounts.

Amber was prized by the Ancient Egyptians who called it the stone of "life and health" as it was thought to promote youthfulness and longevity. In fact, the world would be a far healthier place if amber fulfiled all the claims made for it.

There is no shortage of amber boutiques throughout Poland. Gdańsk is the historic centre, with a guild of amber craftsmen established in the 15th century. The city still has hundreds of shops selling amber jewellery and decorative items. Be careful not to buy amber on the street as it is likely to be fake. Look for a sign of the Amber Association of Poland in shop windows as a guarantee of quality and authenticity. Some of the finest are along Motława Quay and Mariacka, where the Archaeological Museum also has an amber collection. Outside the city is the Bakowo Forest, which includes an amber mine. The most extensive collection of historic amber can be seen at the castle in Malbork (see page 347). ❑

RIGHT: shopping for amber in Gdańsk.

AROUND GDAŃSK

Map on page 344

To follow the route around Gdańsk to the historic towns of Toruń, Frombork and Chełmno is to journey through the 1,000-year history and culture of the country

A t the entrance to the harbour, about 5 km (3 miles) from the city centre, is the Westerplatte peninsula. It was here, at 4.45am on 1 September 1939, that 210 Polish soldiers and officers came under fire from the *Schleswig-Holein*, a German battleship. The garrison held out for seven days before surrenering, after 3,000 Nazi soldiers landed here. The site has become a memorial, ith some of the ruins left exactly as they were after the bombardment, and there a modernistic monument commemorating the bravery of the garrison.

Oliwa is one of Gdańsk's ❶ most attractive suburbs, with a large Cistercian onastery complex including the Oliwa Cathedral. The incredibly slender, twin-wered façade actually houses the longest church in Poland. The Romanesque-othic style, dating from the first half of the 13th century, was partly remodelled the 18th century, adding rococo elements. The 23 side altars date from the 16th d 17th centuries, with a marble tomb of Gdańsk princes who were buried here the 13th century. Many famous musicians have performed on the cathedral's coco Oliwa organ. The work of J. Wulf at the end of the 18th century, the gan has an amazing 1,876 pipes and 110 voices. Organ concerts are a regular traction at the cathedral, and the adjoining park is a delightful place for a stroll.

LEFT:
Szerova Street,
Toruń Old Town.
BELOW:
fountain in front of
the abbey in Oliwa.

Sopot ❷ is full of greenery, open perspectives along tree-lined streets, boulerds and parks. As there was little damage to the town ring World War II, many buildings are original 19th-ntury Seccessionist, with wooden villas providing a ourgeois" character in contrast to the "showcase" chitecture of Gdańsk.

The original settlement of Sopot was established y Oliwa's Cistercian monks. During the 16th cenry the Gdańsk burghers decided that sea air was benicial to their health and began turning the village to a spa. This received a much greater impetus at e beginning of the 19th century, mainly due to the ct that Napoleon's former doctor, Jean Haffner, ected bathing pavilions by the sea in 1823. The evotion of Sopot can be seen in Sopot Museum Muzeum Miasta Sopotu, ul. Poniatowskiego 8 ; open ues–Fri 10am–4pm, Sat, Sun 11am–5pm; entrance e except Thurs; tel: 058 551 22 66).

It's easy to see why Sopot became so popular: a park ns the length of its wide, sandy beaches which provide 1 ideal setting for sun bathing. Some highly eclectic spa ildings can still be seen around the seafront. The pier the longest in Poland, extending 516 metres (1,693 ft) to the sea, which is a favourite place to promenade hile also providing an embarkation point for boat trips Gdańsk, Gdynia and the Hel peninsula. Another vourite place to promenade is the adjacent main thor-ghfare, Bohaterów Monte Cassino (Heroes of Monte assino street): lined with pavement cafés, trendy

boutiques and galleries, it encapsulates Sopot's relaxed spirit. The Grand Hotel is a reminder of Sopot's traditional grandeur. Built in an Art Déco style in 192 and renovated in 1990, the hotel offers a beachside terrace, tea dances, gourme meals and Poland's most elegant, not to mention most historic casino.

Gdynia, 9 km (6 miles) north of Sopot, is Poland's second-largest port. small fishing village until 1921, it was transformed into a "purpose built" po to ensure that Poland would not be entirely dependent on Gdańsk. Tourist attrac tions reflect the maritime character. The museum ships *Błyskawica*, a Worl War II destroyer, and *Dar Pomorza*, a three-masted frigate (both open Tues–Sa 10am–4pm), are moored at the dockyard and have exhibits tracing the histor of the Polish navy. The city also has an excellent Oceanographic Museum an Aquarium (Zjednoczenia 1; tel: 058 621 70 21; open daily 9am–7pm; Sept–Ap 10am–5pm; entrance fee), and a Naval Museum (Bulwar Nadmorski; ope Tues–Sun 10am–5pm; entrance fee; tel 058 732 66 01). Climbing the 50-metr (165-ft) Stone Hill (Kamienna Góra) provides a great view of the harbour.

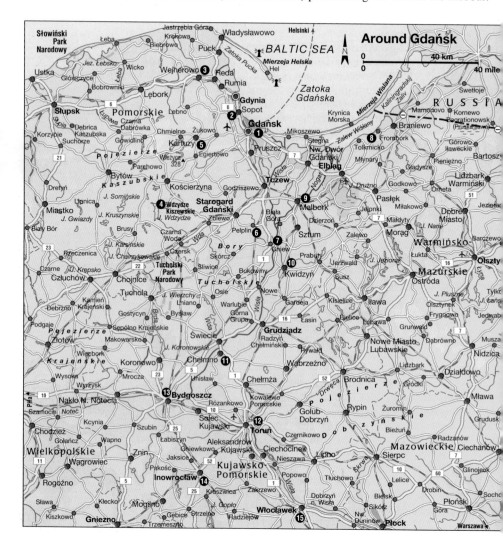

The Bay of Gdańsk and Kashubian Lakes

Curving almost 35 km (20 miles) across the Bay of Gdańsk is the narrow **Hel Peninsula** (Mierzeja Helska). This is an idyllic area, with fishing villages including Jastrzębia Góra, the romantic port of Władysławowo, Chałupy, Kuźnica, Jastarnia, Jurata and, on the tip of the peninsula, the old village of Hel, whose fascinating history is documented in the local fishing museum.

At the beginning of the peninsula is the quiet port of **Puck**, which developed from a Slavic settlement into a naval base for the Polish fleet in the 16th and 17th centuries. The town's buildings are mainly 16th to 18th century with an 18th-century half-timbered former hospital housing the Museum of the Puck region. Southwest of Puck, **Wejherowo** ❸ has a distinctly religious character, with the 16th-century governor establishing the *Kalwaria Wejherowska* (the Wejherowo "Road to Calvary") over the nearby hills. It includes some 26 17th- to 19th-century chapels in total. To the west of the tri-city is the **Pojezierze Kaszubskie**, an extraordinarily scenic combination of lakes and hills, the highest point of which is the Wieżyca at 329 metres (1,080 ft). These uplands are also the source of the rivers Radunia, Wierzyca, Wda, Słupia and Łeba, all of which flow into the Baltic Sea.

The largest lake is the Wdzydze, and around it is **Wdzydze Kiszewskie** ❹, a superb *skansen* (open-air ethnographic museum; open daily 9am–4pm; entrance fee; tel: 058 686 12 88), which extends over an area of 21 hectares (52 acres). This collection of traditional buildings from the Kashubian region, including an exquisite wooden church painted with rustic motifs, provides a wonderful insight into the region's heritage. **Kartuzy** ❺, surrounded by lakes and woods, is the capital of Kashubia. The Carthusian abbey complex has a fascinating 14th-century Gothic church, with a roof shaped like a coffin. The Kashubian Museum's rich collection of folk arts and crafts also details the history and lifestyle of this historic West Slavic tribe (open May–Sept Tues–Sun 9am–4pm; Oct–Apr Tues–Sat 9am–3pm; entrance fee; tel: 058 681 14 42).

A little further southwest is the 1,000-year-old city of **Kościerzyna**, the main centre of Kashubian culture. In June the popular Kashubian tradition of floating wreaths on the lake is followed by a procession around other lakes in the region. With numerous sporting facilities to hand, this makes an ideal base from which to explore the region's towns, such as Chmielno. A popular holiday destination and one of the most historic Kashubian settlements, it is located on the banks of three lakes, the Białe, Kodno and Leckowskie. Traditionally a pottery centre, the renowned Necel workshop can be seen on request. The Kashubian Country Park was established at the centre of this lake district in 1983.

Further south on the River Wierzyca is **Pelplin** ❻, where you can see one of Poland's most beautiful Gothic cathedrals. Originally the church of a Cistercian abbey, this vast triple-naved basilica includes Gothic stalls, as well as Renaissance, Baroque and Rococo works of art by Herman Han and Bartlomej Strobel. The Diocesan Museum's has a collection of sacral art, a Gutenberg Bible printed in 1453, and an

Map
on page
344

TIP

There is a wonderful cultural programme in Sopot. The Opera Leśna (Opera in the Woods), a delightful al fresco auditorium set in a wood, hosts various annual events including the Opera Festival in July, and the International Song Festival in August.

BELOW: Hel beach.

Altar detail in
Malbork Castle
chapel.

amazing collection of musical manuscripts (ks Biskupa Dominika 11; tel: 069 ?
12 21; open Tues–Sun; entrance fee). **Gniew** ❼ is situated on a steep cliff at t
confluence of the Wierzyca and Vistula rivers. Originally settled by the Cister
cians, it was subsequently controlled by the Teutonic Knights – the remains of t
knights' Gothic castle is perched on a hilltop near the town. The original mediev
layout includes churches and town walls, some dating from the 16th centur
while the arcaded burghers' houses are the finest in Pomerania. South of Gnie
and also on the Vistula, is Nowe. Now a centre of the furniture industry, the ou
line of this medieval town with its small castle and two Gothic churches rises hi
above the river.

The **Świecka Uplands** (Wysoczyzna Świecka) run to the south of the Staro
ard Lakes, with the main town being **Świecie**. From 1309 to 1466, Świecie w
the headquarters for a local commander of the Teutonic Knights, with the rui
of the knight's castle, together with a Gothic church, standing above the fork
the Wda and Vistula. One of Poland's largest forests, the **Tuchola Forest** (Bo
Tucholskie), lies to the north and northwest of Świecie beside the rivers Wda a
Brda, which are popular for watersports. Distinctive features in this landsca
are the narrow "channel" lakes, with countless man-made lakes, such as La
Kornowskie near Koronowo. In an isolated and wooded area, the **Cisy Staropo
skie Larch Reserve** (guided tours only) in Wierzchlas, about 32 km (20 mile
southeast of Tuchola, and the Stone Circles (Kręgi Kamienne) archaeologic
and biological reserve (the megalithic site has been dated at the first or seco
century) in Odry north of Czersk, are of particular interest. At the western tip
the forest lies **Tuchola**, the area's main tourist centre, with medieval buildin
and remnants of the town's fortified walls drawing visitors.

BELOW: Frombork
Cathedral.

On the right bank of the Vistula

Poland's most northerly holiday region lies east of the Vistula estuary, where resorts are typically separated from the beach by narrow strips of dunes and woodland. However, resorts such as Mikoszewo, Jantar and Stegna are close to the beaches of the Mierzeja Wiślana spit. The nearby town of Sztutowo was the site of a concentration camp in which 85,000 people of various nationalities died. Near the Russian border, overlooking the Vistula lagoon, is the fishing town of **Frombork** ❽, which has an outstanding 14th-century Gothic cathedral (open daily 9am–5pm, until 4pm Oct–May). This fortified complex includes defensive walls, and a bastion where the famous astronomer Nicolaus Copernicus lived from 1512–43, while writing his celebrated work *De Revolutionibus Orbitium Coelestium* (*On the Revolutions of the Celestial Spheres*). The bastion now houses the Copernicus Museum, with his early treatises and scientific instruments (open Tues–Sun; entrance fee; tel: 055 243 72 18).

A chain of hills covered with beech and oak forests runs alongside the Vistula lagoon (Zalew Wiślany). To the south lies **Elbląg**, the region's second largest city after Gdańsk, and an important centre for industry, culture and tourism. Established in the 9th century, it developed into a flourishing port during the 16th and 17th centuries. Despite devastating losses in World War II, a number of interesting monuments have survived. The Market Gate (1319) includes fragments of the town wall, the Dominican St Mary's Church from the 13th–14th centuries (now an art gallery) and the Gothic Church of St Nicholas, with its 95-metre (312-ft) tower are the main highlights. The city museum is open Tues–Sat 9am–4pm, Sun 9.30am–4pm. Just below Elbląg lies Jezioro Drużno, a nature reserve that harbours around 150 species of waterfowl.

Map on page 344

A strawberry festival is held in June on a hill 2km (1 mile) from Kartuzy, when local strawberry farmers show off their produce.

BELOW: Malbork Castle on the River Nogat.

The town of **Malbork** , on the Nogat river southwest of Elbląg, is domi nated by the monumental Malbork Castle (tel: 055 647 08 00; open daily May Sept 9am–8pm, Oct–Apr 10am–3pm; entrance fee), the largest fortification i Europe. Built by the Great Masters of the Teutonic Knights in the late 13t century, it is actually a castle within a castle, with various chapels, church an refectories. This museum has Poland's finest collection of amber.

There is another Teutonic castle, with an attractive courtyard, further south i **Kwidzyń** ⑩, also now a museum (open Tues–Sun; entrance fee). This is part of Gothic complex including a two-tier chancel, a tower and a triple-naved fortifie cathedral. Massive columns support the cathedral, which also has fin 14th-century frescos. At the northwestern edge of the triangle formed by the river Vistula, Osa and Drwęca lies the small and significant town of **Chełmno** ⑪. Th medieval city walls including several bastions and the Grudiądz Gate, enclose abou 200 monuments of historic interest within the Old Town, perched high up on th banks of the Vistula. Among the most impressive are the 16th-century Italian Renais sance Town Hall with ornamental attics. The design also turns conventional pro portions upside down, with the largest windows at the top of the building diminishing in size as they reach the ground floor. The Town Hall now houses th Regional Museum (open Tues–Fri 10am– 4pm, Sat 10am–3pm, Sun 10am–1pm entrance fee), as well as a bizarre little exhibition dedicated to Ludwig Reideige Poland's most celebrated surgeon. The Gothic parish church of St Mary's, also o the Market Square, features beautiful frescos in the choir and the apostles on pillar

About 30 km (19 miles) to the north of Chełmno lies Grudziądz with it medieval town centre. The Gothic parish church, several Baroque Jesuit churche and a group of warehouses joined by a complex system of defensive walls o

BELOW:
Toruń Old Town.

ᴉe banks of the Vistula, deserve special attention. Near Grudziądz is Radzyń
ᴄhełmiński, noted for its 14th-century Teutonic Knights Castle, an architectural
ᴉasterpiece for this era. About 6 km (4 miles) to the east is Rywałd, where a 1-
ᴉth-century sculpture of the Virgin Mary in the Capuchin monastery draws numer-
ᴜs pilgrims. In the Drwęca valley at the eastern edge of the Chełmno region
ᴮbout 35 km (22 miles) east of Toruń lies the town of Golub-Dobrzyń. At the top
f the steep valley walls is a Gothic castle originally built by the Teutonic Knights,
ᴉough its present appearance reflects Baroque additions. Every July the castle
ᴏsts the International Knights' Tournament, re-enacting medieval jousting. By
ᴉe river's upper reaches is Brodnica, a gateway to Brodnicki Krajobrazowy
ᴏuntry park. Parts of the town's medieval fortifications, including the Mazurian
ᴼwer and Chełminski Gate, have survived, while overlooking the Drwęca are
ᴉe ruins of a Teutonic castle with an 85 metre (278 ft) tower. The remains of
ᴉedieval architecture can also be seen in nearby Nowe Miasto Lubawskie.

ᴼoruń – a Gothic haven

ᴼoruń ⓘ is one of Poland's most interesting cities, with on-going restoration
ᴡork also turning it into one of the most attractive. Numerous buildings that
ᴀrgely survived the Nazis intact provide variations on a historic theme: Renais-
ᴀnce and neo-Renaissance, Gothic and neo-Gothic, not to mention some splen-
ᴉd Baroque and the occasional Secessionist flourish. In fact, the city is full of
ᴇlightful architectural surprises: a decorative frieze here, a stained glass win-
ᴏw there. You have to keep looking, but you'll be rewarded. Comprehensive
ᴉnd compact, Toruń is easily covered on foot, with a day's walking tour taking
ᴉ all the sights, though you obviously need longer to visit museums.

Map on page 344

BELOW: Old
Town Hall, Toruń.

As the largest city in the Chełmno region, with a population of 200,000, Toruń was founded on the right bank of the River Vistula in 1233 by the Teutonic Knights. This order effectively ruled the town for the next 260 years as it developed into an important trading centre within the Hanseatic League. In the 17th century Toruń became a centre for the Protestant movement, and subsequently for the Polish nationalist movement against Prussia after the partition of Poland. Becoming part of an independent Poland in 1920, Toruń is now an educational and cultural centre, with the Mikołaj Kopernik University one of Poland's finest institutions.

The Old Town and New Town have retained their medieval layout, with the 14th-century **Town Hall ⓐ** (Ratusz) at the centre of the Old Town Market Square (Rynek Staromiejski). One of Europe's finest Gothic civic buildings, it houses the Regional Museum (Muzeum Okręgowe; Rynek Staromiejski 1; open Tues–Fri 9am–6pm, Sat 9am–4pm, Sun 9am–1pm; entrance fee except Sun; tel: 056 622 70 38), with a superb collection of Gothic sacred art, exhibited amid Gothic interiors with vaulted ceilings, a portrait gallery of Polish monarchs and impressive 18th- and 19th-century Polish paintings. Climbing the Town Hall Tower is an experience in itself, and the observation terrace at a height of 42 metres (140 ft) provides great views of the Old Town. To the side of the town hall, the Nicholas Copernicus (Mikołaj Kopernik) Monument states *"ruszył ziemię, zatrzymał słońce i niebo"* (*"he put the earth in motion and stopped the sun and sky"*). Every 19 February the University Rector places a bouquet here honouring his status as the university's patron.

Among the surrounding buildings are Arthur's Court (Dwór Artusa) a late 19th-century neo-Renaissance building, formerly the seat of the town's burghers and now

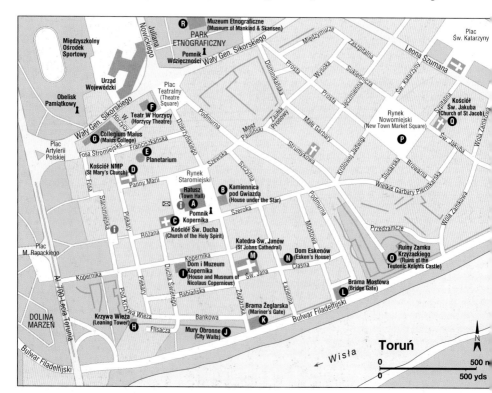

cultural centre, while one of the most extravagant is **House under the Star** ❸ Kamiennica Pod Gwiazdą; tel: 056 622 11 33; open Tues–Sun 10am– 4pm; entrance fee except Sun). Its Baroque architecture, featuring a flourish of fruit and floral motifs culminating in a wonderful gabled roof crowned with a star, dates from 1697. This is now a museum exhibiting the arts and crafts of the Far East (Rynek Staromiejski 35). The neo-Baroque, late-18th century **Church of the Holy Spirit** ❸ (Kościół Św. Ducha; open daily) is next door to the late 19th-century neo-Renaissance main post office. By the edge of the Market Square is the vast **St Mary's Church** ❹ (Kościół Najświętszej Marii Panny; open daily). Built in 1351, it incorporates fragments of two earlier churches and is approached through a cloistered courtyard. In addition to the Baroque altar, the church has an amazing vaulted ceiling, while the walls bear poignant frescos of Christ.

The city's other attractions include Poland's most modern **Planetarium** ❺ (Franciszkańska 19; tel: 056 622 50 66; open Mon–Sat 9am–5pm; entrance fee), while the most impressive of several theatres is the neo-Baroque **Teatr W. Horzycy** (Theatre dedicated to W. Horzyca) ❻. It was built in 1904 by the renowned Viennese architects Ferdinand Fellner and Hermann Helmer, who specialised in theatres and concert halls. Meanwhile, the most historic part of the university is **Maius College** ❼ (Collegium Maius; not open to the public), dating from 1594.

Local explanations for how the **Leaning Tower** ❽ (Krzywa Wieża) acquired its 1.5-metre (5-ft) tilt vary. It may have resulted from a Teutonic Knight caught fraternising with a townswoman. As this monastic order stipulated celibacy, his penance was to build a leaning tower, to remind him of having "deviated" from the rules. A more technical (and probable) explanation is that the foundations are on clay soil. **House and Museum of Nicholaus Copernicus** ❾ (Dom

Map on page 350

BELOW: Church of the Blessed Virgin Mary in Toruń.

The three roofs of the Cathedral of St John date from the 14th century. The Beautiful Madonna statue on the north wall of the apse is a copy of the original statue which disappeared during World War II.

BELOW: leisure boat on the River Vistula.

i Muzeum Kopernika; M Kopernika 15-17; open May–Aug Tues, Thurs, Su 10am–6pm, Wed, Fri, Sat noon–6pm; Sept–Apr Tues–Sun 10am–4pm; entranc fee; tel: 056 622 67 48) is a fine red-brick Gothic house, documenting the li and work of this great astronomer, born here in 1473. The well-preserved **Ci Walls ❿** (Mury Obronne) dating from late 13th century have been preserve virtually in their entirety along the river, with four bastions and three gat including the **Mariner's Gate ❾** (Brama Żeglarska) built in 1432 and **Bridg Gate ❿** (Brama Mostowa). Formerly the parish church of the Old Tow **Cathedral of St John ❿** (Katedra Św. Janów; open daily) dates from the 15 century, built on the site of a church dating from 1250. A combination of restrai and extravagance, Gothic murals and a chapel in which Copernicus was baptise are among the features, together with Baroque and rococo elements. The Renais sance palace **Esken's House ❿** (Dom Eskenów; Łazienna 16; open Tues–Su 10am–4pm; entrance fee; tel: 056 622 70 38) includes 20th-century Polis paintings and military effects from the 15th–19th centuries.

Loathed as a symbol of oppression, the Teutonic castle was pulled down b the town's inhabitants in 1454. However the **Ruins of the Teutonic Knights Castle ❿** (Ruiny Zamku Krzyżackiego) still show what an important buildin this was. Constructed between 1250–1450, it is now a picturesque, romantic sp (Przedzamcze; open daily 9am–7pm).

New Town Market Square ❿ (Rynek Nowomiejski) includes a delightf café, Pod Modrym Fartuchem ("Under the Bright Blue Apron"), first estab lished in 1489 and still going strong. The original Baroque interiors once host Polish kings such as Jan Olbracht and Kazimierz Jagiellończyk. The neigh bouring 19th-century **Church of St Jacob ❿** (Kościół Św. Jakuba; open daily

ncludes beautiful arches, together with Gothic sacred art, including crucifixes.

The **Muzeum Etnograficzne** (Museum of Mankind and *Skansen*) ❼ (Wały Gen Sikorskiego 19; open mid Apr–Sept Mon, Wed, Fri, 9am–4pm, Tues, Thurs, Sat–Sun 10am–6pm; Oct–mid Apr Tues–Fri 9am–4pm, Sat–Sun 10am–4pm; entrance fee; tel: 056 622 80 91) comprises two museums. One is housed within the former Arsenal, built in 1824, and has an incredible collection of fishing items, a traditional occupation in the city. In the *skansen*, you forget the city-centre location as this enchanting village enclave transports you back to 18th- and 19th-century village life. Various farmsteads and households are furnished with period furniture and effects.

Maps:
Area 344
City 350

Bydgoszcz and surroundings

Nearby **Bydgoszcz** ❽ has always had a sense of "rivalry" with Toruń, and the inhabitants of both typically deride each others' city. Toruń is infinitely more attractive to visit, although Bydgoszcz has its moments. An administrative centre with a population of 400,000, it was founded by Casimir the Great in 1346. The city's heyday was in the 15th and 16th centuries, when its warehouses and breweries supplied the entire region, with barges being the mode of transport along the River Vistula to Gdańsk. Destroyed during the Swedish invasion, Bydgoszcz flourished under Prussian rule, but paid the price of being thoroughly "Germanised". Nevertheless, the Nazis were met by fierce resistance from the inhabitants and when the city surrendered mass executions were carried out – some 50,000 by the end of the war.

Known for a time both as Little Venice and as Little Berlin, the heart of the city is Old Town, and the main market square, **Stary Rynek**. This large open

BELOW: the River Vistula.

Map on page 344

The Hollywood actress Apolonia Chalupiec (1896–1987) was born in Lipno about 23 km (14 miles) to the north of Włocławek. She made her name in the silent movie era as Pola Negri and remains a Hollywood icon.

BELOW: lake and tree dwellers.

space is surrounded by brightly painted houses, of which the pick is the former **Jesuit College**, today the city's Town Hall. The square packs out with terraces during the summer months, as does much of **ulica Długa**, old Bydgoszcz's main street, today fully pedestrianised. While the joy of old Bydgoszcz is simply walking around its streets and many embankments (two rivers and a canal converge here), you should make a point of visiting **The Granary** (Spichrza nad Brdą, ul. Grodzka 7-11, open Tues–Fri 10am–4pm, Sat, Sun noon–4pm; entrance fee except Sat; tel: 052 585 98 14), where three separate exhibitions outline the city's somewhat exotic history. The **Bydgoszcz Canal** is itself worthy of note. The 24.7 km (15.34 miles) stretch of water boasts six locks and links up with to the Noteć river, making it possible to travel from Bydgoszcz to Berlin on water. West of Bydgoszcz stretch the Pojezierze Krajeńskie (Krajna Lakes), where deep gorges cutting through the moraine hills provide attractive views, with Sępólno Krajeńskie and Więcbork especially popular holiday destinations.

Kujawy Region

Always one of Poland's wealthiest regions, **Kujawy** became part of the Polanie State at the beginning of the 10th century.

The spa town of **Inowrocław** , the administrative centre for West Kujawy, has a few interesting buildings, including the triple-naved, Romanesque St Mary's Church built from stone, and the Gothic-Baroque Church of St Nicholas.

To the south, on the large Lake Gołpo, is the town of **Kruszwica**. Among the ruins of the 14th-century castle is an ornate Romanesque collegiate church in the form of a basilica, and the Mysza Wieża (Mouse Tower).

A wide variety of waterfowl are protected by the Nadgoplański Park Tysiąclecia nature reserve. The banks of the lakes provide excellent breeding grounds for the birds.

Nearby **Strzelno** has an interesting monastery. The village church here is a combination of the circular, early-Romanesque Church of St Procopius, dating from around 1160, and the interesting Church of the Holy Trinity (1133–1216), where you can see highly artistic 12th-century sculpted pillars and a tympana.

In the eastern part of Kujawy, on the left bank of the Vistula, is the former episcopal see of **Włocławek** . Now an industrial town with a population of 120,000, the most interesting monument is the brick Church of the Assumption, dating from 1411. Baroque elements and chapels were subsequently added around the church. This includes the Chapel of the Mother of God, with late-Gothic carvings by the renowned Wit Stwosz dating from 1493. Soft light from a magnificent window designed in an Art Nouveau style by Józef Mehoffer illuminates the chancel. Try to set aside time to make a visit to the Gothic Church of St Vitalis (dating from 1330) with its famous 1493 triptych depicting the coronation of the Virgin Mary. The 14th-century Church of St John dominates the historic Market Square.

Stretching between the towns of Włocławek and Płock is the vast Gostynińsko-Włocławski Country Park, established in 1979. The pretty Dobrzyński lakes are to be found to the north of Włocławek, between the Vistula, Drwęca and Skrwa rivers. ❏

Nicholas Copernicus

One of the most influential astronomers, Nicholas Copernicus (Mikołaj Kopernik) was born in Toruń in 1473, the son of a prosperous merchant. The house in which Copernicus was born is now a museum detailing his life and works (*see page 352*). The collection includes the original edition of De Revolutionibus Orbium Coelestium, Copernicus's revolutionary theory that the sun and not the earth was the centre of the universe, and that the earth and planets revolved around the sun.

Copernicus studied at the Jagiellonian University in Kraków from 1491–95. As central and eastern Europe's second oldest university (after Prague), it was already renowned for its astronomy and mathematics faculties. Collegium Maius, the oldest college, includes a Copernicus Room, with a collection of astronomical instruments from the 1480s including astrolabes and handwritten sections of the *De revolutionibus* manuscript.

In 1497 Copernicus went to Italy, studying under renowned Italian astronomers including Domenico Maria Novara. It was after arriving there that he witnessed a lunar eclipse, which first led him to question whether the earth was the centre of the universe. Meanwhile, he studied cannon law at Bologna and lectured on astronomy in Rome, before studying medicine at Padua and becoming a doctor of cannon law at Ferrara in 1503.

Returning to Poland in 1503, he was appointed administrator and physician at the Bishop's Castle of Lidzbark Warminski in the Mazurian lake district, where his uncle was Bishop of Warmia. This Gothic castle, built between 1350–1401, is now a museum with part of the collection devoted to Copernicus and his work.From 1510 he was based in Frombork, where he was appointed cannon, although between 1510–19 he spent regular periods of time in Olsztyn. It was in Olsztyn's Gothic Cathedral Chapter and Castle that he created an astonomical table on the walls of the cloisters, where he recorded his findings.Olsztyn's Copernicus Planetarium now provides the opportunity to "experience"

outer space from the perspective of an astronaut. Continuing to study astronomy, it was here that he wrote a treatise questioning the belief that the earth was the centre of the universe. This was the foundation of his famous book, completed in 1530. Popular phraseology in Poland (which every schoolchild learns) sums this up as: "he stopped the sun, and set the earth in motion." However, the book was not published until 1543 in Nuremberg. Copernicus only saw a copy as he lay dying in Frombork, having suffered a brain haemmorage. He was buried in Frombork cathedral.

Copernicus dedicated the book to Pope Paul III, but the Roman Catholic church still considered his theories to be "subversive" and the work was banned until 1757. Yet it provided a basis for subsequent theories by distinguished astronomers including Galileo.

The Nicholaus Copernicus Museum in Frombork exhibits among other items astronomical instruments and an edition of his book inscribed by the 17th-century astronomer Jan Hevelius who lived in Gdańsk.

RIGHT: Copernicus monument in Toruń.

THE NORTHEAST

One of the best ways to explore the "Land of the Great Masurian Lakes" is by a locally-hired yacht, canoe or kayak

An area of outstanding natural beauty, the Masurian Lake district includes more than 1,000 lakes, many of which are linked by rivers and canals, and surrounded by several national parks that shelter various rare species of flora and fauna. Extending across three separate regions of northeastern Poland – Warmia, Mazury and Suwalszczyzna – this area is also known as the "green lungs" of Poland, reflecting the absence of any industrial development. With numerous lakeside resorts in the area, this is the most popular holiday destination for Poles.

Warmia is named after the ancient Prussian tribe known as the Warms, with Mazury also originally part of East Prussia. It was the constant threat to Polish territories posed by the Prussians, that led Duke Konrad Mazowiecki to seek help from the Teutonic Order of Knights in the mid-13th century. However, this resulted in the Order establishing its own territories in the process. Being extremely well-organised and industrious, the Teutonic Knights built a chain of heavily fortified castles to consolidate their presence, and continued to extend their territory through military conquests.

It was only in 1410, during one of the greatest European battles of medieval times, that a combined Polish and Lithuanian army succeeded in defeating the Tuetonic Knights, around the village of Grunwald. Consequently, part of this northeastern region was returned to Poland, and the remainder of the knights' territory became a Polish fiefdom.

Following the Swedish invasion of the 17th century the region came under Swedish rule, and under the partitions of Poland, these regions were annexed by Prussia. Suwalszczyzna was returned to Poland after World War I, and Warmia and Mazury after World War II. ❏

PRECEDING PAGES: a rural estate in Łabędnik near Bartenstein.
LEFT: a trip along one of the canals in northeast Poland.

THE MAZURIAN LAKES

The "Land of a Thousand Lakes" is the ideal place for watersports enthusiasts, anglers and hikers, or visitors who just want to get away from it all

Map on page 362

A region of outstanding natural beauty, the Mazurian landscape is characterised by countless lakes, gentle hills, deep valleys and flat depressions, as well as sandy plains, wooded areas and extensive forests, formed after the Ice Age. Popularly referred to as the "land of a thousand lakes", this is in fact Europe's largest complex of wetlands, with a series of national parks and primeval forests providing a sanctuary for an amazing range of flora and fauna. Many of the region's lakes are linked by rivers and canals, which means you can travel for days entirely on water. Almost the entire region is fully protected, with no industrial development allowed, and even agriculture is strictly monitored to be eco-friendly. Nevertheless, a range of hotels, guesthouses and campsites offer leisure facilities, while organic farms provide a novel and inexpensive option, with board and lodging partly paid by helping out with the work. Moreover, many historic towns throughout the region provide an interesting contrast to "nature's architecture".

Olsztyn

Olsztyn ❶, on the banks of the River Łyna, is an ideal base with various lakes within easy reach. There is also plenty to see in this engaging town – although renovation is on-going, the important buildings are well maintained.

The Old Town, granted its municipal charter in 1353, was largely destroyed by the Red Army in 1945. The key sights are the neo-Renaissance New Town Hall, which is early 20th-century, while several impressive churches include the Gothic St James's Cathedral (Katedra Św. Jakuba). A monumental tower sets the tone of this grand building, and the interior features vaulted ceilings, the altar of the Holy Cross, with its mid-16th-century Renaissance triptych depicting the crucifixion, and the neo-Gothic altar to the Madonna of Ostrobrama, which is late 19th-century. One monument that survived the war intact is the High Gate (Wysoka Brama), a handsome brick construction that continues to provide an "official" entrance into the Old Town. Beyond the Old Town there are wonderful examples of Prussian, Seccessionist and eclectic early 20th-century architecture.

However, Olsztyn's most important historical building is the 14th century Gothic **Castle of the Cathedral Chapter**, a fortified residence of the Bishops of Warmia. Between 1516 and 1521, the astronomer Nicolaus Copernicus was in residence here, in his capacity as the town administrator *(see page 355)*. Fragments of an astronomical chart drawn by him can be seen in the courtyard, and his study has been recreated complete with astronomical instruments.

LEFT: fishing on the lakes.
BELOW: milking in the fields, Talty.

The Castle is now the Warmia and Mazurian Regional Museum (open Tues–Sun 9am–5pm June–Aug, otherwise 10am–4pm; entrance fee). Atmospheri interiors provide a setting for a fine collection of regional art and furniture, a well as folk arts and crafts, the earliest dating from the 17th century. Archaeo logical finds from ancient burial sites in the area can also be seen here.

Several idyllic lakes heighten the appeal of the nearby landscape. The larges Lake Ukiel, has a good beach, as do lakes Skanda and Kortowskie. There ar cruises, or you can hire a boat and travel independently. The Copernicus Plane tarium (al. Zwycięstwa; open Tues–Fri 10.30am–4pm June–Aug, otherwise 10am–5pm; entrance fee) is another aspect of the city's astrological heritage

West of Olsztyn

The delightful lakeside scenery in the Ostróda and Iława regions is very popu lar with holiday-makers from Warsaw, Gdańsk and Germany. The peak summe months, July and August, see the most popular beaches crowded, the camp sites often full and boat-hire companies booked up.

In addition to aqua- and eco-pursuits, the region's sightseeing options include the delightful town of **Morąg** ❷. Key sights include a Gothic Town Hall, frag ments of the town walls and the Baroque Dohn Palace where the German philosopher and writer, Johann Gottfried von Herder, was born in 1744; a museum exhibits details of his life and works (open Tues–Sun; entrance fee). The nearby Narie lake (Jezioro Narie), with almost 20 islands, is a beautiful sight

A principal attraction of **Olsztynek**, located on the northeastern edge of town, is the *skansen* (open-air ethnographic museum; open Tues–Sun 10am–4pm; entrance fee; tel: 089 519 21 64). Set in prime countryside, the traditional timber cottages

Bust of Olsztyn poet Michael Lengowski.

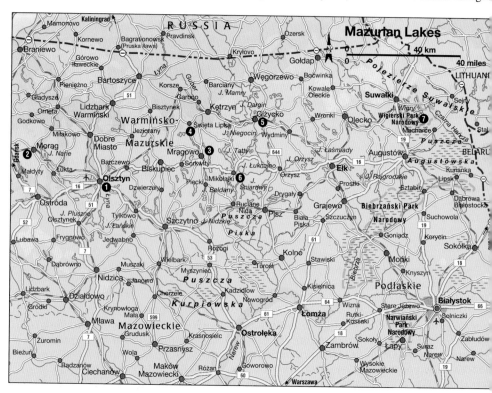

and farmsteads exemplify the Warmia and Mazurian style, together with build-ings from the Vistula Valley and Lithuania. Among the most interesting are a water mill, a Mazurian farmyard, a wooden church and three windmills. To the east of Olsztynek is an attractive forest with numerous small lakes.

Grunwald, 20 km (12.5 miles) southwest of Olsztynek, is chiefly known as the site of one of Poland's most famous battles and one of the greatest battles of the Middle Ages, fought by almost 80,000 men. On 15 July 1410, a combined army of Polish and Lithuanian troops defeated the Teutonic Knights (*see page 263*). A monument erected in the town in 1960 commemorates this victory, which effectively broke the knight's dominance in Poland, while an amphithe-atre houses a museum detailing the battle (open daily; entrance free).

The **Elbląg Canal**, linking Elbląg and Ostróda, is a fascinating feat of engi-neering, completed in 1860. A journey along this almost 130-km (80-mile) stretch is a major tourist attraction and takes around 12 hours (Żegluga Ostródzko-Elbląska, ul. Mickiewicza 9a, tel: 089 646 38 71; www.zegluga.com.pl). Com-prising a network of lakes, canals and locks, there are also special platforms on wheels used to transport ships of up to 50 tonnes across tracts of land with major height differentials of up to 100 metres (330 ft) onto the next stretch of water. This is the only operational system of its kind in the world. The views are also spec-tacular, with the large and shallow Lake Drużno, outside Elbląg, an ornitholog-ical reserve, and numerous lakes and forests between Iława, Ostróda and Morąg.

Being a Baltic port meant that Elbląg was always a priority for invading armies, with each invasion, including World War II, reducing the town to rub-ble. Now known chiefly as a brewing centre, a limited area of the original Old Town is slowly being recreated in its historic style, with the surrounding area

Map on page 362

The beauty of the Mazurian countryside can be enjoyed on Lake Ukiel near Olsztyn.

BELOW: country cottage.

rebuilt using ultra-modern designs. While no longer an important port, Elbląg is still the key departure point for the nearby Russian territory of Kaliningrad

The Great Mazurian Lakes

The Mazurski Landscape Park embraces the central Mazurian Lake district The peaceful town of **Mrągowo ❸** is an ideal base, with its 18th- and 19th-century buildings including the Town Hall and Evangelical Church. The park has the largest number of lakes in the region, with almost a third of its 50,000 hectares (124,000 acres) accounted for by water, including Lake Śniardwy, surrounded by the primeval Piska forest. Lake Łuknajno, near Mikołajki, is listed as a World Biosphere Reserve, and is a nesting ground for mute swans among other rare breeds. Only marked trails can be followed in this protected area.

Near Mrągowo, on the edge of Lake Dejnowa, is **Święta Lipka ❹**, where the church is an important shrine for Roman Catholic pilgrims. This dates from the 13th century, when a roadside wooden statue of the Madonna appeared to have miraculous powers and was moved to a nearby church. During the 16th century the statue and chapel were destroyed by the Protestants who ruled this region, then part of Prussia. However, at the beginning of the 17th century the Polish king was allowed to build a Catholic church on the site where the statue had originally stood. A hundred years later (1687–93), the present Italianate Baroque church was designed by Georg Ertly, a native of South Tyrol who spent nearly all of his working life in Vilnius. Ertly also used his skills as an illusionist: painting frescos to simulate a dome, and the wood chancel to resemble marble. When the organ plays, small gilded figures depicting saints and angels are activated. Organ concerts are held here during the summer season.

BELOW: the castle of the Teutonic Knights in Olsztyn.

The ruins of the **Wolf's Lair**, Adolf Hitler's former headquarters in the Gierłoż Forest near Kętrzyn, are a chilling reminder of the Nazi occupation. Around 70 buildings were constructed here, including seven massive bunkers with walls up to 8 metres (25 ft) thick. With only a few short intervals, Hitler directed much of his military strategy from here between 1941–44, particularly the eastern front. On 20 July 1944, Count Claus von Stauffenberg made his courageous, though unsuccessful, assassination attempt on Hitler. Although the bomb exploded, Hitler was not close enough for it to harm him.

A major centre for various watersports, **Giżycko ❺** is on the edge of Lake Niegocin. The town has a church designed by the German architect Karl-Friedrich Schinkel and a castle built by the Teutonic Knights.

The delightful town of **Mikołajki ❻** is set on the edge of Poland's largest lake, Śniardwy – so large that its also referred to as the Mazurian Sea, while the town is frequently described as the "Venice of Mazuria". This may be an exaggeration, but the small 19th-century houses, fountain and long quayside with pleasure cruisers and sailing boats, create an inviting atmosphere.

Boat excursions

As many of the smaller lakes surrounding Augustów, Ostróda and Iława, not to mention the Great Mazurian Lakes, are linked by a network of canals, an ideal way of seeing them is by taking a pleasure cruise. A popular cruise covers the main lakes in five separate stages. A passenger service operates between Giżycko and Węgorzewo (25 km/16 miles), between Giżycko and Mikołajki (40 km/25 miles), between Mikołajki and Ruciane-Nida (20 km/12 miles), and between Mikołajki and Pisz (25 km/16 miles). Sightseeing trips via Ruciane-Nida can be booked in

Map on page 362

It is sometimes possible to spot a tarpan from the zoological station in Popielno, near Mikołajki. Europe's only wild horse, the tarpan became extinct in the wild in the 18th century. However, some farmers continued using them as workhorses, which provided a means of breeding.

BELOW: sailing on one of the Great Lakes.

Map on page 362

Giżycko and Mikołajki. One of the most attractive sections of the canal network connects Mikołajki and Ruciane-Nida, with the woodland of the Puszcza Piska lining almost the entire route. The lock in Guzianki compensates for the difference in water levels between the Bełdany and Guzianka lakes.

If you'd rather explore in your own boat, an interesting route that extends for 90 km (55 miles) begins in Sorkwity between Biskupiec and Mrągowo, and ends in Lake Bełdany. The River Krutynia changes its name between the various lakes, with a large section running through the untamed woodland of the Puszcza Piska, past several camping and rest areas, and close to nature reserves.

Sorkwity has one of Masuria's few Protestant churches, an attractive brick and white-washed building with a carved baptismal angel suspended above the congregation in the nave. Using a block and tackle the angel can be lowered at christenings, and the head of the child anointed with holy water from the silver dish held by the angel. Another neighbouring attraction is the impressive Sorkwity Palace, a 19th-century neo-Renaissance confection, which is set in a landscaped, wooded park, near Lake Lampackie.

The eastern region

The route along the Czarna Hańcza River (97 km/60 miles) is one of the most attractive and popular in Poland, particularly for kayak enthusiasts. Beginning on the eastern bank of Lake Wigry in Stary Folwark, the river meanders through the beautiful Augustów forest.

The Augustów Canal is also a popular route for boat trips. Engineered in the first half of the 19th century, it linked the Vistula and Niemen rivers in order to transport Polish goods to Baltic ports. Constructed between 1822–39, the Augustów Canal begins in Biebrza and extends through the lakes of the Augustów forest for 100 km (60 miles), reaching Hrodna in Belarus. A total of 18 sluice gates regulate different water levels. The engineers were led by the Polish general Ignacy Prądzyński, and the canal is now considered a historic monument, as well as a great tourist attraction, with canoes and boats cruising the waters.

The Suwałki lake district includes the **Wigry National Park** ❼ (Wigierski Park Narodowy), of which almost two-thirds is forest, mainly fir and pine, with some trees more than 200 years old. It's a natural habitat for rare species including the mute swan, wild boar, wolf, elk and the white-tailed eagle.

Lake Wigry, Poland's second deepest lake, is outstandingly beautiful – if you feel like strolling all the way around it's a 70-km (45-mile) hike. The park also has Poland's deepest lake, Hańcza, at 110 metres (360 ft), while Lake Jaczno is renowned for its amazing malachite coloured water.

The River Biebrza flows into the narrow valley around Sztabin, where it twists and divides to create a stunning vista.

Overflowing during the spring, the river floods the surrounding bogs and meadows supporting a community of beavers, though the area is best known for rare birds, including ruffs, the spotted eagle, whooper swans and the double snipe. ❑

INSIGHT GUIDES

TRAVEL TIPS

POLAND

TRAVEL TIPS

TRANSPORT

GETTING THERE AND GETTING AROUND

GETTING THERE

By Air

The flight time from the UK to Poland is approximately two-and-a-half hours; from Paris, two hours and 15 minutes; from New York, just under 10 hours. Poland has regular connections to almost all capital cities of Europe.

Frederic Chopin Airport, 6 km (4 miles) from the centre of Warsaw, is the hub of most Polish National Airlines worldwide services. There are daily flights to and from London, New York, Chicago and Montreal. Warsaw has regular direct flights to the main cites of former republics of Soviet Union, as well as Minsk, Riga and Vilnius. Most international flights are on B767s and 737s. Some flights are seasonal. From the UK, the two scheduled carriers are Polskie Linie Lotnicze LOT and British Airways, with Ryanair, Easyjet and Wizzair also offering low-cost flights from Stansted and Luton. International flights land at Warsaw and Kraków; internal flights land at the following city airports: Kraków, Gdańsk, Katowice, Poznań, Rzeszów and Szczecin. Frederic Chopin Airport is comfortable and compact, servicing 3.5 million passengers per year. You will find airline offices, banks, post offices and car rental companies in the terminal.

Warsaw International Airport (Frederic Chopin):
Arrivals tel: (022) 650 4220;
Departures tel: (022) 650 3943.
LOT reservations and tickets:
Tel: (0801) 300 952;
Business class tel: (0801) 300 953.
Domestic flights:
Tel: (022) 650 1750
www.polish-airports.com

Travel to and from the Airport

Frederic Chopin Airport is situated only 6 km (4 miles) from the centre of Warsaw. To reach the main city, you could take buses 175 or 188, which take you to the centre. Buy a ticket at the kiosk and validate it immediately on entering the bus. Always watch your luggage, as these routes are more exposed to theft than other regular lines. For large luggage you need to purchase an extra ticket.

FC Airport also has its own bus line, **City Line**. The bus stops at the all the larger hotels and operates every 20 minutes between 6am–11pm. (On Sunday and public holidays every 30 minutes.) Buy a ticket on board the bus. It's a little more expensive than regular buses.

LOT also organises a luxury car service **Fly&Drive** into the centre of the city. Or you could phone for a taxi – do not take a taxi from the taxi station at FC unless you must because they are far more expensive than ordering by phone.

By Train

Take the Eurostar from London St Pancras to Brussels, then a high-speed train to Cologne, then a direct air-conditiioned sleeper from Cologne to Warsaw.

EuroCity trains connect Warsaw with Berlin. Passengers who use this connection also have links with Cologne, Wiesbaden, Karlsruhe, Hamburg, Frankfurt and Munich. Travelling from Germany to Poland by train is relatively cheap. It is not worth obtaining the reduced Interail Pass for people under 26 as travel within Poland is so cheap. Most trains to Poznań and Warsaw pass through Berlin and Frankfurt.

ABOVE: waiting for a train in Kraków.

All fast and express trains run on international links. Trains have first and second class carriages, berths, sleepers and restaurant cars. Almost all international trains arrive at Warsaw Central Station (Warszawa Centralna), located in the heart of the city centre.
International and domestic information: Tel: 9436, 9431
Reservations: Tel: (022) 524 50 40

Direct Trains to Poland

Paris–Cologne–Düsseldorf–Hanover–Berlin–Poznań–Warsaw; Cologne–Hanover–Leipzig–Wrocław–Warsaw; Frankfurt–Bebra–Wrocław–Warsaw; Munich–Dresden–Wrocław–Katowice; East-West Express: London–Hoek van Holland–Berlin–Warsaw–Moscow; Chopin Express: Vienna–Warsaw.

For further information on train times contact: **POLRES**, Al. Jerozolimskie 4400-024 Warsaw, tel: (022) 823 33 43. Tickets can also be bought at Orbis, Ul. Bracka 16, tel: (022) 827 71 40.

By Sea

Passenger ferry services link the Polish ports of Świnoujście and Gdańsk with Denmark and Sweden.

By Road

Coach Services

Regular weekly services are run most of the year in luxury air-conditioned coaches, with bar and toilet facilities. The coaches leave either from London via Amsterdam to Poznań and Warsaw; or from London, Manchester or Birmingham to Wrocław, Katowice and Kraków and many other cities in Poland. The journey time is about 30 hours, with fare reductions for students, senior citizens and children. Coach operators throughout Poland run many services to and from German cities, such as Cologne, Dusseldorf, Essen, Dortmund, Hanover and Braunschweig.

By Car

It is possible to drive to Poland via the Channel (or with the ferry to Hook of Holland or Ostend) and via Holland and Germany to reach the Polish border. At the point of entry you must show your car registration documents and driving licence. There is no limit on buying petrol and no restriction on travelling within Poland.

From the Hook of Holland or Ostend, the driving time to the Polish border is about 12 hours. When Poland became a member of the Schengen group of countries in 2008 all border posts were disbanded, and there are no longer any passport or customs checks on entry. Customs officers can still search vehicles if they have due cause but such searches are rare.

The **Polish Motoring Association** (PZM) can provide information about travelling around Poland and maps.

Vehicles towing caravans require an additional insurance document. Drivers who do not possess the necessary third-party insurance papers will have to obtain them from the Polish Motoring Association (PZM) at the border crossing. Fully comprehensive insurance is recommended.

Main Crossing Points

Germany–Poland:
Ahlbeck–Świnoujście (foot passengers only); Linken–Lubieszyn; Pomellen–Kołbaskowo (near Szczecin); Schwedt–Krajnik Dolny; Frankfurt-am-Oder–Slubice and Swiecko; Guben–Gubin; Forst–Olszyna (motorway to Wrocław); Bad Muskau–Łęknica; Görlitz–Zgorzelec; Zittau–Porajów/Sieniawka; Hohenwutzen–Osinów Dolny.

Poland–Czech Republic:
Jakuszyce–Harrachov, Kudowa–Słone Nachod; Głuchoslazy–Mikulovice; Chałupki Stary–Bohumin; Porajów–Hradek n. Nisou; Lubawka–Kralovec; Boboszów–Dolni Lipka; Cieszyn–Cesky Tesin.

Poland–Slovakia:
Chyxne–Trestena; Piwniczna–Mnisek; Zwardoý–Skalite; Cysa Polana–Javorina.

Poland–Ukraine:
Medyka–Mostiska; Dorohusk–Jagodin; Hrebenne–Rawa Ruska.

Poland–Lithuania:
Ogrodniki–Lazdijai.

Poland–Belarus:
Terespol–Brest.

Poland–Russia:
Bezledy–Bagrationowsk.

Airline Offices

Polish Airlines (LOT) Offices

Information and reservation centres are located throughout Poland. The staff usually speak excellent English. Alternatively, log on to the website: www.lot.com for more details.
Kraków: 15 Basztowa Ul. Tel: (0801) 300 952/3.
Gdańsk: 2/4 Waly Jagiellonskie Ul. Tel: (0801) 300 952/3.
Poznań: 6/1 Piekary Ul. Tel: (0801) 300 952/3.
Warsaw: 65/79 Al. Jerozolimskie. Tel: (0801) 300 952/3.
Wrocław: 36 Piłsudskiego. Tel: (0801) 300 952/3.

LOT Offices Overseas:

Amsterdam: Overtoom 60, 1054 HK, Amsterdam. Tel: (020) 616 92 66. Fax: (020) 616 96 66.
Chicago: 333 N Michigan Avenue, Suite 916. Tel: (1800) 223 05 93.
London: 414 Chiswick High Road, London W4. Tel: (0845) 601 0949 (English-speaking operators).
Los Angeles: 6033 West Century Blvd, Suite 1107.

GETTING AROUND

By Air

The Polish airline LOT operates flights from Warsaw to Gdańsk, Katowice, Koszalin, Kraków, Poznań, Szczecin and Wrocław (see below). While LOT will happily sell you tickets from one regional Polish city to another (Gdansk to Krakow, or Wrocław to Katowice for example), note that there are in fact no direct flights: in all cases you will have to change in Warsaw.

On arrival the Airport City Bus Service runs from the airport to major hotels in downtown Warsaw. Tickets are available from the Orbis desk at the airport, the LOT desk at the Marriott Hotel or from the driver.

By Train

With over 26,500 km (16,450 miles) of railway lines, the Polish railway network covers the whole country, but regular, non-express trains can be slow and overcrowded.

Express trains run between the major cities. Non-stop express trains complete with restaurant cars run between Warsaw and Gdańsk/Gydnia, Poznań and Kraków. For information about connections, enquire directly at the railway station or in the PKP

Tel: (1800) 223 0593.
New York: 500 Fifth Avenue, Suite 408. Tel: 1-718 6562632.
Paris: 27 rue du Quatre Septembre, 75002 Paris. Tel: (01) 4742 05 60. Fax: (331) 4017 02 97.

Overseas Airlines in Warsaw

Air Canada: Tel/fax: (022) 822 5477.
Air France: 21 Krucza Ul. Tel: (022) 628 12 81/3.
American Airlines: 20 Al. Ujazdowskie. Tel: (022) 625 05 17, (022) 625 30 02.
British Airways: 49 Krucza Ul. Tel: (022) 529 9000.
KLM: Żwirki i Wigury 1 (Airport). Tel: (022) 622 80 00. Fax: (022) 622 96 85.
Lufthansa: 19 Nowy Zwiat Ul. Tel: (022) 338 1300.

Low-cost carriers in the UK

www.ryanair.com
www.easyjet.com
www.wizzair.com

(Polish National Railway) offices.
Rail fares are still reasonable.
Tickets can be purchased from the
Orbis offices or in the POLRES offices
(Warsaw, tel: 823 33 43). It is well
worth booking a seat particularly on
express services and paying 50
percent extra for a first-class ticket.
You may also wish to consider buying
a POLRAIL pass. Valid on all PKP railway
lines, these are issued for 7, 14, 21
or 30 days. Users named on the non-
transferable ticket, are entitled to
unlimited rail travel during this period.
    Most stations have left-luggage
offices *(przechowalnia bagazu)*.
www.pkp.com.pl
information and reservations.
www.it.com.pl/pkpdc/eng
Warsaw Central Station schedules.
www.walden.mo.net/jdobek/pkptrav.html
Polish rail page with extensive details
about Polish trains.

ABOVE: taxis are useful for journeys beyond the city centre.

in the metal boxes on the bus or
tram wall. When you change vehicles,
you must punch a new ticket. All-day
tickets and one-week tickets are
available in kiosks or at the ZTM-
Transport Authority (pl. Unii
Lubelskiej or ul. Senatorska 37,
Warsaw). Route maps are usually
displayed inside buses and at stops.

Getting Around Towns

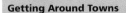

Buses and trams are the main forms
of public transport in the larger
towns (although in Warsaw it is the
metro). They usually operate between
5.30am and 11pm, (Warsaw's metro
closes around 11.30pm). In some
cities there is a night service, but
fares are more expensive.
    In Warsaw, there's an Old Town
tram that begins and ends its route
at Castle Square, taking a 30-minute
guided trip through the Old and New
Towns.
    Tickets *(bilety)* can be purchased
at a RUCH kiosks or from machines at
bus and railway stations. Tickets are
not available from bus drivers.
Tickets must be validated
immediately on entering the vehicle

By Coach

There are two possibilities to choose
from: the state-owned **PKS** or the
private **Polski Express**.
    The **PKS** runs both stopping and
express services. Tickets can be
bought at bus stations, Orbis offices,
travel agencies and, if there are
spare seats, from the driver. In the
Tri-City (Gdańsk-Gdynia-Sopot) and in
the Upper Silesia industrial region, a
zonal system operates. The biggest
private coach company Polski
Express provides several shuttle
services between major cities in
Poland. Prices are higher than PKS,
but the standard is relatively high
(buses with air-conditioning, TV, toilet
and coffee bar). For information
about all available connections you

may ask in any travel office or at PKS
coach stations.
Polski Express tel: 620 0330 (open
7am–9pm).
PKS tel: 9433.

By Taxi

When available for hire taxis display
an illuminated sign. The best places
to find one is at taxi ranks in city
centres and outside hotels, railway
stations and airports. It is also
possible to phone for a radio taxi
(ask in your hotel for details). This
usually works out cheaper, as
independent drivers, who are not
linked to companies, are more likely
to overcharge their passengers. At
night, and for journeys into the
outlying countryside, fares are
usually 50 percent higher.
    In all cases drivers must display
their fares (however exorbitant) in the
window of their cabs. All taxis are
metered, and journeys are charged
per km, plus a small starting fee
(usually around 6–8zł). Check that
the taxi meter is switched on as soon
as your journey starts. Hailing a cab
is not recommended. Taxis hailed in
the street will almost certainly be
unofficial cabs. If it's an emergency,
agree upon the fare in advance.

Taxi Telephone Numbers
MPT-Radio Taxi 91 91
Taxi Plus 96 21
Super-Taxi 96 22
Halo-Taxi 96 23
Korpo-Taxi 96 24
Volfra-Taxi 96 25
Express-Taxi 96 36
O.K. Taxi 96 28
Wawa Taxi 96 44
Super Taxi 2 96 66
Sawa Taxi 644 44 44

Hitchhiking

Hitchhiking is a perfectly acceptable
way of travelling in Poland. The
normal method of signalling to
drivers that you are looking for a lift
is to wave the whole arm. The
thumbs-up signal is, however,

Car and Bus Hire Companies in Warsaw

Avis
65/79 Al. Jerozolimskie,
Hotel Marriott
Tel/fax: (022) 630 73 16; and
Frederic Chopin International
Airport
Tel: (022) 650 48 71/2
Budget
65/79 Al. Jerozolimskie,
Hotel Marriott
Tel: (022) 630 72 80
Fax: (022) 630 69 46; and
Frederic Chopin International
Airport, Terminal 1, Arrivals Hall
Tel/fax: (022) 650 40 62
Europcar
Ul. Żwirki i Wigury 1
(Frederic Chopin Airport)
Tel: (022) 650 25 64
www.europcar.pl
Hertz, Ul. Nowogrodzka 27

Tel: (022) 621 02 39; and
Frederic Chopin International
Airport
Tel: (022) 650 28 96
Joka
Ul. Okopowa 47
Tel: (022) 636 63 93
www.joka.com.pl
National Car Rental
Frederic Chopin International
Airport
Tel: (022) 606 92 02

Bus and Minibus Hire
Europe Tour
Ul. Mokotowska 222/10
Tel/fax: (022) 621 05 08,
(022) 622 04 24, (022) 628 64 62
Mazurkas Travel, Ul. Nowogrodzka
24/26 – Hotel Forum
Tel: (022) 629 18 78

understood by drivers. Sometimes, a small contribution is expected.

Driving

The road network in Poland covers 220,000 km (135,000 miles) and even remote tourist attractions are relatively easy to reach. Roads have internationally recognised signs, and you should drive on the right-hand side of the road. Outside built-up areas, traffic levels are generally lower than in western Europe, but drivers should be on the look-out for motorcyclists, carts and tractors. In main towns during peak hours you will find traffic jams and slow traffic. At night on country roads it is often difficult to spot pedestrians. The main streets and most side roads are usually in good condition. You may also expect heavy traffic during summer weekends.

Petrol Stations

The majority of petrol stations along highways and main routes are open 24 hours a day. They offer similar services to those in western Europe, including small shops and tea and coffee facilities. In small towns, however, you may expect petrol stations to open from 6am to 10pm. Only in the rarest cases are credit cards not accepted.

Lead-free petrol is widely available in all stations. Ten litres (2 gallons) of petrol can be imported into Poland or taken out in fuel containers.

Breakdown Services

The Polish Motoring Association (PZM) is the main breakdown service but there are many other roadside assistance stations. The breakdown emergency service centres usually operate from 7am to 10pm, some closing at 3pm. Membership of the PZM secures assistance to members of automobile clubs affiliated with the Fédération Internationale de

Cruises

In the summer season (1 May to 15 October), the following cruises along the Baltic coast are available: Gdańsk Sopot Hel; Gdynia Jastarnia; Gydnia Hel; Szczecin Świnoujście and Szczecin Midzyzdroje. Also possible are excursions on the Vistula between Warsaw and Gdańsk, on the Mazurian Lakes and on the Elblag-Ostróda Canal.

l'Automobile (FIA) and the Alliance Internationale de Tourisme (AIT), holders of insurance policies issued by the Intermutuelle Assistance, Assistance Internationale and SOS, and ADAC club members. Members should contact the Autotour Motoring Tourism Bureau to check whether they are affiliated.

If your car model has a producer assistance programme (such as Mobilo with Mercedes-Benz), call your dealer and ask for correct telephone numbers in Poland to contact local assistance services.

Polish Motoring Association (PZM)
Tel: 981
ADAC (Warsaw)
Tel: 290 374, 24 hours
Autotour Motoring Tourism Bureau,
63 Al. Jerozlimskie, Warsaw 00-697
Tel: 621 07 89, 628 62 55
Fax: 628 62 54

Rules of the Road

Maximum speed limits are: in built-up areas 60 kmh (37 mph); motorways 130 kmh (80 mph); express roads (specially signed) 110 kmh (68 mph); outside built-up areas 90 kmh (56 mph). Motorists caught exceeding speed limits (radar traps are very frequent) can expect a large fine. The maximum fine for speeding is 500zł.

From 1 November to 1 March, it is necessary to keep dipped headlights on throughout the day. Motorcyclists

should leave their headlights on throughout the year.

Many traffic lights have green arrows, which permit filtering to the right on a red light as long as there are no pedestrians crossing the road. However it's necessary to stop before the lights, and continue turning right after checking that the road is clear. Vehicles on round-abouts have priority over joining traffic. Where priority is not clearly stated, trams always have priority over other road users. Stopping within 100 metres (330 ft) of a level crossing is not permitted. Many of the main trunk roads have slow lanes to allow faster traffic to pass.

The permitted blood alcohol level is virtually zero, so do not drink at all when driving. The penalties are severe. Seat belts must be worn by the driver and front-seat passenger at all times. If belts are fitted on rear seats, they must be worn as well. Children can travel in the car only in special child-seats.

Parking

Parking is a major problem in any of the big cities, especially where historic centres are pedestrian-only. If you are driving, check that your hotel has parking facilities. A car parked in a prohibited zone will be towed away. Only guarded car parks should be used and make sure nothing of value is visible to passers by.

Car Hire

Branches of the main car rental companies are to be found at airports, stations, leading hotels and in the major cities. The following conditions apply: drivers should be at least 21 years old, have a valid passport and a full driving licence. In addition, they must either pay a substantial deposit or leave security in the form of a credit card imprint. Daily rates are similar to those in western Europe.

BELOW: the traditional way of getting around town, by horse and cart.

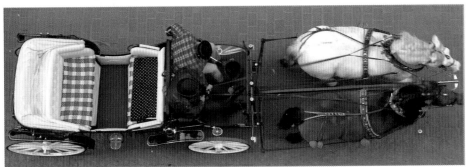

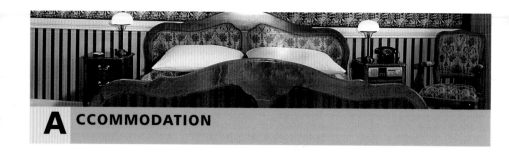

A CCOMMODATION

HOTELS, YOUTH HOSTELS, BED & BREAKFAST

Hotels and Private Rooms

During the height of the season, basic hotels, youth hostels and campsites in the main tourist regions are hopelessly overcrowded, so it is a good idea to reserve accommodation well in advance. However, it is not usually a problem finding a bed in the higher-price range hotels, even in mid-summer. If you find yourself facing a night under the stars, do not despair. Ask at the local tourist information office or rooms agency *(biuro zakwaterowania)* for a list of private houses where overnight guests are welcome. By the coast or in the Mazurian Lakes district, houses with beds available show signs with the words *pokoje* or *noclegi*. If you arrive in a town late at night, ask a taxi driver about likely vacancies.

Hotels are divided into five categories: 1-, 2-, 3-, 4-star and luxury hotels. Luxury hotels provide the same standards of comfort as the international hotel chains of western Europe and the USA, such as Marriott and Holiday Inn. The now privatised tourist organisation Orbis also manages some very good hotels. The number of stars beside the hotel name can be misleading, however, as many have recently taken to reducing their star rating for tax reasons.

Hotels that target business people and tourists will offer guests spacious rooms, translation and secretarial services, fitness suites, bars and restaurants. Prices are comparable with similar hotels in western Europe.

The number of hotels and *pensions* is still growing and many of them do not yet have star ratings, but generally offer good facilities. Almost all hotels and boarding houses accept major credit cards.

ABOVE: Francuski Hotel, Krakow.

Roadhouses and Hostels

The many, often rustic-style, roadhouses *(zajazd)* on the main arterial roads offer good-quality accommodation. They do not claim to provide luxury accommodation but, after a long car journey, they offer a comfortable overnight stay.

The Polish Association for Tourism and Culture (PTTK) arranges accommodation in tourist-class overnight hostels for those interested in activity holidays. They are located in the mountains, along canoeing and sailing routes, as well as in cities, including Kraków, Poznań, Płock, Sandomierz, Sanok, Sopot, Szczecin, Szczyrk, Walbrzych, Warsaw and Zakopane. Some of the larger hostels have cafés.

PTTK, Warsaw, Ul. Senatorska 11 tel: (022) 826 2151.

Student Hotels and Youth Hostels

Between July and October, Almatur, a travel agency run by the Polish Student Association, offers bargain accommodation in student residences. If you have an International Student Card (ISIC), you'll receive a discount. Further information and bookings are available from all Orbis offices, or at **Almatur**, 06-116 Warsaw, Ul. Ordynacka 9, tel: 265381.

During the summer holidays, the Polish Youth Hostel Association (PTSM) arranges accommodation in converted school buildings. The PTSM is a member of the International Youth Hostel Federation (IYHF). Travellers with a valid IYHF card receive a 25 percent discount. You can obtain a listing of 200 or so youth hostels and an official IYHF card at any IYHF office, or directly in Warsaw, from the **PTSM** at Ul. Chocimska 28, tel: 849 83 54, and Ul. Szpitalna, tel: 827 78 43. The hostels promoted by the PTTK are very similar.

Camping

The Polish Camping and Caravanning Federation (PFC) operates 240 campsites. The organisation grades the campsites into three categories. All have access to running water, sanitary facilities and electricity. In addition to these amenities, campsites in Category II have washrooms, those in Category III hot running water in the washrooms and restaurants. Don't expect luxury from these relatively inexpensive alternatives to hotels. Many campsites also rent out modestly furnished bungalows. It is worth seeking out sites with guarded car parks (Category III).

Information is available from the **PFC**, Ul. Grochowska 331, 03838 Warsaw, tel/fax: 810 60 50, www.pfcc.info. Polorbis *(see page 375)* will also supply a list of Polish campsites. The regularly updated map entitled *Campingi w Polsce* is also very useful (available in bookshops and kiosks). The camping season lasts from 15 Jun–30 Sep. A number of unsupervised sites *(miejsca biwakowe)* are located in picturesque lakeside spots or in the forests, but no sanitary amenities whatsoever are provided. Independent camping is not permitted, but often the authorities turn a blind eye. It is always advisable to check with the forestry office or landowner

before erecting your tent. Sometimes a small fee is requested.

Campsites

Warsaw
Wok, Ul. Odrębna 16
Tel: (022) 612 79 51
Fax: (022) 612 61 27
www.wonder.com.pl/wok
First class.
Open: all year round. All facilities.
Bielsko-Biała
Ul. Karbowa 15
Tel: (033) 821 60 80
Fax: (033) 821 61 81
www.camping.bielsko.com.pl
First class.
Open: 1 May–30 Oct. All facilities.
Łeba
Intercamp 84

Ul. Turystyczna 6
Tel: (059) 866 12 06
One of the largest campsites in Poland.
Open: 15 June–30 Aug.
Poznań
Malta
Ul. Krańcowa 98
Tel: (061) 876 62 03
Fax: (061) 876 62 83
Situated overlooking the Malta Lake.
Open all year round.

Agrotourism

For agrotourist holidays contact Gospodarstwa Gościnne,Polish Federation of Rural Tourism, ulica Wspolna 30, Warsaw 00-930, tel: 602 305 330, www.agritourism.pl.

WARSAW

In the capital of Poland you can find a variety of types of accommodation: a few luxury hotels (Bristol Hotel), some international chain hotels (Holiday Inn, Sheraton, Marriot, Mercure), and many inexpensive options as well.

It's a good idea to choose a hotel in the centre of Warsaw, only a short distance from the interesting sights in the Old Town. You should make reservations in advance, particularly in June, July, September and October. Christmas time is also very busy.

Budget

Etap
Ul. Zagórna 1
Tel: (022) 745 36 60
Fax: (022) 622 55 01
www.orbis.pl
Cheap and cheerful, this hotel may not be all that close to the city centre but all its rooms have ensuite facilities, staff are very helpful and it offers great value for money. €
Hit
Ul. Kłopotowskiego 33
Tel: (022) 618 94 70
Fax: (022) 619 57 44.
www.hithotel.pl
Opened in 2008 this hotel

offers a range of cheap accommodation in the Praga area of Warsaw, a short walk from the Old Town. Expect good, clean, no frills rooms, all with their own (if tiny) bathrooms. €
Premiere Classe
Ul. Towarowa 2
Tel: (022) 624 08 00
Fax: (022) 620 26 29
www.premiereclasse.com.pl
In spite of the name this is strictly a one-star establishment, but as one-star hotels go it is good. Bright, if not big rooms, all have bathrooms and the beds are very comfortable. Well located close to the station and PKiN. €

Moderate

Campanile
Ul. Towarowa 2
Tel: (022) 582 72 00
Fax: (022) 582 72 01
www.campanile.com.pl
Great value two-star hotel a short tram ride from the city centre. The small rooms have lots of little extras and the buffet breakfast is excellent. €€
Harenda
Krakowskie Przedmieście 4/6
Tel: (022) 826 00 71
Fax: (022) 826 26 25
www.hotelharenda.com.pl

Excellent location on one of the finest streets in town. Only a few minutes' walk to the Old Town. In the same building as one of the city's best-known restaurants (of the same name). Not all of the 40 rooms are ensuite; some can take an extra bed. €€
Karat
Ul. Słoneczna 37
Tel: (022) 601 4411
Fax: (022) 849 52 94
www.hotelkarat.pl
Close to Łazienki Park, in a quiet location but near Puławska Street – one of Warsaw's main thoroughfares. Newly renovated, the hotel offers 30 ensuite rooms at a reasonable price. €€
Maria
Jana Pawła II 71
Tel: (022) 838 40 62
Fax: (022) 838 38 40
www.hotelmaria.pl
Just outside the city centre, a small hotel (22 rooms) in very good condition. Rooms have ensuite bathrooms; parking, restaurants, bar. €€

Expensive

Belwederski
Belwederska 46/50
Tel: (022) 841 60 21
Fax: (022) 841 60 29

A modest-sized hotel (44 rooms), situated on the same street as the President's Palace. Excellent view of park. All rooms with bath. Sport facilities, bar, restaurant. €€€
Holiday Inn
Złota 48/54
Tel: (022) 697 39 99
Fax: (022) 830 05 68
www.orbis.pl
Located between the main railway station and the Palace of Science and Culture, close to the business and shopping centres. There are 336 room, air-conditioned, with satellite TV; sports, health and disabled facilities; indoor and outdoor parking. €€€
Jan III Sobieski
Pl. Zawiszy 1
Tel: (022) 579 10 00
Fax: (022) 659 88 28
www.sobieski.com
While nowhere near as luxurious as it would have

PRICE CATEGORIES

Approximate price catgories for a standard double room per night:
€ = below 250zł
€€ = 250–425zł
€€€ = 425–600zł
€€€€ = over 600zł

you believe, you can stay here in some comfort for relative peanuts. The catch is that it is a (short) tram ride from the city centre. €€€

MDM
Plac Konstytucji 1
Tel: (022) 339 16 00
Fax: (022) 621 41 73
www.syrena.com.pl
Situated in the centre, the architecture of MDM and surrounding buildings reflects the Communist era. The 111 pleasantly renovated apartments are ensuite; the hotel is air-conditioned and has business and disabled facilities. €€€

Novotel Centrum
Ul. Nowogrodzka 24/26
Tel: (022) 621 02 71
Fax: (022) 625 04 76
www.orbis.pl
Situated in the heart of the commercial district. There are 733 rooms with panoramic views of the city. Restaurant Soplica offers international cuisine and Restaurant Maryla specialises in traditional Polish dishes. Shops, hairdresser. €€€

Luxury

Bristol Le Méridien
Krakowskie Przedmieście 42/44
Tel: (022) 551 10 00
Fax: (022) 625 25 77
www.lemeridien-bristol.com
One of the most elegant and oldest hotels in the city. Art Nouveau, recently renovated. 155 beds (double and single rooms), 43 apartments – all ensuite, with satellite TV. Excellent cuisine in three separate restaurants; café, bars. Health club with indoor swimming pool, sauna, solarium; suitable for the disabled, facilities for children. €€€€

Hilton Warsaw
Ul. Grzybowska 63
Tel: (022) 356 55 55
Fax: (022) 356 55 56
www.warsaw.hilton.com
Just fantastic. A skyscraper of luxury Warsaw's newest five-star is also the best. Boasting the biggest rooms, the biggest swimming pool and

arguably the best views in town, if you have the cash stay here. €€€€

Hyatt Hotel
Ul. Belwederska 23
Tel: (022) 558 12 34
Fax: (022) 558 12 35
www.warsaw.hyatt.com
Set on the tree-lined Belwederska Boulevard not far from the beautiful Łazienki Park. €€€€

Inter Continental
Ul. Emili Plater 49
Tel: (022) 328 88 88
Fax: (022) 328 88 89
www.warsaw.intercontinental.com
Surprisingly accessible in terms of price. The top-floor swimming pool has startling views and the unique design of the lower floors. Rooms are big and have the plushest carpets in Warsaw. €€€€

Marriott
Al. Jerozolimskie 65/79
Tel: (022) 630 63 06
Fax: (022) 830 03 11
www.marriott.com/waw.pl
Situated in Warsaw's centre. It has 521 rooms with luxurious facilities, including health club and indoor swimming pool. On the top floor the Panorama restaurant has a wonderful view of Warsaw, with a choice of several other restaurants, cocktail bars and a nightclub. Guarded car park. Casino. €€€€

Mercure-Fryderyk Chopin
Aleja Jana Pawła II
Tel: (022) 528 03 00
Fax: (022) 528 03 03
Email: mercure@perytnet.pl
In the city centre, close to the Palace of Science and Culture; 250 rooms, all ensuite with satellite TV. Two restaurants (French and international), bar, sauna, guarded car park. Modern furnished rooms. Children's, disabled and health facilities. €€€€

Polonia Palace
Al. Jerozolimskie 45
Tel: (022) 318 28 00
Fax: (022) 318 28 89
www.poloniapalace.com
Given a major refit in 2007 this hotel, built in 1913, boasts a lobby that is in itself one of Warsaw's must-sees, a joyous mix of marble and glass. The rooms are fantastic and

ABOVE: the Polonia Palace Hotel.

have superb views over the busy city-centre streets below, though rest assured the great soundproofing will mean you will not hear a thing. €€€€

Le Regina
Ul. Kościelna 12
Tel: (022) 531 60 00
Fax: (022) 531 60 01
E-mail: leregina@orcogroup.com
Beautifully decorated and meticulously restored 18th-century palace, with a courtyard garden, swimming pool and fitness centre, perfectly located on the edge of the historic Old Town district. €€€€

Sheraton
Ul. Prusa 2
Tel: (022) 450 61 00
Fax: (022) 450 62 00
www.sheraton.com/warsaw
With 350 comfortable, well-equipped rooms, this modern and elegant hotel is located between Łazienki Park and the fashionable Nowy Świat street. Health club, swimming pool, business and conference facilities. Restaurant, café, jazz bar. €€€€

Victoria Sofitel
Ul. Królewska 11
Tel: (022) 657 80 11
Fax: (022) 657 80 57
www.orbis.pl
With 365 rooms, situated in the city centre overlooking the Saxon Gardens; walking distance to the Old Town. Business centre, perfume counter, shop, rooms for disabled, restaurants with Polish and international cuisine. €€€€

Westin
Al. Jana Pawła II 21
Tel: (022) 450 80 00
Fax: (022) 450 81 11
www.westin.com.pl
Another of Warsaw's high-rise gems. A triumph of glass and modern design, even the lifts at this hotel have won architectural awards. Expect only the best of everything in every one of the enormous rooms. €€€€

Youth Hostels

Nathan's Villa
Ul. Piękna 24/26
Tel/Fax: (022) 622 29 46
www.nathansvilla.com
Proof that hostels are not what they used to be. Expect flat screen TVs, free internet, laundry and no threat of either lockout or early check-out. Expect only a good crowd of well-travelled backpackers and the occasional visit from owner Nathan himself. €

Oki Doki
Pl. Dąbrowskiego 3
Tel: (022) 826 51 12
Fax: (022) 826 83 57
www.okidoki.pl
A bizarre place offering dorms and private rooms themed along such offbeat lines as Communist Chic and D.H. Lawrence. There's the usual free internet, a laundry service and you can make use of the well equipped kitchen, A good bar/common room serves cheap beer and buzzes to the early hours. Friendly staff. €

AROUND WARSAW

Courtyard by Marriott
Ul. Żwirki i Wigury 1
(Frederic Chopin Airport)
Tel: (022) 650 01 00
Fax: (022) 650 01 01
www.marriot.com/wawcy
Early morning flight? Stay at the airport. The great value Courtyard – opposite the main terminal – offers superb rooms (with soundproof windows) and the best breakfast in Warsaw. Internet café and a lively bar. Even if you are not staying here it is a good place to relax between flights. €€

Sokrates Hotel
Ul. Smyczkowa 9
Tel: (022) 843 95 51
Under the auspices of Warsaw University. Located 25 minutes from city centre by bus, or faster by metro. Tourist standard, clean. Rooms with bathroom, small restaurant/bar. €€
Gromada
Ul. 17 Stycznia 32a
Tel: (022) 576 46 00
Fax: (022) 846 15 80
Close to the airport, 30 minutes from the city centre by bus. 127 rooms, all with bathrooms. Guarded

parking. Sauna and fitness centre. €€€
Konstancja
Konstancin Jeziorna Zródlana 6/8
Tel: (022) 756 43 25
Fax: (022) 756 43 67
One of the few nice places in the surrounding area, 15 km (9 miles) from the city centre, on the way to Wilanów and near parks and forests. Rooms with air-conditioning. €€€
Novotel
Ul. 1 Sierpnia 1
Tel: (022) 575 60 00
Fax: (022) 575 69 99
www.orbis.pl

Situated 4 km (2 miles) from the city centre, on the way to the airport. 280 rooms with bath. Health and disabled facilities, sauna and fitness centre. Restaurant, cocktail bar. €€€
Wilczeniec Country Club
Łomiankach
Tel/fax: (022) 860 67 65
www.stajniapolska.pl
Located 15 minutes from central Warsaw, by the Vistula river, this is also an equestrian centre with qualified instructors, in a secluded countryside location. €€€

CENTRAL POLAND

Bydgoszcz

Chemik
Al. Wojska Polskiego 48
Tel: (052) 374 89 13
Fax: (052) 361 18 22
Five km (3 miles) from city centre. 20 rooms (single, double) with bathroom, satellite TV. €
Ikar
Ul. Szubińska 32
Tel: (052) 366 80 00
Close to the centre, some ensuite rooms, recently renovated. €
Ratuszowy
Ul. Długa 37
Tel: (052) 339 84 00
www.hotelratuszowy.com.pl
Located in the Old Town, in the city centre. Old architecture and stylish rooms, sauna, solarium, bar. Intimate atmosphere. €€
Hotel Pod Orłem
Ul. Gdańska 14
Tel: (052) 583 05 30
Fax: (052) 584 02 24
www.hotelpodorlem.pl
Renovated to its original splendour of 1896. Surrounded by attractive gardens, 1.3 km (about 1 mile) from the station. The 80 rooms are all ensuite, some with private balcony. Three restaurants, cocktail bar, nightclub, fitness centre, facilities for children and disabled, satellite TV. Some shops, travel service, car hire,

guarded car park. Horse riding 6 km (4 miles) away, yacht charter and fishing 30 km (15 miles) away, watersports 3 km (2 miles) away. €€€
Hotel Brda
Ul. Dworcowa 94
Tel: (052) 585 01 00
Fax: (052) 585 05 85
www.hotelbrda.com
Located right in the centre of the city. 250 rooms, sauna, solarium, exchange bureau, car hire, guarded car park. €€€
City Hotel
Ul. 3 Maja 6
Tel: (052) 325 25 00
Fax: (052) 325 25 05
Email: city@cps.pl
A modern, luxurious hotel located in the city centre, 3 km (2 miles) from the station, 5 km (3 miles) from the airport. Family atmosphere and excellent restaurant. 130 rooms all with bathroom/WC, satellite TV, Viennese coffee house, fitness suite, guarded car park, dogs allowed. €€€€

Kazimierz Dolny

Domek Góralski
Ul. Krakowska 47
Tel: (081) 881 02 63
Rooms in this wooden house with garden have a view of the Vistula, but not all are ensuite. Dogs allowed. Disco, cinema and

museum nearby. €
Aaznia
Ul. Senatorska 21
Tel: (081) 881 02 98
Fax: (081) 881 02 49
In the city centre, near the Town Square; 13 ensuite rooms with satellite TV; restaurant and café; dogs allowed. €€
Dom Architekta
Rynek 20
Tel/fax: (081) 881 05 44
Close to Town Market Square; the favourite place in Kazimierz Dolny to stay; 106 beds with bath; restaurant. €€
Zajazd Piastowski
Ul. Sloneczna 3
24–120 Kazimierz Dolny
Tel: (081) 881 03 51
Only 1 km (half a mile) from the Vistula riverside, ensuite rooms with satellite TV. Horse riding and swimming pool. Dogs allowed. €€

Łódź

Ibis
Al. Piłsudskiego 11
Tel: (042) 638 67 00
Fax: (042) 638 67 77
www.orbis.pl
Not the most original choice but in a city where good value accommodation is thin on the ground, the Ibis is a good option. Well located you can expect standard Ibis rooms and the usual great breakfast

(which comes at an extra cost). €
Centrum
Ul. Kilińskiego 59/63
Tel: (042) 632 86 40
Fax: (042) 636 96 50
In the city centre, close to the station; newly renovated, with 90 ensuite rooms. €€
Qubus
Al. Mickiewicza 7
Tel: (042) 275 51 00
Fax: (042) 275 52 00
www.qubushotel.com
Probably the best hotel in Łodz. Chic rooms decorated in gentle pastel shades, with air-conditioning throughout, offer not a little luxury, while the lobby bar is lively and the restaurant excellent. €€€

Toruń

Trzy Korony
Rynek Staromiejski 21
Tel/fax: (056) 622 60 31/32
www.hotel3korony.pl
Excellent location on the Market Square; 60 rooms, not all ensuite; restaurant, bar. €

PRICE CATEGORIES

Approximate price catgories for a standard double room per night:
€ = below 250zł
€€ = 250–425zł
€€€ = 425–600zł
€€€€ = over 600zł

Hotel Gromada
Ul. Żeglarska 10–14
Tel: (056) 622 60 60
Fax: (056) 622 53 48
Email: zstaropolski@gromada.pl
Ideally located within the Old Town and by the river Vistula; comfortable

rooms in a period building. €€€
Hotel Petite Fleur
Piekary 25
Tel: (056) 663 44 00
Fax: (056) 663 54 54
www.hotel.torun.com.pl
Charming townhouse hotel

with Gothic architecture and traditional decor. €€€
Mercure Helios
Ul. Kraszewskiego 1/3
Tel: (056) 619 65 50
Fax: (056) 619 62 54
Email: helios@orbis.pl
Located close to the Old

Town; 180 beds; (double rooms, single rooms, apartments) all ensuite with satellite TV; restaurant, café, dancing, sight-seeing service, dogs allowed, guarded car park. €€€€

THE COAST

Gdańsk

Dom Aktora
Ul. Straganiarska 55–56
Tel: (058) 301 61 93
Fax: (058) 301 59 01
www.domaktora.pl
Charming pension on the edge of the Old Town. €
Hotel Królewski
Ul. Ołowianka 1
Tel: (058) 326 11 11
Fax: (058) 326 11 10
www.hotelkrolewski.pl
Located amidst the granaries by the Motława Canal, a short walk from the Old Town, offering 30 rooms and six suites. €€
Mercure Hevelius
Ul. Heweliusza 22
Tel: (058) 321 00 00
Fax: (058) 321 00 20
Email: mer.hevelius@orbis.pl
www.orbis.pl
Attractively modern, comfortable hotel, a short walk from the main historic sights, with a bar, nightclub and good restaurant. €€
Novotel
Ul. Pszenna 1.
Tel: (058) 300 27 50
Fax: (058) 300 29 50
Near the city centre, within walking distance of the Old Town, 3 km (2 miles) from the station; 154 double rooms with bathroom/WC, satellite TV, some of them overlooking the Old Town. Restaurant, café, car park, dogs allowed. €€€
Hotel Podewils
Ul. Szafarnia 2
Tel: (058) 300 95 60
Fax: (058) 300 95 70
www.podewils-hotel.pl
A waterfront location, by the Old Town, within an attractive period building; antique furnishings. €€€
Dwór Oliwski
Ul. Bytowska 2
Tel: (058) 554 70 00
Fax: (058) 554 70 10

www.dwor-oliwski.com.pl
Beautifully restored 17th-century manor house with restaurant and fitness centre in the historic Oliwa district between Gdańsk and Sopot. €€€€
Hanza Hotel
Ul. Tokarska 6
Tel: (058) 305 34 27
Fax: (058) 305 33 86
Email: hotel@hanza-hotel.com.pl
Located in the Old Town, with wonderful views of the Motława River. The newest hotel in the city, 104 air-conditioned rooms, car park, health facilities, casino. €€€€

Gdynia

Nadmorski
Ul. Ejsmonda 2
Tel: (058) 667 77 77
Fax: (058) 667 77 00
www.nadmorski.pl
Situated between the sea and the forest this is a real escape from the busy industrial tri-city conurbation. Rooms are kitted out with plush carpets, deep baths and fluffy pillows. €€

Kołobrzeg

Awangarda
Ul. Rubinowa 2/4
Tel: (060) 243 52 06
Fax: (094) 351 65 55
www.awangarda.max.pl
Ten minutes by bus from the city centre, new hotel, 60 beds; rooms all with bath/WC, sauna, solarium, swimming pool, bar, restaurant. €
Górnik
Ul. Kościuszki 3
Tel: (094) 354 00 78
Fax. (0694) 354 00 66
www.gornik.nat.pl
Set in a park by the sea, this pensione offers an

indoor swimming pool and health club with various spa treatments. €€
Hotel Centrum
Ul. Katedralna 12
Tel: (094) 354 55 60
Fax: (094) 352 29 05
www.centrum.info.pl
A new hotel in the city centre, 70 en suite rooms with satellite TV; fitness centre; disco, restaurant. €€
Solny
Ul. Fredry 5, 78–100 Kolobrzeg
Tel: (094) 354 57 00
Fax: (094) 354 58 28
Email: solny@orbis.pl
Two km (1 mile) from the station and 1 km (half a mile) from the beach; 150 double rooms with bathroom/WC, satellite TV; restaurant, café, bars, disco, sports facilities, fitness suite, facilities for children, guarded car park. €€€

Łeba

Arkun
Ul. Wróblewskiego 11
Tel: (059) 866 24 19
Fax: (059) 866 24 95
www.arkun.interleba.com
In the city centre, near the beach and station; 60 ensuite rooms with satellite TV; guarded car park, fitness centre; watersports. €
Wodnik
Ul. Nadmorska 10
Tel: (059) 866 13 66
Fax: (059) 661 542
www.wodnik.leba.pl
Close to the beach and a forest; restaurant, café, bar, indoor swimming pool, sauna. €€
Neptun
Ul. Sosnowa 1
Tel: (059) 866 14 32
Fax: (059) 866 23 57
www.neptun.leba.pl

Situated on the beach; 75 ensuite rooms; guarded car park; tennis court, billiards, fitness centre, playground; watersports, swimming pool. €€€

Słupsk

Staromiejski
Ul. Jedności Narodowej 4–5
Tel: (059) 842 84 64
Fax: (059) 842 50 19
www.staromiejski.maxmedia.pl
Located in town centre; 77 ensuite rooms, satellite TV; restaurant, bar, dogs allowed, guarded car park. €€
Zamkowy
Ul. Dominikańska 4
Tel/fax: (059) 842 52 94
In the town centre; 66 beds (double rooms, single rooms, apartments), satellite TV; restaurant, bar. €€

Sopot

Pensjonat Eden
Ul. Kordeckiego 4–6
Tel/fax: (058) 551 15 03
www.hotel-eden.com.pl
On the beach; close to the town; rooms with shared bathrooms. €
Hotel Haffner
Ul. JJ Haffnera 59
Tel: (058) 550 98 88
Fax: (058) 550 9800
www.hotelhaffner.pl
Stylish hotel, centrally located with pool, fitness centre and spa facilities. €
Maryla
Ul. Sępia 22
Tel: (058) 551 00 34
Fax: (058) 551 00 35
www.hotel.sopot.pl
All 34 rooms are ensuite in this clean and pleasant secessionist-era hotel with a garden. €€
Sheraton
Powstańców Warszawy 10
Tel/fax: (058) 767 10 00

www.sheraton.pl/sopot
New (opened summer 2008) the Sheraton has been built on the Sopot seafront, just yards from the Grand: competition at last. It is everything you could expect of a Sheraton hotel, with fantastic views out to sea. €€€
Sofitel Grand
Ul. Powstańcow Warszawy 12/14
Tel: (058) 520 60 22
Fax: (058) 520 60 69

www.orbis.pl
This hotel *(see pic right)* was built in 1926 in the Art Nouveau style; near the town centre, it overlooks the beach; 65 double rooms, 43 single rooms, 4 apartments – all ensuite; restaurant, café, bar, casino, suitable for the disabled, art and craft gallery, dogs allowed, guarded car park. €€€

THE NORTHEAST

Augustów

Hotel Delfin
Ul. Turystycna 81
Tel: (087) 644 31 12
Fax: (087) 644 35 88
www.hotel-delfin.com.pl
Lake-side setting, with the hotel also offering an aqua park. €€

Białowieża

Hotel Białowieza
Ul. Waszkiewicza 218b
Tel: (085) 744 43 80
Fax: (085) 744 45 34
www.hotel.bialowieza.pl
Set in the national park, this modern hotel has a health centre, as well as offering watersports facilities such as canoeing. €€

Białystok

Hotel Turkus
Al. Jana Pawła II 54
Tel: (085) 662 81 00
Fax: (085) 662 81 02
www.jard.pl
100 ensuite rooms, with restaurant, café, bar and parking. €
Pensjonat Guliwer
Ul. Celownicza 29
Tel: (085) 744 38 37
Fax: (085) 744 34 51
Near the city centre, single, double and family rooms. Horse riding. €
Hotel Gromada
Al. Jana Pawła II 77
Tel: (085) 651 16 41
Fax: (085) 651 17 01
Email: bialystokhotel@gromada.pl
www.gromada.pl
Six km (4 miles) from the city centre, near the forest.

82 rooms and suites, satellite TV, restaurant, guarded car park, dogs allowed. Trips to nearby sights arranged. €€
Hotel Mosir
Ul. Wołodyjowskiego 5
Tel: (085) 749 62 00
Fax: (085) 749 62 33
www.bialystokmosir.com.pl
Newly built six-storey hotel with 93 en suite rooms, restaurant, nightclub, fitness centre. Next door to the athletic stadium with tennis and watersports facilities. €€
Best Western Hotel Cristal
Ul. Lipowa 3–5
Tel: (085) 749 61 00
Fax: (085) 749 61 71
www.cristal.com.pl
Situated in the city centre. Pleasant atmosphere and quality service, 80 rooms and suites, satellite TV, health facilities, nightclub, casino, car park. €€€
Hotel Gołebiewski
Ul. Pałacowa 7
Tel: (087) 678 25 00
Fax: (087) 678 26 00
www.golebiewski.pl
412 ensuite rooms and apartments, restaurant, nightclub, car park, swimming pool, disabled facilities. €€€

Elbląg

Stadion Hotel
Ul. Brzeska 41
Tel: (055) 641 11 05
Fax: (055) 234 40 42
40 rooms, pets allowed, car park. Facilities include grill, solarium. Museum and watersports 3 km (2 miles) away. €

Gromada
Pl. Slowiański 2
Tel: (055) 230 61 91
Fax: (055) 232 40 83
www.polhotels.com/Elblag/Gromada
Located in the town centre; 112 rooms with bathroom/WC, satellite TV; restaurant, nightclub, sauna, disabled facilities, car park, travel agency. €€
Żuławy
Ul. Królewiecka 126
Tel: (055) 234 57 11
Fax: (055) 232 95 00
www.hotel-zulawy.com.pl
Conveniently located in the city centre, 50 attractive, ensuite rooms with satellite TV. Facilities include sauna, billiards table, ticket reservation, restaurant. Sailing 20 km (10 miles) away. €€
Kadyny Palace
Tolkmicko
Tel: (055) 231 61 20
Fax: (055) 231 62 00
www.kadyny.com.pl
Located 90 minutes southeast of Gdańsk Airport, close to the national park. 40 bedrooms all ensuite, restaurant, sauna, tennis, mountain biking, horse-riding. €€€

Malbork

Parkowy
Ul. Portowa 3
Tel: (055) 272 24 13
Near to the Teutonic Knights' castle in the park; 40 beds (double, single rooms) in hotel and 10 camping houses. All rooms and camping places have bath/WC. €

Zamek
Ul. Starościńska 14
Tel: (055) 272 33 67
Fax: (055) 272 27 38
www.hotel-zamek.e-tur.com.pl
Close to the castle; 80 ensuite rooms; two restaurants, café, guarded car park. €€€

Olsztyn

Gromada
Pl. Konstytucji 3 Maja 4
Tel: (089) 534 58 64
Fax: (089) 534 63 30
Email: kormoran@gromada.pl
www.gromada.pl
In the town centre; 100 double rooms, 2 apartments – all ensuite, satellite TV; restaurant, café, bars and guarded car park. €€
Novotel
Ul. Sielska 4a
Tel: (089) 522 05 00
Fax: (089) 527 54 03
www.orbis.pl
Situated on the bank of Ukiel Lake, close to the forest, with 97 double rooms with bath/WC and satellite TV; rooms for disabled people; car, bicycle rental; guarded parking, pets allowed, watersports (sailing, windsurfing), horse riding, biking and hiking nearby. €€€

PRICE CATEGORIES

Approximate price catgories for a standard double room per night:
€ = below 250zł
€€ = 250–425zł
€€€ = 425–600zł
€€€€ = over 600zł

The Northwest

Poznań

Hotel Royal
Ul. Św Marcin 71
Tel: 858 2300
www.hotel-royal.com.pl
Located on the principal shopping street, near the old town, the hotel occupies a pair of period townhouses. €€

Vivaldi
Ul. Winogrady 9
Tel: (061) 858 81 00
Fax: (061) 853 29 77
www.vivaldi.pl
Close to the city centre and by the edge of a park; all rooms ensuite; restaurant, café, swimming pool. €€€

Hotel Royal
Ul. Św Marcina 71
Tel: (061) 858 23 00
Fax: (061) 853 78 84
www.hotel-royal.com.pl
Stylish hotel within the city centre, dating from 1910 and retaining a period feel. €€€€

Polonez
Al. Niepodległości 36
Tel: (061) 864 71 00
Fax: (061) 852 37 62
www.orbis.pl
Located in the city centre, near to the historical part; 203 single rooms, 192 double rooms, 12 apartments – all with bathroom/ WC, satellite TV; restaurant, café, bar,

dancing, casino; guarded car park, dogs allowed. €€€€

Szczecin

Neptun
Ul. Matejki 18
Tel: (091) 488 38 83
Fax: (091) 488 41 17
www.orbis.pl
In city centre, close to the Old Town and business district; 179 double rooms, 96 single rooms, 8 apartments, all ensuite with satellite TV; restaurant, bar, nightclub, outdoor swimming pool, casino, horse riding and downhill skiing 5 km (3 miles) away. €€€

Victoria
Pl. Batorego 2
Tel: (091) 434 38 55
Fax: (091) 433 73 68
www.hotelvictoria.com.pl
Set in an old house in the city centre; 60 ensuite rooms. €€€

Radisson SAS
Pl. Rodła 10
Tel: (091) 359 55 95
Fax: (091) 359 45 94
www.radisson.com.pl
Situated in the city centre; 370 rooms all with satellite TV; two restaurants, café, bars, nightclub, casino, fitness suite, indoor swimming pool, guarded car park. €€€€

The Southeast

Lublin

Grand Hotel Lublinianka
Krakowskie Przedmieście 56
Tel: (081) 446 63 33
Fax: (081) 446 62 00
www.lublinianka.com
Centrally located, with attractive period architecture, restaurant, café and bar. €€

Huzar
Ul. Spadochroniarzy 7
Tel: (081) 533 05 36
www.hotelhuzar.pl

Close to city centre; 116 rooms all ensuite; restaurant, billiards. €€

Unia Mercure
Al. Racławickie 12
Tel: (081) 533 20 61
Fax: (081) 533 35 01
www.mercure.pl
Located in the city centre; 3 km (2 miles) from the station, 70 double rooms, 35 single rooms, 5 apartments, all ensuite with TV; restaurant, café, bar, dancing, guarded car

park, dogs allowed. €€€€

Nowy Sącz

Max Motel
Ul. Graniczna 95
Tel: (018) 443 97 15
24 bedrooms, all ensuite with satellite TV; restaurant, guarded car park. €

Beskid
Ul. Limanowskiego 1
Tel: (018) 443 57 70

Fax: (018) 443 51 44
www.orbis.pl
In the town centre; at the junction of three rivers Dunajec, Poprad and Kamienica. 56 double rooms, 8 single rooms, 10 apartments – all with bathroom/WC; restaurant, café, dancing, dogs allowed, guarded car park; downhill skiing 20 km (12 miles) away, fishing 5 km (3 miles) away. €€€

The Southwest

Jelenia Góra

Cieplice
Ul. Cervi 11
Tel: (075) 755 10 41
Email: cieplice@ptkarkonosze.pl
Situated in the district of Jelenia Góra-Cieplice, 7 km (4 miles) from the city centre, close to the spa and spa park. €€

Europa
Ul. 1 Maja 16–18
Tel: (075) 649 55 00
Fax: (075) 752 44 95
Email: europa@ptkarkonosze.pl
In the city centre. 29 rooms, near the museum and concert hall. Ski lift nearby, sailing 30 km (19 miles) away. €€

Mercure Jelenia Góra
Ul. Sudecka 63
Tel: (075) 754 91 48
Fax: (075) 752 62 66
www.mercure.com
Near the town centre; with a swimming pool, brasserie, bars, fitness suite, guarded car park. €€€€

Wrocław

Mleczarnia Hostel
Ul. Włodkowica 5
Tel/Fax: (071) 787 75 70
www.mleczarniahostel.pl
Well located hostel whose ground floor is given over to one of the liveliest bars in the city. Dorms are clean,

bathrooms equally so and there is a range of private rooms with en-suites if you can afford a bit more cash. €

Mercure Panorama
Pl. Dominikański 1
Tel: (071) 323 27 00
Fax: (071) 344 36 81
www.mercure.com
In the city centre; 70 double rooms, 34 single rooms, 8 apartments – all with bathroom/WC, satellite TV; restaurant, café, dancing, dogs allowed, guarded car park. €€

Sofitel
Ul. Św. Mikołaja 67
Tel: (071) 358 83 00

Fax: (071) 358 83 01
www.orbisonline.pl
You know you have chosen well when you walk into the huge rooms and see Bang and Olufsen stereos on the walls. Add in marble bathrooms with jacuzzis and you have yourself a treat (though it doesn't come cheap). €€€

Hotel HP Plaza
Ul. Drobnera 11–13
Tel: (071) 320 84 00
Fax: (071) 320 84 59
www.parkplaza.pl
Ultra-modern central, deluxe hotel with river views, sauna and fitness centre. €€€€

THE SOUTH

ABOVE: the colourful interior of The Secret Garden Hostel.

Close to motorway (E40), in residential district of the town. From some rooms there is a view of the park and private garden. Air-conditioned, satellite TV, sauna, swimming pool, tennis courts; restaurant, cocktail bar, summer grill bar, casino watersports in Kryspinów Lake 15 km (10 miles) away, horse riding 2 km (1 mile) away. €€€€

Kraków

In high season Kraków is overcrowded so it is advisable to make a reservation at least a month before your stay.

Hotel Wyspiański
Ul. Westerplatte 15
Tel: (012) 422 95 66
Fax: (012) 422 57 19
www.hotel-wyspianski.pl
Budget option, conveniently located. €

Hotel Saski
Ul. Sławkowska 3
Tel: (012) 421 42 22
Fax: (012) 421 48 30
www.hotelsaski.com.pl
In the centre of the Old Town, in a 16th-century townhouse; some rooms ensuite. €€

Hotel Senacki
Ul. Grodzka 51
Tel: (012) 422 11 61
Fax: (012) 422 79 34
www.senacki.krakow.pl
Pleasant hotel overlooking the 17th century church of SS Peter and Paul. Ensuite rooms, restaurant and bar. €€

Klezmer-Hois
Ul. Szeroka 6
Tel/fax: (012) 411 12 45
www.klezmer.pl
Original 1930s' decor perfectly located in the Kazimierz district. €€

Pod Białym Orłem
Ul. Pijarska 17
Tel/fax: (012) 422 11 44
www.podorlem.com.pl
Located in the historic centre of town. Small, traditional; 90 rooms, restaurant. €€

Pod Różą
Ul. Floriańska 14
Tel: (012) 424 33 00

www.hotel.com.pl
Located in a renovated building in the Old Town. Family atmosphere, ensuite rooms. €€

Rycerski
Pl. Na Groblach 22
Tel: (012) 422 60 82
Small but smart boarding house, close to the Royal Castle Wawel; 16 double rooms and 2 suites. Restaurant. €€

Francuski
Ul. Pijarska 13
Tel: (012) 627 37 77
Fax: (012) 627 37 00
Email: francuski@orbis.pl
Traditional hotel dating from 1912, recently renovated, located in historic centre of Kraków; 80 rooms all with bathroom/WC, satellite TV, some with view of the Old Town; restaurant (Polish and French cuisine), café, dogs allowed, guarded car park. €€€

Palac Bonerowski
Ul. Św. Jana 1
Tel: (012) 374 13 00
Fax: (012) 374 13 05
www.palacbonerowski.pl
Want to stay on Kraków's main square? Do it in style. The Bonerowski oozes class from every corner, from the Secession façade to the dark wooden furnishings. The onsite restaurant is Kraków's best. €€€

Pollera
Ul. Szpitalna 30
Tel: (012) 422 10 44
www.pollera.com.pl
The Pollera Hotel in the centre of Kraków offers large rooms, some suitable for disabled. Family

atmosphere, hotel taxi service, car park, restaurant. €€

Radisson SAS
Ul. Straszewskiego 17
Tel: (012) 618 88 88
Fax: (012) 618 88 89
www.radissonsas.com
With great views of Planty Park the Radisson is everything you would expect, and more. More than 400 paintings by graduates of the city's academy of art cover the walls, the kind of touch that makes all the difference. €€€

Wentzl
Rynek Główny 19
Tel: (012) 430 26 64
Fax: (012) 430 26 65
www.wentzl.pl
Historic hotel on Krakow's main square. Every room is individually furnished in a surprisingly modern and fresh mix of bright and breezy colours. €€€

Ester
Ul. Szeroka 20
Tel: (012) 429 11 88
Fax: (012) 429 12 33
In the city centre, close to the Old Town; 24 ensuite double rooms with TV, phone. €€€

Hotel Copernicus
Ul. Kanoniczna 16
Tel: (012) 424 3400
Fax: (012) 424 3405
www.hotel.com.pl
Attractive modern interiors behind a period façade. €€€€

Novotel Krakow Bronowice
Al. Armii Krajowej 11
Tel: (012) 622 64 00
Fax: (012) 622 64 05
www.orbisonline.pl

Częstochowa

Zajazd Vegas
Ul. Św. Rocha 24
Tel: (034) 362 05 30
Located close to the city centre, some rooms ensuite. €

Etap Hotel
Ul. Wojska Polskiego 281/291,
42-200 Częstochowa
Tel: (034) 366 90 75
Fax: (034) 368 19 66
www.orbis.pl
A perfect place to stay while travelling, next to the Warsaw-Katowice motorway and 1.5km (1 mile) from the railway station, overlooking meadows. Restaurant, café, bars, car hire, parking. Downhill skiing 10 km (5 miles) away, tennis court 3 km (1½ miles) away. €€€€

Mercure Patria
Ul. Ks. Popiełuszki 2,
42-200 Częstochowa
Tel: (034) 360 31 00
Fax: (034) 360 32 00
Email: mer.patria@orbis.pl
Located in the town centre, on the E16 (Lódź and Warsaw direction), near the Jasna Góra Monastery; 30 single rooms, 66 double rooms with bathroom/WC and satellite TV. Restaurant serves Polish, French and Hungarian cuisine, bars, disco, facilities for the disabled, currency

PRICE CATEGORIES

Approximate price catgories for a standard double room per night:
€ = below 250zł
€€ = 250–425zł
€€€ = 425–600zł
€€€€ = over 600zł

exchange, guarded car park, dogs allowed. Tennis courts, volleyball, basketball. €€€€

Gliwice

Argenteum
Ul. Sowińskiego 5
Tel: (032) 238 04 80
Fax: (032) 231 69 33
www.argentum.gliwice.pl
Near the railway station; a good value choice, with 30 ensuite rooms, and a car park. Sailing and fishing just 10 km (6 miles) away. €
Diament
Ul. Zwycięstwa 30
Tel: (032) 231 22 44
Fax: (032) 231 72 16
www.hoteldiament.pl
Restaurant, café, bar, dogs allowed. Tennis court and disco 1 km (half a mile) away; sailing,

fishing 10 km (6 miles away). €€
Piast
Ul. Chodkiewicza 33
Tel/fax: (032) 279 11 37
www.piasthotel.pl
132 ensuite rooms with satellite TV. Car park, hairdresser, ticket reservations on-site. €€

Katowice

Hotel Katowice
Al. Korfantego 9
Tel: (032) 258 82 81
Fax: (032) 259 75 26
www.hotel-katowice.com.pl
In the city centre. €
Novotel Katowice Centrum
Ul. Rozdzieńskiego 16
Tel: (032) 200 44 44
Fax: (032) 200 44 11
www.orbis.pl
In city centre; with restaurant, café, nightclub,

indoor pool, sauna. Dogs allowed, guarded car park. €€€€

Opole

Weneda
Ul. 1 Maja 77.
Tel: (077) 442 10 00
Fax: (077) 442 10 02
www.hotel-weneda.opole.pl
Centrally located hotel with a traditional style. €€
Mercure Opole
Ul. Krakowska 59
Tel: (077) 451 81 00
Fax: (077) 451 81 99
www.mercure.com
Newly renovated, in the town centre; 34 double rooms, 59 single rooms, 5 apartments – all with bathroom/WC; café-restaurant, garages and guarded car park. €€€

Youth Hostels

Good Bye Lenin
Ul. Joselewicza 23
Tel/Fax: 012 421 20 30
www.goodbyelenin.pl
A communist-era themed hostel predictably popular with visiting students. No lockout, free internet, a bar and TV room make it a good choice for a cheap Krakow sleep. €
The Secret Garden Hostel
Ul. Skawińska 7
Tel: (012) 430 54 55
This colourful place has comfortable dorm rooms as well as simple, immaculately clean private doubles, triples and quad rooms. Use of washing machine, lockers and luggage storage. The perfect backpacker stopover. €

THE MOUNTAINS

Bielsko-Biała

Hotel Ondraszek
Ul. Warszawska 185
Tel: (033) 812 20 37
Fax: (033) 812 20 37
Email: ondraszek@skg.pl
Two km (1 mile) from the station and 4 km (2 miles) from the city centre. With 39 comfortable rooms. €€
Hotel Prezydent
Ul. 3 Maja 12
Tel: (033) 822 72 11
www.hotelprezydent.pl
In the city centre, in a restored 19th-century building, one of the best hotels in town. 74 ensuite rooms. Smart restaurant. €€€
Magura
Ul. Żywiecka 93
Tel: (033) 819 91 99
Fax: (033) 819 91 59
www.orbis.pl
Situated 4 km (2 miles) from the station, beside the Beskidy Mountains, with wonderful views, satellite TV. Restaurant offers traditional Polish and international cuisine. Vegetarian food available. Business centre, hairdresser, café, bar, disco. Outdoor guarded car park. Pets permitted.

Sixteen km (10 miles) to Szczyrk, well known resort for downhill skiing. €€€

Promnice

Noma Residence
Tel/fax: (032) 219 46 78
www.promnice.com.pl
Located about 50 km (30 miles) north of Bielsko-Biała. Built in 1861, this neo-Gothic hunter's castle is one of the best architectural sights from the 19th century. A traditional atmosphere, with 24 rooms. Horse riding, balloon flights, sailing and mountain biking. €€€€

Szczyrk

Pensjonat Czak
Ul. Kampingowa 7
Tel: (033) 817 93 89
Fifteen minutes' walk from the city centre; 25 rooms with bath/WC; bar, small restaurant. €
Klimczok
Ul. Poziomkowa 20
Tel: (033) 826 01 00
Fax: (033) 826 01 10
www.klimczok.pl
Two km (1 mile) from the

city centre; 270 beds, high standard, two restaurants, Scottish pub, nightclub, casino, indoor tennis court, indoor swimming pool, fitness centre. €€€€

Zakopane

Hotel Gromada
Ul. Zaruskiego 2
Tel: (018) 201 50 11
Fax: (018) 201 53 30
www.gromada.pl
Just off the main thoroughfare, Ul. Krupówki, this modern hotel also offers a sauna, gym and regional cuisine. €€
Belvedere
Droga do Białego 3
Tel: (018) 202 12 00
Fax: (018) 202 12 50
www.belvederehotel.pl
Traditional style hotel with good modern facilities: swimming pool, fitness centre, "Thalgo" spa treatments, two restaurants, café and bar. €€€
Litwor
Ul. Krupówki 40
Tel: (018) 201 71 89
Fax: (018) 202 42 05
www.litwor.pl

Perfectly located by the town's central thoroughfare; attractive, well-appointed rooms, a great restaurant, swimming pool, fitness centre, all within a traditional architectural style. €€€

Youth Hostels

Zakopane
Dom Turysty PTTK
Ul. Zaruskiego 5
Tel/fax: (018) 206 32 81
www.domturysty.z-ne.pl
Located in the city centre in a 19th-century building; 640 beds, price depends on the standard, restaurant, bar, shop, TV room, billiards. €
Schronisko Mlodzielowe
Ul. Marusarzówny 15.
Tel: (018) 201 56 06
Fifty beds; tourist standard but nice atmosphere. €

E ATING OUT

RECOMMENDED RESTAURANTS, CAFES & BARS

What to Eat

Polish cuisine ranges from rich and substantial to light and elegant. Poles allow themselves a generous amount of time in order to enjoy their meals.

A typical lunch is usually composed of at least three courses, starting with a soup, such as *barszcz* (beet) or *żurek* (sour rye), followed perhaps by an appetiser of salmon or herring (prepared in either cream, oil or vinegar). Other popular appetisers are various meats, vegetables or fish in aspic. For the main course you may want to try the national dish, *bigos* (sauerkraut with pieces of meat and sausage) or *kotlet schabowy* (breaded pork chops). Finish on a sweet note with ice cream or a piece of *makowiec*, poppy seed cake, or *droż dzówka*, a type of yeast cake.

Other Polish specialities include *chłodnik* (a chilled beet soup), *golonka* (pork knuckles cooked with vegetables), *kołduny* (meat dumplings), *zrazy* (slices of beef served with buckwheat) and *flaki* (tripe).

What to Drink

Coffee or lemon tea *(herbata)* are favourite drinks and usually follow a meal, Poles prefer to drink vodka or *piwo* (beer) with their meals. Among the best known brands are: EB, Żywiec, Okocim and Warka. Most restaurants offer a selection of German and Czech beers. Stronger alcoholic drinks, usually brands of vodka such as Żubrówka, Wyborowa, Premium and Żytnia, are invariably present on every festive table. Finding good wine is easy but it tends to be expensive.

Where to Eat

It is common that good, smart, well-managed restaurants are located in the Old Town of major cities. More and more restaurants are also serving foreign specialities, particularly Italian, Chinese, Japanese, Vietnamese and French cuisine. A few restaurants serve traditional kosher Jewish fare. Most hotels have details of nearby restaurants.

A service charge is usually included in the price at restaurants, but it is customary to pay a figure rounded up by 5–10 percent in recognition of good service.

BELOW: a table with a view at Café Camelot, Kraków.

Milk bars *(bar mleczny)* are now almost a thing of the past but if you can find one, they make a good alternative to restaurants and are excellent value for money. Mainly self-service, cafeteria-style, they occupy simple premises and have a limited choice of basic dishes. Often you get a home-cooked and filling plate for very little. There are also a number of popular Oriental food bars (usually run by Chinese or Vietnamese) located in the city centres. During the summer season in the tourist resorts along the Baltic Sea coast, stalls sell freshly caught baked or smoked fish.

WARSAW

RESTAURANTS

Adler
Ul. Mokotowska 69
Tel: (022) 628 73 84
www.adlerrestauracja.pl
Nice setting, one of the few places offering typical German food. Very good wine and beer. €€

Bazyliszek
Rynek Starego Miasta 1/3
Tel: (022) 831 18 41
Open: 11am–11pm.
Noted for its duck with apples; the magnificent view over the Market Square is just as impressive. €€€

Belvedere
Ul. Agrykoli 1
Tel: (022) 841 22 50/48 06
www.belvedere.com.pl
Open: noon–late.
Located in the Orangery in the park, an impressive French and Polish menu includes żurek (a Polish soup) with ham and mushrooms, sirloin steak cooked to the recipe of King Stanisław August's chef. In the summer there

is an open-air café where you can simply order a coffee and cake. €€€

Blue Cactus
Ul. Zajaczkowska 11
Tel: (022) 851 23 23
Open: Mon–Sat noon–11pm, Sun 11am–3pm.
www.bluecactus.pl
Mexican style cuisine. Always crowded, so it is wise to make a reservation. €€

Casa Valdemar
Ul. Piekna 7/9
Tel: (022) 628 81 40
www.warsawvoice.pl/view/3909
Open: noon–last customer.
Excellent restaurant serving Spanish cuisine. Tastefully arranged interior, magnificent clay oven. Great atmosphere. €€€

Champions
Al. Jerozolimskie 65/79 (Marriott Hotel)
Tel: (022) 630 51 19
www.champions.pl
Open: 11am–midnight.
Superior burger bar food at the Marriott. Ribs, steaks and fajitas come at decent prices, and the myriad TV screens showing non-stop sport mean you will not

miss a kick. Good kids menu. €€

Dom Polski
Ul. Francuska 11
Tel: (022) 616 24 88
www.restauracjadompolski.pl
Choose from a table in the garden, conservatory or dining room in this elegant villa serving superb Polish dishes. €€

Essencia
Ul. Marszałkowska 94/98 (Novotel Warszawa Centrum)
Tel: (022) 596 12 34
www.essencia.pagi.pl
Open: Mon–Sat 6.30–10.30am, noon–3pm, 6–11pm, Sun 7–11am.
High-quality, modern European food where the soft lighting and staff in designer outfits set the scene for long, lazy dinners with friends. €€€

Flik
Ul. Puławska 43
Tel: (022) 849 44 34
www.flik.com.pl
Open: 10am–last customer.
Good restaurant serving Polish food at reasonable prices. Delicious meat dishes with herb sauces and dumplings; good wine list. €€€

Fukier
Rynek Starego Miasta 27
Tel: (022) 831 10 13
www.ufukiera.pl
Open: noon–midnight.
Polish and Jewish cuisine in the heart of the Old Town, in a lovely atmosphere. €€€

Fusion at the Westin
Al. Jana Pawła II 21
Tel: (022) 450 86 31
www.westin.com.pl/fusion
Open: Mon–Fri 6.30–10.30am, noon–10.30pm, Sat 7–10.30am, noon–10.30pm, Sun 7–10.30am, 12.30–10.30pm
Try Sunday brunch, an expat institution, at the Westin's showpiece eatery. From noon–4pm every Sunday you can try a variety of cuisines as you sip champagne and enjoy some light live jazz.

Lemon Grass
Al. Ujazdowskie 8
Tel: (022) 696 33 00
www.lemongrass.waw.pl
Open: noon–11pm.
For something exotic in Warsaw try this convincingly authentic Thai restaurant. All the key ingredients are imported fresh daily, from the giant prawns to the chili that laces the beef dishes. €€€

Malinowa
Ul. Krakowskie Przedmieście 42/44
Tel: (022) 551 10 00
Open: 6pm–11pm.
French and Polish award-winning restaurant in the Bristol Le Meridien (see page 378). Excellent menu. €€€

Montmartre
Ul. Nowy Świat 7
Tel: (022) 628 63 15
www.warsawvoice.pl/view/3909
Open: noon–late.
Delicious French cuisine at a relatively low price. Menu includes frogs legs, snails, fresh oysters, and apple tart for dessert. €€€

Pierogarnia
Ul. Bednarska 28/30
Tel: (022) 828 03 92
www.pierogarnianabednarskiej.pl
Open: 11am–9pm.

BELOW: eating alfresco in Warsaw.

For a cheap feed in Warsaw you can do no better. Come here to feast on vegetarian *pierogi* filled withy cheese or jam, sold by weight and eaten at canteen-style tables. €€
Podwale
Ul. Podwale 25
Tel: (022) 635 63 14
www.podwale25.pl
Traditional Polish cuisine in a classic setting with a large courtyard for al fresco dining. €€
Restauracja Polska Tradycja
Ul. Belwederska 18a
Tel: (022) 840 0901
www.restauracjatradycja.pl
Elegant, traditional town house setting with delicious sophisticated Polish dishes. €€–€€€
Santorini
Ul. Egipska 7
Tel: (022) 672 05 25
www.kregliccy.pl
Open: noon–11pm.
Traditional Greek restaurant outside the city centre. €€
Tokio
Ul. Dobra 17

Tel: (022) 827 46 32
Japanese restaurant popular with resident Japanese. €€
Sense
Ul. Nowy Świat 19
Tel: (022) 826 65 70
www.sensecafe.com.pl
Open: Mon–Thur noon–11pm, Fri–Sat noon–12.30am, Sun noon–10pm.
Easily Warsaw's best restaurant. Expect only the most inventive Asian-European fusion cuisine served in a stylish setting. €€€

CAFÉS

Batida
Ul. Nowogrodzka 1/3
Tel: (022) 621 45 34
www.batida.com.pl
Open: Mon–Fri 7am–8pm, Sat 8am–4pm, Sun 9am–3pm.
Suitable place for breakfast or lunch. Variety of salads and freshly baked croissants. Delicious cakes and tarts with fruit. Excellent coffee.

Blikle
Nowy Świat 33
Tel: (022) 826 66 19
www.blikle.pl
Open: 10am–8pm.
Elegant café and one of Warsaw's most popular meeting places. Delicious doughnuts, ice cream and snacks.
Café Bristol
Bristol Hotel, Ul. Krakowskie Przedmieście 42/44
Tel: (022) 551 18 28
Open: 10am–1am.
Elegant Viennese-style café that serves delicious desserts, coffee and lunches.
Calypso
Ul. Chłodna 15
Tel: (022) 652 36 60
Open: 10am–10pm.
The best ice cream café in Warsaw; also has delicious cakes.
Coffee Karma
Pl. Zbawiciela 3/5
Tel: (022) 875 87 09
www.coffeekarma.pl
Open: Mon–Fri 7.30–10pm, Sat 9am–10pm, Sun 10am–10pm.
The city's best coffee is served at this otherwise

non-descript place overlooking bustling Plac Zbawiciela.
Literatka
Krakowskie Przedmiecie 87/89
Tel: (022) 827 30 54
www.literatka.com.pl
Good coffee and delicious desserts in a bohemian atmosphere.
Mercers
Ul. Chmielna 21
Tel: (022) 826 35 80
www.mercers.pl
Open: Mon–Fri 7am–11pm, Sat–Sun 9am–11pm.
This is where Warsaw's ladies-who-lunch come for their mid-morning coffee. A superior range of cakes and sandwiches, though note there is no table service: order and pay at the counter.
Pożegnanie z Afryką
Ul. Freta 4/6
Tel: (050) 138 30 91
Open: 7am–10pm.
www.pozegnaniezafryka.pl
Situated in the Old Town, serving more than 40 types of coffee, which is offered for sale as well. Part of a national chain.

CENTRAL POLAND

RESTAURANTS

Bydgoszcz

Capri
Ul. Niedzwiedzia 11
Tel: (052) 322 49 81
www.company.yellowpages.pl
Open: 11am–11pm.
Italian cuisine, featuring 50 different types of pizza. €€
Chopin
Ul. 3 Maja 6
Tel: (052) 325 25 00
www.city-hotel.pl
Open: 6.30am–10am, noon–11pm.
Polish and French cuisine in the centre of Bydgoszcz; the speciality is fried Norwegian salmon, but also try the beef medallions in various sauces, vegetables à la chinoise, and a wide selection of wines and desserts. €€€
Torbyd
Ul. Chopina 11a

Tel: (052) 341 60 25
Open: 9am–10pm.
Traditional Polish cuisine. The speciality of the house are sautéed cutlets with mushrooms, pork shoulder with plums, as well as fine desserts and wines. €€

Kazimierz Dolny

Domu Michalakow
Ul. Nadrzeczna 24
Tel: (081) 881 05 79
Open: from 1pm.
Range of salads, meats and soups. The ribs and trout are recommended. Good wines. €€
Obiady Domowe
Ul. Tyszkiewicza 22
Tel: (081) 881 07 31
Open: 1–5pm.
Homemade hot meals, delicious ravioli. €
Staropolska
Ul. Nadrzeczna 14
Tel: (081) 881 02 36
www.staropolska.kazimierz-dolny.pl
Open: 9am–last customer.

Inn-style, excellent food, reportedly one of the best in the city at this long-established restaurant. Traditional Polish cuisine. €
Zielona Tawerna
Ul. Nadwiślańska 4
Tel: (081) 881 03 08
www.gastronauci.pl
All decorated in green. *Ruskie pierogi* (Polish ravioli) and sirloin steak with pumpkin are the specialities. €

Łódź

Dworek
Ul. Rogowska 24
Tel: (042) 659 76 40
www.restauracja-dworek.dot.pl
Open: noon–11pm.
Polish cuisine outside the city centre. Speciality is sirloin steak with mushrooms. €€€
Figaro
Ul. Piotrowska 92
Tel: (042) 630 20 08
www.restauracjafigaro.pl

A chic contemporary setting serving imaginative cuisine. €€
Irish Pub 77
Ul. Piotrkowska 77
Tel: (042) 632 48 76
www.irishpub.pl
Open: noon–3am.
Polish cuisine. The speciality is pot-roast pork knuckle. €
Łódź Kaliska Bar
Ul. Piotrkowska 102
Tel: (042) 630 69 55
www.klub.lodzkaliska.pl
Tasty, traditional Polish dishes, and popular meeting place. €
Maharaja
Ul. Traugutta 4

PRICE CATEGORIES

Prices are for a two-course meal for two with a bottle of wine:
€ = below 50zł
€€ = 50–100zł
€€€ = 100–170zł
€€€€ = over 170zł

Tel: (042) 633 40 45
Open: noon–11pm.
Indian cuisine. Big menu, with particularly good chicken and mutton dishes. €€€

Toruń

Hungaria
Ul. Prosta 19
Tel: (056) 622 41 89
Open: 10am–10pm.
Polish and Hungarian cuisine, located in the Old Town. Specialities include goulash soup and Hungarian style poultry delicacies. €
Kuranty
Ul. Rynek Staromiejski 29

Tel: (056) 662 52 52
A bohemian atmosphere with Polish and Italian dishes. €
Staromiejska
Ul. Szczytna 2/4
Tel: (056) 622 6725
Open: 10am–10pm.
Italian and Polish cuisine – perhaps the best Italian food in Poland. Delicious tortellini pasta with cheese and spinach, good wines. €€
Staropolski Zajazd
Ul. Żeglarska 10/14
Tel: (056) 622 60 60/3
Open: 7am–10pm.
Traditional Polish cuisine. Located in the Old Town in a Gothic building. *Lurek*, *pierogi* and a selection of

meat dishes. €
Zielony Wieloryb
Ul. Rynek Nowomiejski 13
Tel: (056) 653 92 53
Open: Mon–Fri 1pm–last customer, Sat–Sun 2pm–last customer.
Funky and popular basement with live music serving traditional Polish cuisine. €

CAFÉS

Kazimierz Dolny

Galeria U Dziwisza
Ul. Krakowska 1
Tel: (502) 628 220
The only tea-shop in town,

also doubles as an art gallery. Good cakes.

Łódź

Blikle Cafe
Ul. Piotrkowski 89 80/82
Tel: (042) 632 05 45
www.blikle.pl
Open: 10am–10pm, Sun 10am–6pm.
Small modern patisserie with a selection of French, Italian and Polish cakes.
Cafeteria u Michała i Darka
Al. Kozciuszki 80/82
Tel: (042) 636 50 55 ext 308
www.puby.pl
Open: 10am–10pm.
Delicious range of coffees.

THE COAST

RESTAURANTS

Gdańsk

Bar Pod Ryba
Długi Targ 35/38/1
Tel: (058) 305 13 07
www.barpodryba.pl
Open: 11am–9pm.
Serves one thing: jacket potatoes, with as many fillings as you can imagine. Right off the main square it is perfect for a cheap lunch. €
Chłopskie Jadło
Ul. Szeroka 33-35
Tel: (058) 301 46 54

www.chlopskiejadlo.pl
Open: Sun–Thur noon–10pm, Fri–Sat noon–midnight.
This Kraków legend has made it to the seaside. Expect the same high standards – including some great hand-rolled *pierogi* – and the same decent prices. €€
Kubicki
Ul. Wartka 5
Tel: (058) 301 00 50
Open: noon–9pm (in summer until the last customer).
Traditional Polish restaurant in the Old Town on the banks of the Motława River. Pork knuckle, smoked eel and duck are recommended.

Vodka is served in flasks. €€
Pod Lososiem
Ul. Szeroka 54
Tel: (058) 301 76 52
www.podlososiem.com.pl
Open: 11am–last customer.
Old, elegant setting; known for its excellent cuisine, mainly fish, but also for its "golden water" – pieces of gold leaf floating in a herbal liqueur. €€€
Pod Złotym Kurem
Ul. Długa 4
Tel: (058) 301 61 63
Open: 11am–10pm.
Polish and European cuisine. Quick, tasty and inexpensive. €

Targ Rybny
Ul. Targ Rybny 6c
Tel: (058) 320 90 11
www.targrybny.pl
Open: 11am–11pm.
The name means fish market, and the menu is a predictably excellent selection of fish dishes. Brilliant décor makes it feel like you're dining in your grandmother's kitchen. €€
Tawerna
Ul. Powroźnicza 19/20
Tel: (058) 301 41 14
www.tawerna.pl
One of the few restaurants reflecting on the maritime atmosphere of the city, decorated with model ships. Try the duck or fish with a large jug of beer. €€
U Hubertusa
Ul. Piwna 59
Tel: (058) 301 03 22
Fax: (058) 305 76 71
Open: noon–last customer.
Polish cuisine, with an emphasis on game. Located in the Old Town. The house speciality is a tasty wild boar chop. €€€

Kołobrzeg

Monte Christo Inn
Ul. Morska 7c/6
Tel: (094) 354 53 19
Open: from 2pm.
Traditional Polish cuisine. Close to the lighthouse. Speciality is trout and cod "à la Baltic". €

BELOW: there are plenty of excellent cafés in Poland.

Skandynawia
Ul. Dworcowa 10
Tel: (094) 352 82 11 ext 150
Fax: (094) 352 44 78
Open: 11am–1am.
Expensive restaurant located
in the Skandia hotel. Wide
range of meals. Specialities
include wild boar roast; good
selection of wines. €€€
Smażalnia ryb
Ul. Morska 6
Excellent fresh fish. €

Łeba

Wodnik
Ul. Nadmorska 10

Tel: (059) 866 13 66
Fax: (059) 866 15 42
www.wodnik.leba.pl
Open: 7am–10pm.
Basic Polish cuisine. €

Słupsk

Franciszkańska
Ul. Jednozci Narodowej 3
Tel: (059) 842 52 86
Open: 7.30am–10pm.
Polish cuisine in the city
centre. Specialities are
pierogi ruskie. €€
Staromiejska
Ul. Jednozci Narodowej 4
Tel: (059) 842 03 36

Open: 11am–11pm.
Polish and Hungarian
cuisine. Specialities include
cutlets cooked Hungarian
style, and deer fillet. €€

CAFÉS

Gdańsk

Capri
Ul. Długa 59/61
Tel: (058) 301 24 75
Open: 10am–10pm.
Stylish, crowded café,
serving excellent desserts.

Choose from a
mouthwatering selection of
ice cream, cakes and pies.
Irish
Ul. Korzenna 33/35
Tel: (058) 320 24 74
www.irish.pl
Stylish pub located in the
cavernous, historic cellars of
the old town hall.

Kołobrzeg

Polegnanie z Afryką
Ul. Giełdowa 8c/2
Open: 10am–10pm.
Chain café serving delicious
coffees.

THE NORTHEAST

RESTAURANTS

Białystok

Cristal
Ul. Lipowa 3
Tel: (085) 749 61 59
www.cristal-restaurant.pl
Open: 7–11am, 1pm–3am.
In the Cristal Hotel (see
page 381), serving French
and Polish cuisine. The
best place to eat in the city.
€€
Oaza
Ul. Świętojańska 4
Tel: (085) 32 80 20
Open: 10am–10pm.
Arabic cuisine. €€
U Cezara
Ul. Sienkiewicza 26
Tel: (085) 743 60 83
Open: 9am–11pm.
Traditional Polish cuisine
offering good value for
money. €

Białowieża

Karczma u Jankiela
Ul. Krzyże 2a
Tel: (085) 681 28 40
Regional Polish cuisine in a
charming country-inn
setting. €

Elbląg

Europejska
Pl. Słowiański 2
Tel: (055) 234 81 11
Fax: (055) 232 40 83
Open: 6am–11am, 1pm–midnight.
European cuisine and

elegant atmosphere.
Specialities include pork
croissant in a wine sauce.
€€
Mandaryn
Ul. Zw. Ducha 8
Tel: (055) 232 77 86
Open: noon–midnight.
Chinese restaurant in the
Old Town. Good food at
reasonable prices. €
Myśliwska
Ul. Marymoncka 5
Tel: (055) 234 28 61
Open: 10am–8pm, 10am–10pm
(high season).
Traditional Polish cuisine,
specialising in game. The
place is designed in a
hunters' style, with a huge
fireplace in the centre and
hunters' trophies on the
walls. Discotheque and
billiards. €€

Malbork

Nad Nogatem
Pl. Słowiański 5
Tel/fax: (055) 272 31 31
Open: 1pm–2am.
Polish and Chinese cuisine.
Beautiful waterfront
location. €
Piwniczka
Ul. Strościńska 1
Tel: (055) 273 36 68
Open: 9am–10pm.
Located in the cellars f the
Middle Castle. Meat
features heavily on the
menu, but there are
vegetarian options too. €
Grot
Ul. Kościuszki 22d
Tel: (055) 646 96 60

Open: noon–10.30pm.
International menu serving
veal and trout. Located in
Hotel Grot. €€
Zamkowa
Ul. Starozcimska 14
Tel/fax: (055) 272 27 38
www.hotelprodus.pl
Open: 7am–10pm.
Polish cuisine. Located
close to the castle, in a
hotel. Offers about 60
main courses, plus soups
and starters. Specialities
include castle pottage and
vegetarians mushroom
ragout. €€€

Olsztyn

Nowoczesna
Ul. Kościuszki 49
Tel/fax: (089) 533 46 72
Open: 8am–11pm (until 2am
Sat–Sun).
Polish cuisine in the
Warmiński Hotel. Disco on
Saturday nights. €€
U Piotra
Ul. Pana Tadeusza 6
Tel: (089) 533 50 77
www.u-piotra.pl
Open: 11am–11pm.
Chinese cuisine, with about
80 main courses, plus
soups and starters.
Specialities are Peking
duck and rice cakes. €€
Yu Grill Boro
Ul. Nowowiejskiego 11
Tel: (089) 523 53 01
Open: 10am–11pm.
Yugoslavian cuisine, run by
Serbs. Excellent food,
delicious soups, grilled
meat, and more. €€

CAFÉS

Białystok

Hortex
Ul. Curie-Skłodowskiej 15
Tel: (085) 723 69
Open: 11am–10pm.
Cakes, ice cream and
snacks.
Pożegnanie z Afryką
Ul. Warynskiego 3/5
Tel: (085) 652 55 05
Open: 10am–10pm.
Small, pleasant place with
excellent coffee.

Elbląg

Zagłoba
Stary Rynek 11
Tel: (055) 641 00 13
Open: noon–midnight.
Country style café.

Olsztyn

Pozegnanie z Afryką
Ul. Podwale 2
Tel: (089) 534 91 31
Open: 10am–10pm.
Small café and coffee shop
offering over 40 different
varieties.

PRICE CATEGORIES

Prices are for a two-course
meal for two with a bottle
of wine:
€ = below 50zł
€€ = 50–100zł
€€€ = 100–170zł
€€€€ = over 170zł

THE NORTHWEST

Poznań

Adria
Ul. Głogowska 14
Tel: (061) 865 83 74
www.adria.poznan.pl
Open: 9am–10pm.
Polish and French cuisine.
Next to the station.
Speciality is pork knuckle
Bavarian style. €€

Avanti/Pod Koziołkami
Ul. Stary Rynek 95
Tel: (061) 851 78 68
www.podkoziolkami.pl
Good salad bar. €

Bażanciarnia
Stary Rynek 94
Tel: 855 33 59
www.bazanciarnia.pl
Distinguished Polish

cuisine in a sophisticated
townhouse setting looking
over the market square.
Pheasant, duck and fish
are on the menu. €€

Meridian
Ul. Litewska 22
Tel: (061) 656 53 53
Fax: (061) 656 55 26
www.hotelmeridian.com.pl
Open: from 1pm.
European cuisine; one of
the most expensive
restaurants in the city.
Seafood is a speciality.
€€€

Mysliwska
Ul. Libetta 37
Tel/fax: (061) 852 95 60
Open: 1pm–last customer.
www.pandacatering.pl/mysliwska.htm

Polish cuisine. Located in
the centre of the city.
Specialities include deer
leg and roast piglet with
stuffing. €€

Szczecin

Chief
Ul. Rayskiego 16
Tel: (091) 434 37 65
www.chief.com.pl
Open: 10am–last customer.
Polish cuisine, and
reportedly the best fish
restaurant in Poland.
Perfect shark goulash,
zander in three ways,
salmon tartare. €€€

Hotel Park
Ul. Plantowa 1

Tel: (091) 434 00 50
www.parkhotel.szczecin.pl
Fashionable place. €€

Radisson
Pl. Rodla 10
Tel: (091) 359 55 95
www.szczecin.radissonsas.com
Open: 7am–midnight.
Polish and Italian cuisine
served in two elegant
restaurants. Shrimp soup,
rabbit Maltese style and
bigos og pierogi are
particularly good. €€€

Szmaragd
Ul. Kopalniana 2
Tel: (091) 460 81 32
Open: 9am–10pm.
Polish cuisine outside the
city centre. Fish is a
speciality. €€

THE SOUTHEAST

Lublin

Karczma Słupska
Al. Racławickie 22
Tel: (081) 533 88 13
Open: 10am–10pm.
Traditional Polish cuisine

with a choice of about 40
main courses. A speciality
is grilled pork loin and
ravioli with lentils. €

Bel Etage
Ul. Krakowskie Przedmieście 56
Tel: (081) 44 66 33

Located in the Lublinianka
Hotel. Classic Polish and
European dishes. Rooftop
cafe in summer. €€

Unia
Al. Racławickie 12
Tel: (081) 533 20 61

Open: 1pm–midnight.
European cuisine. Many
Polish dishes. Specialities
includes pork loin cooked
the Hungarian way, meat
casserole in a pancake
with asparagus, quails. €€

THE SOUTHWEST

Jelenia Góra

Grodzka Karczma
Ul. Grodzka 5
Tel: (075) 752 53 91
www.hotelbaron.pl
Polish and German cuisine,
as well as pizzas. €

Joland
Ul. Krótka 23/24
Tel: (075) 764 63 04
Open: noon–midnight.
Polish cuisine. Specialities
include roast duck in gravy.
Also a discotheque. €€

Mama
Pl. Piastowski 21b
Tel: (075) 755 9112

PRICE CATEGORIES

Prices are for a two-course
meal for two with a bottle
of wine:
€ = below 50zł
€€ = 50–100zł
€€€ = 100–170zł
€€€€ = over 170zł

Open: 11am–11pm.
Serving Polish and Italian
cuisine, including a variety of
pizzas, fondue, grilled meat;
great selection of wines. €€

Nefryt
Ul. Sudecka 63
Tel: (075) 764 64 81
European cuisine.
Specialities include:
fondue, rabbit roulade; for
vegetarians, *pierogi ruskie*
(a kind of ravioli filled with
cottage cheese and potato
paste). €€€

Wrocław

Belle Epoque
Rynek 20–21
Tel: (071) 343 56 17
Fax: (071) 342 08 12
Open: noon–11pm.
French cuisine in the heart
of the Old Town.
Specialities include fondue
Burgundian style and sole
cooked with orange. €€€

Dwór Polski
Ul. Rynek 5
Tel: (071) 372 48 96/8
www.dworpolski.wroclaw.pl
Open: 11am–last customer.
Polish cuisine, including
beef roulade with
buckwheat groats and
beetroot salad, *pierogi*,
and *krupnik* (barley soup).
€€

Karczma Lwowska
Rynek 4
Tel: (071) 343 98 87
www.lwowska.com.pl
Open: 11am–midnight.
Game dishes abound in
this huge space on the
main square, which
specializes in the cuisine of
eastern Poland. €€€

Karczma Piastów
Ul. Kiełbasnicza 6
Tel: (071) 372 48 96
Open: 11am–midnight.
www.dworpolski.wroclaw.pl
Traditional Polish cuisine.
The interior is arranged in a

folk style. *Pierogi*, filled
roulade, delicious *bigos*
(sauerkraut stewed with
sausages and mushrooms)
and *faramuszka* (a beer
soup with caraway seeds
and cottage cheese) are
recommended. €€

Novocaina
Rynek 13
Tel: (071) 343 69 15
www.novocaina.pl
Open: 11am–11pm.
Modern European cuisine
at its best in a classy
setting on the main market
square. Good pizzas are a
decent option if the budget
is a bit tight. €€€

Pod Złotym Jeleniem
Rynek 44
Tel: (071) 372 39 51
www.restauracjekrawczyk.com.pl
Open: 11am–2am.
Grilled meats are the
speciality here, such as
pork shoulder rissole with
honey. €€

THE SOUTH

RESTAURANTS

Kraków

Arka Noego
Ul. Szeroka 2
Tel: (012) 429 15 28
Open: 10.30am–11pm.
All aboard Noah's Ark for all sorts of kosher treates, from Czech wines to Israeli beers. The food is unfussy but comes in huge portions at cheap prices. There is live music most evenings, which warrants a compulsory surcharge. €€

Ariel
Ul. Szeroka 17
Tel: (012) 421 79 20
www.ariel-krakow.pl
Open: 9am–11pm.
Non-kosher Jewish cuisine. Vegetarian dishes available. €€

Carlito
Ul. Florianska 28
Tel: (012) 429 19 12
Open: 10am–11pm.
Offering perhaps the best views of Ul. Florianska, Carlito's is one of those great restaurants that attracts a loyal clientele who come her time after time. Serving great pizza baked on a clay oven amidst a full menu of good trattoria food. Ebullient atmosphere. €€

Chimera
Ul. Św. Anny 3
Tel: (012) 423 21 78
www.chimera.com.pl
Open: noon–11pm.
Taking Polish cuisine to new heights this place offers modern takes on Polish classics, such as roasted duck with a selection of fruit pate. Very expensive. €€€

Chłopskie Jadło
Ul. Św. Jana 3
Tel: (012) 429 51 57
www.chlopskiejadlo.pl
Open: noon–midnight (later Sat–Sun).
Traditional Polish cuisine served in a country inn atmosphere. Always crowded, so make a reservation unless you are willing to wait for a table. Reportedly the best *golabki* (stuffed cabbage leaves) in the country, as well as dumplings and potato cakes. €€

Cyrano de Bergerac
Ul. Sławkowska 26
Tel: (012) 411 72 88
Open:dily noon–11pm.
www.cyranodebergerac.pl
Open: noon–last customer.
French cuisine, with an emphasis on fish. Located in the heart of the Old Town. The duck foie gras is particularly recommended, as is the lamb curry with apples. €€€€

Floriańska
Ul. Floriańska 43
Tel: (012) 421 08 70
www.restauracja-florianska.pl
Open: 1–11pm.
Polish classics and Mediterranean fusion treats. €€€

Metropolitan
Ul. Sławkowska 3
Tel: (012) 421 98 03
www.metropolitan-krakow.com
A contemporary, stylish setting serving great European dishes. €€

Orient Ekspres
Ul. Stolarska 13
Tel: (012) 422 66 72
www.orient-ekspres.krakow.pl
Open: 1pm–last customer.
Delicious European cuisine, highly recommended. The specialities include veal escalopes in Roquefort sauce and the vegetarian tart. €€

Pod Aniołami
Ul. Grodzka 35
Tel: (012) 421 39 99
www.podaniolami.pl
A large, atmospheric cellar serving excellent Polish and regional cuisine. €€

Wierzynek
Rynek Główny 15
Tel: (012) 424 96 00
www.wierzynek.com.pl
Open: 8am–midnight.
Polish, French and vegetarian cuisine. A historic restaurant where kings, dukes and princes dined in

the 14th century. Nowadays everybody can eat there, if their wallet can bear it. €€€

Polskie Jadło
Ul. Św. Jana 30
Tel: (012) 433 98 25
www.polskiejadlo.com.pl
Open: noon–3am.
Upmarket Polish food in a glorious setting on the Rynek. The pork knuckle with steamed cabbage is a treat. €€

Smak Ukraiński
Ul. Kanonicza 15
Tel: (012) 421 92 94 ext 25
www.ukrainska.pl
Open: noon–10pm.
At the foot of Wawel Hill this fantastic Ukrainian restaurant has one of the most glorious gardens in the city. Dining here on a summer evening is perfect. €€€

Vega
Ul. Św. Gertrudy 7
Tel: (012) 422 34 94
www.vegarestauracja.com.pl
Open: 9am–9pm.
Eating in Krakow can often be a bit of a meat fest, so for something different try this excellent vegetarian restaurant with splendid views of Planty Park. €€

Vinoteca La Bodega
Ul. Sławkowska 12
Tel: (012) 425 49 81
www.bodega.pl
Open: 10am–midnight.
Traditional Spanish tapas bar with an astonishing wine list. €€

Częstochowa

Chinska
Ul. Racławicka 3
Tel: (034) 324 62 35
Open: noon–last customer.
Chinese cuisine. Delicious sweet and sour chicken with fruit, sirloin and mushrooms, or hot pork and leeks. Excellent value. €€

Gia Long
Ul. Warszawska 9
Tel: (034) 324 67 35
Open: noon–11pm.
Vietnamese. Specialities include "burning" shrimps. €€€

Orbis
Al. Wojska Polskiego 281/291
Tel: (034) 366 90 75

BELOW: Arka Noego in Kazimierz.

www.orbis.pl
Open: 7am–11pm.
Traditional Polish cuisine. Specialities include broccoli cream, Hetman sirloin and wild rice. €€€

Viking
Ul. Nowowiejskiego 10/12
Tel: (034) 324 57 68
www.restauracjaviking.pl
Open: 10am–midnight.
Polish, Chinese and Swedish cuisine! The speciality is Polish "noblemen soup", and Viking beef with asparagus spears. €€

Gliwice

Kim Lan
Rynek 21
Tel: (032) 231 04 68
www.kim-lan.pl
Open: 10am–10pm.
Chinese and Vietnamese. €€€

Katowice

C'est si Bon
Ul. Ligonia 4
Tel: (032) 781 68 48
www.cestsibon.pl
Open: Mon–Sat 1–10pm, Sun 1–8pm.
All is indeed well at Katowice's best French restaurant. The selection of fresh fish dishes on the menu is impressive for a

city found so far from the coast. €€€
Czerwona Oberża
Ul. Wita Stwosza 5.
Tel: (032) 251 60 30
Open: noon–last customer.
Fashionable and expensive. Located in cellars with a nice atmosphere and live music. €€€

Tatiana
Ul. Staromiejska 5
Tel: (032) 203 74 13
www.tatiana.arg.pl
Open: Mon–Sat 10am–midnight, Sun 11am–midnight.
Russian restaurants are few and far between in Poland, which is perhaps why this one is always full. Giant portions of Moscow borsch and beef stew are served by smart, friendly staff. €€

Wunderbar
Ul. Plebiscytowa 2
Tel: (032) 781 76 90
www.wunderbar.pl
Open: noon–midnight.
Wonderful in every way, the bratwurst here are made on the premises and you can taste the difference. A Katowice legend. €€

Zielone Oczko
Ul. Kozciuszki 101
Tel: (032) 205 30 77
www.zieloneoczko.pl
Open: 11am–midnight.
Polish and Italian cuisine.

Pleasantly located in a park with a large, open-air café. The *lurek* (sour soup) with sausage is recommended. €€

Łańcut

Zabytkowa
Ul. Dominikańska 1
Tel: (017) 225 29 23.
Open: 10am–midnight.
Polish cuisine in the Old Town with a homely atmosphere. €

Zajazd Dymarka
Dabrówki
Tel: (017) 225 14 07
www.zajazd-dymarka.pl
Open: 8am–10pm.
Polish and Greek cuisine. Hunter's soup is a speciality. €€

Zamkowa
Ul. Zamkowa 1
Tel: (017) 225 28 05
Traditional Polish cuisine in the castle. *Lurek* (sour soup) and Counts' roulade are specialities. €€

CAFÉS

Kraków

Café Camelot
Ul. Św. Tomasza 17
Tel: (012) 423 06 38

Hot cherry wine and apple pie are some of the favourites. Loch Camelot cabaret and jazz are in the basement.

Café Larousse
Ul. Św. Tomasza 22
Open: 10am–10pm.
Nice place for a coffee break. €

Jama Michalika
Ul. Floriańska 45
Tel: (012) 422 15 61
www.jamamichalika.pl
Situated in the heart of the Old Town, the Secessionist-era Jama Michalika is the best-known café in Poland.

Maska
Ul. Jagiellońska 1
Tel: (012) 429 60 44
Open: 9am–3am.
Close to the Old Theatre.

Noworolski
Rynek Główny 1/3
Tel: (012) 422 47 71
www.noworolski.com.pl
Open: 9am–last customer.
A tourists' favourite in the arcade of the Cloth Hall.

Pożegnanie z Afryk
Ul. Św. Tomasza 21
Tel: (012) 644 47 45
www.pozegnanie.com
Open: 10am–10pm.
This Kraków café company has many branches in numerous cities, offering more than 40 types of coffee.

THE MOUNTAINS

RESTAURANTS

Bielsko-Biała

Klimczok Zajazd
Ul. Bystrzańska 94
Tel: (033) 814 15 67
Open: 9am–10pm.
Polish cuisine, homely atmosphere in a wooden house with fireplace. On the road to Szczyrk. €€

Patria
Ul. Wzgórze 19
Tel: (033) 812 24 08
Open: 10am–2am.
Traditional Polish cuisine. Art Nouveau interior with pleasant atmosphere. €€

Prezydent
Ul. 3 Maja 12
Tel: (033) 822 72 11

www.hotelprezydent.pl
Open: 7am–midnight.
Polish, Italian and French cuisine served in a smart restaurant in a 19th-century hotel building. €€€

Szczyrk

Impresja
Ul. Poziomkowa 20
Tel: (033) 817 867 83
Fax: (033) 817 89 07
Open: noon–11pm.
Polish and European cuisine. Specialities are hot smoked ribs, *zur* (sour soup). €€

Klimczok
Ul. Poziomkowa 20
Tel: (033) 826 01 00/10
www.klimczok.pl
Open: 10am–midnight.

Polish and European cuisine 2 km (1 mile) from the city centre. Elegant hotel restaurant serving veal with mushrooms, cream and cranberries among other dishes. €€€

Stara Karczma
Ul. Myśliwska 2
Tel/fax: (033) 817 86 53
www.karczma.szczyrk.pl
Open: 10am–last customer.
Polish cuisine in the city centre. €€

CAFÉS

Bielsko-Biała

Farma Café
Pl. Smolki 7
Tel: (033) 812 31 63

Open: Mon–Sat 8.30am–10pm.
Toasted sandwiches and cakes.

Pożegnanie z Afryką
Ul. Cechowa 18
Open: 10am–10pm.
Coffee shop set in a historic building.

Tex Mex (Indiana Steak)
Ul. Cechowa 8
Tel: (033) 811 02 55
Set in an Old Town cellar, you can taste wines here from all over the world.

PRICE CATEGORIES

Prices are for a two-course meal for two with a bottle of wine:
€ = below 50zł
€€ = 50–100zł
€€€ = 100–170zł
€€€€ = over 170zł

ACTIVITIES

THE ARTS, NIGHTLIFE, SHOPPING AND SPECTATOR SPORTS

THE ARTS

Theatre

Poles are stalwart supporters of the performing arts. Theatre is very popular in Poland. In Warsaw alone there are 23 theatres to choose from. Theatre groups such as the Teatr Stary in Kraków are usually present at international theatre festivals.

Polish drama ranges from productions of classical works by both Polish and international dramatists to contemporary experimental plays. Kraków's Cricot 2 (Kanonicza 5) acquired its reputation from the avant garde playwright Tadeusz Kantor (1915–91) and the theatre specialises in the production of his works. In Warsaw, the Jewish Theatre

BELOW: Juliusz Slowacki Theatre.

(Teatr Żydowski) performs Jewish popular drama in Yiddish with the audience able to follow the action with the aid of a translation played on headphones. No words are necessary at the Warszawski Teatr Pantomimy and in Wrocław's Teatr Polski, where Henryk Tomaszewski's world-famous mime group once played. The repertoire of the Wybrzeźe-Theatre in Gdańsk often includes plays by Shakespeare. Children and adults are fascinated by the puppet theatres: the Miniatura in Gdańsk and Szczecin's Pleciuga.

Cabaret is often performed in Warsaw's Stodoła student club, in Gdańsk's Zak or in Kraków's famous Piwnica pod Baranami.

Theatres and Concert Halls

Kraków
Karol Szymanowski State Philharmonic
1 Zwierzyniecka
Tel: (012) 422 43 64
www.filharmonia.krakow.pl
Helena Modrzejewska Stary Theatre
1 Jagielloński
Tel: (012) 422 40 40
www.stary-teatr.pl
Juliusz Slowacki Theatre
1 Plac sw. Ducha
Tel: (012) 422 45 44
www.slowacki.krakow.pl

Gdańsk
Wybrzeźe Theatre
Ul. Sw. Ducha 2
Tel: (058) 301 13 28
www.teatrwybrzeze.pl
Baltic State Opera and Philharmonic
15 Aleja Zwycięstwa
Tel: (058) 763 49 12
www.operabaltycka.pl
Miniature Puppet and Actor Theatre

16 Grunwaldzka
Tel: (058) 341 94 83

Poznań
Stanislaw Moniuszko Grand Theatre
9 Aleksandra Fredry
Tel: (061) 852 82 91
Music Theatre
1e Niezlomnych
Tel: (061) 852 17 86
Poznań State Philharmonic
81 Sw. Marcin
Tel: (061) 852 47 08
www.filharmoniapoznanska.pl
Polish Dance Theatre
4 Kozia
Tel: (061) 852 42 41
www.pyy-poznan.pl

Warsaw
Grand Theatre of Opera and Ballet
1 Plac Teatralny
Tel: (022) 826 50 90
www.teatrwielki.pl
Ateneum Theatre
2 Jaracza
Tel: (022) 625 73 30
www.teatrateneum.pl
Dramatyczny Theatre, Palace of Science and Culture
Tel: (022) 656 68 44
Polski Theatre
2 Karasia
Tel: (022) 826 79 92
Jewish Theatre
12/16 Plac Grzybowski
Tel: (022) 620 62 81
National Philharmonic Hall
10 Sienkiewicza
Tel: (022) 551 71 31
Roma Musical Theatre
49 Nowogrodzka
Tel: (022) 628 0360
www.teatrroma.pl
Rampa Musical Theatre
20 Kołowa
Tel: (022) 679 89 76
www.teatr-rampa.pl

Classical Music

Poland's concert halls do not just offer Chopin's piano concertos, which are most people's idea of Polish classical music. Other options include experimental works by Krzysztof Penderecki or Witold Lutosławski – composers whose reputation has admittedly not spread that far afield.

Opera and ballet are performed at The Grand Theatre in Warsaw (Teatr Wielki). If the Polish National Opera is performing *Halka* during your stay, do try to get a ticket. Even if you cannot understand a word of Polish, you will still be able to follow this sad love story about a poor girl from the mountains.

The finest musicals in Warsaw can be enjoyed at the Roma and Rampa Musical Theatres.

Information and Tickets

Information about all cultural events can be found in local newspapers. In the *Gazeta Wyborcza-Cojest grane*, in the Friday supplement, there is everything about the latest films, exhibitions and performances taking place in Warsaw. The *WIK – Warszawski Informator Kulturalny* is a good way to find out what's on if you understand Polish. The following websites also give information about cultural events in English: www.culture.pl and www.warsawvoice.pl.

Tickets for theatres, concerts and all cultural events can be bought at major hotels, at theatre box offices or these locations:

ZASP Box Office
Ul. Al. Jerozolimskie 25
Tel: (022) 621 93 83/94 54
Open: Mon–Fri 11am–2pm and 2.30–6pm, Sat 11am–2pm
Stołeczna Estrada
Ul. Flory 9
Tel: (022) 849 32 93
Open: Mon–Fri 8am–4pm

Cultural Centres in Warsaw

Austrian Institute of Culture
8 Próżna
Tel: (022) 620 96 20
www.whatsup.pl/cultural.html
British Council
59 Jerozolimskie
Tel: (022) 695 59 00
Goethe Institute
Ul. Chmielna 13a
Tel: (022) 505 90 00
French Institute
38 Senatorska
Tel: (022) 505 98 00
Italian Institute of Culture
Ul. Marszałkowska 72
Tel: (022) 628 06 10

Russian Culture and Information Centre
25 Belwederska
Tel: (022) 849 27 30
The Institute of Polish for Foreigners
Ul. Kopernika 3
Tel: (022) 826 22 59
www.iko.com.pl

NIGHTLIFE

Where to Go

Poland is quite simply a hedonist's dream. There are pubs, bars, discos, clubs and live music venues in every major city, and finding something to do when the sun goes down will not be difficult. The big student cities of Wrocław and Poznań are particularly lively during term time, while Sopot's strip – all beach bars and open air discos – comes to life in summer, and while Kraków's nightlife is perhaps more cerebral than that in the capital, you can still find plenty of places to dance to the latest sounds.

High rollers are well catered for in the shape of casinos: every major city has at least one, with the most famous being in the Sofitel Grand Hotel in Sopot. Europe's richest people have been gambling here for almost a century. For live music look out for big name concerts during the summer, with the country's former national football stadium in Chorzow often used to host the biggest names in rock and pop.

Warsaw Nightlife

Warsaw nightlife is exciting, edgy, expensive, and everyone loves it. Trendy cocktail bars abound. So much is there to see and do that there are now tour companies offering guided or themed nights out. Try Night Guides at www.night-guides.pl.

Discos/Nightclubs

Club 70
Ul. Waliców 9
Tel: (022) 654 71 41
www.club70.pl
Open: Mon–Sat 8pm–4am
A good, low-brow choice to kick off your nocturnal Warsaw experience. Expect 1970s disco classics and a student-heavy crowd.
Dekada
Ul. Grójecka 19/25
Tel: (022) 668 97 77
www.dekada.pl

Diary of Events

April
Polish Student Pop Festival (Kraków); Springtime Music (Poznań).
May
Contemporary Polish Theatre Festival (Wrocław); Chamber Music Days (Łańcut).
June
Polish Pop Festival (Opole); Jan Kiepura Festival (Krynica, Żegiestów and Nowy Sącz). International Short Film Festival (Kraków).
July
Organ Music Festival (Gdańsk-Oliwa).
August
International Pop Festival (Sopot); Chopin Festival (Duszniki Zdroj); Country Picnic (Mragowo).
September
Swietokrzyskie-Fire Race (Słupia Nowa); International Festival of Contemporary Music Warszawska Jesien (Warsaw).
October
International Jazz Jamboree (Warsaw); Warsaw Theatre Rendez Vous.

Open: Wed–Fri 7pm–6am, Sat 8pm–6am
Trendy and enjoyably over the top, Dekada's huge dance floor fills up with smart locals dancing to mainstream club classics.
Enklawa
Ul. Mazowiecka 12
Tel: (022) 827 31 51
www.enklawa.com
Open: Tue–Sat 9pm–4am
An enclave of Warsaw chic where only the best-looking get in to mingle with the beautiful set inside. Good mix of music of salsa and chart hits.
Vinyl
Ul. Żurawia 22
Tel: (022) 438 92 95
www.vinyl-club.pl
Open: Sept–July Sun–Thur 11am–11pm, Fri–Sat 11am–5am
The cellar club is about the best choice in Warsaw for up-to-the-minute house sounds. The crowd is more hedonistic and less pretentious than elsewhere.

Pubs

Bar Below
Ul. Marszałkowska 64
Tel: (022) 621 18 50
www.barbelow.pl
Open: Sun–Fri 5pm–midnight, Sat noon–midnight
If you visit one pub in Warsaw, make it this place. It is the perfect mix of local pub and trendy

cocktail bar. Both locals and foreigners love it.

Bierhalle
Ul. Nowy Świat 64
Tel: (022) 827 61 77
www.bierhalle.pl
Open: Mon–Fri noon–11pm, Sat–Sun 11am–11.30pm
Also at
Al. Jana Pawła II 82 (Arkadia Shopping Mall)
Tel: (060) 167 79 62
www.bierhalle.pl
Open: Mon–Thur 11am–11pm, Fri 11am–midnight, Sat 10am–midnight, Sun 10am–11pm
A genuine beer hall and microbrewery serving what many people insist is Warsaw's best pint of beer. Live music most evenings.

Porto Praga
Ul. Stefana Okrzei 23
Tel: (022) 698 50 01
www.portopraga.pl
Open: Mon–Wed noon–1am, Thur–Sat noon–2am, Sun noon–midnight
Warsaw's top cocktail bar. Expect to meet only the trendiest and most beautiful people drinking some of the city's most expensive drinks.

SomePlace Else
Ul. Prusa 2 (Sheraton Warsaw Hotel)
Tel: (022) 450 67 10
www.sheraton.com.pl
Open: Mon noon–midnight, Tue–Thur noon–1am, Fri–Sat noon–2am, Sun noon–11pm
Something of an expat legend with a great bar menu and live music most evenings. If you're after live sports on TV, this is the default option.

Around Poland

Bydgoszcz

Atelier 74
Ul. Zaułek 3
Tel: (066) 367 17 88
www.atelier74.xt.pl
Open: Sun–Thur 6pm–midnight, Fri–Sat 6pm–4am
The city's top night time venue where a good, mixed crowd dances to the latest sounds shipped direct by top DJs from London.

El Jazz
Ul. Kręta 3
Tel: (052) 322 15 74
www.eljazz.com.pl
Open: Sun–Thur 4pm–2am, Fri–Sat 4pm–4am
Even when the resident jazz band falls silent this place is still a very cool place to enjoy quiet beers and good conversation.

Kraków

Mechanoff
Ul. Estery 8
Tel: (012) 422 70 98

Open: Mon–Thur 10am–1am, Fri 10am–2am, Sat 10am–3am, Sun 9am–1am
Best of the many bars and pubs that have sprung up on Plac Nowy, in the once rundown part of Kazimierz. Cheap beer, good, mixed crowd and good staff.

Nic Nowego
Ul. Św. Krzyża 15
Tel: (012) 421 61 88
www.nicnowego.com
Open: Mon–Fri 7am–3am, Sat–Sun 10am–3am
The orginal Kraków expat pub. Great pub food served until late alongside the wide range of decently priced drinks.

Paparazzi
Ul. Mikołajska 9
Tel: (012) 429 45 97
www.paparazzi.com.pl
Open: daily 4pm–1am
Kraków's leading cocktail bar for as many years as anyone can remember, yet still the first choice for the city's trendiest revellers.

Rdza
Ul. Bracka 3-5
Tel: (060) 039 55 41
www.rdza.pl
Open: Wed–Sat 7pm–4am
Currently Kraków's premiere club. Expect the cream of Polish Europe's DJs to be playing the latest music for a lively crowd of serious clubbers.

Łodz

Cabaret
Ul. Tuwima 1/3
Tel: (042) 630 05 13
www.cabaret.pl
Open: Fri–Sat 10am–4am
Blissfully student-free club where the city's grown ups come to enjoy themselves. The music is a mix of club classics and mainstream house, and the permanently full

dance floor would suggest punters approve.

Czekolada
Ul. Piotrkowska 55
Tel: (042) 630 60 20
www.klubczekolada.pl
Open: Sun–Tue 9am–midnight, Wed–Sat 9am–4am
An enjoyably eclectic club where students and arty-types dance to a good mix of rock and pop. There are occasional live concerts too.

Irish Pub
Ul. Piotrkowska 77
Tel: (042) 632 48 76
www.irishpub.pl
Open: Sun–Thur noon–1am, Fri–Sat noon–2am
Probably Poland's best Irish pub in that it serves a great Guinness. It is just a pub, and a sound one at that.

Poznan

Academic Pub
Ul. Taczaka 11
Tel: (061) 853 69 80
Open: Mon–Sat 9am–midnight, Sun noon–midnight
Fitting name for the most popular drinking den in what is widely regarded as Poland's student capital. By day this place is a great café, by nightfall it becomes a lively pub.

Brovaria
Stary Rynek 73-74 (Brovaria Hotel)
Tel: (061) 858 68 68
www.brovaria.pl
Open: daily 10am–1am
This pub is owned and run by the makers of Brovaria, Poznan's very own beer. Reputedly the cleanest, clearest pint the city this place is a decent choice if you want to avoid students.

Morphine
Ul. Wrocławska 18
Tel: (061) 855 40 06
www.morphineclub.pl

BELOW: cocktails for two in Kraków.

Open: daily 5pm–4am
Great sounds from the 1970s
dominate the music menu at this hip
spot in the very centre of Poznań.

Sopot

Bulaj
Al. Mamuszki 22
Tel: (058) 551 51 29
www.bulaj.pl
Open: Mon–Fri 11am–10pm,
Sat–Sun 11am–11pm
The best of the pubs that ply their
trade on the Sopot beach front. A
good, young crowd throngs here for
the beach bar that stays open until
very late.

Coctailo
Ul. Bohaterów Monte Cassino 53
Lively bar on Sopot's main
pedestrian street. The drinks are
overpriced but the superb
atmosphere and decent music more
than make up for that.

Viva Club
Al. Mamuszki 2
Tel: (058) 551 62 68
www.vivaclub.pl
Open: daily 10pm–5am
Offering views of the beach from
its upper levels this place is
a Sopot legend. Arrive early
if you want to be sure of getting
in, it gets packed out on summer
weekends.

Wrocław

Obsesja
Ul. Św. Mikołaja 8-11
Tel: (071) 341 84 25
www.klubobsesja.com
Open: Sun and Tue–Wed 5pm–1am,
Thur–Sat 5pm–4am
There may be other discos in
Wrocław, but this is the only one that
counts. Expect the latest house
music, serious clubbers and
surprisingly cheap drinks.

Pod Papugami
Ul. Sukiennice 9a
Tel: (071) 343 92 75
www.podpapugami.com.pl
Open: Mon–Thur noon–1am, Fri
11am–2am, Sat 1pm–2am, Sun
1pm–midnight
Everything you could want and more.
Pub, cocktail bar and disco rolled into
one. There's live music most
weekend evenings too.

Wagon Club
Pl. Orląt Lwowskich 20a
Tel: (071) 341 29 48
www.wagonclub.com
Open: daily 11am–1am
A favourite of the university set,
this warren of an underground
venue offers loads of different
rooms playing different types
of music. Everyone will find
something they like.

Music

Jazz

If live jazz is more to your liking,
there are a number of clubs in the
main cities, such as Zak in Gdańsk,
on Waly Jagielonshie, Akwarium in
Warsaw at Emilii Plater 49 and Pod
Jaszczurami in Kraków at Rynek
Główny 8.
 Urszula Dudziak, Zbigniew
Namysłowski and Michał Urbaniak,
the top names on the contemporary
Polish jazz scene, are regular
performers at these venues.

Rock and Pop

Poland has been on the radar of
major international acts for some
time, and the chances of you
catching a concert when in the
country is high. While the biggest
names play the old national football
stadium in Chorzow, near Katowice,
you can also expect to see a decent
number of acts in Warsaw too. A
good source of concert info are the
In Your Pocket guides, English
language publications published bi-
monthly in eight Polish cities. Tickets
for almost all events can be bought
online, or at branches of the
ubiquitous Empik book and music
stores.

CINEMA

In main cities in Poland you will
find modern cinemas usually
equipped with Dolby stereo sound
system. Check in the local
newspapers for titles and times.
Small towns, however, still have

simple, old-fashioned cinema halls.
 Foreign films are shown in their
language with Polish sub-titles.

SHOPPING

Where to Shop

Shopping in Poland is as good as
anywhere in Europe. Indeed, Warsaw
is now one of the world's great
shopping locations, and many people
come here specifically to roam its
many mega-malls; Arkadia, close to
the centre of Warsaw, is the biggest
mall in Central Europe. Every city in
the country has at least one major
shopping centre, while most also
retain a decent sprinkling of unique,
quirky stores selling antiques and
local handicrafts. Amber remains big
in these parts: you will find amber
shops everywhere, especially in
Gdańsk, Sopot and Gdynia. For
antique seekers the myriad streets of
Kraków's Old Town are a treat.
 Poles do not usually haggle: the
price displayed is the price paid.
Most shops open at 9am and close
at 7pm, few – if any – close for lunch.
Most shops now open on Sunday –
especially in tourist centres such as
Kraków – though close a little earlier.
Malls are open from 10am–10pm,
seven days a week.

What to Buy

Folk Art

Polish folk art, such as embroidered
tablecloths, brightly painted wooden
eggs, leather goods made by the
people of the High Tatra region and

Shopping Centres

Warsaw

Arkadia
Al. Jana Pawła II 82
Tel: (022) 331 34 00
www.arkadia.com.pl
Open 10am–10pm, Sun 10am–9pm
Blue City
Al. Jerozolimskie 179
Tel: (022) 824 45 55
www.bluecity.pl
Open 10am–10pm, Sun 10am–8pm
Galeria Mokotow
Ul. Wołoska 12
Tel: (022) 541 41 41
www.galeriamokotow.pl
Open 10am–10pm, Sun 10am–9pm
Złoty Tarasy
Ul. Złota 59
Tel: (022) 222 22 00
www.zlotetarasy.pl
Open 10am–10pm, Sun 10am–8pm

Gdansk

Galeria Bałtycka
Al. Grunwaldzka 141
Tel: (058) 521 85 50
www.galeriabaltycka.pl
Open 9am–9pm, Sun 10am–8pm

Kraków

Galeria Krakowska
Ul. Pawia 5
Tel: (012) 428 99 00
www.galeria-krakowska.pl
Open 9am–10pm, Sun
10am–9pm

Wrocław

Magnolia Park
Ul. Legnicka 58
Tel: (071) 787 75 80
www.magnoliapark.pl
Open 9am–9pm

ABOVE: Zloty Tarasy in Warsaw.

Kashubian pottery, are sold in the Cepelia shops found throughout Poland.

Hand-carved figures have greatly appreciated in value in recent years. These are often Christian in origin, depicting angels or nativity figures, but may also show characters from Polish village life. Also very popular are folk artists' naïve and glass paintings.

Amber

Amber of varying quality is sold along the Baltic coast and throughout Poland *(see page 341).* It is often arranged in necklaces, either polished or unpolished form, but rings, paperweights and lamp bases are also made from this semiprecious material. Potential buyers should, however, take care. Street sellers often sell reasonably good imitations made from plastic. The general rule is, the clearer the stone, the more expensive it will be. Particularly valuable are those pieces of amber that contain the tiny creatures and insects that were trapped within this hard, brown substance (not really a stone, but fossilised resin) many thousands of years ago.

Jewellery is also made with what is sometimes called black amber, but it is in fact not amber at all but jet, polished black lignite. Mounted in silver, jet rings and brooches make very attractive gifts.

Art and Antiques

Antiques, prints, paintings, sculptures and *objets d'art* are sold in the Desa shops. Take care before handing over large amounts of money for anything resembling an antique, as customs regulations now restrict the export of anything made before

1945. The abundance of contemporary works of art more than makes up for these difficulties.

Books

Well-illustrated coffee table books are widely available in Poland and make good souvenirs. Many are published in German, English or in multi-language editions.

The following shops sell Englishlanguage books and guides in Warsaw:

Academic Bookshop
Ul. Grzybowska 37a
Tel: (022) 682 22 33
Open: Mon–Fri 9am–6pm, Sat 10am–2pm
www.abe.com.pl

American Bookstore
Ul. Krakowskie Przedmieście 45
Tel: (022) 826 01 61
Open: Mon–Fri 11am–7pm, Sat 11am–8pm, Sun 11am–6pm
Fiction, classic guidebooks and dictionaries.
www.americanbookstore.pl

Travellers' Shop
Ul. Kaliska 8/10
Tel: (022) 658 46 26
Open: Mon–Fri 11am–7pm, Sat 10am–4pm
Guidebooks and maps.

Odeon
Ul. Hola 19
Tel: (022) 622 51 73
Open: Mon–Fri 11am–7pm, Sat 11am–8pm, Sun 11am–6pm
Albums and biographies.

Empik
Ul. Marszalkowska 116/122
Tel: (022) 827 82 96
Ul. Nowy Zwiat 15/17
Tel: (022) 627 06 50
www.empik.com
Open: Mon–Sat 9am–10pm, Sun 11am–5pm

Offering a large selection of foreign language newspapers and magazines.

SPORTS

Horse Riding

Poland has many riding centres for holiday-makers who wish to explore on horseback. In the tourist regions, particularly Mazuria, some large hotels have their own stables.

In Kraków the options include **Decjusz**, Ul. Kasztanowa 1, tel: (012) 425 24 21, and **Krakowski Klub Jazdy Konnej**, Ul. Kobierzyńska 175A, tel: (012) 262 14 18.

The choices in Warsaw include **Podkowa, TKKF Horseriding Club**, Ul. Głogów 11, Podkowa Leśna, tel: (022) 758 94 26.

For further information, contact the local tourist offices *(see page 405)* or the **Polish Prestige** office, tel: (022) 620 9817, fax: 624 3628, which organises auctions and transports horses in Poland.

Skiing

Zakopane and Szczyrk, to the south of Katowice, are Poland's main skiing regions. Unfortunately, during busy periods, skiers can expect long waits at the ski lifts at all the centres. In the Silesian Beskid Mountains, an alternative is a welldeveloped network of cross-country tracks. Nevertheless, the downhill runs are good and overall costs are much lower, when compared with the more expensive Alpine skiing regions of Europe, so it is often worth the wait.

Hiking

Buy a good map from one of the kiosks or bookshops and you can explore Poland along colour-marked footpaths. Walkers are well catered for in the magnificent national parks *(see page 399).* The routes through the High Tatras are quite demanding and hikers need to have a good head for heights and some climbing experience. The best months for a walking holiday are August and September. The PTTK *(see page 376)* run a number of hostels in walking country.

Watersports

Sailing and watersports enthusiasts adore the lakes and rivers of Poland, particularly in Mazuria. These waterways are becoming increasingly popular with canoeists, rowers and amateur sailors, with many people making overnight stops in the waterside campsites. If all you want to do is swim, windsurf or paddle, then, wherever you are, you are sure to find an attractive lake close by.

For information about the best routes and campsites, contact one of the following clubs:

Polish Sailing Association (Polski Zwiazek Zeglarski)
Ul. Chocimska 14, 00791 Warsaw
Tel: (022) 849 57 31/848 04 83
Fax: (022) 848 04 82
Regional Sailing Association
Tel: (022) 379 223
Polish Kayaking Union (Polski Zwiazek Kajakowy)
Ul. Ciołka 17, 01445 Warsaw
Tel: (022) 837 4059
Fax: (022) 371 470

Cycling

Northern Poland attracts many cycling enthusiasts. The surfaced roads are not too busy, the countryside not too hilly and the scenery is quite varied. Country roads often follow ancient oak-lined tracks through picturesque villages. Keep well away from the main highways at all costs. As well as a tyre repair kit, make sure you have a heavy-duty bike lock. If you don't have your own bike, don't worry. In many hotels and boarding houses you can rent mountain bikes.

SIGHTSEEING TOURS

Since the political upheavals of 1989, a large number of small, privately owned travel companies have emerged that run coach excursions or organise tours. We recommend using well known and recognisable companies such as Orbis, Mazurkas Travel or PTTK *(see below)*.
Almatur, the travel agency run by the Polish Student Association, arranges reasonably priced individual or group tours for students, including educational and cultural programmes, international student lodgings along the coast, on lakes and in the mountains. They also organise tours for film, fishing and horse-riding enthusiasts. Contact:
Almatur, Ul. Copernicus 23, 00-359 Warsaw. Tel: (22) 826 26.39. Fax: (22) 827 08 16
www.almatur.pl
    Other useful tour operators include:

Polish Travel Quo Vadis Ltd.
Ul. Ptasia 2, Warsaw
Tel: (22) 322 85 85
Fax (22) 322 85 42
www.polishtravel.com.pl
Open: Mon–Fri 9am–5pm.
English-speaking guides, organised tours of Poland.
Mazurkas Travel
Al. Wojska Polskiego 27, Warsaw
Tel: (22) 389 41 50
Fax: (22) 831 91 75
E-mail: euromic@mazurkas.pol.pl
www.mazurkas.com.pl
Open: Mon–Fri 8.30am–8pm
Tour operator or travel agency for groups only.
PTTK
Ul. Litewska 11/13
Tel: (022) 629 39 47
www.pttk.com.pl
Open: Mon–Fri 9am–6pm, Sat 10am–2pm
Run by the Polish Countryside Association, PTTK offers plenty of tours for individuals and groups around Poland, with an emphasis on the great outdoors.

Suggested Tours

From Kraków to Wieliczka and the famous 13th-century **salt mine**.
Oświęcim, the World War II concentration camp, better known by its German name, Auschwitz.
Ojców National Park, by the Pradnik River. The PTTK *(see page 391)* organises hiking, canoeing, sailing and motorcycling tours within the park, as well as excursions on foot, on skis and in the mountains. Local tour guides are available.
From Gdańsk to Westerplatte and the **National Memorial** to 1 September 1939.
Oliwa and organ recitals in the old cathedral.

Malbork and the Castle of the Teutonic Knights.
Sztutowo, formerly Stutthof concentration camp.
Frombork, where Nicholas Copernicus (Mikołaj Kopernik) spent 28 years of his life.
From Warsaw to Zelazowa Woła, **Chopin's birthplace**.
Wilanów, the former residence of Jan III Sobieski.
Puszcza Kampinowska, with woods, marshland and dunes populated by elk, fox, boar and bird species.
Zalew Zegrzyński, a large reservoir offering leisure and watersports opportunities.

OUTDOOR ACTIVITIES

National Parks

No one should visit Poland without exploring at least one of the 23 national parks *(see page 129)*. There is a huge variety of preserved terrains: from the rocky, Alpine Tatras to wooded Pieniny or Bieszczady ranges, from the ancient Białowieska Forest to the shifting dunes in the mini-desert on the shores of the Baltic, from the rivers and lakes hidden away among the forests of the Suwalski region to the Roztocze plateau.
    All the parks are open to tourists, many accessible only on foot. The only exception is the Białowieski Park, where visitors must explore the forest in the company of a local guide. Basic overnight accommodation is available.

Białowieski National Park
5 Park Palacowy,
17-230 Białowieża
Tel: (085) 681 23 06/23 23
www.pl-info.net/poland/parks/

BELOW: windsurfing at Puck Bay, along the Baltic Coast.

bialowieski_park.html
www.bpn.com.pl
The oldest forested park in the
country (founded 1921) and the most
extensive wooded area in Europe,
covering 5,348 hectares (13,200
acres); a breeding centre for
European bison, tarpan (Polish
horses), stag, roe deer and wild boar.

Babiogórski National Park
34-223 Zawoja
Tel: (033) 877 51 10
Park management:
34-223 Zawoja 1403
Tel: (033) 877 51 10/51 24
www.bgpn.pl
Contains the highest portions of the
Western Bieszczady Mountains,
including Mount Tarnica, from
700–1,725 metres (2,300–5,560 ft).

Kampinoski National Park
38 Tetmajera Ul.,
05-080 Izabelin
Tel: (022) 722 60 01/65 59
www.kampinoski-pn.gov.pl
The largest national park in Poland
covers the Vistula River Valley.

Bieszczadzki
Tel: 461 06 10
Park management:
38-714 Ustrzyki Górne
Tel: (090) 309 156/(134) 610 650
www.bdpn.pl
In the Krośnienskie Province covers
27,064 hectares (66,848 acres) and
rises 660–1,346 metres (1,950–
4,414 ft) over the West Bieszczady
Mountains and part of the
Carpathians. Traces of old charcoal
burning kilns and ancient sacred
sites; the Bieszczadzkie Museum is
in Ustrzyki Dolne.

Drawieński
Park management:
73-220 Drawno,
Ul. Leśnikow 2
Tel/fax: (095) 768 2051/2510
www.dpn.pl
In Gorzowskie Province, covering
9,068 hectares (22,397 acres):
between the Drawa and Płociczna
rivers; mud turtles, beavers, otters
and many rare bird species.

Gorczański
Park management:
Poreba Wielka 590,
34–735 Niedzwiedz
Tel: (018) 331 72 07
www.gorczanskipark.pl
In Nowosadeckie Province, covering
6,763 hectares (16,700 acres): the
central section of the Gorce massif
(part of the West Beskid
Mountains).

Karkonoski
Park management:
58-570 Jelenia Góra,
Ul. Chałubinskiego 23
Tel: (075) 755 33 48/37 26
www.kpnmab.pl

Park Information

For further details of national
parks and nature reserves, try:
National Parks Association
00-922 Warsaw,
Ul. Wawelska 52/54
Tel: (022) 825 1493/5748
www.mos.gov.pl/kzpn

In Jeleniogórskie Province covering
5,562 hectares (13,738 acres):
Alpine park with post-glacial features
in the Karkonosze Mountains.

Magurski
Krempna 59,
38-232 Krempna,
woj-podkarpackie
Park management:
38-232 Nowy Zmigród,
Ul. Krampna 59
Tel: (013) 441 40 99
www.magurskipn.pl
In the Krośnienskie Province,
covering 19,962 hectares (49,306
acres): it takes in part of the Beskid
Niski Mountains.

Ojcowski
Park management:
32-047 Ojców, Ojców 9,
Skała 39
Tel: (012) 389 10 39/20 05
www.opn.pan.krakow.pl
In Krakowskie Province, covering
1,890 hectares (4,668 acres) and
part of the Kraków-Częstochowa
Upland and the Prandik valley;
numerous underground springs.

Pieniński
Park management:
34-450 Krościenko,
Ul. Jagiellońska 107B
Tel: (018) 262 56 01/2
www.pieninypn.pl
In Nowosadeckie Province covering
2,231 hectares (5,510 acres): takes
in the middle section of the Pieniny
mountains; very varied landscape – try
a raft ride through the Dunajec valley.

Poleski
Park management:
22-234 Urszulin,
Ul. Lubelska 3A
Tel: (082) 571 3071/2
www.poleskipn.pl
In Chełmskie Province covering 9,647
hectares (2,382 acres): countless
lakes and marshland.

Roztoczanski
Park management:
22-470 Zwierzyniec,
Ul. Płazowa 2
Tel: (084) 687 22 86/22 07
www.roztoczanskipn.pl
In Zamojskie Province
covering 7,886 hectares
(19,478 acres): the geologically
varied region in the western part
of the park.

Słowiński National Park
Park management:
Bohaterów Warszawy Ul,
76-214 Smoldzino
Tel: (059) 811 72 04/73 39
www.slowinskipn.pl
Beside the Baltic, with moving sand
dunes over 50 m (160 ft) high and
desert landscape which includes a
100-metre (328-ft) wide beach.

Świętokrzyski
Park management:
26-010 Bodzentyn,
Ul. Suchedniowska 4
Tel: (041) 311 50 25
www.swietokrzyskipn.org.pl
In Kieleckie Province, covering 6,054
hectares (14,953 acres): covers the
oldest Polish mountain range, the Gory
Świętorkrzyskie. The remains of an
early smelting furnace were discovered
near Nowa Słupia, a village that is now
home to the Museum of Ancient
Metallurgy; Święty Krzyż abbey nearby.

Tatrzański
Park management:
34-500 Zakopane,
Ul. Chałubińskiego 42 A
Tel: (018) 206 32 03
www.tpn.pl
In Nowosądeckie Province covering
21,164 hectares (52,275 acres):
Alpine park containing Poland's
highest mountain range, the Tatras,
and Mount Rysy (2,499 metres/
8,196 ft). Tytus Chałubiński Tatra
Museum (www.muzeumtatrzanskie.pl) is at
34-500 Zakopane, Ul. Krupówki 10,
tel: (018) 201 52 05.

Wielkopolski
Park management:
Jeziory, 62-050 Mosina
Tel: (061) 813 22 06
www.wielkopolskipn.pl
In Poznańskie Province covering
5,337 hectares (13,182 acres); post-
glacial landscape with typical
geological formations.

Wigierski
Park management:
16-400 Suwałki,
Krzywe 82
Tel: (087) 563 25 40
www.wigry.win.pl
In Suwałskie Province covering
15,113 hectares (37,329 acres);
surrounds one of the largest and
deepest lakes in Poland, Lake Wigry;
45 other lakes and a section of the
Augustówski Forest.

Wolinski
Park management:
72-510 Międzyzdroje,
Ul. Niepodległości, 3
Tel: (091) 328 07 37/27
www.wolinpn.pl
In Szczecińskie Province covering
5,001 hectares (12,352 acres):
Wolin Island and a part of Szczecin
Lagoon.

A – Z

A HANDY SUMMARY OF PRACTICAL INFORMATION, ARRANGED ALPHABETICALLY

A dmission Charges

Most Polish museums, art galleries and other attractions now have at least a nominal entrance fee, though usually offer free entry one day a week (mostly on Sundays). There are reductions for children, but not for pensioners or students. Most places charge fairly high fees for the use of video cameras; some will charge simply for taking photos. Almost all clubs and discos have admission fees, though in most cases this includes at least one free drink.

B udgeting for Your Trip

While certain things such as public transport and train travel, taxis and museum admission fees and snacks remain almost ridiculously cheap, life and travel in Poland is becoming increasingly expensive, especially in Warsaw and Kraków.

The biggest expense, anywhere in the country, will always be accommodation. Good, cheap hotels can be hard to find, especially during the week. The mid-range hotel sector is still in its infancy, with most new hotels still being five star, luxury

establishments aimed at business people. Make sure you book accommodation well in advance, and expect to spend upwards of 160zł (approx. €50) per night for even the most basic hotel room.

Business Hours

Offices are generally open Monday to Friday 9am–6pm. Shops open 10am–6pm Monday to Friday and 9am–2pm on Saturdays. In general shops are closed on Sundays, but more and more larger stores are staying open all week. Shopping centres are an exception staying open until late, seven days a week. There are plenty of small neighbourhood shops open 24 hours a day.

Banks open Monday to Friday 8am–6pm without lunch break. Post Offices open Monday to Saturday, 8am–8pm. The main post office in major cities is open 24 hours.

Shop Opening Hours

Opening times vary. Whatever the time, whatever the day, you will almost certainly find a shop open somewhere. In general, the bigger the town, the longer the opening times. Most shops open at 8am (some food

shops at 6am) and close at 7pm, on Saturday a little earlier. Department stores generally close at 6pm. Most shops are closed on Sunday.

Business Travellers

Many of Poland's cities are geared well towards business travellers, especially Warsaw – now one of Europe's great business cities – and Poznań, which, at the heart of

Warsaw Banks

Narodowy Bank Polski
Ul. Swietokrzyska 11/12
Tel: (022) 653 10 00. www.nbp.pl
Bank Pekao
Ul. Grzybowska 53/57
Tel: (022) 656 06 05.
www.pekao.com.pl
Bank Millenium
Stanislawazaryna 2A
Tel: (022) 598 40 40. www.millenet.pl
Bank Handlowy Warszawie SA
Ul. Senatorska 16
Tel: (022) 657 72 00. www.citibank.pl
ING Towarzystwo Ubezpieczen na Zycie SA
Ul. Ludna 2
Tel: (022) 522 00 00. www3.ing.pl

CLIMATE CHART

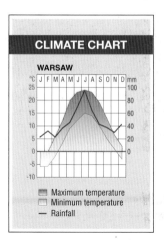

WARSAW

- ▦ Maximum temperature
- ▢ Minimum temperature
- — Rainfall

Europe, has been hosting trade fairs for centuries. Such hotels in these cities charge far more during the week for accommodation than they do at weekends.

C hildren

Children have always been welcomed in Poland, and they are increasingly well catered for. Hotels will rarely charge for children staying in their parents' room, and it is now common for restaurants to offer special children's portions and menus. Especially good in this regard is the Rooster chain of upmarket burger bars, which also offers small children's play areas in most of its restaurants. Of all Poland's destinations, Kraków is probably the most geared to children, its parks and attractions all having something to offer even the smallest kids. Note that on public transport in Poland children over the age of five are expected to possess a ticket, and there are rarely reductions. Children do get excellent reductions however on Inter City trains and on LOT internal flights.

Climate

Due to the country's lengthy coastline, the climate in Poland varies between oceanic and continental. Therefore, weather conditions are subject to change. From May until October Poland enjoys beautiful weather. In March spring begins – a little windy and rainy and averaging -1–15°C (30–60°F). In May to June temperatures rise to 21°C (70°F) and remain as such through the summer. August can be very warm with temperatures often climbing beyond 30°C (86°F).

The traditional "golden Polish autumn" in September is usually sunny and dry, with temperatures around 15°C (60°F). In November the first foggy and cold days begin, complemented by shorter days. Winter lasts about three months (December–February), but can be so severe that in many northern regions temperatures drop to -30°C (-22°F). Snow in the mountain regions makes for excellent skiing. It remains in the mountains until around Easter.

Crime and Security

Theft is not unusual in places frequented by tourists. It is better to keep any valuables and jewellery in the hotel safe. If you are travelling by car, it is essential to park it for longer periods or overnight in a guarded car park – even the smaller towns have them. If you are the victim of a theft, report it immediately to the reception desk at your hotel or to the police. The emergency police number is 997. If you lose all your money or your passport, you will have to seek advice from your nearest consulate or embassy (see below).

Customs Regulations

The following articles may be imported into Poland duty-free:
Alcohol: 2 litres of wine, 5 litres of beer, 1 litre of spirits.
Tobacco products: up to 200 cigarettes or 50 cigars or 250g of tobacco (for people aged 18 and above).
Food: up to 200g of coffee, up to 1 kg of chocolate products and presents to the value of $100.

Two cameras and one video camera can be imported duty-free. Expensive articles such as photographic, film or hi-tech equipment, jewellery and furs should be declared on entry.

Dogs and cats may be imported, but they must have been immunised against rabies at least three weeks before arrival at the border. The official vaccination certificate (not older than 12 months) must be produced. Many hotels accept dogs, but will make a surcharge.

Works of art bought in Poland, such as antiques and books printed before 9 May 1945, can only be exported if an authorisation from the relevant Curator of Art Works or the National Museum in Warsaw is produced.

Polish customs regulations are subject to frequent alterations. Before buying anything of value, check that customs will issue an export licence

Electricity

220 volts. Sockets take two round pins.

and whether any special documentation is required.
Warsaw Customs Headquarters Hotel Marriot, Al. Jerozolimskie 65/69
Tel: 630 5162

D isabled Travellers

This is an area, alas, where Poland still generally struggles to meet European Union standards. While legislation has been passed to make all public buildings accessible, few actually are, and little is done to enforce the rules. Most forms of public transport are still inaccessible to all but the fittest, and while recent repairs of sidewalks in major cities means that getting around is easier than before, crossing the street can still be a trial. When it comes to the private sector there has been more progress, with hotels all over the country – especially those at the top end – now more than able to take disabled guests with ease. Even so, disabled guests planning on visiting Poland are advised to do their homework well before travelling.

E mbassies and Consulates

Australia:
Ul. Nowogrodzka 11, Warsaw 00-513
Tel: (022) 521 34 44
Austria:
34 Gagarina Ul, 00-748 Warsaw
Tel: (022) 841 0081/4
Fax: 841 0085
www.ambasadaaustrii.pl
Belgium:
34 Senatorska Ul, 00-950 Warsaw
Tel: (022) 827 0233/5
Fax: 635 5711
www.diplomatie.de/warsaw
Canada:
Ul. Matejki 1/5, Warsaw
Tel: (022) 584 31 00
www.canada.pl
Denmark:
19 Rakowiecka Ul, 02-517 Warsaw
Tel: (022) 565 2900
www.ambwarszawa.um.dk
France:
Ul. Piekna 1
Tel: (022) 529 30 00
www.ambafrance-pl.org
Germany:
Ul. Jazdow 12, 00-467 Warsaw
Tel: (022) 584 17 00
Fax: (022) 584 17 39
www.warszawa.diplo.de
Italy:
6 Dabrowskiego Pl, 00-055 Warsaw
Tel: (022) 826 34 71
www.ambvarsavia.esteri.it
Japan:
Szwolerzów 8, Warsaw
Tel: (022) 696 50 00
www.pl.emb-japan.go.jp

TRANSPORT · ACCOMMODATION · EATING OUT · ACTIVITIES · A – Z · LANGUAGE

Emergency Numbers

Ambulance (public): 999
Police: 997, from a mobile dial 12, for foreign tourists 0 800 200 300.
Fire: 998
Please note: do not expect anyone at these numbers to be able to speak English.

Norway:
2a Fryderyka Chopina Ul,
00-559 Warsaw
Tel: (022) 696 40 30
Fax: 628 93 83
www.amb-norwegia.pl
Russia:
49 Belwederska Ul, 00-761 Warsaw
Tel: (022) 621 34 53
Fax: 625 30 16
www.poland.mid.ru
Switzerland:
Al. Ujazdowskie 27, 00-540 Warsaw
Tel: (022) 628 04 81, 621 05 48
Spain:
4 Myśliwiecka Ul, Warsaw
Tel: (022) 583 40 00
Sweden:
3 Bagatela Ul, 00-585 Warsaw
Tel: (022) 640 89 00
Fax: 640 89 83
www.swedenabroad.com/warsaw
UK: Al. Róż 1, 00-556 Warsaw
Tel: (022) 311 00 00
Fax: 621 71 61
www.britishembassy.pl
USA: 29/31 Al. Ujazdowskie,
00-540 Warsaw
Tel: (022) 625 14 01
http://poland.usembassy.gov

Entry Requirements

Visas can be obtained from a Polish consulate in your country of residence or from Warsaw airport on arrival. Visa extensions can be obtained from the offices of the Ministry of Internal Affairs, Foreign Visitors' Department, 11 Floor, 47a/49 Wspólna Ulica, Warsaw. Children on their parents' passports are not charged for visas.

Transit visas are valid for 48 hours. If you want a transit visa, you will need a visa for your destination country. Passport and visa regulations can change quite quickly so it's wise to check with the Polish consulate in your country of residence before setting off.

British visitors can stay in Poland for six months without a visa but passports must be valid for at least six months after the date of your departure. Passport holders from most European countries, the USA and the Commonwealth can stay for up to 90 days without a visa. Visitors

from Bulgaria, Estonia, Macedonia, Mongolia and Romania can remain for up to 30 days without a visa, while visitors from Hong Kong are allowed two weeks. Visas remain valid for six months from the date of issue.

Visitors to Poland are obliged to register their stay within 48 hours after crossing the border. Registration is performed by the hotel or camp site reception desk.

Etiquette

Poles are great hosts – especially in their own homes – but do note that they are a conservative bunch. If you can manage to get yourself invited to a Polish home (and to do so is worthwhile) always bring something; flowers go down especially well. On entering a Pole's home you should at least offer to take your shoes off. You should expect to be asked some rather personal and direct questions, which may include your views on the Catholic church, homosexuality and Poland itself. Be diplomatic in response, even if you do not like what you hear.

When entering churches make sure you are respectfully dressed. Women should cover their shoulders and shorts are by and large unacceptable, though increasingly tolerated, at least for men.

G ay and Lesbian Travellers

Poland gets a bad reputation for its attitude to gays, yet in reality there are few better places in Europe to be out and proud. Kraków tends to be more liberal than Warsaw, though there are gay nightspots in both cities. Sopot in summer is another place gays will be more than welcome. For more information on gay nightspots check the specialist site www.gayguide.net.

H ealth and Medical Care

The Polish authorities do not require any special inoculations, but protection against tetanus, polio and diphtheria (the latest booster should have been carried out within the past 10 years) is recommended. If, however, you are planning to spend a lot of time in country areas, particularly those close to the Russian, Lithuanian or Belarus border, then it is wise to see your doctor about the symptoms and treatment of Lyme Disease before leaving home.

It is also advisable to take out a private health insurance policy.

In an emergency, you will be taken to a hospital where you will receive

immediate treatment, but for any course of treatment or hospital stay you will be expected to pay in cash. Make sure you take out medical insurance to cover all eventualities.

British passports holders are covered by a bi-lateral agreement concerning emergency treatment and do not pay even if they do have medical insurance.

Chemists

Chemists are open from 10am to 7pm. An emergency system operates in most towns. The address of the chemist providing out-of-hours service is usually posted in chemists' windows. To be on the safe side it is advisable to bring a supply of any special medication you might need on your trip.

Chemists serve as the first place to ask for help in minor medical problems. There is a rota system with one chemist (*Apteka*) in the area staying open 24 hours for emergencies. Most standard drugs are available in Poland without a prescription, but are sometimes marketed under different names. It is always a good idea to show the chemist the empty container to ensure you get the right drug.

Doctors and Dentists

Most of the doctors and dentists in the cities speak English and are trained to western standards. Most four- and five-star hotels have a doctor on call.

Hospitals and Ambulances

Hospitals in Poland do not always meet western standards of nursing and accommodation, but medical care is usually sufficient in an emergency. There are public and private ambulance companies operating in major cities and a public ambulance service covering the whole country. Ambulances are usually equipped according to western standards. Depending on their speciality different hospitals cover different emergencies. Patients are referred to an appropriate hospital by a doctor or ambulance crew. Self referral is also possible via the Accident and Emergency departments (*Izba przyj*).

Warsaw Hospitals and Clinics

Szpital Damiana: Ul. Wałbrzyska 46
Tel: (022) 566 22 22. www.damian.pl
CM Medical Centre: Al. Jerozolimskie 65/79 (LIM Hotel Mariott). Tel: (022) 458 70 70. www.cm-lim.com.pl
FALCK: Groszowicka 11–13. Tel: (022) 517 34 00. Ambulance service, not a clinic.
FALCK Medycyna: Ul. Obozowa 20.
Tel: (022) 535 91 01. www.falck.pl.

KLINIKA ProMed: Ul. Uniwersytecka 5 at Pl. Narutowicza. Tel: (022) 822 18 11. Open: Mon–Fri 7.30am–8pm; Sat 9am–5pm.
German Embassy Medical Centre: Ul. Katowicka 31. Tel: (022) 617 30 21/30 11 ext. 240. Mon–Fri 7am–3pm. For all foreigners; appointments only.

Dental Treatment

Austria Dental Centre: Ul. Zelazna 54. Tel: (022) 654 21 16; 821 31 84. www.austriadent.pl. Mon–Fri 9am–9pm; Sat 9am–1pm. English- and German-speaking dentists.
Eurodental: 8-20 Ul. Andersa 15, Tel: (022) 831 31 61/20 90; Ul. Nowowiejska 37, Tel: (022) 875 0088; Ul. Śniadeckich 14, Tel: (022) 627 58 88. www.eurodental.pl. English-speaking dentists.

Internet

Getting online in Poland has never been easier. Almost all hotels now offer some kind of internet connection, almost always Wifi, though usually at quite exorbitant prices (as much as 65zł, €20 for 24 hours access). You can avoid these charges by buying a pre-pay access card from Orange stores (which are ubiquitous all over Poland). These provide unlimited access to the Orange Wifi network for a set period of time. You simply buy a card, find a hotspot, open your web browser and follow the simple instructions.

Maps

Several words are frequently abbreviated on Polish maps. Aleja (abbreviated as Al.) means avenue, Ulica (abbreviated as Ul.) means street, Plac means square, and Rynek is Market Square. In addresses, house numbers usually follow the name of the street.

Media

In recent years Poland has greatly increased the amount of newspapers, magazines and books that it publishes and television and radio have more interesting channels, especially independent stations.

Newspapers

In March 1990, the government's monopoly on the press was lifted and the powerful state-owned Ruch publishing co-operative dissolved. Within four months of the introduction of a market economy, some 90 magazines had ceased trading. In October 1990, the press was privatised and

over 100 magazines sold off, in most cases to foreign companies. About 70 titles passed to newly formed co-operatives, one of which was the respected Warsaw weekly magazine *Polityka*. The daily *Gazeta Wyborcza*, once the mouthpiece of the Solidarity trade union, increased its circulation to about 1,850,000 copies, becoming the country's largest and most influential daily paper. During the presidency of Lech Wałęsa it frequently incurred his wrath for criticising his style of government.

By 1999, the Polish media published 76 daily newspapers (19 national and 57 regional) and more than 150 magazines. Many of these magazines are international titles published in Polish, such as *Elle*, *Marie Clare*, or *Cosmopolitan*. International newspapers and magazines are available from hotel kiosks, good bookshops, EMPIK'S (a special bookshop network found at www.@empik.com.pl). British newspapers usually arrive a day after publication. *Gazeta Wyborcza* and *Życie Warszawy* produce weekend supplements in English. The *Warsaw Voice* is probably the most authoritative English-language publication. It gives a good insight into Polish politics, business and culture and also has a listings section for tourists. The second important publication in English is *Business Journal Magazine*.

Radio and Television

In October 1992 the monopoly on radio and TV was abandoned and the private broadcasters who had been working illegally since 1990 were legalised. Polish radio now offers four main stations, the most important being Polskie Radio. There are also numerous local channels. During the summer, Polish Radio 1 provides a summary of the news and weather in English.

Polish television consists of two state-run and several private stations; in addition, a range of regional programmes is also produced. Large hotels in the main cities have western satellite channels. These channels are also very popular among Poles. It is reckoned that one in four households now has a satellite dish or at least access to one. Since 1998 two digital broadcast TV platforms have been available between them offering up to 100 TV channels.

Money

Polish złoty (zł or PLN), divided into 100 groszy (gr).

Notes (for 10, 20, 50, 100 and 200 złoty) come in different sizes

and are easily recognisable. The nine coins are: 1, 2, 5, 10, 20 and 50 groszy and 1, 2 and 5 złoty.

Currency and Exchange

The currency is Polish *złoty* (zł). Since the economic reforms of 1990, złoty can be changed in privately run *bureaux de change* (*kantor*). Some travel agents and hotels will change money too, although you should check the commission rate first. Eurocheques (maximum amount per cheque – 500 new złoty) are not accepted in all *bureaux de change*, so it may be necessary to go to a bank.

Banks are plentiful in Poland (*see page 400* for opening times), but with the increasing number of cash dispensers you can easily go your whole stay without entering one. There are often long queues in banks, so be prepared for a wait.

A *kantor* is usually the best place to exchange foreign currency, almost always offering a better rate than banks. These offices rarely accept travellers cheques. Most *kantor* can be found in hotels, main railway and bus stations and in main streets.

Credit Cards and Travellers' Cheques

Most hotels, petrol stations, car rental firms, good quality restaurants, luxury goods shops and large supermarkets will accept payment with credit cards (check for appropriate signs on entrance). American Express, Visa, Eurocard, MasterCard, Diners' Club and JCB credit cards are the most commonly accepted. Cash against Visa cards can be obtained in banks or in cash dispensers (*bankomat*).

Travellers' cheques are accepted all over Poland. These can be cashed at the foreign exchange desk only of banks. Loss or theft of credit cards can be reported at the following credit card hot lines:
American Express:
Tel: (022) 625 4030
Diners' Club, MasterCard, EuroCard and Visa:
Tel: (022) 515 3000 or 513 3150
Visa and Master Cards:
Tel: (022) 659 2713.

Cash Dispensers

There are 24-hour cash dispensers, accepting credit and bank cards (with pin numbers) on many main streets in larger cities.

The machines usually offer a choice of three languages in which to conduct your transaction, but they issue only Polish złoty. There may be a few day's delay in the transaction reaching your home account.

TRANSPORT ACCOMMODATION EATING OUT ACTIVITIES A–Z LANGUAGE

P hotography

Most international brands of camera film are available throughout Poland. Developing and repairs are also quite cheap. Some shops in the larger cities will process films in one hour. Film and video cassettes are generally available in larger shops or specialist stores, where you can also develop film. Camera film is also available at many petrol stations.

Those buildings and locations that the authorities regard as strategically important, such as stations, bridges, port installations, police and military buildings, may not be photographed. If you wish to take photographs of people, it is polite to ask permission first: *"Czy mogę zrobić zd ęcie?"*

Postal Services

Post offices (*poczta*) are marked by a blue sign with the white letters POCZTA POLSKA, and are usually open Monday to Saturday 8am–8pm, earlier on Saturdays. Services at the *pocztas* include stamps, tokens and cards for public phones, postcards, sending letters, faxes, etc.

To send a letter within Europe costs 1zł, postcards 70 gr. Airmail letters to European destinations take about a week to arrive, two to three weeks elsewhere.

R eligion

95 percent Catholic (Roman and Greek). The remaining population is composed of about 1.5 percent Orthodox, 1 percent Protestant, and small pockets of Muslims and Jews. Throughout the country there are more than 12,500 churches.

Religious Services

A large majority of the Polish population is Roman Catholic, and Poles attend church regularly. Services in English can be found at the following in Warsaw:
Warsaw International Church: Christian Theological Academy, 21 Ul. Miodowa Protestant, Sunday worship at 11am (summer 10am).
Mokotwska Christian Fellowship: 6 Zbawiciela Square. New Testament. Sunday 6pm.
Roman Catholic Service for Catholics Abroad: Caritas, 14 Ul. Radna Sunday 11am.
Basilica of St John the Baptist: 6 Ul. Kanonia (Old Town). Holy mass at 11am.
Augsburg Evangelical Church of the Holy Trinity: 6 Ul. Kreytowa Confession 10.15am on Sunday, service and holy communion 10.30am.

Public Holidays

- **January** New Year's Day (1)
- **March/April** Easter Monday (variable)
- **May** Labour Day (1); Constitution Day (3)
- **June** Corpus Christi (variable)
- **August** Feast of the Assumption (15)
- **November** All Saints' Day (1); National Independence Day (11)
- **December** Christmas Day (25); St Stephen's Day (26)

Warsaw Eastern Orthodox Church: 52 Al. Solidarno, ci. Sunday 10am.
Nożyków Synagogue: 6 Ul. Twarda Saturday service at 10am.
Warsaw Mosque: 103 Ul. Wiertnicza Friday prayers at 1pm (summer); 12 noon (winter).

S tudent Travellers

Poland has a massive student population, with many locals staying in at least part-time education well into their 30s (this is a legacy of the past, when compulsory military service could be avoided by registered students). As such, Poland is a great place for students, not least because general living costs remain relatively low. Those in possession of recognised International Student Cards can get discounts at most attractions (at least publicly owned ones); though note that only Polish students are entitled to discount travel. Poznań, Warsaw and Kraków are the city's biggest university cities, Poznań especially buzzing during term time with thousands of partying students.

Dialling codes

When calling any number in Poland you need to dial both the number and the city code (even if you are in the city in question).

Białystok 085
Bielski-Biała 033
Częstochowa 034
Elblag 055
Gdańsk 058
Gliwice 032
Jelenia Góra 075
Katowice 032
Kazimierz Dolny 081
Kołobrzeg 094
Kraków 012
Lublin 081
Łańcut 017
Łeba 059
Łódź 042
Malbork 055

Nowy Sącz 018
Olsztyn 089
Opole 077
Poznań 061
Sopot 058
Szczecin 091
Toruń 056
Warsaw 022
Wrocław 071
Zakopane 018
Zamość 084

If dialling abroad from Poland, dial 00, then the international dialling code of the country you are calling:
Australia 61
Canada 1
Ireland 353
New Zealand 64
USA 1
UK 44

T elecommunications

Public Telephones

The telephone service belongs to Telekomunikacja Polska. There are both token (*leton*) and card (*karta*) public phones. There are plenty of public phone boxes, although many of them don't work, so it is often better to head for a post office if you need to make a call. For a long-distance call it is better use a credit-card phone; there are credit-card phones at airports and in the foyers of almost all hotels. These are considerably cheaper than making calls from your room. To call abroad from Poland, first dial 00 and then the country code, eg UK = 44. To call Poland from abroad, dial 00 48 then the number required.

It is advisable to purchase phone cards (remove a corner before use), available as 25, 50 or 100 units from post offices and kiosks. If you have to use coin phones you will need to buy one or more of the tokens (A = 1 unit, C = 6 units) from a post office or kiosk.

Until recently, it was often necessary in smaller towns to dial out via the operator, but now almost everywhere has its own dialling code. A leaflet listing dialling codes can be obtained at post offices.

Useful Numbers

Roadside Assistance (PZM): Tel: 981
Long-distance Operator: Tel: 900
International Operator: Tel: 901
International Directory Enquiries: Tel: 908
Inland Directory Enquiries: Tel: 913
Radio Taxi: Tel: 919
Speaking Clock: Tel: 962
Weather Information: Tel: 9221

Medical Information: Tel: 9439
City Information: Tel: 911

Mobile Phones

Large numbers of Poles now have
mobile phones – at the last count
there were more than 3 million
users. The main reason for this is the
increasing speed of life and the
frustration of using private and public
phones. Although the network is still
being developed, there remain some
areas where only mobiles work.

There are currently three GSM
operators that provide roaming
facilities for foreign tourists with their
own mobiles. Plus GSM or PL01 (on
telephone display) operates in almost
the entire country. Era GSM or PL02
also operates almost everywhere.
Idea or PL03 (using the DCS system)
operates only in Warsaw, Gdańsk,
Szczecin, Katowice, Kraków, Pozań
and Wrocław. Contact your local GSM
dealer for information on facilities
and roaming costs.

Tipping

Tipping is the norm in Poland and it is
usual to leave about 10 percent of
the total bill as a tip in a restaurant,
hairdressers and for taxi drivers.

Toilets

Decent public toilets are few and far
between in Poland. Exceptions are
those in railway stations (for which
you be expected to pay a few groszy)
and in the many underpasses in
central Warsaw. Some parks in
Poland have portaloos, but they do
rather leave much to be desired on
the hygiene front.

Tourist Offices

Local Tourist Offices

Bielsko-Biała: 2 Willowa Ul,
1 Warszawska Ul, 43-300 Bielsko-
Biała. Tel: (033) 827 93 22.
www.bielsko.pl
Częstochowa: Slaska 11/13, 42-
217 Częstochowa. Tel: (034) 370 71
00. www.czestochowa.um.gov.pl
Kielce: 12 Piotrkowska Ul, Kielce 25-
510. Tel: (041) 367 64 36.
Kraków: Rynek Główny (Main Market
Sq) 1–3, Sukiennice, 31-042 Kraków.
Tel: (012) 421 77 06. www.mcit.pl
Lublin: Ul. Krakowskie Przedmieście
78, Lublin 20-400. Tel: (081) 532 44
12.
Nowy Sącz: 46a Jagiellońska Ul,
Nowy Sącz 30-300. Tel: (018) 444
24 22.
Płock: 38 Al. Jachowicza, Płock 09-
400. Tel: (024) 262 94 97.
Poznań: Ul. Ratajczaka 44, Poznań

Time Zone

GMT plus one hour. When it is
noon in Warsaw it is 6am in New
York and 8pm in Tokyo. Daylight
Saving is in effect May–October
when one hour is added.

61-728. Tel: (061) 851 96 45. Fax:
(061) 856 04 54. www.cim.poznan.pl
Szczecin: Ul. Korsarzy 34. Tel: (091)
433 88 41. Fax: (091) 434 79 84.
www.zamek.szczecin.pl
Toruń: 25 Rynek Staromiejski, Toruń
87-100. Tel: (056) 621 09 31.
www.it.torun.pl
Warsaw: Branches at: 10 Plac
Zamkowy; Krakowskie Przedmieście
39; Main Hall of the Central Railway
Station; and Arrivals Hall of the
International Terminal of Warsaw
Airport. Tel: (022) 94 31/474 11 42.
www.warsawtour.pl

Polish Tourist Offices

Germany: Polnisches Informations-
zentrum für Touristik, Marburger
Strasse 1, 10789 Berlin. Tel: (030)
210 09 20. Fax: (030) 210 092 14.
www.polen-info.de
Netherlands: Pool Informatiebureau
voor Toerisme, Leidsestraat 64,
Amsterdam 1017PD. Tel: (020) 625
35 70. Fax: (020) 623 09 29.
www.members.tripod.com/~poleninfo
Sweden: Polska Statens Turistbyrå,
Kungsgatan 66, Box 449, S-10128
Stockholm. Tel: (08) 21 60 75, 21
81 45. Fax: (08) 21 04 65.
www.poland.travel/sv
UK: Polish National Tourist Office,
310–312 Regent Street, London
W1B 3AX. Tel: (020) 7580 8811.
Fax: (020) 7580 8866. E-mail:
info@visitpoland.org
USA: Polish National Tourist Office,
275 Madison Avenue, Suite 1711,
New York, NY 10016. Tel: (212) 338
94 12. Fax: (212) 338 92 83. E-mail:
pntonyc@polandtour.org.
www.poland.travel/en-us

Tour Operators

UK Tour Operators

Polorbis Holidays Ltd
Suite 530–532 Walmar House,
288–300 Regent Street, London
W1B 3AL. Tel: (020) 7636 2217.
www.polorbis.co.uk
Fregata Travel Ltd
83 Whitechapel High Street, London
E1 7QX. Tel: (020) 7375 3187. Fax:
(020) 7247 7884. www.fregatatravel.co.uk
Bogdan Travel
5a Broadway, Gunnersbury Lane,
London W3 8HR. Tel: (020) 8992
6004. Fax: (020) 8896 9044.
www.polish-travel.com

US Tour Operators

Happy Holidays Travel
5324 W Lawrence Avenue, Chicago,
IL 60630. Tel: (312) 282 1188.
American Travel Abroad Ltd
250 West 57th Street, New York,
NY 10107. Tel: (212) 586 5230. Fax:
(212) 581 7925.
4801 W Peterson Ave, Chicago,
IL 60646. Tel: (312) 725 9500.
Fax: (312) 725 8089.

Websites

Poland's shop window on the net
contains useful tourist information,
including visa requirements:
www.poland.pl or **www.polska.pl**
an introductory site with maps,
places, the present situation, etc.
www.explorepoland.pl
large, general guide to Poland.
www.hotelspoland.com
hotels; on-line reservation system.
www.polhotels.com
secure on-line hotel reservation
system; car rental.
www.discoverpoland.com
hotels, excursions and car rental.
www.inyourpocket.com
www.gopoland.com

What to Bring

If you are taking prescription drugs it
is advisable to bring enough for your
full trip, as though they may be
available in Poland they may well be
marketed under different names.
Bring baby milk if travelling with
young children: this is relatively
expensive in Poland, as are nappies.

What To Wear

The summer months are similar to
that of the UK with less humidity. The
winter, however, is cold with heavy
falls of snow in the mountains and
temperatures falling below 0°C
(32°F). In winter it is necessary to
bring a thick coat, boots, and
especially, hat and gloves. In autumn
it rains often so bring a waterproof.

Women Travellers

Poland poses no particular threat to
women travelers. Indeed, the country
– especially its cities – is perhaps far
safer for women travellers than many
places in Western Europe. Employ
common sense at all times and you
should have little problem beyond the
annoying glances of leering men.

Weights and Measures

Poland uses the metric system.

L ANGUAGE

UNDERSTANDING THE LANGUAGE

General

Polish, a Slavic language, is the mother tongue of 99 percent of the population. The most widely known foreign language is german, though English is quickly gaining on it and is far more popular than German among younger people. In the cities English speakers are unlikely to find many problems, as most people they'll encounter speak at least some English (many Poles are fluent in English and other languages). In the countryside, communication difficulties are to be expected.

The Polish language is extremely difficult and can be quite daunting at first, but it is pronounced exactly as it is spelt. Learning even a handful of key phrases is a good idea and will prove helpful. As a general rule, the accent falls on the second-last syllable.

Useful Phrases

Hi/bye *Cześć (chesh)*
Yes *Tak (tack)*
No *Nie (nee-ar)*
Thank you *Dziękuje (gen-coo-yea)*
Please *Proszę (proshay)*
Good morning *Dzień dobry*
/afternoon *(jane dobray)*
Good evening *Dobry wieczór (dobray vieer-chew)*
Goodbye *Do widzenia (do-vitzania)*
Sorry/Excuse me *Przepraszam (puh-shay prusham)*
How much is it? *Ile to kosztuje? (e-lay toe coshtu yea)*
I would like... *Chciałabym (chow bim)*
Where is...? *Gdzie jest? (jay yest)*
How far? *Jak daleko? (yak daleko)*
How long? *Jak długo? (yak dwugo)*
Good/OK *Dobry (dobray)*
Bad/no good *Zły (zuh-wee)*

Cheap *Tanio (tan-yo)*
Expensive *Drogo (drogo)*
Hot *Gorąco (gorronso)*
Cold *Zimno (zhim-no)*
Free *Wolny (volney)*
Occupied *Zajęty (zigh-yente)*
I don't understand *Ja nie rozumiem (ya nie rozumee-em)*
Help! *Pomocy! (po-mo-tsay)*

Signs

Open *Otwarty*
Closed *Zamknięte*
Exit *Wyjście*
Pharmacy *Apteka*
Post Office *Poczta*
Avenue *Aleja (Al.)*
Street *ulica (ul.)*
Old Town *Stare Miasto*
Police Station *Posterunek Policji*
Information *Informacja*
Toilets/WC *Toalety*
　Men *Panowie*
　Women *Panie*
No Smoking *Palenie Wzbronione*
Cash Desk *Kasa*

Pronunciation

Polish vowels:
a = as the u in "cut"
ą = a nasal vowel, as in the French "Jean"
ę = as in the French "un"
i = as in feet
ó = as the English u
u = as in book

Polish consonants:
Pronounced as in English except ć is pronounced in a much softer way than the Polish c

ch = as in the Scottish loch
cz = ch as in church
dź = as in beds
dż = j as in jam
ł = w
ń = ny (as in canyon)
rz = zh as in pleasure
ś = like s but much softer
sz = sh as in show
szcz = shch as in pushchair
w = v

BELOW: an assortment of Polish publications.

FURTHER READING

General

Between East and West by Anne Applebaum. US journalist's account of her travels through Poland.
Old Polish Legends by F. C. Anstrutter. Enjoyable book of traditional Polish tales and legends.
Hiking Guide to Poland and Ukraine by Tim Burford. Best hiking guide to the region.
Poland's Jewish Heritage by Joram Kagan. Short history of Jews in Poland.
Colloquial Polish by B.W. Mazur.
Jewish Roots in Poland: Pages from the Past and Archival Inventories by Miriam Weiner. The most comprehensive guide to Polish Jewry.

History

The Jews in Poland by Chimen Abramsky, Maciej Jachimczyk and Anthony Polonsky. Comprehensive historical background to the Jewish community in Poland.
The Struggles for Poland by Neal Ascherson. Book to accompany the UK Channel 4 series. Good introduction to modern Polish history and politics.
Winter in the Morning by Janina Bauman. Moving account of life in the Warsaw Ghetto written by survivor.
God's Playground: A History of Poland by Norman Davies. Intelligent and entertaining history of pre-Solidarity Poland.
Heart of Europe: A Short History of Poland by Norman Davies. Balanced and entertaining history from World War II onwards.
The Holocaust by Martin Gilbert. Most-read account of the Polish role in the Holocaust.
Nice Promises by Tim Sebastian. Accessible account of Poland in the early 1980s by former BBC correspondent in Warsaw.
The Poles by Stewart Stevens. Personal journalistic account of Poland in the 1980s.
A Path of Hope by Lech Wałęsa. Autobiography of the Solidarity leader of his pre-presidential days.
The Polish Way by Adam Zamoyski. Accessible history of Poland going up to the 1989 elections.

Rising '44 by Norman Davies. Gripping account of the Warsaw uprising.

Literature

The Burning Forest ed Adam Czerniawski. Anthology of modern Polish poetry from the 19th century to the present day.
Selected Poems by Zbigniew Herbert (1977). Probably the best Polish poet. Political contemporary observations. Herbert's death in 1998 was mourned throughout the nation.
Insatiability by Stanisław Ignacy Witkiewicz. In-depth twelfth century account of artistic lifestyle, not an easy read but worth it.
A Minor Apocalypse by Tadeusz Konwicki. Highly political novel narrating a day in the life of a political activist.
The History of Polish Literature by Czesław Miłosz. Written in the 1960s this is still the most comprehensive book on Polish literature.
The Issa Valley by Czesław Miłosz. Semi-autobiographical account of childhood in a Lithuanian rural community.

Culture, Art and Architecture

Atlas of Warsaw's Architecture by J.A. Chrościcki and A. Rottermund. Interesting and informative atlas of Warsaw's architectural treasures.
Kraków: City of Museums by Jerzy Banach (ed). Book detailing Kraków's many museums.
Book of Warsaw Palaces by T.S. Jaroszewski.
Warsaw: the Royal Way by Jerzy Lileyko. Details the sights and history of the Royal Way.
Double Vision: My Life in Film by Andrzej Wajda. Autobiography of Poland's greatest director.

Send Us Your Thoughts

We do our best to ensure the information in our books is as accurate and up-to-date as possible. The books are updated on a regular basis using local contacts, who painstakingly add, amend and correct as required. However, some details (such as telephone numbers and opening times) are liable to change, and we are ultimately reliant on our readers to put us in the picture.

We welcome your feedback, especially your experience of using the book "on the road". Maybe we recommended a hotel that you liked (or another that you didn't), or you came across a great bar or new attraction we missed.

We will acknowledge all contributions, and we'll offer an Insight Guide to the best letters received.

Please write to us at:
Insight Guides
PO Box 7910
London SE1 1WE
Or email us at:
insight@apaguide.co.uk

Other Insight Guides

Insight Guides cover nearly 200 destinations, providing information on culture and all the top sights. Other **Insight Guides** to Eastern Europe include: **Baltic States**, **Bulgaria** and **Romania**.

Insight Guides **Step by Step Krakow** brings you the very best of the city with tailor-made walks and tours.

ART & PHOTO CREDITS

Map Production:
Colourmap Scanning Ltd

© 2009 Apa Publications GmbH & Co.
Verlag KG (Singapore branch)

INSIGHT GUIDE
POLAND

Cartographic Editor **Zoë Goodwin**
Production **Linton Donaldson**
Design Consultants
Carlotta Junger, Graham Mitchener
Picture Research **Hilary Genin**

INDEX

Numbers in italics refer to photographs